Strategic Opportunities for Bridging the University-Employer Divide

William E. Donald
University of Southampton, UK & Ronin Institute, USA

A volume in the Advances in Educational Marketing, Administration, and Leadership (AEMAL) Book Series

IGI Global
PUBLISHER of TIMELY KNOWLEDGE

Published in the United States of America by
IGI Global
Information Science Reference (an imprint of IGI Global)
701 E. Chocolate Avenue
Hershey PA, USA 17033
Tel: 717-533-8845
Fax: 717-533-8661
E-mail: cust@igi-global.com
Web site: http://www.igi-global.com

Library of Congress Cataloging-in-Publication Data

Names: Donald, William (William Edward), 1987- author.
Title: Strategic opportunities for bridging the university-employer divide / by William Donald.
Description: Hershey PA : Information Science Reference, 2024. | Includes bibliographical references. | Summary: "The book is a comprehensive resource that captures the current landscape, identifies opportunities, and addresses challenges in enhancing collaboration between universities and employers"-- Provided by publisher.
Identifiers: LCCN 2023037169 (print) | LCCN 2023037170 (ebook) | ISBN 9781668498279 (hardcover) | ISBN 9781668498316 (paperback) | ISBN 9781668498286 (ebook)
Subjects: LCSH: Graduate students--Employment. | School-to-work transition. | Vocational guidance. | Employees--Recruiting. | Academic-industrial collaboration.
Classification: LCC HD6277 .D56 2024 (print) | LCC HD6277 (ebook) | DDC 331.702--dc23/eng/20240214
LC record available at https://lccn.loc.gov/2023037169
LC ebook record available at https://lccn.loc.gov/2023037170

This book is published in the IGI Global book series Advances in Educational Marketing, Administration, and Leadership (AEMAL) (ISSN: 2326-9022; eISSN: 2326-9030)

British Cataloguing in Publication Data
A Cataloguing in Publication record for this book is available from the British Library.

Advances in Educational Marketing, Administration, and Leadership (AEMAL) Book Series

ISSN:2326-9022
EISSN:2326-9030

Editor-in-Chief: Siran Mukerji, IGNOU, India & Purnendu Tripathi, IGNOU, India

MISSION

With more educational institutions entering into public, higher, and professional education, the educational environment has grown increasingly competitive. With this increase in competitiveness has come the need for a greater focus on leadership within the institutions, on administrative handling of educational matters, and on the marketing of the services offered.

The **Advances in Educational Marketing, Administration, & Leadership (AEMAL) Book Series** strives to provide publications that address all these areas and present trending, current research to assist professionals, administrators, and others involved in the education sector in making their decisions.

COVERAGE

- Academic Administration
- Educational Finance
- Students as Consumers
- Governance in P-12 and Higher Education
- Faculty Administration and Management
- Technologies and Educational Marketing
- Educational Management
- Direct marketing of educational programs
- Educational Marketing Campaigns
- Academic Pricing

The Advances in Educational Marketing, Administration, and Leadership (AEMAL) Book Series (ISSN 2326-9022) is published by IGI Global, 701 E. Chocolate Avenue, Hershey, PA 17033-1240, USA, www.igi-global.com. This series is composed of titles available for purchase individually; each title is edited to be contextually exclusive from any other title within the series. For pricing and ordering information please visit http://www.igi-global.com/book-series/advances-educational-marketing-administration-leadership/73677. Postmaster: Send all address changes to above address.

Titles in this Series

For a list of additional titles in this series, please visit:
http://www.igi-global.com/book-series/advances-educational-marketing-administration-leadership/73677

Handbook of Research on Critical Issues and Global Trends in International Education
Megel R. Barker (ABA Oman International School, Oman) Robyn Conrad Hansen (Northern Arizona University, USA) and Liam Hammer (International School of Lusaka, Zambia)
Information Science Reference • © 2024 • 420pp • H/C (ISBN: 9781668487952) • US $270.00

Autoethnographic Tactics to Closing the Gap on Educational Attainment
Anika Chanell Thrower (Borough of Manhattan Community College/CUNY, USA) and Alex Evangelista (Borough of Manhattan Community College/CUNY, USA)
Information Science Reference • © 2024 • 300pp • H/C (ISBN: 9798369310748) • US $230.00

Interrogating Race and Racism in Postsecondary Language Classrooms
Xiangying Huo (University of Toronto, Canada) and Clayton Smith (University of Windsor, Canada)
Information Science Reference • © 2024 • 300pp • H/C (ISBN: 9781668490297) • US $215.00

Academic Framework for 21st-Century Schooling Promoting Global Peace and Harmony
Marmar Mukhopadhyay (Educational Technology and Management Academy Council, India) and Arnab Kundu (Chhinpur Jr. High School, India)
Information Science Reference • © 2023 • 349pp • H/C (ISBN: 9781668470053) • US $230.00

Promoting Crisis Management and Creative Problem-Solving Skills in Educational Leadership
Afzal Sayed Munna (University of Sunderland in London, UK) Uzoechi Nwagbara (University of Sunderland in London, UK) and Yahaya Alhassan (University of Sunderland in London, UK)
Information Science Reference • © 2024 • 300pp • H/C (ISBN: 9781668483329) • US $215.00

IGI Global
PUBLISHER of TIMELY KNOWLEDGE

701 East Chocolate Avenue, Hershey, PA 17033, USA
Tel: 717-533-8845 x100 • Fax: 717-533-8661
E-Mail: cust@igi-global.com • www.igi-global.com

To my darling Wife, Eleanor Donald.
Thank you for your unwavering support, belief, and patience.
Without you, this book would not have been possible.

To our wonderful Daughter, Grace Donald.
Thank you for your hugs, whiteboard cleaning services, and eternal optimism.
Our dancing to Bruce Springsteen songs was a welcome interlude to writing.

To our plucky Pug, Stanley Donald.
Thank you for your disgruntled grunts, looks of disdain, and loud snoring.
I hope the book does not induce similar occurrences in the reader.

Table of Contents

Section 3
Graduate Recruiters

Section 4
Challenges, Opportunities, and Future Workplace Trends

Foreword

There is ongoing interest and literature on the importance of employability and ways to better prepare students for transition to work and sustainable careers. The complexities of employability, the graduate labor market and influential external factors, including migration and visa policy and global economic trends, make this no easy task. Yet employability is critical in different ways to many stakeholders.

For students, it supports a return on their significant investment in attending university. This could be intrinsic satisfaction from achieving personal career goals or increased capacity for job attainment and higher earnings. For some, the foregone years of much-needed income to support their family and the accrual of sizeable debt mean that employability, although they may not realize it, is a critical part of their tertiary education journey.

Industry relies on higher education, alongside other education systems, as a facilitator of quality talent pipelines, enabling them to advance productivity, competitiveness, and innovation at organizational and national levels. Meanwhile, graduate employability assures governments that their investment in public universities effectively contributes to meeting economic and societal needs.

There has been a subtle shift in expectations that universities will 'produce' work-ready graduates (with employers as consumers) to shared responsibility and university-employer collaboration in developing talent for the future. Collaboration is mutually beneficial given global talent shortages and the linking of graduate employability-related metrics to university profiles and possibly funding.

Recognizing that university-employer partnerships have multiple purposes and levels, this book considers the challenges and strategic opportunities for greater collaboration between university career advisors and graduate recruiters. The book initially explores the critical yet possibly undervalued role of university career services. An important part of this is the complexities around student engagement in the offerings of career services. We know this can be influenced in many ways, including sociocultural factors, personal agency, and how provision is designed, structured and delivered. The book highlights the importance of career services for developing aspects of employability, particularly supporting students in creating, curating, and communicating their professional brand and employability narrative to prospective employers.

The book's exploration of the perspectives of those at the 'coal face' of graduate recruitment in different regions is of particular value. This provides critical insights into their thinking and practices, including the challenges and opportunities of efficiently attracting and selecting early career talent. Prioritizing person-organization fit can also position early career talent as a means for establishing and maintaining competitive advantage and organizational sustainability. The book extends beyond hiring practices and considers many ways employers can partner with universities to develop employability and better prepare students for the university-work transition. Insights from graduates themselves further crystalize the need to address the university-employer divide. Combining these viewpoints with macro-level insights into graduate recruitment and employment patterns and relevant economic mega-trends inform discussion of practical strategies for better supporting employability and sustainable careers to benefit all actors.

My final comment relates to the interweaving of lived experiences throughout the book. The author's own career journey and experiences mean the book considers the challenges and opportunities for bridging the university-employer divide through many lenses and with careful consideration of universities' diverse student cohorts. This is to be applauded as collaboratively supporting the sustainable careers of all students can reduce inequalities and encourage employers to think beyond standardized notions of successful graduate recruits. The book's accessible integration of theory and lived experience insights make this a valuable text for anyone interested in ensuring the sustainability of a career ecosystem.

Denise Jackson
Edith Cowan University, Australia

Preface

For the last fifteen years, I have been captivated by the production and flow of graduate talent from universities into the labor market. My journey commenced as a graduate recruiter within a talent management team for an investment bank in London, responsible for attracting, hiring, developing, and retaining early career talent. During my tenure, I made three intriguing observations. Firstly, the high turnover rates among personnel in graduate recruitment and university career services made it challenging to establish and maintain sustainable strategic partnerships. Secondly, resource restrictions often limited the support university career services could provide their students. Similarly, our relatively small recruitment team could only physically visit a limited number of universities between the start of the academic year (late September or early October) and the closing date for internship and graduate program applications (mid to late November). Thirdly, despite receiving an exceedingly high volume of applicants, we often struggled to meet the headcount demands of the business. The most promising candidates frequently received multiple job offers from our competitors, leading to the practice of accepting several offers and then reneging at the last minute on all of the agreed contracts except the one with their preferred employer. On the other hand, less competitive candidates lacked knowledge of the sector, the organization, job roles, or how to navigate the application and selection process. Consequently, these individuals often faced multiple rejection decisions, undermining their confidence and self-perceived employability.

In 2012, my career in the industry ended abruptly due to a life-changing disability. However, I successfully adapted and pursued a PhD from 2014 to 2017 under the supervision of Professor Yehuda Baruch and Associate Professor Melanie Ashleigh at Southampton Business School, University of Southampton. My PhD research employed a mixed methods approach to explore students' perceptions of graduate employability – a topic largely overlooked in the graduate employability and career literature at the time. To highlight this fact, according to Google Scholar, the two empirical papers from my PhD research have garnered over 500 citations and according to ResearchGate, they have been read over 17,250 times by individuals from over 100 countries. My PhD research yielded four notable findings. Firstly, the students who would benefit the most from accessing university career services were least likely to seek career support. Secondly, men exhibited higher self-perceived employability compared to women. Thirdly, students pursuing specialized degrees (e.g., Engineering, Law, or Mathematics) demonstrated higher self-perceived employability than those undertaking generalist degrees (e.g., English, History, or Philosophy). Lastly, self-perceived employability declined between the penultimate and final year of undergraduate study, influenced by contextual factors such as labor market competitiveness and individuals receiving rejection decisions during the application and selection process. These findings raised concerns regarding student engagement with university career services and the potential impact on social mobility, particularly the disparities by gender and degree discipline.

In the seven years since completing my PhD, I have made significant contributions to the academic community by publishing conceptual, empirical, literature review, opinion, and theoretical manuscripts in internationally accredited journals. Through collaborations with scholars from Australia, Canada, China, India, the United Arab Emirates, the United Kingdom, and the United States of America, I have explored the perspectives of students, graduates, graduate recruiters, and university career services. One notable observation is the limited integration between theory and practice. Primarily, academics publish in journals read by other academics, while practitioners publish in magazines read by other practitioners. Another intriguing observation from my time in academia has been the need for more integration between research areas and research groups. To address these two concerns, I took on the role of sole Editor for a book titled ‘Handbook of Research on Sustainable Career Ecosystems for University Students and Graduates’, published by IGI Global in June 2023. The book aimed to bridge the fragmented Vocational Behavior and Human Resource Management fields as well as academic and practitioner perspectives in the context of early-career talent. The twenty-four chapters provided original and thought-provoking discussions encouraging readers to think broadly about sustainable career ecosystems. The handbook featured contributions from forty-four individuals representing institutions across five continents (Africa, Asia, Europe, North America, and Oceania) and twelve countries (Australia, Canada, China, Germany, Hungary, India, Italy, Nigeria, South Africa, United Arab Emirates, United Kingdom, and the United States of America). These contributors included academics and practitioners at various career stages and across diverse disciplines, capturing national and global perspectives from established and emerging voices.

Whilst working on the handbook of research, I uncovered another significant gap in the existing literature. In January 2023, I searched Google Scholar using the phrase "career advisors and graduate recruiters". Surprisingly, the top 10 results revealed that I was listed as an author in positions 1 (2022), 2 (2022), 3 (2022), 6 (2019), and 10 (2022). The remaining works in positions 4 (1989), 5 (1984), 7 (2006), 8 (2006), and 9 (2011) were all published over a decade ago. Yet, significant changes have occurred in the higher education landscape in the past decade. We have witnessed the introduction and substantial increases in student tuition fees, leading to higher student loans and associated debt. The number of students pursuing higher education has also dramatically risen, resulting in heightened competition for graduate jobs and ongoing debates regarding student and graduate visas. Furthermore, various global events such as recessions, pandemics, wars, and rising inflation have significantly impacted the labor market and the recruitment of early career talent. Moving forward, climate change will likely take center stage alongside the advancement of Artificial Intelligence (AI) and automation.

Drawing upon my unique combination of lived experience as a practitioner and academic, as well as my extensive networks within the industry and higher education institutions, I gained valuable insights that led to engaging discussions with the publisher IGI Global. These discussions resulted in the commissioning of this book in Spring 2023 titled 'Strategic Opportunities for Bridging the University-Employer Divide'. The primary objective of this timely publication is to bring together academic and practitioner perspectives, offering pragmatic strategies for university career advisors and graduate recruiters to act as catalysts for fostering sustainable career ecosystems whereby all actors benefit. The book is a comprehensive resource that captures the current landscape, identifies opportunities, and addresses challenges in enhancing collaboration between universities and employers. In the aftermath of the COVID-19 pandemic, which has created an unprecedented demand for university career support from students, and with organizations worldwide engaged in a fierce war for talent, the book takes on added significance. Against this backdrop, I aim to present a consolidated view of how university career advisors and graduate recruiters (alongside other actors within a career ecosystem) can work collaboratively and strategically to prepare university students for sustainable careers. The book's primary audience is agents of university career services and organizations involved in preparing university students for sustainable careers. The secondary audience is academics and policymakers involved in research and strategic decision-making concerning preparing university students for sustainable graduate careers. The tertiary audience is university students interested in understanding how university career services and organizations can support them in preparing for transitioning across the university-work divide.

The resulting book is organized into four sections, comprising ten chapters. Section One serves as an introduction, whereby Chapter 1 presents an overview of university career advisors, graduate recruiters, and sustainable graduate careers. Section Two delves into the role of university career advisors in preparing students for sustainable careers, covering topics such as graduate employability and employability capital (Chapter 2), student engagement strategies (Chapter 3), and signaling employability (Chapter 4). In Section Three, the focus shifts to the role of graduate recruiters as agents for organizations, exploring their role in attracting early career talent (Chapter 5), preparing students for the university-to-work transition (Chapter 6), and assessing person-organization fit (Chapter 7). Section Four addresses the challenges (Chapter 8) and opportunities (Chapter 9) for greater collaboration between university career services and graduate employers, concluding with a discussion of future workplace trends and implications (Chapter 10).

This book distinguishes itself through its distinctive approach of seamlessly integrating diverse streams of academic literature with practitioner insights. One notable feature is the inclusion of a series of Lived Experience Insights, which provide firsthand accounts of real-world scenarios. Each insight presents the challenge, context, action taken, outcome, lessons learned, and advice in circa 500 words. These insights, shared by individuals including university career advisors, academics, recruitment agency employees, and graduate recruiters worldwide, offer 32 perspectives, with four presented at the end of Chapters 2-9. By combining these lived experiences with academic theory, the book brings the topics addressed in each chapter to life, providing a holistic view of the subject matter.

The preface now concludes by providing a brief overview of the ten chapters.

Chapter 1 serves as a comprehensive introduction and overview, setting the scene for the book. It begins by examining the contrasting landscapes of traditional and contemporary universities, where neoliberalization has brought about significant changes. These include the massification of higher education participation, the emergence of students as consumers facing increased tuition fees and student loans, a strong emphasis on employability outcomes (often measured as employment outcomes), and a failure to effectively address inclusion and social mobility concerns. In this context, the role of university career advisors as agents within contemporary universities has become increasingly significant. However, university career advisors often face resource constraints, particularly exacerbated by the challenges posed by the COVID-19 pandemic, which has heightened students' demand for career support. Thus, it becomes imperative for these actors to collaborate with academics to embed employability into the curriculum and with graduate recruiters as representatives of graduate employers to establish a sustainable career ecosystem. Yet, graduate recruiters also face resource limitations. Additionally, the increased reliance on technology in the attraction and selection processes has brought benefits (such as targeted outreach to specific student groups) and challenges (including the potential for biased algorithms impacting the selection process and perpetuating social inequality). The chapter explores sustainable careers and clearly defines a sustainable career ecosystem. Finally, it offers an overview of the remaining three sections of the book, which build upon the foundations established in Chapter 1.

Chapter 2 marks the beginning of Section 2 in the book, delving into the topic of graduate employability. It starts by exploring different definitions of graduate employability and the evolution of the skills agenda, transitioning from a narrow focus to a more comprehensive framework known as employability capital. In collaboration with Professor Yehuda Baruch and Associate Professor Melanie Ashleigh, we developed one of the most cited conceptual models of capital within the context of self-perceived graduate employability, published online in 2017 (the same year as two other influential models). Recognizing the benefits and limitations of each of these three models in isolation, our research team subsequently undertook a systematic literature review of publications between 2016 and 2022 to integrate various literature streams and models into a single comprehensive framework known as the Employability Capital Growth (ECG) model, published online in 2023. This chapter presents the ECG model, which encompasses nine forms of capital: (i) social capital, (ii) cultural capital, (iii) psychological capital, (iv) personal identity capital, (v) health capital, (vi) scholastic capital, (vii) market-value capital, (viii) career identity capital, and (ix) economic capital. Additionally, it considers external factors such as (i) access to career counseling, (ii) labor market supply and demand, (iii) location of jobs, (iv) recruitment process bias, (v) chance events and career shocks, (vi) cost of living versus wages, (vii) flexible working opportunities, and (viii) the impact of automation and AI. The ECG model also highlights personal outcomes, including (i) self-perceived employability, (ii) personal resources, (iii) personal brand, (iv) job attainment and quality, (v) job performance and productivity, (vi) career progression and success, (vii) earnings and financial security, and (viii) wellbeing and career satisfaction. Concluding this chapter, practical applications and operationalizations of the ECG model are discussed from the perspectives of university career services and their students. The chapter also features four lived experience insights, providing real-world examples that shed light on the concepts discussed and prompt readers to reflect upon pertinent questions concerning graduate employability and employability capital.

Chapter 3 highlights the pivotal role of university career services in assisting students to acquire employability capital and personal resources, ultimately enhancing their self-perceived employability, employment outcomes, and indicators of career sustainability, such as health, happiness, and productivity (as discussed in Chapter 1 and Chapter 2). Additionally, university career services play a vital role in helping students effectively communicate their employability to potential employers, a topic that will be explored further in Chapter 4. However, this chapter acknowledges that student engagement poses the primary challenge faced by university career services. In response, it examines four interconnected challenges: (i) limited student awareness and engagement, (ii) insufficient institutional commitment, (iii) growing student demands for health and wellbeing support, and (iv) difficulties in promoting social mobility. To address these challenges, the chapter presents five effective engagement strategies: (i) raising awareness and visibility, (ii) providing accessible, timely, and tailored support, (iii) implementing peer mentoring and alum mentoring programs, (iv) embedding employability within the curriculum, and (v) establishing additional partnerships and resources. Concluding the chapter, four lived experience insights are shared, offering real-world examples that illustrate challenges encountered, strategic approaches adopted, and outcomes achieved concerning student engagement.

Chapter 4 marks the conclusion of Section 2, focusing on the development and operationalization of employability capital for university students through effective signaling strategies to prospective employers. This approach recognizes the interconnectedness of signals and capitals during the university-to-work transition. The chapter begins by providing an overview of signaling theory and then delves into three avenues for students to develop and signal their employability. The first approach is personal branding, which involves individuals marketing themselves as a brand to enhance employment opportunities and career sustainability. Establishing a personal brand requires time, effort, and authenticity, with individuals needing to refine and adapt their brand as their career progresses. The second method of signaling employability is through career metaphors, which allow individuals to make sense of their evolving careers by framing their future as mental objects for exploration and reflection. One metaphor I created is the Weather as a Career Metaphor (WCM), comprising ten weather elements. These elements include the Sun, representing intrinsically rewarding employment; Rain, symbolizing personal growth and resource acquisition; Drought, indicating career stagnation; Thunder and Lightning, representing visible conflicts with others; Ice, denoting hidden challenges; Fog, representing uncertainty and an inability to see ahead; Tailwind, symbolizing support mechanisms for career progression; Headwind, indicating barriers to career progression; Tornado, representing adverse outcomes of career shocks or chance events; and Rainbow, signifying positive outcomes of career shocks or chance events. The third opportunity for signaling employability lies in career narratives, which help students identify and align their purpose, significance, and meaning in life. Career narratives also capture the importance of reciprocity and the need for mutually beneficial relationships. Concluding the chapter, four lived insights offer practical application of the themes discussed, allowing readers to understand how these concepts can be applied in real-world scenarios.

Chapter 5 marks the beginning of Section 3, shifting our focus to the role of graduate recruiters operating as agents for organizations. This chapter examines the critical task of attracting early career talent, which is essential for the sustainability of organizations and the overall career ecosystem. The chapter initially provides an overview of Generation Z, graduate migration patterns, Industry 4.0, and holistic identity formation. It then delves into the challenges faced in attracting early career talent, including (i) the war for talent and skills shortages, (ii) the importance of attracting diverse applicants, (iii) considering mental health, wellbeing, and flexible working, and (iv) the significance of corporate citizenship through social and environmental impacts. Subsequently, the chapter explores opportunities for attracting early career talent, such as (i) early engagement strategies, (ii) the cultivation of authentic branding, values, and culture, and (iii) the provision of competitive compensation, benefits, and development opportunities. Concluding the chapter, four lived experience insights are presented, showcasing examples from the media and entertainment industry and the fundraising sector in the United Kingdom, teaching in Canada, and the aviation industry in the United States of America. These insights provide a captivating glimpse into the challenges and opportunities surrounding the attraction of early career talent. They underscore the importance of adopting a multidimensional strategy and fostering collaborative engagement with other actors within the career ecosystem to increase the likelihood of successful and sustainable outcomes.

Chapter 6 continues Section 3, exploring how graduate recruiters and recruitment agency representatives acting on behalf of organizations can effectively prepare students to transition from university to the professional world. The chapter begins by giving an overview of the university-to-work transition, which refers to the period when students move from their academic lives to their professional careers, usually after graduating. The benefits organizations can expect from hiring graduate talent are also discussed. Attention then turns to the Graduate Recruitment Attraction Matrix (GRAM), which encompasses twenty-five activities to enhance talent attraction efforts and prepare students for undertaking the university-to-work transition. The four quadrants that form the GRAM are subsequently explored, followed by the activities grouped into six themes: (i) careers fairs, (ii) presentations and panel events, (iii) sponsorship and ambassador roles, (iv) networking and mentoring, (v) experience opportunities, and (vi) diversity-focused events. Finally, the chapter concludes by providing four lived experience insights. These insights offer perspectives from graduate recruiters, professionals engaged in preparing and sourcing graduate talent through agencies, and representatives from a foundation in Hungary that provides free or subsidized workshops and training sessions to help young people develop essential skills and competencies.

Chapter 7 concludes Section 3 by exploring how to establish and maintain Person-Organization Fit (POF). The chapter begins with an overview of the Person-Environment Fit (PEF) and POF theories. Next, the focus shifts to selecting graduate talent by introducing the Graduate Recruitment Selection Process (GRSP) model, which outlines thirteen stages from online application to hiring and induction. A discussion of the significance of sustainable talent pipelines is then presented along with an Early Career Talent Pipeline (ECTP) conceptual framework, emphasizing the importance to organizations of seeking feedback from interns and recent graduate hires to inform process improvements in their selection procedures. The chapter continues by considering challenges and strategies in assessing person-organization fit via four themes: (i) volume of applicants, (ii) selection stage choices, (iii) use of technology, and (iv) bias in the selection process. Furthermore, an Early Career Attraction and Retention (ECAR) model is presented, encompassing key themes of company culture, supply and demand, career progression, health and wellbeing, and remuneration. This model is based on interviews with employees who graduated in 2020 and 2008, providing insights into the factors that influence early career professionals' attraction to and retention within organizations. Additionally, the chapter introduces the Person-Organization Fit Assessment Matrix (POFAM), which demonstrates how person-organization fit can evolve over time. It includes examples where talent retention may be desirable or undesirable from either the employee's perspective, the organization's perspective, or both. The chapter concludes with four insights evidencing the challenges various organizations face and their actions to ensure alignment of POF during the attraction and selection process.

Chapter 8 begins Section 4 by considering the challenges of fostering greater collaboration among actors in pursuing a sustainable career ecosystem. The chapter identifies five challenges for university career advisors, including: (i) resource constraints, (ii) range of employers, (iii) alignment of goals and objectives, (iv) league table rankings, and (v) recruitment agencies. Next, five challenges for graduate recruiters are presented, including: (i) resource constraints, (ii) targeting universities, (iii) cultural differences, (iv) compliance approval, and (v) evolving business demands. Furthermore, the chapter explores the challenges additional actors face, including students, lecturers, alums, professional bodies, and national governments. The chapter concludes by presenting four lived experience insights from Australia, Canada, the USA, and the UK that shed light on collaboration challenges between actors.

Chapter 9 continues Section 4 by exploring the opportunities for enhanced collaboration among actors to sustain the career ecosystem. The chapter emphasizes the importance of collaboration between university career advisors and graduate recruiters, calling for the prioritization of open dialogue and the optimization of resources. Subsequently, the State Progress Checklist is introduced, consisting of three endeavor elements and nine themes. The three endeavor elements are (i) potential, (ii) agendas, and (iii) effects. The nine themes are (i) resources, (ii) motivations, (iii) interactions, (iv) assumptions, (v) scenarios, (vi) plans, (vii) actions, (viii) outcomes, and (ix) reuses. Fifty questions are then provided, mapped to the nine themes, for university career advisors and graduate recruiters to consider separately and then collaboratively. Additional actors that play integral roles in determining the sustainability of the career ecosystem are then briefly discussed, including students, lecturers, alums, professional bodies, and national governments. The chapter concludes with the final set of four lived experience insights from Canada, India, and the UK.

Chapter 10 concludes Section 4 and the book with some thoughts about future workplace trends and their implications. The chapter begins by considering recent developments and the current landscape, which suggests the future of work will likely be volatile, uncertain, complex, and ambiguous, particularly around the impacts of technological advancement and climate change. From an organizational standpoint, fifteen key areas across three themes are identified concerning the future of work. Theme one, attraction and selection, includes (i) the war for talent, (ii) the skills gap, (iii) skill-based hiring, (iv) automation and AI, and (v) diversity, equity, and inclusion outcomes. Theme two, human-centric work design, incorporates (vi) I-Deals, (vii) Automation and AI, (viii) flexible working, (ix) a 4-day work week, and (x) inclusive culture. The final theme, talent retention, includes (xi) upskilling and reskilling, (xii) purpose and autonomy, (xiii) feedback, (xiv) promotion, and (xv) remuneration. The chapter continues by considering the future of work from the graduate perspective. Four themes are identified based on qualitative interviews with graduates from 2020 and 2008, including (i) skill development (e.g., human skills and technical skills), (ii) motivation (e.g., growth mindset, industry knowledge, work experience, and attitude), (iii) career ownership (e.g., lifelong learning and career progression), and (iv) wellbeing (e.g., flexible working and work-life balance). Implications for universities include a sense of belonging, creating global citizens, curriculum design, and the evolving role of career counselors. Implications for students include university participation, lifewide learning, work experience, and a sense of purpose. Finally, implications for bridging the university-employer divide include dialogue between actors, resource-sharing, access to a broader range of employers, and using recruitment agencies as intermediaries. The chapter concludes with ten reflections, a future research agenda, and the key takeaway messages.

Thank you for taking the time to read this book. I hope that you find it informative and thought-provoking.

William E. Donald
University of Southampton, UK & Ronin Institute, USA

Acknowledgment

First, the author would like to thank each of the collaborators of the various projects which have helped inform this book's content.

Second, the author would like to thank the individuals who contributed to the 32 Lived Experience Insights, which enabled the book to bridge theory and practice.

Third, the author would like to thank the anonymous peer reviewers and also the following individuals who provided critical feedback on earlier drafts of the various chapters of the book:

Yehuda Baruch, *University of Southampton, UK*
Thomas J. Buckholtz, *Ronin Institute, USA*
Dinuka Gunaratne, *Northeastern University, Canada*
Helen P. N. Hughes, *University of Leeds, UK*
Maria Jakubik, *Ronin Institute, USA; University of Pécs, Hungary*
Oliver Jenkin, *Career Development Institute, UK*
Emily W. Lankau, *Ronin Institute, USA*
Maria Mouratidou, *University of Cumbria, UK*
Thanh Pham, *Monash University, Australia*
Philip Saxon, *Corvinus University of Budapest, Hungary*
Jenny Surridge, *Talent Acquisition and Projects Specialist, UK*
Jennifer Woodside, *University of Waterloo, Canada*

Fourth, the author would like to thank Denise Jackson, *Edith Cowan University, Australia, for* voluntarily giving up her time to write the foreword for this book.

Fifth, the author would like to thank the *University of Southampton, UK*, and the *Ronin Institute, USA,* for their ongoing support and the opportunity to be affiliated with them.

Sixth, the author would like to thank the team at *IGI Global, USA*, for their support in commissioning, developing, and publishing this book. Special thanks to Mikaela Felty, *Senior Acquisitions Editor*; Jan Travers, *Director of Intellectual Property and Contracts*; Ryan Cruz, *Editorial Integrity & Contracting Coordinator*; Nina Eddinger, *Assistant Book Development Editor*; and Jocelynn Hessler, *Managing Editor of Book Development*.

Seventh, the author would like to thank Hayley Lewis of HALO Psychology Limited for kindly allowing me to include her '10 Red Flags of Faulty Org Design' figure in this book.

Finally, the author would like to thank you, the reader. I hope that you find this book engaging and that it stimulates new ways of thinking to theoretically and practically advance strategic approaches to bridging the university-employer divide.

William E. Donald
University of Southampton, UK & Ronin Institute, USA

Section 1
Introduction and Overview

Chapter 1
Setting the Scene

ABSTRACT

This chapter builds on the preface by setting the scene for the book. The chapter provides an overview of the contemporary university, including a discussion of the influence of neoliberal policies. Next, university career advisors are introduced as agents of the university. The focus then shifts to graduate employers to consider their needs concerning early career talent. Graduate recruiters are then introduced as agents of the employer. Next, the concept of sustainable graduate careers is introduced, capturing the dimensions of person, context, and time, whereby time at university can act as an antecedent to a sustainable career. The chapter concludes by giving a brief overview of the remainder of the book.

INTRODUCTION

We live in interesting, complex, and challenging times. The pursuit and dissemination of knowledge as a function of the contemporary university must seek to address these challenges from systemic, local, national, and international perspectives. The rise of disinformation and 'fake news' places increased significance on critical thinking and challenging assumptions rather than adopting a dogmatic and entrenched perspective to any given situation. Complex and evolving labor markets mean an individual's learning is no longer confined to educational settings. Instead, learning must occur as a lifewide and lifelong pursuit (Cole & Coulson, 2022; Jackson, 2011). Lifewide learning refers to the various opportunities for learning at any given time, whilst lifelong learning captures a commitment to self-improvement and development across the lifespan. Moreover, The Fourth Industrial Revolution (Industry 4.0) has the potential to dramatically change our lives during a period

DOI: 10.4018/978-1-6684-9827-9.ch001

of rapid technological advancement. Baruch and Sullivan (2022) observe how the workforce will need to upskill and reskill across their career span in response to the increased prevalence of automation and artificial intelligence and the evolving needs of society and civilization. Concurrently, the increased risks of "chance events such as the COVID-19 pandemic and climate change mean that individuals must embrace change" (Donald & Mouratidou, 2022, p. 3). We also know that the potential impacts of these chance events are most significant for young people in the labor market due to increased risks of unemployment, underemployment, or wage suppression (Donald, 2020; Lee et al., 2020).

Another dimension at play is the role of universities in fostering social mobility. Current agendas and metrics addressing widening participation focus predominantly on transitioning from secondary to tertiary education. Yet, such approaches often fail to consider the impacts of time spent at university on students' social mobility and, subsequently, of graduates in the labor market (Bukodi, 2017). The lack of focus is problematic since the COVID-19 pandemic has exacerbated pre-existing social mobility issues and seen unprecedented demand for career support, whereby university career services often lack the resources to meet such demands from their students and recent graduates (Donald et al., 2022). In response, it has been proposed that graduate recruiters can play a valuable role by partnering with universities to achieve win-win outcomes (Buckholtz & Donald, 2022). Unfortunately, the high levels of personnel turnover within graduate recruitment teams make it difficult to establish and maintain relationships between universities and organizations (Reedy, 2022). Moreover, academics researching areas related to graduate employability, vocational behavior, talent acquisition, human resource management, and human resource development tend to publish most of their work in academic journals, often behind paywalls, where it is beyond the reach of practitioners and can take months or even years to reach the publication stage. Conversely, practitioners tend to write for blogs and practitioner magazines, which academics are less likely to access, and, although published promptly, are less likely to have undergone a thorough peer review process.

In response to these challenges, this book aims to draw together theoretical and practitioner insights to offer pragmatic strategies for university career advisers and graduate recruiters to act as agents for fostering sustainable graduate careers. The primary audience is agents of university career services and organizations involved in preparing university students for sustainable careers. The secondary audience is university students interested in understanding how university career services and organizations can prepare them for sustainable careers and support them in the university-to-work transition. The tertiary audience is academics and policymakers involved in research and strategic decision-making.

This opening chapter sets the scene by introducing contemporary universities, university career advisors, graduate employers, graduate recruiters, and sustainable graduate careers. The chapter concludes with an overview of the remaining three sections of the book, which develop on the foundations of chapter one to provide strategic opportunities for bridging the university-employer divide.

CONTEMPORARY UNIVERSITIES

The traditional view of the university, rooted in the 19th and 20th Centuries, afforded the protection of academic freedom to physical spaces (e.g., classrooms and labs) and the dialogue and discourse between scholars and their students. Yet, this closed approach risked abdication of social responsibility and failed to adapt to the evolving needs of broader society. Subsequently, the contemporary or social-engaged view, rooted in the late 20th and 21st Centuries, extends the coverage of such academic protections. Application occurs in the context of a willingness to be persuaded by new information, evidence, and discourse when conducted per ethical and professional standards determined by subject matter experts. The contemporary university is driven by a two-way exchange of knowledge between the university and broader society, with the goal of maximizing the benefits to society via a commitment to public service. In other words, higher education is tasked with developing "authentic and responsible citizens who will be able to act and solve global problems" (Jakubik, 2022, p. 285). As the British philosopher Nicholas Maxwell writes in the preface to his book titled *The World Crisis – And What to Do About It: Revolution for Thought and Action*, examples of global problems that threaten our future include:

the climate crisis; the current pandemic; the destruction of the natural world, catastrophic loss of wild life, and mass extinction of species; lethal modern war; the spread of modern armaments; the menace of nuclear weapons; pollution of earth, sea and air; rapid rise in the human population; increasing antibiotic resistance; the degradation of democratic politics, brought about in part by the internet. (Maxwell, 2021, Preface)

However, the shift from traditional to contemporary universities has also witnessed an increased influence of neoliberal policies. These manifestations include massification and globalization of participation in higher education, increased reliance on student fees and grants for university funding, and emphasis on metrics and associated league table rankings (Maisuria & Cole, 2017). Each of these dimensions brings its own challenges. The massification of higher education means that as a more significant proportion of the population holds a university degree, the value of the qualification reduces. The Dearing Report also saw the United Kingdom (UK) government shift the responsibility for the funding of university degrees from the state to the individual student (Dearing, 1997), which in turn positioned students as consumers, and led universities to seek to increase the representation of international students who paid higher fees than their domestic counterparts. Nevertheless, Brooks et al. (2021) found that although student perspectives are influenced by the fees they are charged, many students recognize universities as offering spaces for networking, learning, and knowledge-sharing to achieve personal growth, leading to decent employment, and contributing to broader society.

Another challenge stems from how student satisfaction scores and employment outcomes heavily influence the metrics that drive league table rankings. Prospective students subsequently use these rankings to inform their choice of university, meaning that universities that feature higher in the ranking tables can attract more students and the associated revenue from them. The need to ensure high student satisfaction scores, which are self-reported by the students, has led to accusations of grade inflation since student evaluations of teaching have been shown to increase when a student's grades increase for the corresponding course (Berezvai et al., 2021). Again, when combined with the massification of participation in higher education, accusations of grade inflation make it more difficult for employers to differentiate between graduates based on the degree classification, further undermining the value of a university degree. In fact, when combined with the shift of responsibility for the funding of a degree from the state to the individual, students perceive the benefits of participation in higher education to begin to narrow compared to the associated costs (Donald et al., 2018).

The challenges of contemporary universities also impact academics. The supply of individuals securing a Doctor of Philosophy (PhD), a Doctor of Business Administration (DBA), or a Doctorate in Education (EdD) greatly exceeds the availability of academic jobs, particularly tenure track and Professor roles. Subsequently, many academics are given low-paid and temporary contracts, whereby in the initial phase of their career, they often have to move nationally or internationally every couple of years. The assessment by the university of an individual's teaching quality is also driven by self-reported student evaluations whereby higher satisfaction scores are deemed to indicate a higher quality of teaching provision. Unfortunately, not only do courses perceived to be 'easier' by the students secure higher satisfaction scores, but student evaluations are influenced by "racist, sexist and homophobic prejudices, and are biased against discipline and subject area" (Heffernan, p. 144). Subsequently, academics can experience high levels of stress, especially given that in addition to the design, delivery, and assessment of curriculum content, they are also expected to conduct and publish research and contribute via academic service (e.g., peer review, organizing conferences, etc.). For academics like me who are housebound and disabled, there are also significant barriers to accessing shared spaces for knowledge exchange since many conferences that were run virtually during the restriction periods of the COVID-19 pandemic have since returned to an in-person-only format. Examples of other academics impacted by these systemic barriers to inclusion are caregivers for family members, individuals unable to secure a visa to enter the host country, or those who cannot secure funding to cover the conference fee, travel and accommodation costs (Donald, 2022).

Risks to inclusion also present themselves to prospective and current university students (Ingram & Allen, 2019). One of the primary concerns is that higher education "primarily serves to maintain, rather than narrow, inequalities attached to social origins" (Bukodi, 2017, p. 367). Yet, social mobility data focusing on widening participation has predominantly captured admissions data, whereby data on the impacts during the degree course and across the career span remain embryonic (Donald & Ford, 2023). Consequently, there have been calls for a more inclusive and diverse curriculum design (Jackson, 2020), particularly concerning access to work-integrated learning experiences (Lloyd et al., 2019). Such calls are timely, given that the COVID-19 pandemic further exacerbated social inequalities by disrupting education provision and assessment, restricting social interactions, and limiting opportunities to gain work experience (Daniel, 2020; Dougherty, 2022). Additionally, research shows that university students who would benefit the most from seeking career guidance from their university career service are those least likely to do so (Donald et al., 2018).

The role of university career advisors as agents of contemporary universities thus takes on increased significance. Enhancing employability can promote social mobility, increase league table rankings, and benefit broader society via a diverse and innovative workforce to address the challenges of a changing world. A caveat to mention here is that employability (the ability to do a job) is distinct from employment (a snapshot in time metric of whether an individual currently has a job), highlighting the influence of contextual factors that sit beyond an individual's agency (Jackson & Bridgstock, 2018). Such a distinction is often lost in league table rankings, whereby metrics claiming to measure the employability of graduates often measure employment outcomes instead. In areas where there is an oversupply of graduates compared to the demand, employers have historically relied on the university's reputation as an initial filter, meaning that the higher-ranked universities are less impacted by contextual factors than lower-ranked universities–presenting a further concern for inclusion and social mobility.

UNIVERSITY CAREER ADVISORS

Traditionally, university career advisors tended to be centralized within a single physical building on each university's main campus with the narrow remit of supporting their students to draft and polish Curriculum Vitae (CVs) and cover letters for job applications. However, the role of university career advisors in the UK expanded following the Dearing Report (Dearing, 1997). Universities were incentivized to increase their students' and graduates' employability and employment outcomes because it influenced league table rankings. Yet, the evolution of the role of a university career advisor driven by such policies and approaches was not confined to the UK. Yoon and Hutchinson (2018) observe the uniformity of the role of career advisors within universities around the globe, grounded in response to two societal concerns, "filling gaps between education and employment needs" and "being responsive to the growing demands of the 21st Century global economy" (p. 220). Subsequently, the scope of career guidance has expanded across the centralized career service and the decentralized school or faculty levels in recognition of the social responsibility of the contemporary university to prepare their students for the labor market (Bridgstock & Jackson, 2019; López-Miguens et al., 2021). Career advisors usually require specific qualifications, training, and certification, whereby typical services provided include:

1) assessment (exploration); 2) employment information (exploration); 3) coaching/ counseling (exploration and choices); 4) career fairs (career exploration, choices, preparation, and first job selection); 5) career workshops/trainings (preparation); 6) internships (preparation); 7) employer engagement (first job selection); and 8) application assistance including resume, cover letter, job interview, and selection training (first job selection). (Yoon & Hutchinson, 2018, p. 221)

Career advisors also became tasked with engaging academics, students, and employers, by acting as agents for the university operating within an evolving career ecosystem. Baruch (2015) defines a career ecosystem as a dynamic environment consisting of interconnected and interdependent actors whose interactions determine the effectiveness of the overall system by facilitating a constant flow of human capital. Therefore, for the purpose of this book, a career advisor is defined as an agent of the university responsible for enhancing the employability of their students (either in a centralized or decentralized setup) by engaging with other actors operating within a career ecosystem such that the flow of talent from the university to the labor market benefits all actors.

Academics can act as role models for their students and engage them in discussions about their future careers, which in turn, can increase self-efficacy (Zhang et al., 2018). Their knowledge of the labor market and associated contacts can also help identify student networking and employment opportunities, including internships, placements, and graduate scheme opportunities (Donald et al., 2018). Academics can also provide critical insights regarding the abilities and needs of their students to career advisors, either via the centralized university career service or via the decentralized representatives at the faculty or school level. The approach can subsequently enable career advisors to articulate what their students can offer to employees and where they need additional support. Similarly, employers know their respective demands of graduates and the resources that they have available to support university students in preparing for the university-to-work transition. Therefore, fostering such partnerships between interconnected and interdepending actors operating within a career ecosystem can lead to win-win outcomes (Buckholtz & Donald, 2022). The collaboration between actors, including university alums, within a career ecosystem can also enhance students' self-perceived employability and employment outcomes (Cody et al., 2018) and operationalize holistic engagement across the ecosystem (Ferns et al., 2019).

Another benefit of fostering partnerships within a career ecosystem comes from increased opportunities for student engagement. Partnerships between career advisors, academics, and industry can help tailor approaches to individual students to increase their readiness for the global labor market following graduation (Hennings et al., 2022). We know that (i) students who need career guidance the most are least likely to seek it (Donald et al., 2018), (ii) many students do not access support early enough in their degree (Lynch & Lungrin, 2018), and (iii) the COVID-19 pandemic has led to unprecedented demand from students and graduates for career guidance (Donald et al., 2022). Academics can play a crucial role in helping their students connect lived experiences, interests, and goals with the curriculum, assessment approaches, and learning outcomes (Lynch & Lungrin, 2018). The approach can help students identify opportunities to enhance their employability whilst promoting social mobility via improved retention outcomes (Ayoubi, 2017). My own collaborative research has also shown the potential for embedding employability into the curriculum, whereby students' confidence in their self-perceived employability rose from 37.5% to 92.5% during a 10-week compulsory module (Padgett & Donald, 2023). Students cited the benefits of the module to include "increased confidence, interactive classes, skills development, knowledge of the recruitment process, CV development, proactive career ownership, interview guidance and networking" (p. 1). These findings developed calls to use the curriculum as a vehicle to enhance self-perceived employability and practical wisdom in students (Jakubik, 2021; Jakubik & Müürsepp, 2022). They are also supported by Petruzziello et al. (2022), who found that online environments as part of the university curriculum in Italy, used during the COVID-19 pandemic, enhanced career engagement and facilitated the acquisition of career-related resources. Consequently, career advisors can benefit themselves and their students by establishing and maintaining partnerships with academics and working with organizations to provide guidance on curriculum content and design.

Career advisors were also significantly impacted by the COVID-19 pandemic-related restrictions, with fundamental shifts in their relationship with organizations. Instead of their traditional role as 'event organizers' charging employers for access to talent on campus, career advisors were now 'partnership managers' (O'Brien, 2022). The disruption to on-campus events in 2020 and 2021 saw a temporary shift from in-person to online events, raising questions from late 2021 onwards concerning which events should stay online and which should eventually return to an in-person format (Donald et al., 2022). Career services had a crucial role to play in advocating for their students regarding what works best for them from an engagement and employability development perspective (O'Brien, 2022). Simultaneously, university career advisors became more aware of the benefits of engaging with the local community and promoting access to career opportunities within Small and Medium Enterprises (SMEs; Vincent & Chahal, 2022). Students benefit from such a strategic evolution since it increases the diversity and location of employment opportunities beyond the multinational and often London-centric corporations that traditionally have dominated the in-person and 'pay-to-play' university career fairs (Donald et al., 2022).

Our focus now shifts from university career advisors as agents of universities to the needs of graduate employers before introducing graduate recruiters as agents of organizations.

GRADUATE EMPLOYERS

Earlier in the chapter, we considered how the rise of automation and artificial intelligence as part of Industry 4.0 will drive the need for upskilling and reskilling of talent to meet the needs of society (Baruch & Sullivan, 2022). Routine and repetitive jobs are likely to be replaced with higher-skilled jobs (Ghani & Muhammad, 2019), increasing the pressure on universities to produce highly skilled graduates (Teng et al., 2019). Unfortunately, graduates tend to perceive their skills development more favorably than employers at the point of university-to-work transition, further highlighting the need for collaboration between the interdependent actors operating within a career ecosystem (Lisá et al., 2019). There is also a lack of alignment between what universities think employers want and what employers actually want regarding graduates entering the labor market (Osmani et al., 2019). A similar theme appears when considering what the term 'quality' means in the context of higher education provision based on the perceptions of academics, students, and employers. Students and academics emphasize the quality of teaching and learning and the professional relationships between academics and students, whilst employers emphasize the value of personal qualities (Dicker et al., 2019). Dicker and colleagues subsequently call for greater collaboration between organizations and universities to ensure the curriculum design helps to produce employable graduates capable of meeting the current and future demands of the labor market and broader society. The value of an undergraduate degree as a differentiator and determinant of talent has also been eroded due to the massification of participation in higher education. For example, Verhaest et al. (2018) found that when an employer lists an undergraduate degree as a minimum requirement on a job specification, applicants who hold a Master's degree are 19 per cent more likely to be invited to the interview stage compared to applicants who only hold an undergraduate degree (Verhaest et al., 2018). The value of a Master's degree can be even more influential in certain sectors and for specific roles where there are high levels of competition for employment opportunities.

The Careers 2032 Project (2022) found that the top strategic challenge cited by graduate employers for the upcoming decade (2022-2032) was attracting and retaining diverse talent, deemed critical for organizational sustainability. The findings align with a report by the Bright Network (2022), which found that 62% of students and 77% of employers did not think graduate recruitment was inclusive. Historically, there have been concerns that employers give the illusion of inclusion without providing equitable graduate outcomes. For example, Ingram and Allen (2019) found that whilst employers provided employment opportunities to graduates from lower socioeconomic backgrounds, the graduates from the most privileged backgrounds tended to secure the best-paid and most prestigious roles. Once in the labor market, such issues continue to play out whereby the employees who would benefit the most from voluntary opt-in programmes such as mentorship are those least likely to participate (Sandvik et al., 2022), re-enforcing the same trend with career guidance in university settings (Donald et al., 2018). University students and recent graduates also voice concerns around diversity initiatives of graduate employers, citing the most significant barriers as lacking a network of contacts, a lack of relevant work experience, competition from other graduates, and economic factors (Bright Network, 2022). My own collaborative research also shows how the COVID-19 pandemic widened pre-existing inequalities. Individuals undertaking the university-to-work transition since 2020 are less prepared than previous cohorts since the pandemic-related restrictions disrupted their education, limited opportunities to gain work experience, and undermined their confidence (Donald & Jackson, 2022).

The COVID-19 pandemic also influenced what employers and graduates look for in each other. My discussions with graduate employers found an increased emphasis on commercial acumen, previous labor market experience, resilience, and taking the initiative, whilst one's degree classification became less significant (Donald et al., 2022). A study of university students and recent graduates found that 54% of respondents felt the pandemic would impact their graduate prospects, whilst 95% thought employers should be playing a more active role in upskilling students during their degree (Bright Network, 2022). Another study captured the desire for job crafting, flexible working opportunities, meaning, and purpose, as the COVID-19 pandemic gave them time to reflect on what they truly want from life (Afshari & Nasab, 2021). Increased emphasis is also being placed on wellbeing and work-life balance since three in four university students and recent graduates reported reduced levels of subjective wellbeing due to the pandemic-related restrictions (Donald & Jackson, 2022). Further research that I carried out collaboratively in India suggests that employers can facilitate graduates to manage their stress levels, acquire and replenish personal resources, and increase workplace wellbeing by providing opportunities to participate in serious leisure activities (Nimmi & Donald, 2022). Therefore, it seems logical that graduate employers who offer the greatest flexibility and support to early career talent concerning working hours, location, job role, and career progression will gain a competitive advantage by attracting prospective talent and retaining existing talent.

Our focus now shifts to exploring the role of graduate recruiters operating as agents for graduate employers.

GRADUATE RECRUITERS

University career advisors and graduate recruiters represent the meso-level actors responsible for preparing students for the university-to-work transition, whereby graduate recruiters act as agents of organizations and can be considered gatekeepers (Holmes, 2013). Organizations tend to adopt one of three approaches, (i) graduate recruiters are employed by the organization, (ii) organizations outsource their recruitment whereby graduate recruiters are employed by an agency and may work with multiple organizations concurrently, or (iii) organizations supplement an internal team of graduate recruiters with expertise from an external agency. Regardless of the approach, the overall objective is broadly the same: attract and select diverse early career talent cost-effectively and efficiently to meet the organization's current and future needs. Therefore, this book adopts Donald et al.'s (2022) definition of a graduate recruiter as *an employee of a graduate recruitment team within a human resources (HR) department of an organization, an employee of a graduate recruitment agency or an employee of other such organizations specializing in student and graduate talent. Their remit includes responsibility for or support of (e.g., through research and strategic planning) the attraction and selection of current university students and recent graduates for spring week (opportunities for fresher students), summer internship, year-in-industry placement, and, most importantly, graduate roles. (p. 2)*

From a career ecosystem perspective, graduate recruiters work with managers of graduates to understand the specific business needs and headcount demands, the marketing team to attract talent, and university career advisors or agencies to access students at specific universities or with specific demographics. Unfortunately, the cyclical nature of annual recruitment means that graduate recruiters employed within HR teams tend to move roles every couple of years, either to a competitor organization, a recruitment agency or, internally, into a different HR function with fewer travel and event commitments (Donald et al., 2022). The movement of graduate recruiters captures the dynamic nature of career ecosystems. It also highlights the challenges for relationship management between universities and organizations, and the difficulties in delivering long-term strategic agendas for the organization. However, understanding the views of graduate recruiters remains imperative for universities to prepare their students for an evolving labor market (Boffo, 2018), acknowledging how each actor in the career ecosystem impacts the path, progress, and direction of the other actors (Bhaskar et al., 2023). Graduate recruiters operating within recruitment agencies may be able to help overcome the high mobility of internal graduate recruiters operating within the HR departments of organizations. Yet, university career advisors were wary of such relationships amid concerns that organizations pivot their strategic partnerships from university career services to graduate recruitment agencies (Donald et al., 2022).

The COVID-19 pandemic represented a significant chance event whereby restrictions to daily life accompanied by socio-technical change caused unprecedented challenges and disruption for recruitment agencies, organizations and their talent management strategies (Cooke et al., 2021; Mulder, 2021). Graduate recruiters were temporarily forced into pivoting their attraction and selection activities from an in-person to a virtual format, requiring significant investment in digital transformation technologies (Soto-Acosta, 2020). Despite such challenges, organizations were keen to continue hiring graduates for the recruitment cycle, albeit with some adjustments to the headcount demands from specific business areas. The Institute of Student Employers (ISE) and the International Network of Employers and University Career Services (INEUCS) claimed that organizations had learnt their lessons from aggressively cutting headcount targets for early career talent in response to the

2007-2008 Global Financial Crisis, which resulted in a lack of sustainable talent pipelines to meet future business demands when market conditions improved (ISE & INEUCS, 2020). The same report also found that students were considering delaying their entry into the labor market by undertaking postgraduate study (e.g., a Master's degree) in the hope that any volatility in the graduate labor market would be short-lived. However, the report's authors raised concerns about a repeat of the aftermath of the 2007-2008 Global Financial Crisis, whereby a similar approach led to a temporary reduction in the flow of talent into the labor market, resulting in an oversupply of graduates in the subsequent years.

During the initial lockdown phase of the COVID-19 pandemic, I had the opportunity to interview graduate recruiters (operating internally within an organization's HR team or externally for a recruitment agency) from the accounting, banking, and finance sectors (Donald et al., 2023). The perceived benefits of the disruption included overcoming resistance to change, embracing technology, and environmental impacts (e.g., reduced travel and printing of marketing and assessment materials). Conversely, the perceived risks included difficulties differentiating marketing and branding from competitors in a virtual environment, the absence of any in-person assessment phase during the selection process, and problems conducting onboarding virtually (e.g., performing identity checks). Perhaps the most interesting finding was the impact of the pandemic on the diversity of hires. Graduate recruiters operating within HR teams assumed that the increased reliance on technology in the selection process would reduce bias, leading to an increased diversity of hires. Unfortunately, the reality was quite different, whereby bias was often inadvertently embedded into the design process and the decision-making algorithms, negatively impacting the diversity of graduate hires. External graduate recruiters operating within recruitment agencies tended to report more favorable outcomes since a virtual format meant they could invite students representing specific demographics from multiple universities simultaneously instead of having to visit a limited number of universities in person.

The easing of pandemic-related restrictions raised some interesting questions for graduate recruiters (Donald et al., 2023). These include:

- What aspects of the attraction and selection process should remain virtual to gain a return on the significant investment in digital transformation technologies?
- What aspects are best delivered via an in-person format?
- Has the role of a graduate recruiter fundamentally changed, whereby time spent travelling around various universities can now be spent running tailored and personalized virtual events?
- Does this mean that technological competence will become a crucial requirement for graduate recruiters?

- What do the changes mean for the actors within a career ecosystem?
- Can collaboration between actors help to distribute individual risk factors?
- Can digital transformation lead to win-win outcomes?

The remaining part of this introductory chapter focuses on sustainable graduate careers before offering a brief overview of the upcoming topics addressed in this book.

SUSTAINABLE GRADUATE CAREERS

Hughes (1937, cited in Baruch, 2006) defined a career as "the moving perspectives in which persons orient themselves in reference to the social order, and of the typical sequences and concatenations of office" (p. 126). The word career originates from the Latin word *carrus,* meaning *wheeled vehicle*. It emerged in English in the mid-16th Century from the French word *carrière* and the Italian word *carriera* and originally referred to a *road* or *racecourse*. Language development over time resulted in a career representing the road or course taken by an individual during their working life. Arthur et al. (1989) capture this in their definition of a career as "the evolving sequence of a person's work experiences over time" (p. 8). Historically, organizations adopted a predictable, stable, and predefined structure, offering an authority-based hierarchical career system (Super, 1957). The traditional career involved a linear pathway of upward mobility through hierarchical progression (Wilensky, 1961), whereby a psychological contract saw an employee exchange loyalty to an organization for security via a job for life. A psychological contract is defined by Rousseau (1995) as "individual beliefs, shaped by the organization, regarding terms of an exchange agreement between individuals and their organizations" (p. 9). The definition was subsequently amended by Baruch and Hind (1999), who defined the psychological contract as "the unspoken promise, not present in the small print of the employment contract, of what the employer gives, and what employees give in return (p. 299).

The late 20th Century witnessed a significant shift with the emergence of a contemporary career, characterized by unstable and unpredictable career environments, low levels of job security, and increased movement within and across different organizations, whereby the individual commits to themselves or a profession rather than an organization (Gubler et al., 2014). Concurrently, the old psychological contract of stability, loyalty, and mutual commitment was replaced by a new psychological contract of dynamism, breach of the old contract, and competence-based relationships (Baruch, 2015). However, that is not to say that traditional careers no longer exist, rather that contemporary careers have greater prevalence in the labor market (Dries & Verbruggen, 2012). The shift from traditional to contemporary careers places increased significance on a sustainable career, particularly for graduates who now have multiple paths to employability (Donald, 2017; Donald et al., 2017). A sustainable career is defined as "sequences of career experiences reflected through a variety of patterns of continuity over time, thereby crossing several social spaces, characterized by individual agency, herewith providing meaning to the individual" (Van der Heijden & De Vos, 2015, p. 7). Their definition captures three dimensions of person, context and time, whereby education is an antecedent to career sustainability (De Vos et al., 2020), with three key indicators of a sustainable career being happiness, health, and productivity (Van der Heijden, 2005). For the purpose of this book, the *person* is a university student or recent graduate, the *context* is the various higher education institutions and employers of graduates, and *time* represents the progression through university and into the labor market. The approach acknowledges the shared tenants of graduate employability and worker employability, responding to calls to bridge these two research areas, which have historically developed independently (Akkermans et al., 2023). The contemporary career and the new psychological contract mean that the responsibility for a sustainable career is shared by individuals and employers (Fan & Potočnik, 2021). Students and graduates need to take ownership of their careers, whilst universities and employers need to facilitate them in acquiring employability capital and personal resources (Freire & Bettencourt, 2021). Consequently, individuals benefit from career success and wellbeing, whilst organizations benefit from increased competitive advantage, productivity, and financial performance (Donald et al., 2020; Ybema et al., 2020).

For the purpose of this book, I combine the definitions of a *Career Ecosystem* (Baruch, 2015) and *Sustainable Careers* (Van der Heijden & De Vos, 2015) to define the construct of a *Sustainable Career Ecosystem* as

a variety of interconnected and interdependent actors across higher education institutions and workplace contexts, whereby the lives and careers of individuals evolve and play out over time with an emphasis on sustainable outcomes for the individual, organizations, and broader society. Indicators at the individual level include employability, lifewide and lifelong learning via a growth mindset, health, happiness, productivity, and financial security. Indicators at the organizational level include the attraction and retention of talent, innovation, competitive advantage, financial performance, and productivity. Indicators for broader society include increased levels of taxation for investment in public services, increased standards of living, national competitiveness, national wellbeing, and acknowledgement of the need for collaborative approaches to the future of work. (Donald, 2023a, Preface)

A sustainable career ecosystem provides the framework for understanding the roles that university career advisors and graduate recruiters, as the respective agents of the university and organizational contexts, can play in facilitating and establishing sustainable careers for university students and graduates. The objective is to foster win-win outcomes for all actors operating within a sustainable career ecosystem whereby such benefits continue to play out over time. This book builds on an emerging area of interest, combining career ecosystems and the new psychological contract to strive for sustainable career and organizational outcomes (e.g., Baruch & Rousseau, 2019; Donald, 2023b; Donald et al., 2020).

OVERVIEW OF THE BOOK

Section One has set the scene for this book by introducing contemporary universities, university career advisors, graduate employers, graduate recruiters, and sustainable graduate careers (Chapter 1). Next, Section Two focuses on the role of university career advisors in helping their students prepare for a sustainable career by exploring graduate employability and employability capital (Chapter 2), engagement strategies (Chapter 3), and signaling employability (Chapter 4). Attention then turns to Section Three to explore the role of graduate recruiters operating as agents for an organization to attract early career talent (Chapter 5), prepare students for the university-to-work transition (Chapter 6), and assess person-organization fit (Chapter 7). Finally, Section Four considers the challenges of greater collaboration between university career services and graduate employers (Chapter 8), the opportunities for fostering such a collaboration (Chapter 9), and a discussion of future workplace trends (Chapter 10). Sections Two, Three, and Four also incorporate a series of real-world 'Lived Experience Insights' since this book aims to draw together theoretical and practical dimensions to offer pragmatic strategies for university career advisors and graduate recruiters to act as agents for bridging the university-employer divide and fostering sustainable careers by preparing university students to undertake the university-to-work transition.

REFERENCES

Afshari, L., & Nasab, A. H. (2021). Enhancing Organizational Learning Capability Through Managing Talent: Mediation Effect Of Intellectual Capital. *Human Resource Development International*, *24*(1), 48–64. doi:10.1080/13678868.2020.1727239

Akkermans, J., Donald, W. E., Jackson, D., & Forrier, A. (2023). Are we talking about the same thing? The case for stronger connections between graduate and worker employability research. *Career Development International*. Advance online publication. doi:10.1108/CDI-08-2023-0278

Arthur, M. B., Hall, D. T., & Lawrence, B. S. (1989). *Handbook of Career Theory*. Cambridge University Press. doi:10.1017/CBO9780511625459

Ayoubi, A. (2017). *The Tremendous Benefits of Connecting Academic and Career Advising*. The Career Leadership Collective.

Baruch, Y. (2006). Career development in organizations and beyond: Balancing traditional and contemporary viewpoints. *Human Resource Management Review*, *16*(2), 125–138. doi:10.1016/j.hrmr.2006.03.002

Baruch, Y. (2015). Organizational and labor market as career eco-system. In A. De Vos & B. I. J. M. Van der Heijden (Eds.), *Handbook of Research on Sustainable Careers* (pp. 164–180). Edward Elgar. doi:10.4337/9781782547037.00029

Baruch, Y., & Hind, P. (1999). Perpetual motion in organizations: Effective management and the impact of the new psychological contracts on 'Survivor Syndrome'. *European Journal of Work and Organizational Psychology*, *8*(2), 295–306. doi:10.1080/135943299398375

Baruch, Y., & Rousseau, D. M. (2019). Integrating psychological contracts and ecosystems in career studies and management. *The Academy of Management Annals*, *13*(1), 84–111. doi:10.5465/annals.2016.0103

Baruch, Y., & Sullivan, S. E. (2022). The why, what and how of career research: A review and recommendations for future study. *Career Development International*, *27*(1), 135–159. doi:10.1108/CDI-10-2021-0251

Berezvai, Z., Lukáts, G. D., & Molontay, R. (2021). Can professors buy better evaluation with lenient grading? The effect of grade inflation on student evaluation of teaching. *Assessment & Evaluation in Higher Education*, *46*(5), 793–808. doi:10.1080/02602938.2020.1821866

Bhaskar, A. U., Baruch, Y., & Seeta, G. (2023). Drivers of career success among the visually impaired: Improving career inclusivity and sustainability in a career ecosystem. *Human Relations*, *76*(10), 1507–1544. doi:10.1177/00187267221103529

Boffo, V. (2018). Employability and transitions: fostering the future of young adult graduates. In V. Boffo & M. Fedeli (Eds.), *Employability and Competences: Innovative Curricula for New Professions*, (pp. 117-128). Firenze University Press. doi:10.36253/978-88-6453-672-9.19

Bridgstock, R., & Jackson, D. (2019). Strategic institutional approaches to graduate employability: Navigating meanings, measurements and what really matters. *Journal of Higher Education Policy and Management*, *41*(5), 468–484. doi:10.1080/1360080X.2019.1646378

Bright Network. (2022). *What do graduates want? 2022/23*. Bright Network. https://employers.brightnetwork.co.uk/what-do-graduates-want-report-and-video

Brooks, R., Gupta, A., Jayadeva, S., & Abrahams, J. (2021). Students' views about the purpose of higher education: A comparative analysis of six European countries. *Higher Education Research & Development*, *40*(7), 1375–1388. doi:10.1080/07294360.2020.1830039

Buckholtz, T. J., & Donald, W. E. (2022). Direct outcomes and win-win relationships between university careers advisors and graduate recruiters. *GiLE Journal of Skills Development*, *2*(1), 9–25. doi:10.52398/gjsd.2022.v2.i1.pp9-25

Bukodi, E. (2017). Cumulative inequalities over the life course: Life-long learning and social mobility in Britain. *Journal of Social Policy*, *46*(2), 367–404. doi:10.1017/S0047279416000635

Cody, E. E., Kryst, E. L., & Smith, K. K. (2018). Collaboration as a cornerstone for change. *Career Planning and Adult Development Journal*, *34*(2), 20–31.

Cole, D., & Coulson, B. (2022). Through and beyond COVID-19, promoting whole person, lifelong and lifewide learning. *Journal of Innovation in Polytechnic Education*, *4*(1), 81–90.

Cooke, F. J., Dickmann, M., & Parry, E. (2021). IJHRM after 30 years: Taking stock in times of COVID-19 and looking towards the future of HR research. *International Journal of Human Resource Management*, *32*(1), 1–23. doi:10.1080/09585192.2020.1833070

Daniel, J. (2020). Education and the COVID-19 pandemic. *Prospects*, *49*(1), 91–96. doi:10.100711125-020-09464-3 PMID:32313309

De Vos, A., Van der Heijden, B. I. J. M. & Akkermans, J. (2020). Sustainable careers: Towards a conceptual model. *Journal of Vocational Behavior, 117*, a.103196. doi:10.1016/j.jvb.2018.06.011

Dearing, R. (1997). *Higher Education in the Learning Society: Report of the National Committee of Inquiry into Higher Education*. Her Majesty's Stationary Office.

Dicker, R., Garcia, M., Kelly, A., & Mulrooney, H. (2019). What does 'quality' in higher education mean? Perceptions of staff, students and employers. *Studies in Higher Education, 44*(8), 1425–1441. doi:10.1080/03075079.2018.1445987

Donald, W. E. (2017). *Students' Perceptions of Graduate Employability: A Sequential Explanatory Approach.* [Doctoral Thesis, University of Southampton]. https://eprints.soton.ac.uk/id/eprint/415935

Donald, W. E. (2020). *Viewpoint: COVID-19 and the Future of Careers.* Graduate Recruitment Bureau. doi:10.13140/RG.2.2.19306.13760

Donald, W. E. (2022). *Overcoming Systemic Barriers to Inclusion in Academia: The Case for a Hybrid Conference Format.* Times Higher Education. doi:10.13140/RG.2.2.13284.65926

Donald, W. E. (2023a). Preface. In W. E. Donald (Ed.), *Handbook of Research on Sustainable Career Ecosystems for University Students and Graduates,* (Preface). IGI Global. doi:10.4018/978-1-6684-7442-6

Donald, W. E. (2023b). Application of career ecosystems theory and the new psychological contract to the field of project management: Toward a conceptual model. *Project Management Journal, 54*(1), 7–18. doi:10.1177/87569728221118873

Donald, W. E., Ashleigh, M. J., & Baruch, Y. (2018). Students' perceptions of education and employability: Facilitating career transition from higher education into the labour market. *Career Development International, 23*(5), 513–540. doi:10.1108/CDI-09-2017-0171

Donald, W. E., Ashleigh, M. J., & Baruch, Y. (2022). The university-to-work transition: Responses of universities and organizations to the COVID-19 pandemic. *Personnel Review, 51*(9), 2201–2221. doi:10.1108/PR-03-2021-0170

Donald, W. E., Baruch, Y., & Ashleigh, M. J. (2017). Boundaryless and protean career orientation: A multitude of pathways to graduate employability. In M. Tomlinson & L. Holmes (Eds.), *Graduate Employability in Context: Theory, Research and Debate* (pp. 129–150). Palgrave Macmillan. doi:10.1057/978-1-137-57168-7_6

Donald, W. E., Baruch, Y., & Ashleigh, M. J. (2020). Striving for sustainable graduate careers: Conceptualization via career ecosystems and the new psychological contract. *Career Development International, 25*(2), 90–110. doi:10.1108/CDI-03-2019-0079

Donald, W. E., Baruch, Y., & Ashleigh, M. J. (2023). Technological transformation and human resource development of early career talent: Insights from accounting, banking, and finance. *Human Resource Development Quarterly*, *34*(3), 329–348. doi:10.1002/hrdq.21491

Donald, W. E., & Ford, N. (2023). Fostering social mobility and employability: The case for peer learning. *Teaching in Higher Education*, *28*(3), 672–678. doi:10.1080/13562517.2022.2145467

Donald, W. E., & Jackson, D. (2022). Subjective wellbeing among university students and recent graduates: Evidence from the United Kingdom. *International Journal of Environmental Research and Public Health*, *19*(11), 6911. doi:10.3390/ijerph19116911 PMID:35682494

Donald, W. E., & Mouratidou, M. (2022). Preparing for a sustainable career: Challenges and opportunities. *GiLE Journal of Skills Development*, *2*(2), 3–5. doi:10.52398/gjsd.2022.v2.i2.pp3-5

Dougherty, S. M., Ecton, W. G., Bonilla, S., & McGuinness, S. (2022). The effects of the COVID-19 pandemic and recession on career preparation during high school. *Peabody Journal of Education*, *97*(1), 326–343. doi:10.1080/0161956X.2022.2079911

Dries, N., & Pepermans, R. (2008). 'Real' high-potential careers: An empirical study into the perspectives of organisations and high potentials. *Personnel Review*, *37*(1), 85–108. doi:10.1108/00483480810839987

Fan, Y., & Potočnik, K. (2021). The impact of the depletion, accumulation, and investment of personal resources on work-life balance satisfaction and job retention: A longitudinal study on working mothers. *Journal of Vocational Behavior*, *131*(1), 103656. doi:10.1016/j.jvb.2021.103656

Ferns, S., Dawson, V., & Howitt, C. (2019). A collaborative framework for enhancing graduate employability. *International Journal of Work-Integrated Learning*, *20*(2), 99–111.

Freire, C., & Bettencourt, C. (2021). The effect of work-family conflict and hindrance on nurses' satisfaction: The role of ethical leadership. *Personnel Review*, *51*(3), 966–979. doi:10.1108/PR-05-2020-0379

Ghani, E. K., & Muhammad, K. (2019). Industry 4.0: Employers' expectations of accounting graduates and its implications on teaching and learning practices. *International Journal of Education and Practice*, *7*(1), 19–29. doi:10.18488/journal.61.2019.71.19.29

Gubler, M., Arnold, J., & Coombs, C. (2014). Reassessing the protean career concept: Empirical findings, conceptual components, and measurement. *Journal of Organizational Behavior*, *35*(S1), S23–S40. doi:10.1002/job.1908

Heffernan, T. (2022). Sexism, racism, prejudice, and bias: A literature review and synthesis of research surrounding student evaluations of courses and teaching. *Assessment & Evaluation in Higher Education*, *47*(1), 144–154. doi:10.1080/02602938.2021.1888075

Hennings, M., Zhu, Y., & Van der Veen, R. (2022). Developing the capacity for a proactively self-managed career: An analysis of aspiring new-generation employees in Japan. *Asia Pacific Journal of Human Resources*, *60*(3), 682–699. doi:10.1111/1744-7941.12296

Holmes, L. (2013). Competing perspectives on graduate employability: Possession, position or process? *Studies in Higher Education*, *38*(4), 538–554. doi:10.1080/03075079.2011.587140

Ingram, N., & Allen, K. (2019). 'Talent-spotting' or 'social magic'? Inequality, cultural sorting and constructions of the ideal graduate in elite professions. *The Sociological Review*, *67*(3), 723–740. doi:10.1177/0038026118790949

Institute of Student Employers, & International Network of Employers and University Career Services. (2020). *Covid-19: Global impacts on graduate recruitment*. Institute of Student Employers, & International Network of Employers and University Career Services https://cdn.ymaws.com/ise.org.uk/ resource/collection/78C3D824-D17B-4316-8E69-15A054E40F1E/Covid-19-international_final.pdf

Jackson, D. (2020). Applying academic selection criterion to work-integrated learning programmes: Risk management or perpetuating inequality? *Teaching in Higher Education*, *25*(1), 98–115. doi:10.1080/13562517.2018.1541884

Jackson, D., & Bridgstock, R. (2018). Evidencing student success and graduate employability in the contemporary world-of-work: Renewing our thinking. *Higher Education Research & Development*, *37*(5), 984–998. doi:10.1080/07294360.2018.1469603

Jackson, N. J. (2011). *Learning for A Complex World: A Lifewide Concept of Learning, Education and Personal Development*. AuthorHouse.

Jakubik, M. (2021). Searching for practical wisdom in higher education with logos, pathos and ethos. Case: Finnish Universities of Sciences. *Philosophies*, *6*(3), 63. doi:10.3390/philosophies6030063

Jakubik, M. (2022). The role of higher education in solving global problems. *International Journal of Management. Knowledge and Learning*, *11*, 285–295. doi:10.53615/2232-5697.11.285-295

Jakubik, M., & Müürsepp, P. (2022). From knowledge to wisdom. Will wisdom management replace knowledge management? *European Journal of Management and Business Economics*, *31*(3), 367–389. doi:10.1108/EJMBE-07-2021-0219

Lee, S., Schmidt-Klau, D., & Verik, S. (2020). The labour market impacts of the COVID-19: A global perspective. *The Indian Journal of Labour Economics : the Quarterly Journal of the Indian Society of Labour Economics*, *63*(S1), 11–15. doi:10.100741027-020-00249-y PMID:33041544

Lisá, E., Hennelová, K., & Newman, D. (2019). Comparison between employers' and students' expectations in respect of employability skills of university graduates. *International Journal of Work-Integrated Learning*, *20*(1), 71–82.

Lloyd, N. A., Paull, M., Clerke, T., & Male, S. A. (2019). *Access, Quality and Wellbeing In Engineering Work Integrated Learning Placements*. National Centre for Student Equity in Higher Education.

López-Miguens, M. J., Caballero, G., & Álvarez-González, P. (2021). Responsibility of the University in Employability: Development and validation of a measurement scale across five studies. *Business Ethics, the Environment & Responsibility*, *30*(1), 143–156. doi:10.1111/beer.12319

Lynch, J., & Lungrin, T. (2018). Integrating academic and career advising toward student success. *New Directions for Higher Education*, *184*(184), 69–79. doi:10.1002/he.20304

Maisuria, A., & Cole, M. (2017). The neoliberalization of higher education in England: An alternative is possible. *Policy Futures in Education*, *15*(5), 602–619. doi:10.1177/1478210317719792

Maxwell, N. (2021). *The World Crisis – And What To Do About It: A Revolution for Thought and Action*. World Scientific.

Mulder, R. H. (2021). The impact of new technologies on work and its implication for human resource development research. *Human Resource Development Quarterly*, *32*(1), 105–109. doi:10.1002/hrdq.21447

O'Brien, G. (2022). Making campus attraction work for employers: Aligning employer-led experiences to the student journey. *Phoenix*, *166*(2022), 6-7

Osmani, M., Weerakkody, V., Hindi, N., & Eldabi, T. (2019). Graduates employability skills: A review of literature against market demand. *Journal of Education for Business*, *94*(7), 423–432. doi:10.1080/08832323.2018.1545629

Padgett, R., & Donald, W. E. (2023). Preparing graduates for sustainable careers: A case of 'The Global Marketing Professional' module. *Higher Education, Skills, and Work-Based Learning*, *13*(1), 22–35. doi:10.1108/HESWBL-03-2022-0073

Petruzziello, G., Antonio, A. A., Chiesa, R., & Mariani, M. G. (2022). It takes more than agency: Linking support from teaching staff, career engagement, and movement capital among university students. *Frontiers in Psychology*, *13*, 1083698. Advance online publication. doi:10.3389/fpsyg.2022.1083698 PMID:36600715

Reedy, F. (2022). Fostering connections between industry and universities. *Phoenix*, 166(2022), 13.

Rousseau, D. M. (1995). *Psychological Contracts in Organizations: Understanding Written and Unwritten Agreements*. Sage (Atlanta, Ga.). doi:10.4135/9781452231594

Sandvik, J., Saouma, R., Seegert, N., & Stanton, C. T. (2022). *Should Workplace Programs Be Voluntary or Mandatory? Evidence From a Field Experiment on Mentorship* (Working Paper 29148). National Bureau of Economic Research. doi:10.3386/w29148

Soto-Acosta, P. (2020). COVID-19 pandemic: Shifting digital transformation to a high-speed gear. *Information Systems Management*, *37*(4), 260–266. doi:10.1080/10580530.2020.1814461

Super, D. E. (1957). *The Psychology of Careers*. Harper & Row.

Teng, W., Ma, C., Pahlevansharif, S., & Turner, J. J. (2019). Graduate readiness for the employment market of the 4th industrial revolution: The development of soft employability skills. *Education + Training*, *61*(5), 590–604. doi:10.1108/ET-07-2018-0154

The Careers 2032 Project. (2022). *An Industry Research Project Co-Produced By AGCAS, ISE, Wonkhe and Handshake, Looking at The Careers Sector of 2032 and The Role Technology Could Play in Facilitating Human Connections*. Handshake. https://joinhandshake.co.uk/careers2032

Van der Heijden, B. I. J. M. (2005). No one has ever promised you a rose garden. *On shared responsibility and employability enhancing strategies throughout careers*. Heerlen: Open University of the Netherlands. Van Gorcum.

Van der Heijden, B. I. J. M., & De Vos, A. (2015). Sustainable careers: Introductory chapter. In A. De Vos & B. I. J. M. Van der Heijden (Eds.), *Handbook of Research on Sustainable Careers* (pp. 1–19). Edward Elgar. doi:10.4337/9781782547037.00006

Verhaest, D., Bogaert, E., Dereymaeker, J., Mestdagh, L., & Baert, S. (2018). Do employers prefer overqualified graduates? A field experiment. *Industrial Relations*, *57*(3), 361–388. doi:10.1111/irel.12212

Vincent, M., & Chahal, G. (2022). Supporting local SMEs to access talent. *Phoenix, 166*(2022), 8-9.

Wilensky, H. L. (1961). Orderly careers and social participation: The impact of work history on social integration in the middle mass. *American Sociological Review*, *26*(4), 521–539. doi:10.2307/2090251

Ybema, J. F., van Vuuren, T., & van Dam, K. (2020). HR practices for enhancing sustainable employability: Implementation, use, and outcomes. *International Journal of Human Resource Management*, *31*(7), 886–907. doi:10.1080/09585192.2017.1387865

Yoon, H. J., & Hutchinson, B. (2018). Syntheses and future directions for career services, credentials, and training. In H. J. Yoon (Ed.), *International Practices of Career Services, Credentials, and Training* (pp. 217–238). National Career Development Association.

Zhang, J., Yuen, M., & Chen, G. (2018). Teacher support for career development: An integrative review and research agenda. *Career Development International*, *23*(1), 122–144. doi:10.1108/CDI-09-2016-0155

Section 2

University Career Advisors

Chapter 2
Graduate Employability and Employability Capital

ABSTRACT

The meaning of the term graduate employability continues to evolve. Where skills and competencies development dominated the discourse of the late 20th and early 21st centuries, recent definitions of graduate employability take a more holistic approach. An area of nascent interest in literature is the development of different forms of employability capital. This chapter briefly presents the evolution of graduate employability before offering a more in-depth focus on employability capital. The different conceptualizations of employability capital are presented, culminating in the Employability Capital Growth (ECG) model consisting of nine forms of capital, external factors, and personal outcomes. Next, the focus shifts to the operationalization and practical application of the ECG model, offering benefits to various actors operating within a sustainable career ecosystem. The chapter concludes with real-world examples of developing graduate employability and using employability capital to bridge our understanding of theory and practice.

INTRODUCTION

Section One of the book set the scene by introducing university career advisors, graduate recruiters, and sustainable graduate careers. In Section Two, our focus shifts to the role of university career advisors in helping their students prepare for a successful and sustainable career. This chapter focuses on graduate employability and employability capital, including operationalization and practical applications for the benefit of all actors operating within a sustainable career ecosystem. It should be

DOI: 10.4018/978-1-6684-9827-9.ch002

acknowledged, however, that it is also possible for a career ecosystem to be considered non-sustainable or fragile if actors fail to acknowledge their interdependencies. Chapters 3 and 4 subsequently discuss how university career services can engage their students and help them to develop and signal their employability to prospective employers.

GRADUATE EMPLOYABILITY

Employability is a psychosocial construct and "a constellation of individual differences that predispose employees to (pro)actively adapt to their work and career environments" (Fugate, 2006, p. 20). The term employability has also been defined as "the capability to move self-sufficiently within the labour market to realise potential through sustainable employment" (Hillage & Pollard, 1998, p. 12) or "the individual's ability to keep the job one has, or to get the job one desires" (Rothwell & Arnold, 2007, p. 25). Employability has been posited to predict career success and workplace wellbeing (De Vos et al., 2021). Perceptions of one's own employability are also important to help individuals to traverse turbulent labor market movements and maintain employment (Forrier et al., 2015), with perceived employability defined as "the individual's perception of his or her possibilities of obtaining and maintaining employment" (Vanhercke et al., 2014, p. 594). The specific type of employability which forms the focus of this book is graduate employability.

You may like to take a moment to reflect on what the term graduate employability means to you. You might also like to ask a friend, colleague, or family member what the term means to them. Where do your respective definitions align, and where do they diverge? One of the challenges when discussing graduate employability is that it can often mean different things to different people, either because the meaning is constantly evolving or because different definitions suit different agendas (Small et al., 2018).

During the late 20th and early 21st centuries, skills and competencies development dominated the graduate employability discourse. As Tomlinson (2012) observes, using the UK as a case, this was driven by "a policy climate of heavy central planning and target-setting around the coordination of skills-based education and training" (p. 412). The most influential impact in the UK came from 'The Dearing Report: Report for the National Committee of Inquiry into Higher Education', which called for universities to focus on equipping their students with the necessary skills to meet industry needs (Dearing, 1997). The dominance of skills and competencies development was reflected in definitions of graduate employability at the time. For example, Yorke (2004) defined graduate employability as

A set of achievements–skills, understanding and personal attributes–that make graduates more likely to gain employment and be successful in their chosen occupations, which benefits themselves, the workforce, the community and the economy. (p. 8)

In collaboration with Universities UK, the Confederation of British Industry (2009) offered a comparable definition of graduate employability as

A set of attributes, skills and knowledge that all labour market participants should possess to ensure they have the capability of being effective in the workplace–to the benefit of themselves, their employer and the wider economy. (p. 9)

Whilst these remain the two most cited definitions of graduate employability, the terminology has continued to progress in response to calls for a more holistic approach to address an overreliance on the skills and competencies agenda (Keep & Mayhew, 2010; Holmes, 2015). A new definition was subsequently suggested based on the views of various stakeholders, whereby

Graduate employability means that higher education alumni have developed the capacity to obtain and/or create work. Furthermore, employability means that institutions and employers have supported the student knowledge, skills, attributes, reflective disposition and identity that graduates need to be successful in the workforce. (Kinash & Crane, 2015, p. vi)

However, as discussed in Chapter 1, university metrics that claim to assess graduate employability often assess the existing employment status of a graduate instead (Jackson & Bridgstock, 2018). This is problematic since an individual can be employable (capable of doing a job) without being employed (captured as a snapshot in time status).

More recently, views of graduate employability have been influenced by sustainable careers and various forms of employability capital. Bennet (2020) defines graduate employability as the ability to "find, create and sustain meaningful work across the career lifespan" (p. 5). The definition maps to the person, context, and time dimensions of a sustainable career (Van der Heijden & De Vos. 2015; De Vos et al., 2020). My own work on graduate employability also bridges employability capital and sustainable careers, whereby employability capital and career ownership are antecedents of a sustainable career (Donald et al., 2020; 2023a; Donald, Van der Heijden et al., 2023). Other scholars also acknowledge the need for career ownership via proactive behaviors (Ma & Yue, 2023) to operationalize strengths and overcome challenges (Pham, 2020; Tang, 2022) by combining individual resources, agency, and an understanding of local labor markets (Pham & Jackson, 2020).

Most of the above definitions stem from the individual's perspective, whereas employers and wider national and global bodies may have a different stand on graduate employability. Whilst not a definition, Nilsson (2017) operationalizes graduate employability from a recruitment perspective and states

One important aspect of employability, especially in areas with high competition for jobs, is the ability to market oneself, to negotiate and to accentuate the appropriate forms of individual competence, personal capital, social capital, and cultural capital to a recruiter. (p. 71)

The array of different definitions of graduate employability, combined with the evolving nature of global labor markets and broader society, probably explains why different people often have different views of what graduate employability actually is. Such disconnects are also seen between what universities think employers want and what employers actually need from graduates (Osmani et al., 2019). There are also geographical and cultural differences, as evidenced in a study by Teng et al. (2019), which found that students in Malaysia felt that attending university improved their personal skills to a greater extent than students in China. Subsequently, Cole and Coulson (2022) and Cole and Donald (2022) suggest the need for lifewide and lifelong learning, whereby lifewide learning during university can capture the relative value of curricular learning, co-curricular learning, extra-curricular learning, and paid work to enhance self-perceived employability (Jackson & Bridgstock, 2021).

Our focus now shifts to an emerging area of interest in developing different forms of employability capital (e.g., Clarke, 2018; Donald et al., 2019; 2023a; Nimmi, Zakkariya et al., 2021; Peeters et al., 2019; Pham, 2021; Pham et al., 2019; Römgens et al., 2020; Tomlinson, 2017).

EMPLOYABILITY CAPITAL

Human capital theory (Becker, 1964; Schultz, 1961) posits how investment in people leads to economic benefits and sustainable outcomes for individuals, organizations, and society (Vithana et al., 2023). A literature review that I co-conducted found that when preparing university students for the labor market, there are three established and highly cited models based on two theoretical underpinnings (Donald et al.,

2023a). The first model positions human capital as a distinct capital whereby the accumulation of human capital, social capital, cultural capital, identity capital, and psychological capital is termed graduate capital (Tomlinson, 2017). The second model follows a similar theoretical underpinning whereby the six dimensions of graduate employability are offered as human capital, social capital, individual attributes, individual behaviors, perceived employability, and labor market factors (Clarke, 2018). The third model builds on earlier conceptualizations of human capital offered by Useem and Karabel (1986) and Baruch et al. (2005), whereby human capital is presented as an accumulation of six capitals: social capital, cultural capital, psychological capital, scholastic capital, market-value capital, and skills capital (Donald, 2017; Donald et al., 2019). Each of these three models has been empirically validated in various contexts. Tomlinson's (2017) model in Australia (Benati & Fischer, 2021; Pham et al., 2019), Spain (Caballero et al., 2020) and the UK (Tomlinson et al., 2022). Clarke's (2018) model in China (Ma & Bennett, 2021) and Australia (Le Rossignol & Kelly, 2023), and Donald et al.'s (2019) model in India (Nimmi, Kuriakose et al., 2021; Nimmi, Zakkariya et al., 2021) and the UK (Donald, 2017; Donald et al., 2018; 2019).

When conducting our literature review (Donald et al., 2023a), we were concerned about how different scholars use the same terminology in different ways, supporting the view that the conceptualization of employability capital remains inconclusive (Peeters et al., 2019). A citation network analysis of graduate employability and career development literature also found little theoretical or practical exchange of ideas between the two fields (Healy, Hammer et al., 2022). Our literature review aimed to create a new model to provide a shared foundation for researchers in recognition that existing models can reinforce and complement each other (Römgens et al., 2020). For example, a strength of Tomlinson's (2017) model is the inclusion of identity capital to acknowledge concerns in the human capital literature that class conflict is often overlooked (Bowels & Gintis, 1975). A strength of Clarke's (2018) model is the inclusion of external factors captured via labor market supply and demand, which are often neglected when conceptualizing employability capital (Peeters et al., 2019). A strength of Donald et al.'s (2019) model is the inclusion of career ownership and career advice, whereby their influence on self-perceived graduate employability highlights the need for the operationalization of capital for personal outcomes (Islam & Amin, 2022).

The corpus for our literature review consisted of 94 publications (see Donald et al., 2023a for a detailed explanation of the systematic literature review process). Following qualitative content analysis of the manuscripts within the corpus, we identified nine forms of employability capital. Table 1 provides definitions, and Table 2 provides examples for each of these.

Table 1. Defining the nine forms of employability capital

ID	Capital	Definition
1	Social Capital	The resources an individual gains via establishing and nurturing relationships through networks with various other individuals and groups leading to enhanced self-perceived employability via an understanding of values, norms, and practices.
2	Cultural Capital	The influence of the situations experienced by an individual leading to the accumulation of culturally valued knowledge to determine one's self-perceived employability and functionality within the labor market.
3	Psychological Capital	The characteristics of an individual that determine 'who you are', building on social cognitive theory and positive psychology to offer a personal resource for enhancing self-perceived employability and navigating volatile and global labor market environments.
4	Personal Identity Capital	How prospective employers and others judge an individual based on their background and the associated signals they present. Personal identity capital can enhance or detract from other forms of capital, but an individual's agency is restricted by external systems.
5	Health Capital	An accumulation (or lack) of resources related to an individual's mental and physical state, including health dimensions within and outside their control, that impacts their self-perceived employability and ability to perform a job.
6	Scholastic Capital	The resources from pre-university education, university education, and additional professional qualifications that cumulatively determine self-perceived employability.
7	Market-Value Capital	The cumulative resources from experiences gained from the labor market combined with technical and personal skills that determine self-perceived employability.
8	Career Identity Capital	The cumulative resources from engaging in reflective practices, seeking career counseling, and adopting personal agency to increase one's ability to signal their self-perceived employability to prospective employers.
9	Economic Capital	An individual's access (or lack of) to material resources and the associated revenue that can be generated directly or indirectly from these resources to enhance one's self-perceived employability.

Source: Adapted from Donald et al. (2023a, p. 7).

You will notice two things from the two tables: (1) human capital is not mentioned explicitly, and (2) employability capital is adopted as the collective term for the nine forms of capital per Peeters et al. (2019). The decision not to use the term *human capital* stemmed from wanting to find shared ground between the three dominant existing models. The choice of the term *employability capital* also helped to overcome my own misgivings around the terminology of graduate capital since non-graduates can also possess and develop some of these forms of capital.

Table 2. Examples for each of the nine forms of employability capital

ID	Capital	Examples
1	Social Capital	Parents and family; friends; mentors; memberships; networks; social media.
2	Cultural Capital	Sports; clubs; societies; volunteering; travelling; school/university reputation.
3	Psychological Capital	Hope; self-efficacy; confidence; resilience; optimism; adaptability.
4	Personal Identity Capital	Gender; age; social class; ethnicity; sexual orientation; dialect; attire.
5	Health Capital	Physical health; mental health; lifestyle choices; access to healthcare.
6	Scholastic Capital	School subjects; school grades; university degree subject; degree classification.
7	Market-Value Capital	Internship; placement; work experience; technical skills; personal skills.
8	Career Identity Capital	Career ownership; growth mindset; lifewide learning; lifelong learning.
9	Economic Capital	Parental financial support; student loans; living expenses; financial return.

Source: Adapted from Donald et al. (2023a, p. 7).

Based on the literature review, we also identified external factors and personal outcomes. External factors were defined as "dimensions beyond the individual's own agency that play a role in determining self-perceived employability and employment outcomes by acknowledging the notion of contingent employability" (Donald et al., 2023, p. 7). Personal outcomes were defined as "the benefits an individual experiences from enhancing their employability capital as an accumulation of nine forms of capital" (p. 7). Table 3 provides examples of eight external factors and eight personal outcomes. Figure 1 then presents our model.

Table 3. Examples of external factors and personal outcomes

Theme	Examples
External Factors	Access to career counselling; labor market supply and demand; location of jobs; recruitment process bias; chance events and career shocks; cost of living versus wages; flexible working opportunities; automation and Artificial Intelligence (AI) impacts.
Personal Outcomes	Self-perceived employability; personal resources; personal brand; job attainment and quality; job performance and productivity; career progression and success; earnings and financial security; wellbeing and career satisfaction.

Source: Adapted from Donald et al. (2023a, p. 8).

Figure 1. Employability capital growth (ECG) model
(C) 2023 Donald, Baruch & Ashleigh. Used with permission.)

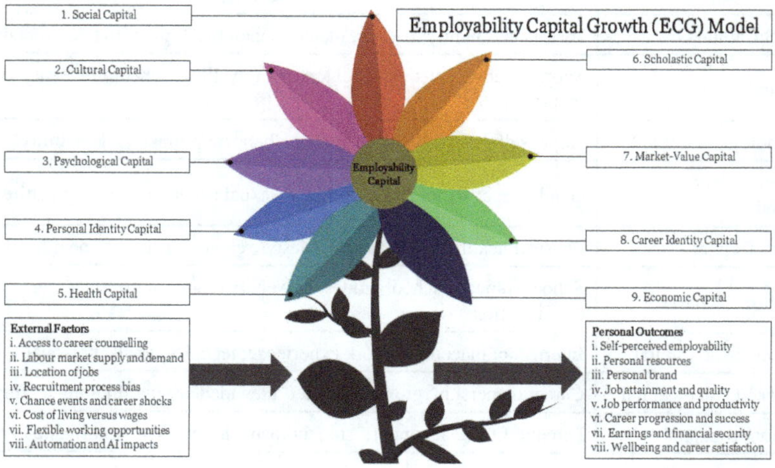

OPERATIONALIZATION AND PRACTICAL APPLICATION

Our focus now shifts to thinking about the operationalization of the Employability Capital Growth (ECG) model and its practical applications from the perspectives of university career services, lecturers, alums, and students. Subsequently, four 'Lived Experience Insights' are provided to offer real-world applications of the aspects discussed in this chapter.

For clarification, in this book, I use 'alum/alums' as the gender-neutral single and plural terms that encompass all graduates of an alma mater, regardless of their gender identity–since it is more inclusive than using 'alumnus'/'alumni' (male single/plural) or 'alumna'/'alumnae' (female single/plural). The only exception is where 'alumni' occurs within a direct quote.

University Career Services

Ingram and Allen (2019) conducted intriguing research on the different forms of capital and the related social inclusion outcomes. They found that the demographics of applicants combined with their ability to embody various forms of capital meant that certain graduates were more likely to receive offers for higher-paid roles than others. Effectively, many employers apply impression management by giving the illusion of social inclusion when reporting diversity, equity, and inclusion statistics of graduates as a single entity - whilst disproportionately favoring certain applicants for well-paid employment opportunities. Additionally, gender, class, and ethnicity can all impact students' self-perceived employability and the employment outcomes of graduates (Hooley et al., 2023). Interestingly, these students who could benefit the most from career guidance during their university studies are least likely to access it (Donald et al., 2018) - a theme we explore further in Chapter 3 when discussing student engagement strategies. Consequently, the university career service can play a valuable role in facilitating social mobility by providing career counseling to as many students as possible (positioned as an external factor in Donald et al.'s 2023a ECG model).

The university career service also needs to make students aware of the interplay between individual agency and contextual factors (Fugate et al., 2021) in acknowledgement that employability is malleable, requiring collaborative approaches that provide benefits to all actors (Rodrigues et al., 2020). Encouraging students to take ownership of their careers, acquire various forms of employability capital, commit to lifewide and lifelong learning, and proactively seek career advice can enhance self-perceived employability (Cole & Coulson, 2022; Cole & Donald, 2022; Donald et al., 2019; 2023a; 2023b). University career services should also make their students aware of the value of undertaking work experience during their university studies and help source opportunities so that all students can participate and gain the associated benefits, including enhanced employability capital and increased self-perceived employability (Jackson et al., 2022). Building further on the external factors of Donald et al.'s (2023a) ECG model, university career services also need to promote work experience and employment opportunities at the local and regional levels, develop partnerships with Small and Medium-Sized Enterprises (SMEs), and provide greater support to students interested in entrepreneurial pursuits.

Later in this book, we will explore the employer perspective of preparing students for the university-to-work transition (Chapter 6) and the challenges and opportunities for greater collaboration between different actors operating within a sustainable career ecosystem (Chapters 8 and 9, respectively). However, we now proceed by focusing on the contributions offered by lecturers and alums to enhance the self-perceived employability of students within the university context (Abelha et al., 2020).

Lecturers and Alums

University lecturers (also referred to as Professors in some countries) can play a crucial role in enhancing the self-perceived employability of their students via curriculum-based interventions. For example, Padgett and Donald (2023) showed how the self-perceived employability of postgraduate masters students rose from 37.5% to 92.5% during a nine-week compulsory module focusing on increasing confidence, interactive classes, skills development, knowledge of the recruitment process, Curriculum Vitae

(CV)/Resume development, proactive career ownership, interview guidance, and networking opportunities. Additionally, authentic assessment can help to develop personal skills such as teamwork and real-world problem-solving (Manville et al., 2022) and cultivate creativity (Jakubik, 2022). There is also an emerging interest in how academics can take a more active role during year-in-industry placements or shorter period placements, whereby support and reflective assessments can enhance the benefits of work placement learning on students' readiness for the university-to-work transition (Donald & Hughes, 2023; Okolie, 2022).

Alums can also help to prepare students for sustainable careers (Donald et al., 2018). For example, they may be invited to provide guest lectures on contemporary topics related to a specific university module (Cownie & Gallo, 2021). Alternatively, they may offer insights into their lived experiences covering aspects of the application process, selection process, undertaking the university-to-work transition, or life as a graduate (Donald et al., 2018). There may be the opportunity for alums to mentor students to help them develop and operationalize the different forms of employability capital, including providing access to industry networks (Cownie & Gallo, 2021). Alums can also play a valuable role in helping to address gaps between the university curriculum and the needs of employers (Nabulsi et al., 2021), encouraging students to become entrepreneurs (Jones et al., 2021) or enhancing the reputational capital of their alma mater (Obeng-Ofori & Kwarteng, 2021).

Students

In Homer's Odyssey, the Greek Sea-God Proteus could change shape at will to adapt to the needs of any given situation (Inkson, 2006). Thus, the protean careerist can change themselves according to their own need. Hall (1976; 1996; 2004) offered the protean career metaphor to draw on an individual's motive to follow a particular career path characterized by values-driven and self-directed career moves. Protean career orientation captures how individuals define their own concept of a successful career and subsequently look to achieve this vision of success through their actions (Gubler et al., 2014), leading to an increased likelihood of job and career satisfaction (Li et al., 2019; Wiernik & Kostal, 2019). Time spent at university can act as the foundation for taking ownership of one's career, leading to enhanced levels of self-perceived employability (Cortellazzo et al., 2020; Donald et al., 2019). Exploration of opportunities can help students to reconcile their personal and professional values (Tomlinson & Jackson, 2021) and identify their passion which is essential for employment success (Pham et al., 2019). Additionally, students should participate in curricular learning, co-curricular learning, extra-curricular learning, and paid work to enhance self-perceived employability (Jackson & Bridgstock, 2021).

From an employability capital perspective, a study of management students in India showed social capital as the strongest predictor of self-perceived employability, whilst investment in psychological capital had the largest return for enhancing one's self-perceived employability (Agnihotri et al., 2023). Previous research has also shown how parental support has a positive association with their offspring's career adaptability and career decision-making self-efficacy (Guan et al., 2015; 2016). Engineering students in Australia also defined their own concept of a successful career, emphasizing the significance of networking and work experience to increase their self-perceived employability (Howell et al., 2023). Graduates in India further highlighted the significance of developing psychological capital to enhance life wellbeing and career sustainability (Nimmi, Kuriakose et al., 2022), emphasizing the HERO elements of hope, self-efficacy, resilience, and optimism. A study of university students in China also found links between self-perceived employability and life satisfaction (Ma & Chen, 2022).

Additional Operationalization Opportunities

The Appendix offers some additional opportunities that career practitioners can use to operationalize the ECG model in a university setting (and also in an industry setting).

LIVED EXPERIENCE INSIGHTS

Lived Experience Insight

Shared By Nalayini Thambar, University of Nottingham, UK

The Challenge

The University of Nottingham has a diverse student body with typically high levels of scholastic capital. Highly targeted by well-known graduate recruiters with a well-resourced Careers and Employability Service (CES) and strong graduate outcomes scores, the institutional student employability narrative was rightly confident. However, based on our interactions with students, we were concerned that our institutional employability culture was not encouraging and enabling all of our students to engage and succeed, favoring those with high levels of social and cultural capital, particularly when it came to securing work experience that would directly strengthen their career prospects.

The Context

We ran some focus groups with students identifying as 'first generation' to gain further insight into their perception of their own employability and the prospects of securing work experience. They told us that when they saw messages about employers targeting Nottingham graduates, they interpreted it as a certain type of graduate, "not people like me". They also explained how they did not have the same access and insight to professional work settings as some of their peers and would be happy to learn of targeted schemes and approaches to make them feel seen and supported.

Action Taken

Within our work experience provision, we ringfenced opportunities or gave priority access to specific schemes for those students (traditionally identified as 'widening participation' students), often unable to participate in traditional work experience activities such as spring weeks or internships during the easter or summer vacations due to socio-economic reasons. Our offer included: (i) a regional internship program (combining spring micro-internships and summer 8-week internships), (ii) a multi-disciplinary team-based 'Consultancy Challenge', and (iii) an 'International Work Experience Grant'. Concurrently, we developed our overseas offer to enable all students to engage, removing upfront costs for widening participation students and creating remote international experiences.

The Outcome

We saw increases in Graduate Outcomes (+5%) and degree attainment (+6%) for students who participated when benchmarked against peers who did not. Increases in Graduate Outcomes (+6%) were highest for students previously unable to secure work experience. Additionally, we contributed to regional graduate retention since 19.3% of students who participated in our schemes remained in the region following graduation compared to 15.5% of students who did not participate. The growth of this provision has also enabled the CES to develop effective and long-lasting employer partnerships with over 200 SMEs and charitable organizations across the region.

Lessons Learned and Advice

Consulting with students is key. We developed an understanding of the barriers to engagement that informed how we prepare students without previous work experience. Concurrently, our work with Care Experienced and Estranged Students, in partnership with specialist support colleagues, ensures our offer is inclusive and accessible. Our provision has developed to offer over 750 individual opportunities a year, whereby each strand has evolved, with pilots of further activity phased in over those five years. My advice when setting up a similar scheme would be to avoid trying to deliver everything simultaneously. Instead, adopt a phased approach and be prepared to tweak or change aspects which, although well-intentioned, may not achieve the anticipated outcome.

Lived Experience Insight

Shared By Warren Frehse, The University of Melbourne, Australia

The Challenge

Many students who come to me for career-related support believe their job following graduation should align with their university degree. Consequently, these students often believe that only work experiences during their degree that align with their degree are worthwhile. For example, a data scientist often does not view a retail job as providing any valuable skills for securing employment in the data science field. However, teamwork and communication skills are highly valued by employers and crucial to maximizing one's employability.

The Context

Students tend to exclude experiences from their application letters and CVs that do not develop technical skills. Of course, technical skills are critical for undertaking many specialized careers. Yet, employers recruiting for graduate roles often look for examples of how applicants demonstrate leadership, influence others, work under pressure, and other personal skills (also called soft skills).

Action Taken

When delivering career guidance sessions to students, I carefully emphasize the importance of building these crucial personal skills from within and outside the curriculum. I advise students how they can draw on their experiences of group projects within the curriculum to evidence their ability to work in teams. I also ensure that students know the areas within a university environment where they can take on volunteering roles in student clubs and associations, for example, where leadership can be practiced with evidence-based examples to include on their CVs. Finally, I highlight the value of part-time employment opportunities for developing personal skills to complement the technical skills from the degree.

The Outcome

Since running these career guidance sessions, more students now include evidence of their personal skills in their job applications. However, more must be done to inform students and constantly remind them of what employers seek. Consequently, I also use data from the Australian Association of Graduate Employers to support students in writing their application documents. The data provides additional support for the significance of communication skills, resilience, teamworking and emotional intelligence when employers assess the employability of graduates.

Lessons Learned and Advice

I strongly advocate that students attend employer insight talks and seminars to see firsthand what employers look for when determining the employability and suitability of graduate hires. This should be complemented by attending careers fairs and expos where students can speak directly to recruiters. Such actions will shift students' perception away from only undertaking discipline-related work experiences, encouraging them to gain a broader perspective and enhance their employability. Such an approach is particularly valuable for students at The University of Melbourne, where it is common to change study majors between undergraduate and postgraduate study without needing to complete another undergraduate degree. Consequently, a flexible approach to developing employability acknowledges that career interests can change. Universities have a responsibility to produce graduates who are agile and resilient to overcome challenges that will inevitably occur during their careers. Such an outlook can enable graduates to undertake the university-to-work transition and to thrive in the workplace.

Lived Experience Insight

Shared by William E. Donald, Ronin Institute, USA

The Challenge

Many years ago, when I started mentoring university students, I observed how their self-perceived employability often decreased between their penultimate and final year of undergraduate study. At face value, this would seem counterintuitive, given the increased opportunity to accumulate additional forms of employability capital and personal resources with each additional year of university study. Interestingly, I saw this phenomenon play out in my mentees regardless of their nationality or the country where they were studying, suggesting a global-level phenomenon.

The Context

The fact that these mentees had lower levels of self-perceived employability in their final year of study was somewhat confusing, as it was clear to me as a mentor that their employability had increased over the time we worked together. When I asked my mentees why they perceived themselves to be less employable in their final year of university study, they would usually respond by talking about the volume of rejections they had received during the application and selection phases on applying for graduate schemes or other employment opportunities. I realized at this point that contextual factors were impacting their confidence.

Action Taken

The first step that I took with my mentees was to normalize rejection. Many factors lie beyond our individual control, and every single one of us experiences rejection in our lives. The second step was to ensure my mentees knew the difference between being employable (which they all were) and being employed (which was their objective). The third step was to help them to operationalize their employability capital and personal resources to make it clear to hiring managers what they could offer the organization. The fourth step was to foster peer learning by encouraging my mentees to share their experiences with each other as part of a knowledge-sharing and growth mindset approach.

The Outcome

The cumulative effect of the four-step process resulted in an increased sense of confidence and restoration of their self-perceived employability. The mentees also identified areas of the application and selection process where they struggled and sought to improve their performance. Naturally, the positive framing at the individual level translated to increased desirable outcomes. Many mentees received multiple job offers and were able to decide which offer was best for them at that given point in time. Where necessary, mentees also explored alternative opportunities that mapped to their strengths, particularly during periods of fierce competition for jobs, such as during the aftermath of the Global Financial Crisis 2007-2008.

Lessons Learned and Advice

From a mentor perspective, I learnt that supporting my mentees to feel confident was essential to ensuring that their self-perceptions reflected their employability. I also learnt to talk openly about my experiences with rejection and how sometimes things happen which are beyond our agency. I advise my mentees to speak to each other to share their experiences and speak with recent graduates I have previously mentored to enhance their knowledge and help them to develop valuable professional networks. I also signpost my mentees to other support services that would benefit them in acknowledging the multiple actors involved in a sustainable career ecosystem.

Lived Experience Insight

Shared By Heather Pasero, University of Southampton, UK

The Challenge

Since the late 1980s, increased opportunities to participate in higher education have disproportionately benefited those from more affluent backgrounds. Students from lower-income backgrounds have a lower chance of attending university, graduating, and securing employment. In 2015, concerned with this trajectory, the Office for Students (OfS) and the Higher Education Funding Council for England (HEFCE) developed a national strategy for student access and success in higher education with the vision 'that all those with the potential to benefit from higher education have equal opportunity to participate and succeed'. Consequently, new national, regional and institutional initiatives were funded.

The Context

The University of Southampton launched the 'My Generation Career Coaching Programme' (MGCCP) pilot stage in 2019. The aim was to address the unique challenges that first-generation university students face by helping them to establish career goals and prepare for the university-to-work transition. Funding was provided for a one-year pilot covering marketing, coaching materials, books, events, and student items such as interview attire. In partnership with the 'Widening Participation and Social Mobility Team', the project sought to implement a marketing strategy targeting first-generation UK-domiciled undergraduates across all degrees and years of study.

Action Taken

Participants in the MGCCP took the 'Career-Readiness Test' (based on Tomlinson's (2017) Graduate Capital Model) at the start and end of the one-year pilot program. Participants also provided other self-reported information (e.g., engagement with student societies, part-time work, self-confidence, self-awareness, etc.) at the end of each coaching appointment. The coaches involved in the MGCCP were qualified/

experienced career consultants who initially attended a 2-hour training session. They subsequently met monthly with 2-3 other coaches to reflect and share experiences and best practices.

The Outcome

The success of the MGCCP was determined by three metrics assessing the impact of the one-to-one career coaching sessions across the 12 months on the program participants: 1) self-confidence increased by 39%, 2) engagement factors increased from 36% to 65%, and 3) 'Career Readiness Test' scores were between 9 and 15 percentage points higher than for first-generation students not involved in the MGCCP. Future data from the 'Graduate Outcomes Survey' will also be used to assess the effectiveness of the MGCCP as an intervention. The pilot's success means the MGCCP is now an ongoing initiative.

Lessons Learned and Advice

One-to-one coaching sessions lasting for one hour at a time and running across 12 months allow for in-depth discussions to understand the individual student's motivations, needs, and barriers. I also observed that the 'Career Readiness Test' offered a valuable framework for students to identify where to build graduate capital and for coaches to provide support on how to achieve this. Finally, for first-generation students, a strong determination to succeed is often hampered by a lack of knowledge of the labor market and opportunities to build networks (social capital). We invited students from the MGCCP to a networking event for underrepresented students, which was well attended, and something I would recommend to other universities.

Reflection on Lived Experience Insights

The four lived experience insights covering Australia, the UK and the USA, evidence some similar trends concerning the employability of university students. For example, students need access to career counseling and mentoring to establish career goals and consider career options beyond those immediately related to their degree. There is also an emphasis on building confidence, gaining industry experience, and establishing networks to gain knowledge of specific industries and/or job roles.

The insights also emphasize how specific groups of students may need targeted support (e.g., first-generation students) and how the year of study can impact confidence and self-perceived employability (lower for final-year students than penultimate-year students). These factors are also captured within the ECG model presented in this chapter, and the hope is that the ECG model can act as a framework, complemented by the lived experience insights, for the benefit of all actors operating within a sustainable career ecosystem.

CONCLUSION

In this chapter, we (i) explored different definitions of graduate employability, (ii) reviewed the literature on employability capital, (iii) evidenced how the ECG model came about, and (iv) offered suggestions for operationalization and practical application.

If you are a student reading this book, you may like to consider:

- How can you use the ECG model to enhance your employability?
- Which forms of capital do you already possess as personal resources?
- Which forms of capital do you feel you need to develop to maximize your chances of securing a job in your desired field following graduation?
- What actions can you take on your own by adopting a protean career orientation?
- How might university career services, lecturers, and alums be able to provide support to you?

I encourage you to consider these questions at the very beginning of your university degree, and periodically re-visit them throughout your university studies. The approach will give you the necessary time to identify and acquire personal resources whilst becoming aware of contextual and external factors.

If you are a practitioner involved in providing career guidance to university students, I invite you to consider how you might be able to make the best use of the ECG model to enhance the self-perceived employability of the individuals you support. Tables 1 and 2 provide definitions and examples for each of the forms of employability capital. Perhaps you could use these as the basis for one-to-one or group-based sessions with students to increase their awareness of these capitals, before talking through Figure 1, which captures external factors and personal outcomes. The Appendix may also be of interest to you. There may also be an opportunity to encourage peer learning, whereby final-year students provide support to penultimate-year students, who in turn provide support to first-year students. You may also wish to consider partnerships with lecturers to embed these sessions into the university curriculum, or guest lectures by alums to share their lived experiences and insights to support specific groups of students.

Keep these thoughts in the front of your mind as we move through the two remaining chapters of Section Two, which discuss how university career services can engage their students (Chapter 3) and help them to develop and signal their employability to prospective employers (Chapter 4). Taken together, these three chapters offer a platform for university students and university career advisors to consider innovative ways to collaborate for the benefit of all actors operating within a sustainable career ecosystem.

REFERENCES

Abelha, M., Fernandes, S., Mesquita, D., Seabra, F., & Ferreira-Oliveira, A. T. (2020). Graduate employability and competence development in higher education – A systematic literature review using PRISMA. *Sustainability (Basel), 12*(15), 5900. doi:10.3390u12155900

Agnihotri, S., Shiva, A., & Khan, F. N. (2023). Investigating forms of graduate capital and their relationship to perceived employability: An application of PLS predict and IPMA. *Higher Education and Work-Based Learning, 13*(1), 179–197. doi:10.1108/HESWBL-07-2022-0146

Baruch, Y., Bell, M. P., & Gray, D. (2005). Generalist and specialist graduate business degrees: Tangible and intangible value. *Journal of Vocational Behavior, 67*(1), 51–68. doi:10.1016/j.jvb.2003.06.002

Becker, G. S. (1964). *Human Capital: A Theoretical and Empirical Analysis with Special Reference to Education.* University of Chicago Press.

Benati, K., & Fischer, J. (2021). Beyond human capital: Student preparation for graduate life. *Education + Training, 63*(1), 151–163. doi:10.1108/ET-10-2019-0244

Bennett, D. (2020). *Embedding employABILITY thinking across higher education. Australian Government Department of Education and Training*. LTR. https://ltr.edu.au/resources/FS16-0274_Bennett_Report_2020.pdf

Bennett, D., & Ananthram, S. (2022). Development, validation and deployment of the EmployABILITY scale. *Studies in Higher Education, 47*(7), 1311–1325. doi:10.1080/03075079.2021.1888079

Bowels, S., & Gintis, H. (1975). The problem with human capital theory – A Marxian critique. *The American Economic Review, 65*(2), 74–82.

Caballero, G., Álvarez-González, P., & López-Miguens, M. J. (2020). How to promote the employability capital of university students? Developing and validating scales. *Studies in Higher Education*, *45*(12), 2634–2652. doi:10.1080/03075079.2020.1807494

Clarke, M. (2018). Rethinking graduate employability: The role of capital, individual attributes and context. *Studies in Higher Education*, *43*(11), 1923–1937. doi:10.1080/03075079.2017.1294152

Cole, D., & Coulson, B. (2022). Through and beyond COVID-19, promoting whole person, lifelong and lifewide learning. *Journal of Innovation in Polytechnic Education*, *4*(1), 81–90.

Cole, D., & Donald, W. E. (2022). Shifting the narrative: Towards a more holistic approach to learning. *GiLE Journal of Skills Development*, *2*(1), 3–4. doi:10.52398/gjsd.2022.v2.i1.pp3-4

Confederation of British Business. (2009). *Future Fit: Preparing Graduates For the World of Work*. Confederation of British Business.

Cortellazzo, L., Bonesso, S., Gerli, F., & Batista-Foguet, J. M. (2020). Protean career orientation: Behavioral antecedents and employability outcomes. *Journal of Vocational Behavior*, *116*, 103343. doi:10.1016/j.jvb.2019.103343

Cownie, F., & Gallo, M. (2021). Alumni gratitude and academics: Implications for engagement. *Journal of Further and Higher Education*, *45*(6), 788–802. doi:10.1080/0309877X.2020.1820457

De Vos, A., Jacobs, S., & Verbruggen, M. (2021). Career transitions and employability. *Journal of Vocational Behavior*, *126*, 103475. doi:10.1016/j.jvb.2020.103475

De Vos, A., Van der Heijden, B. I. J. M. & Akkermans, J. (2020). Sustainable careers: Towards a conceptual model. *Journal of Vocational Behavior, 117*, a.103196. doi:10.1016/j.jvb.2018.06.011

Dearing, R. (1997). *The Dearing Report: Report for the National Committee of Inquiry into Higher Education*. Higher Education in the Learning Society, HMSO.

Donald, W. E. (2017). Students' perceptions of graduate employability: A sequential explanatory approach. [Doctoral Thesis, University of Southampton]. https://eprints.soton.ac.uk/id/eprint/415935

Donald, W. E., Ashleigh, M. J., & Baruch, Y. (2018). Students' perceptions of education and employability: Facilitating career transition from higher education into the labor market. *Career Development International, 23*(5), 513–540. doi:10.1108/CDI-09-2017-0171

Donald, W. E., Baruch, Y., & Ashleigh, M. J. (2019). The undergraduate self-perception of employability: Human capital, careers advice and career ownership. *Studies in Higher Education, 44*(4), 599–614. doi:10.1080/03075079.2017.1387107

Donald, W. E., Baruch, Y., & Ashleigh, M. J. (2020). Striving for sustainable graduate careers: Conceptualization via career ecosystems and the new psychological contract. *Career Development International, 25*(2), 90–110. doi:10.1108/CDI-03-2019-0079

Donald, W. E., Baruch, Y., & Ashleigh, M. J. (2023a). Construction and operationalisation of an Employability Capital Growth Model (ECGM) via A systematic literature review. *Studies in Higher Education*, 1–15. Advance online publication. doi:10.1080/03075079.2023.2219270

Donald, W. E., Baruch, Y., & Ashleigh, M. J. (2023b). *Application of the Employability Capital Growth Model in University and Industry Settings*. CareerWise Blog, Canadian Education and Research Institute for Counselling (CERIC). https://careerwise.ceric.ca/2023/10/04/how-the-employability-capital-growth-model-supports-student-success/

Donald, W. E., & Hughes, H. P. N. (2023). How academics can play a more influential role during a year-in-industry placement: A contemporary critique and call for action. *Industry and Higher Education*. doi:10.1177/09504222231162059

Donald, W. E., Van der Heijden, B. I. J. M., & Manville, G. (2023). *Sustainable Careers and Organisations: Development of a Conceptual Framework and Future Research Agenda*. British Academy of Management Conference 2023.

Forrier, A., Verbruggen, M., & De Cuyper, N. (2015). Integrating different notions of employability in a dynamic chain: The relationship between job transitions, movement capital and perceived employability. *Journal of Vocational Behavior, 89*, 56–64. doi:10.1016/j.jvb.2015.04.007

Fugate, M. (2006). *Employability*. Sage.

Fugate, M., Van der Heijden, B. I. J. M., De Vos, A., Forrier, A., & De Cuyper, N. (2021). Is what's past prologue? A review and agenda for contemporary employability research. *The Academy of Management Annals, 15*(1), 266–298. doi:10.5465/annals.2018.0171

Guan, P., Capezio, A., Restubog, S. L. D., Read, S., Lajom, J. A. L., & Li, M. (2016). The role of traditionality in the relationships among parental support, career decision-making self-efficacy and career adaptability. *Journal of Vocational Behavior*, *94*, 114–123. doi:10.1016/j.jvb.2016.02.018

Guan, Y., Wang, F., Liu, H., Ji, Y., Jia, X., Fang, Z., Li, Y., Hua, H., & Li, C. (2015). Career-specific parental behaviors, career exploration and career adaptability: A three-wave investigation among Chinese undergraduates. *Journal of Vocational Behavior*, *86*, 95–103. doi:10.1016/j.jvb.2014.10.007

Gubler, M., Arnold, J., & Coombs, C. (2014). Reassessing the protean career concept: Empirical findings, conceptual components, and measurement. *Journal of Organizational Behavior*, *35*(S1), S23–S40. doi:10.1002/job.1908

Hall, D. T. (1976). *Career in Organizations*. Goodyear.

Hall, D. T. (1996). Protean careers of the 21st century. *The Academy of Management Perspectives*, *10*(4), 8–16. doi:10.5465/ame.1996.3145315

Hall, D. T. (2004). The protean career: A quarter-century journey. *Journal of Vocational Behavior*, *65*(1), 1–13. doi:10.1016/j.jvb.2003.10.006

Healy, M., Hammer, S., & Mcllveen, P. (2022). Mapping graduate employability and career development in higher education research: A citation network analysis. *Studies in Higher Education*, *47*(4), 799–811. doi:10.1080/03075079.2020.1804851

Hillage, J., & Pollard, E. (1998). *Employability: Developing A Framework for Policy Analysis*. The Institute for Employment Studies.

Holmes, L. (2013). Competing perspectives on graduate employability: Possession, position or process? *Studies in Higher Education*, *38*(4), 538–554. doi:10.1080/03075079.2011.587140

Hooley, T., Hanson, J., & Clark, L. (2023). Exploring students' and graduates' attitudes to the process of transition to the labour market. *Industry and Higher Education*, *37*(1), 121–134. doi:10.1177/09504222221111298

Howell, S., Hall, W., & Geelan, D. (2023). Exploring the perspectives of engineering undergraduates on employability and employability building activities. *Higher Education. Skills and Work-Based Learning*, *13*(1), 161–178. doi:10.1108/HESWBL-05-2022-0111

Ingram, N., & Allen, K. (2019). 'Talent-spotting' or 'social magic'? Inequality, cultural sorting and constructions of the ideal graduate in elite professions. *The Sociological Review*, *67*(3), 723–740. doi:10.1177/0038026118790949

Inkson, K. (2006). Protean and boundaryless careers as metaphors. *Journal of Vocational Behavior*, *69*(1), 48–63. doi:10.1016/j.jvb.2005.09.004

Islam, M. S., & Amin, M. (2022). A systematic review of human capital and employee well-being: Putting human capital back on track. *European Journal of Training and Development*, *46*(5/6), 99–115. doi:10.1108/EJTD-12-2020-0177

Jackson, D., & Bridgstock, R. (2018). Evidencing student success and graduate employability in the contemporary world-of-work: Renewing our thinking. *Higher Education Research & Development*, *37*(5), 984–998. doi:10.1080/07294360.2018.1469603

Jackson, D., & Bridgstock, R. (2021). What actually works to enhance graduate employability? The relative value of curricular, co-curricular, and extra-curricular learning and paid work. *Higher Education*, *81*(4), 723–739. doi:10.100710734-020-00570-x

Jackson, D., Riebe, L., & Macau, F. (2022). Determining factors in graduate recruitment and preparing students for success. *Education + Training*, *64*(5), 681–699. doi:10.1108/ET-11-2020-0348

Jakubik, M. (2022). Cultivating creativity case: Higher education in Finland. In D. Bylieva & A. Nordmann (Eds.), *Technology, Innovation and Creativity in Digital Society* (pp. 242–255). Springer. doi:10.1007/978-3-030-89708-6_21

Jones, O., Meckel, P., & Taylor, D. (2021). Situated learning in a business incubator: Encouraging students to become real entrepreneurs. *Industry and Higher Education*, *35*(4), 367–383. doi:10.1177/0950422221 1008117

Keep, E., & Mayhew, K. (2010). Moving beyond skills as a social and economic panacea. *Work, Employment and Society*, *24*(3), 565–577. doi:10.1177/0950017010371663

Kinash, S., & Crane, L. (2015). *Supporting Graduate Employability from Generalist Disciplines through Employer and Private Institution Collaboration*. Office for Learning & Teaching, Australian Government.

Le Rossignol, K., & Kelly, M. (2023). A career ecosystem approach to developing student agency through digital storymaking. In W. E. Donald (Ed.), *Handbook of Research on Sustainable Career Ecosystems for University Students and Graduates* (pp. 158–175). IGI Global. doi:10.4018/978-1-6684-7442-6.ch009

Li, H., Ngo, H. Y., & Cheung, F. (2019). Linking protean career orientation and career decidedness: The mediating role of career decision self-efficacy. *Journal of Vocational Behavior*, *115*, 103322. doi:10.1016/j.jvb.2019.103322

Ma, Y., & Bennett, D. (2021). The relationship between higher education students' perceived employability, academic engagement and stress among students in China. *Education + Training*, *63*(5), 744–762. doi:10.1108/ET-07-2020-0219

Ma, Y., & Chen, S.-C. (2022). Understanding the determinants and consequences of perceived employability in graduate labor market in China. *International Journal for Educational and Vocational Guidance*. Advance online publication. doi:10.100710775-022-09567-7

Ma, Y., & Yue, Y. (2023). Student insights on fostering sustainable careers in China: Implications for universities and employers. In W. E. Donald (Ed.), *Handbook of Research on Sustainable Career Ecosystems for University Students and Graduates* (pp. 342–360). IGI Global. doi:10.4018/978-1-6684-7442-6.ch018

Manville, G., Donald, W. E., & Eves, A. (2022). Can embedding authentic assessment into the curriculum enhance the employability of business school students? *GiLE Journal of Skills Development*, *2*(2), 73–87. doi:10.52398/gjsd.2022.v2.i2.pp73-87

Nabulsi, N., McNally, B., & Khoury, G. (2021). Improving graduateness: Addressing the gap between employer needs and graduate employability in Palestine. *Education + Training*, *63*(6), 947–963. doi:10.1108/ET-06-2020-0170

Nilsson, S. (2017). Employability, employment and the establishment of higher education graduates in the labour market. In M. Tomlinson & L. Holmes (Eds.), *Graduate Employability in Context: Theory, Research, and Debate* (pp. 65–86). Palgrave Macmillan. doi:10.1057/978-1-137-57168-7_3

Nimmi, P. M., Joseph, G., & Donald, W. E. (2022). Is it all about perception? A sustainability viewpoint on psychological capital and life wellbeing of management graduates. *Higher Education. Skills and Work-Based Learning*, *12*(2), 384–398. doi:10.1108/HESWBL-01-2021-0004

Nimmi, P. M., Kuriakose, V., Donald, W. E., & Nowfal, M. (2021). HERO Elements of Psychological Capital: Fostering Career Sustainability via Resource Caravans. *Australian Journal of Career Development*, *30*(3), 199–210. doi:10.1177/10384162211066378

Nimmi, P. M., Zakkariya, K. A., & Rahul, P. R. (2021). Channelling employability perceptions through lifelong learning: An empirical investigation. *Education + Training*, *63*(5), 763–776. doi:10.1108/ET-10-2020-0295

Obeng-Ofori, D., & Kwarteng, H. O. (2021). Enhancing the role of alumni in the growth of higher education institutions. *International Journal of Multidisciplinary Studies and Innovative Research*, *4*, 40–48. doi:10.21681/IJMSIR-1.3.831.049173-20201

Okolie, U. C. (2022). Work placement learning and students' readiness for school-to-work transition: Do perceived employability and faculty supervisor support matter? *Journal of Vocational Behavior*, *139*(3), 103805. doi:10.1016/j.jvb.2022.103805

Osmani, M., Weerakkody, V., Hindi, N., & Eldabi, T. (2019). Graduates employability skills: A review of literature against market demand. *Journal of Education for Business*, *94*(7), 423–432. doi:10.1080/08832323.2018.1545629

Padgett, R. C., & Donald, W. E. (2023). Preparing graduates for sustainable careers: A case of 'The Global Marketing Professional' module. *Higher Education, Skills, and Work-Based Learning*, *13*(1), 22–35. doi:10.1108/HESWBL-03-2022-0073

Peeters, E., Nelissen, J., De Cuyper, N., Forrier, A., Verbruggen, M., & De Witte, H. (2019). Employability capital: A conceptual framework tested through expert analysis. *Journal of Career Development*, *46*(2), 79–93. doi:10.1177/0894845317731865

Pham, T. (2020). Reconceptualising employability of returnees: What really matters and strategic navigating approaches. *Higher Education*, *81*(6), 1329–1345. doi:10.100710734-020-00614-2

Pham, T. (2021). Communication Competencies and International Graduates' Employability Outcomes: Strategies to Navigate the Host Labour Market. *Journal of International Migration and Integration*. doi:10.100712134-021-00869-3

Pham, T., & Jackson, D. (2020). Employability and determinants of employment outcomes. In N. Tran, T. Pham, M. Tomlinson, K. Medica, & C. Thompson (Eds.), *Developing and Utilizing Employability Capitals: Graduates' Strategies Across Labour Markets* (pp. 237–255). Routledge. 10.4324/9781003004660-17

Pham, T., Tomlinson, M., & Thompson, C. (2019). Forms of capital and agency as mediations in negotiating employability of international graduate migrants. *Globalisation, Societies and Education*, *17*(3), 394–405. doi:10.1080/14767724.2019.1583091

Rodrigues, R., Butler, C. L., & Guest, D. (2020). Evaluating the employability paradox: When does organizational investment in human capital pay off? *International Journal of Human Resource Management*, *31*(9), 1134–1156. doi:10.1080/09585192.2019.1704825

Römgens, I., Scoupe, R., & Beausaert, S. (2020). Unraveling the concept of employability, bringing together research on employability in higher education and the workplace. *Studies in Higher Education*, *45*(12), 2588–2603. doi:10.1080/03075079.2019.1623770

Rothwell, A., & Arnold, J. (2007). Self-perceived employability: Development and validation of a scale. *Personnel Review*, *36*(1), 23–41. doi:10.1108/00483480710716704

Schultz, T. W. (1961). Investment in human capital. *The American Economic Review*, *11*(1), 1–17.

Small, L., Shacklock, K., & Marchant, T. (2018). Employability: A contemporary review for higher education stakeholders. *Journal of Vocational Education and Training*, *70*(1), 148–166. doi:10.1080/13636820.2017.1394355

Tang, M. (2022). Challenges Associated with Employability Capitals Facing Chinese International Graduates in Australia. In B. Ng (Ed.), *Graduate Employability and Workplace-Based Learning Development: Insights from Sociocultural Perspectives* (pp. 83–99). Springer Nature Singapore. doi:10.1007/978-981-19-5622-5_6

Teng, W., Ma, C., Pahlevansharif, S., & Turner, J. J. (2019). Graduate readiness for the employment market of the 4th industrial revolution: The development of soft employability skills. *Education + Training*, *61*(5), 590–604. doi:10.1108/ET-07-2018-0154

Tomlinson, M. (2012). Graduate employability: A review of conceptual and empirical themes. *Higher Education Policy*, *25*(4), 407–431. doi:10.1057/hep.2011.26

Tomlinson, M. (2017). Forms of graduate capital and their relationship to graduate employability. *Education + Training*, *59*(4), 338–352. doi:10.1108/ET-05-2016-0090

Tomlinson, M., & Jackson, D. (2021). Professional identity formation in contemporary higher education students. *Studies in Higher Education*, *46*(4), 885–900. doi:10.1080/03075079.2019.1659763

Tomlinson, M., McCafferty, H., Port, A., Maguire, N., Zableski, A. E., Butnaru, A., Charles, M., & Kirby, S. (2022). Developing graduate employability for a challenging labour market: The validation of the graduate capital scale. *Journal of Applied Research in Higher Education*, *14*(3), 1193–1209. doi:10.1108/JARHE-04-2021-0151

Useem, M., & Karabel, J. (1986). Pathways to top corporate management. *American Sociological Review*, *51*(2), 184–200. doi:10.2307/2095515

Van der Heijden, B. I. J. M., & De Vos, A. (2015). Sustainable careers: Introductory chapter. In A. De Vos & B. I. J. M. Van der Heijden (Eds.), *Handbook of Research on Sustainable Careers* (pp. 1–19). Edward Elgar. doi:10.4337/9781782547037.00006

Vanhercke, D., de Cuyper, N., Peeters, E., & De Witte, H. (2014). Defining perceived employability: A psychological approach. *Personnel Review*, *43*(4), 592–605. doi:10.1108/PR-07-2012-0110

Vithana, K., Jayasekera, R., Choudhry, T., & Baruch, Y. (2023). Human Capital resource as cost or investment: A market-based analysis. *International Journal of Human Resource Management*, *34*(6), 1213–1245. doi:10.1080/09585192.2021.1986105

Whitmore, J. (1992). *Coaching For Performance: A Practical Guide To Growing Your Own Skills*. Nicholas Brealey Publishing.

Wiernik, B. M., & Kostal, J. W. (2019). Protean and boundaryless career orientations: A critical review and meta-analysis. *Journal of Counseling Psychology*, *66*(3), 280–307. doi:10.1037/cou0000324 PMID:30777774

Yorke, M. (2004). *Employability in Higher Education – What is it – and what it is not*. Higher Education Academy.

ADDITIONAL READING

Bryne, C. (2022). What determines perceived graduate employability? Exploring the effects of personal characteristics, academic achievements and graduate skills in a survey experiment. *Studies in Higher Education*, *47*(1), 159–176. doi:10.1080/03075079.2020.1735329

Cook, E. J. (2022). A narrative review of graduate employability models: Their paradigms, and relationships to teaching and curricula. *Journal of Teaching and Learning for Graduate Employability*, *13*(1), 37–64. doi:10.21153/jtlge2022vol13no1art1483

Hargreaves, A., & Fullan, M. (2012). *Professional Capital: Transforming Teaching in Every School*. Teachers College Press.

Jackson, D., & Dean, B. A. (2023). The contribution of different types of work-integrated learning to graduate employability. *Higher Education Research & Development*, *42*(1), 93–110. doi:10.1080/07294360.2022.2048638

Lehmann, W. (2019). Forms of capital in working-class students' transition from university to employment. *Journal of Education and Work*, *32*(4), 347–359. doi:10.1080/13639080.2019.1617841

Nghia, T. L. H., Singh, J. K. N., Pham, T., & Medica, K. (2020). Employability, Employability Capital, and Career Development. In: T. L. H. Nghia, T. Pham, M., Tomlinson, K. Medica, & C. Thompson (Eds.), *Developing and Utilizing Employability Capitals*. Routledge.

Pitan, O. S., & Muller, C. (2020). Students' self-perceived employability (SPE): Main effects and interactions of gender and field of study. *Higher Education. Skills and Work-Based Learning*, *10*(2), 355–368. doi:10.1108/HESWBL-03-2019-0040

Souto-Otero, M., & Bialowolski, P. (2021). Graduate employability in Europe: The role of human capital, institutional reputation and network ties in European graduate labour markets. *Journal of Education and Work*, *34*(5-6), 611–631. doi:10.1080/13639080.2021.1965969

Wallis, R. (2021). Career readiness: Developing graduate employability capitals in aspiring media workers. *Journal of Education and Work*, *34*(4), 533–543. doi:10.1080/13639080.2021.1931666

Xu, C. L., & Ma, Y. (2023). Geography-mediated institutionalised cultural capital: Regional inequalities in graduate employment. *Journal of Education and Work*, *36*(1), 22–36. doi:10.1080/13639080.2022.2162018

Zou, H., Ullah, A., Qazi, Z., Naeem, A., & Rehan, S. (2023). Impact of micro-credential learning on students' perceived employability: The mediating role of human capital. *International Journal of Educational Management*.. doi:10.1108/IJEM-01-2023-0002

APPENDIX: ADDITIONAL OPERATIONALIZATION OPPORTUNITIES

The Appendix offers some additional opportunities that career practitioners can use to operationalize the ECG model in a university setting or an industry setting. The content first appeared on the CareerWise Blog of the Canadian Education and Research Institute for Counselling (CERIC) in Autumn 2023 (Donald et al., 2023b).

Application in a University Setting

Within a university setting, the primary objective of deploying the ECG model is to prepare students for sustainable careers and for undertaking the university-to-work transition. Career practitioners (e.g., university career advisors, recruitment agency representatives and graduate recruiters) can follow a three-phase approach to support university students: (i) exploring the forms of capital, (ii) fostering a personalized plan, and (iii) considering external factors and personal outcomes.

Phase One: Exploring the Forms of Capital

Initially, students reflect sequentially on each of the nine forms of employability capital under the guidance of a career practitioner. They should also consider how the various dimensions of each form of capital can interact with each other.

Phase Two: Fostering A Personalized Plan

After exploring the nine forms of capital, students are prompted to assess their own strengths and areas for development. They identify which aspects of the various forms of capital they currently possess and how these can be advantageous for employers in showcasing employability during the selection process. Consequently, the student creates a personalized plan identifying the areas they need to enhance with specific and achievable goals for regular evaluation. The tailored approach ensures that each student's needs are addressed effectively, fostering their growth and employability.

Phase Three: Considering External Factors and Personal Outcomes

In the final phase, students need to consider the entire ECG model. When providing career guidance, there is often an excessive focus on individual control, giving students the false impression of complete power (agency) over their employment outcomes. However, students can be capable of performing a job (employable) whilst not necessarily being able to secure a job at a specific point in time (employed).

By discussing external factors with students, career practitioners can help students manage their expectations and understand the role of circumstances beyond their control.

The final dimension of the ECG model focuses on personal outcomes, representing the potential benefits students can gain from proactively developing various forms of employability capital in preparation for the university-work transition. By discussing personal outcomes with students (e.g. self-perceived employability, career progression, earnings, and wellbeing), career practitioners can motivate students to acquire various forms of capital and prepare them for the university-work transition and sustainable careers.

Application in an Industry Setting

Although the ECG model is primarily intended for career practitioners working with university students and graduates, many components of the nine forms of capital, external factors and personal outcomes hold value for individuals throughout their careers. In an industry setting, the focus shifts to organizational agents (e.g. human resource professionals and line managers) supporting employees to embrace lifewide learning, prepare for career transitions and navigate unforeseen circumstances for career sustainability.

For these three focus areas, we now explore how the ECG model can be combined with the GROW (Goals, Reality, Options and Will) model (Whitmore, 1992) to offer various perspectives for employees to consider during career counseling sessions.

Fostering Lifewide Learning

- **G**oal: Explore strategies for acquiring different forms of employability capital in the present or near future.
- **R**eality: Assess current practices and methods of acquiring employability capital.
- **O**ptions: Identify additional avenues to obtain employability capital within and outside the work environment. Determine the necessary resources you require and any support your employer could provide.
- **W**ill: Clarify motivation to acquire various forms of employability capital at any particular moment or stage.

Preparing for Career Transitions

- **G**oal: Develop strategies to acquire different forms of employability capital for long-term career benefits.
- **R**eality: Evaluate upcoming career steps and identify long-term aspirations.
- **O**ptions: Determine which forms of employability capital will be most advantageous in reaching your long-term goals. Establish plans to acquire these resources.
- **W**ill: Define motivation for your next career move and long-term vision. Examine personal outcomes of the ECG model to aid this step. Let this drive your commitment to obtaining relevant employability capital with a long-term perspective.

Navigating Unforeseen Circumstances

- **G**oal: Develop the ability to effectively navigate unexpected events and adverse career shocks that may arise during your career (e.g. being made redundant).
- **R**eality: Acknowledge and be prepared for the possibility of unforeseen circumstances and career shocks. Recognize the influence of external factors beyond your direct control, including those outlined in the ECG model.
- **O**ptions: Proactively identify opportunities to establish strategies and be prepared in advance. Recognize the importance of adaptability, flexibility and building a professional network as crucial aspects of employability capital and career sustainability.
- **W**ill: Use the personal outcomes from the ECG model to act as motivation to acquire the various forms of capital proactively in preparation for navigating unforeseen events (e.g. unexpected redundancy) that may occur during one's career.

Chapter 3
Student Engagement Strategies

ABSTRACT

University career services face several challenges when seeking to provide career support to their students. Examples of these challenges include (i) a lack of student awareness and engagement, (ii) a lack of institutional commitment, (iii) student demands for health and wellbeing support, and (iv) issues promoting social mobility. Each of these challenges has been exacerbated by the COVID-19 pandemic, which has seen record levels of demand for career-related and wellbeing-related support from university students. A lack of resources to meet such demands requires innovative strategies to engage students, foster social mobility, and produce diverse talent for organizations. In this chapter, the authors explore each of these challenges before offering five engagement strategies, including (i) raising awareness and visibility, (ii) accessible, timely and tailored support, (iii) peer mentoring and alums mentoring, (iv) embedding employability into the curriculum, and (v) additional partnerships and resources. Four lived experience insights conclude the chapter.

INTRODUCTION

University career services can play a crucial role in helping their students acquire employability capital and personal resources to enhance self-perceived employability, employment outcomes, and career sustainability indicators of health, happiness, and productivity (as discussed in Chapters 1 and 2). University career services can also help their students signal employability to prospective employers (which we will explore further in Chapter 4). However, Gradleaders (2022) reported that student

DOI: 10.4018/978-1-6684-9827-9.ch003

engagement is the number one issue that university career services currently face. The same survey of 236 career services worldwide found that 67% struggled with student engagement, whilst only 22% of their cumulative students had engaged with them in the last year. In response, the aim of this chapter is to look at four interlinked challenges:

- A lack of student awareness and engagement
- A lack of institutional commitment
- Student demands for health and wellbeing support
- Issues promoting social mobility

Five engagement strategies are then presented:

- Raising awareness and visibility
- Accessible, timely and tailored support
- Peer mentoring and alums mentoring
- Embedding employability into the curriculum
- Additional partnerships and resources

The chapter concludes with a series of four lived experience insights providing examples of real-world challenges, strategic approaches, and outcomes related to the issue of student engagement.

CHALLENGES

Lack of Student Awareness and Engagement

When we think of engagement practices between students and university career services as two actors within a sustainable career ecosystem, there is a tendency to place the responsibility for initiating engagement on the university career service rather than on the individual student. Such views are not without merit, particularly given that contextual factors and structural barriers limit what a student can achieve through career agency/ownership (Forrier et al., 2018). University career services can undoubtedly do more to engage their students and raise awareness of the various support available. For example, in the UK, 28% of university career services do not have a student engagement strategy but plan to in the future, whilst another 19% have no strategy and no plans to develop one (Association of Graduate Careers Advisory Services (AGCAS) & Symplicity, 2022). Moreover, university career services are often based at the main university campus, risking the exclusion of students whose degree-related activities occur at alternative locations (Donald et al., 2018). There also appears to be a disconnect between the coverage that university career services believe they provide and the perceptions of their students. For example, AGCAS and Simplicity (2022) found that 97% of career services reported having a digital platform or website compared to 69% of students thinking they do, and 90% of career services claiming to have a social media presence compared to 72% of students being aware of it. The same report also found that 30% of university students seek career and employability support via social media. However, only 12% of university career services use one of the most popular social media channels, TikTok, to communicate with their students.

Yet, students themselves also need to take responsibility for their own actions since taking ownership of one's career via a protean career orientation has been shown to increase self-perceived employability (Baruch et al., 2020; Donald et al., 2019) and entrepreneurial intention (Bell, 2019). Seeking career advice has also been linked to increased pay, career progression, and job satisfaction (González-Romá et al., 2018), whereby career ownership and career counseling represent antecedents of a sustainable career (Donald et al., 2020; Donald, Van der Heijden et al., 2023). Nevertheless, many students are not actively seeking career guidance via their university career service. Bradley et al. (2019) found that only 4% of first-year, 25% of second-year, and 51% of final-year undergraduate psychology students engaged with a career advisor. The findings are a concern for two key reasons. First, nearly half of the students were not seeking career guidance at any stage of their degree studies. Second, by not seeking career advice early in a degree, students have less time to identify, acquire, and operationalize personal resources and employability capital (Brooks & Youngson, 2016; Donald et al., 2023b; Tomlinson, 2017).

Lack of Institutional Commitment

According to Gradleaders (2022), "career center budgets continue to get slashed with 54% reporting that there is not enough time, money, people or resources available to them" (Online). The position is supported by AGCAS and Symplicity (2022), who found that university career services struggle due to budget constraints, unrealistic expectations from students around what support can be provided, and challenges engaging with academics. The mismatch between career advisor capacity and students' needs is particularly problematic since most degree courses have no formal employability or work experience module embedded into the curriculum–leaving career provision to run in parallel as a separate entity (High Ed Partners, 2021). The scarcity of resources and lack of prioritization means that international students often fail to receive the career-related support they need (Rickmann et al., 2020).

I remember my own experience of witnessing the challenge of lack of resources play out in a discussion with one university career service in the 2020/2021 academic year. I had put together a slide deck that career services could send out to their students to increase engagement during the second lockdown period of the COVID-19 pandemic. Several universities used the resource and saw increased demand for their services. However, one university career service told me they could not use the resource since they could not manage the increased demand that it would generate. It turned out that this particular career service only had four career advisors, of which two worked part-time to support around 14,000 undergraduates and 3,500 postgraduates.

Another challenge linked to a lack of resources is how university career services use their data. Gradleaders (2022) found that despite all respondents using a career management system, 11% of career advisors still lacked easy access to key metrics for reporting their data. Furthermore, the same report observed how 48% of career advisors said they needed additional help to collect employment outcomes data from their graduates. Poor use of data for informing career guidance strategies or enabling students to take ownership of their own journey compounds the problem of a lack of people and budgets available for university career service provisions (Higher Ed Partners, 2021).

Health and Wellbeing

Young people, particularly university students, are more likely to suffer from mental health issues than the general population (Evans et al., 2020). Unfortunately, whilst funding for mental health services by institutions and governments has increased, timely access to such services remains problematic, and where support is provided, it is not always sufficiently connected with promoting wellbeing (Redekopp & Huston, 2020). Concurrently, the pandemic-related restrictions implemented by national governments to try and protect health services and limit the loss of life exacerbated this pre-existing challenge (Cage et al., 2021). Subsequently, addressing mental health issues among university students was declared a global priority (Xiong et al., 2020). Yet, the effects of the pandemic impacted all aspects of health and wellbeing. Donald and Jackson (2022) conducted a study to compare self-perceived wellbeing scores of university students and recent graduates from just before the pandemic (March 2020) and 18 months into the pandemic (September 2021). We examined six positive characteristic aspects of hedonic subjective wellbeing (emotional stability, optimism, resilience, positive emotion, self-esteem, and vitality) and four positive functioning aspects of eudaimonic subjective wellbeing (competence, engagement, meaning, and positive relationships). We found that composite wellbeing scores fell for almost three-quarters of our 414 participants, whereby "adverse outcomes included feelings of isolation, reduced mental and physical health, difficulties undertaking degree studies and work, travel restrictions, and concerns for labour market competitiveness" (Donald & Jackson, 2022, p. 1). Figure 1 shows the pandemic's impacts on the ten dimensions of wellbeing.

The sustainable career theory, discussed in Chapter 1, identifies three dominant indicators of sustainable careers: happiness, health, and productivity (Van der Heijden, 2005; Van der Heijden & De Vos, 2015). Moreover, research has shown that effective career development can strengthen mental health (Redekopp & Huston, 2020). Unfortunately, the reduced levels of health and wellbeing caused by the disruption to daily life of the COVID-19 pandemic are exacerbated by a lack of joined-up thinking across different student support services (Higher Ed Partners, 2021). Subsequently, existing wellbeing support provided by universities is perceived as insufficient by students (Baik et al., 2019), who call for greater access to services (Cage et al., 2021). Such challenges at the university level also play out at the local and national levels. A lack of qualified mental health practitioners means individuals (particularly young people) face long waiting times to access critical support services (Plewes, 2022).

Social Mobility

An additional challenge for university career services concerns how to improve social mobility outcomes for their students, given the apprehensions that higher education "primarily serves to maintain, rather than narrow, inequalities attached to social origins" (Bukodi, 2017, p. 367). We also know that students from disadvantaged backgrounds are less likely to attend prestigious universities and have lower employability outcomes following graduation, impacting their career progression and lifetime earnings (Britton et al., 2019).

Worryingly, even when a student from a disadvantaged background attends the same university, undertakes the same degree course, and receives the same degree classification as someone from a more advantaged background, they still have a lower chance of accessing the best-paid graduate roles and the most prestigious employers (Friedman & Laurison, 2019).

The emergence of internships as a class strategy to 'get ahead' compounds the challenge since upper-middle-class students can "mobilise family resources to progressively 'stack' multiple and 'high-status' internships, resultantly pulling away from their peers in preparing for the graduate labour market" (Wright & Mulvey, 2021, p. 339).

Figure 1. Wellbeing scores for students and graduates pre and during the COVID-19 pandemic
(C) 2022 Donald & Jackson. Used with permission.
Key: Light Gray = Pre-COVID-19 pandemic; Dark Gray = 18 months into the COVID-19 pandemic.

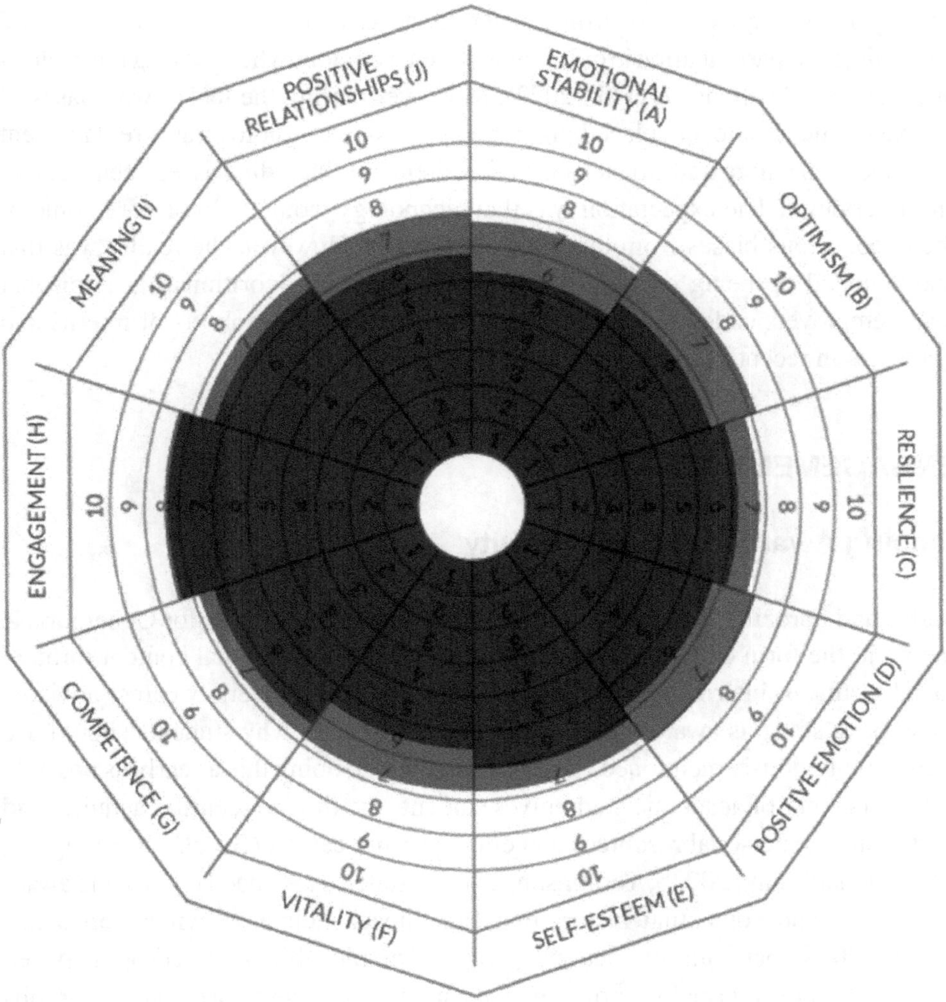

Even when university career services offer schemes aimed at enhancing employability outcomes for diverse groups of students, these often only serve a relatively small percentage of those eligible (Higher Ed Partners, 2021), supporting my findings in the UK that students who need career support the most are least likely to access it (Donald et al., 2018). In Canada, for example, "although racialized people are generally more likely than their non-racialized, non-Indigenous counterparts to earn a bachelor's degree or higher, they are less likely to find jobs that offer the same pay and benefits in the years following graduation" (The Daily, 2023, Paragraph 1). Again, the COVID-19 pandemic exacerbated these pre-existing inequalities due to the disruption to education and reduced opportunities to gain work experience (Haelermans et al., 2022). Less advantaged students also faced issues with digital poverty impacting access to learning materials, access to online career guidance, and hindering their participation in online assessment activities when seeking internships or graduate roles (Donald et al., 2022). Moreover, during the lockdown phases of the pandemic, employers placed greater emphasis on technology as a replacement for some of the more traditional face-to-face elements, including assessment centers and interviews. The expectation was that technology would help remove some of the unconscious biases from the selection process. However, the reality was that biases ended up being embedded into the coding and algorithms, meaning that many employers ended up hiring some of the least diverse cohorts of interns and graduates in recent years (Donald et al., 2023a).

ENGAGEMENT STRATEGIES

Raising Awareness and Visibility

Nadya and Farozin (2021) suggest that "career guidance services for Generation Z can be in the form of 1) coaching, 2) workshops, 3) inspirational content through social media, 4) internship programs" (p. 20). However, university career advisors must make students aware of these services and explain why students should use them. As previously mentioned earlier in this chapter, doing this as early as possible in the first year of academic study gives students the time to identify, acquire, and operationalize personal resources and employability capital (Brooks & Youngson, 2016; Donald et al., 2023b; Tomlinson, 2017). Students also need to be made aware of external and contextual factors that can impact their employment prospects (Clarke, 2018), particularly since self-perceived employability often drops between the penultimate and final year of university study as students start to apply for jobs and receive rejections (Donald et al., 2018). In particular, the increased occurrence of chance events and career shocks places significant emphasis on being prepared for when these inevitably occur during one's career to avoid being overwhelmed (Akkermans et al., 2018; Blokker et al., 2019).

Technology can also play a valuable role when seeking to raise awareness and visibility of the services available to students. Using social media effectively can lead to increased engagement and attendance at career events (Scattergood & Donald, 2023). The approach is explored further in the lived experience later in this chapter, where Kaz Scattergood provides a case from the University of Liverpool, UK, using the social media platform TikTok to enhance student engagement. Research by Higher Ed Partners (2021) also shows how providing online resources can help students build confidence, improve resilience, and facilitate networking opportunities. Using on-demand and micro-engagement technology activities (e.g., case studies or short videos) can also increase engagement when delivered via social media platforms that students are likely to engage with, such as TikTok, Instagram, and Twitter (AGCAS & Symplicity, 2022). Career services can also use technology to measure student engagement, capture student outcomes data, inform strategic direction, optimize data management, and offer students access to on-demand self-assessment tools (Higher Ed Partners, 2021).

Accessible, Timely, and Tailored Support

In February 2022, I had the privilege of interviewing 28 graduates, of which 15 had graduated in 2008 during the Global Financial Crisis and 13 in 2020 during the COVID-19 pandemic. The interviews aimed to understand how individuals who graduated during a global-level chance event felt that university career services could best engage and support their students to prepare them for entry into the labor market (Donald, Jakubik et al., 2023). Graduates called for career advisors to increase the visibility of services offered, provide greater access to these services, and access students as early as possible during their degree studies. There were additional calls to tailor career advice to the individual student, with a greater provision of degree-specific and industry-specific guidance, including access to networking, industry insights, and work experience opportunities. There was also a feeling that university career services should invite a wider range of employers since on-campus events tend to be dominated by multinational companies. In particular, establishing partnerships with local employers and SMEs was viewed as an opportunity to increase access to internship and graduate employment opportunities and retain graduate talent in the local area. Of course, achieving these objectives requires investment and a commitment to social mobility at institutional and government levels.

Previous interviews that I conducted in January 2017 with undergraduate students showed significant alignment with the 2022 findings from graduates. However, undergraduates also emphasized the need for university career advisors to actively visit the various university campuses rather than expect students to travel to the main campus–which, in some cases, can be quite a distance away (Donald, 2017; Donald et al., 2018). However, the increase in virtual and hybrid offerings by university career services since the pandemic restrictions may have helped to overcome this particular concern assuming such offerings reflect a long-lasting shift. Both studies also highlighted the need for support in developing a personal brand and narratives to signal employability (Donald et al., 2018; Donald, Jakubik et al., 2023), an aspect we focus on in-depth in Chapter 4 of this book. Bates et al. (2018) emphasized the benefits of career guidance by showing that students who enrolled on a thirteen-week professional development course in their final year of undergraduate study had greater employment outcomes in the four months following graduation compared to their peers who were not part of the employability intervention. The need for personalized delivery and tailored career support was also echoed by AGCAS and Symplicity (2022), whilst acknowledging that universities will need to invest additional resources into their career services to facilitate such provisions.

Peer Mentoring and Alums Mentoring

Cage et al. (2021) conducted a series of focus groups with university students to understand what would help them to transition between different years of university study and, subsequently, into the labor market. The students asked for support to equip them to cope with mental health challenges and called for the development of peer networks to foster an inclusive environment and learning culture. In parallel, I conducted research via questionnaires with students to understand their needs following the disruption of the COVID-19 pandemic to their daily lives. Students called for guidance on career and finances, as well as opportunities to interact with peers due to reduced chances for in-person interaction during the lockdown phases of the pandemic (Donald & Jackson, 2022). The authors of both of these research studies recommended using mentoring or buddying schemes to achieve such objectives (Cage et al., 2021; Donald & Jackson, 2022). The calls for mentoring opportunities have also come from practitioner-focused publications focusing on how alums can offer mentorship opportunities to improve confidence in university students (AGCAS & Symplicity, 2022; Higher Ed Partners, 2021).

Mentoring provided by peers and alums can address several of the challenges discussed earlier in this chapter by creating networks where a diversity of lived experiences is represented. Donald and Ford (2023) believe that peer learning can foster social mobility within universities leading to enhanced employment outcomes. For example, by increasing visibility and access to support services and enhancing social capital via alum networks. Donald and Scattergood (2023) also found that peer-led social media content proved popular, whereby students were initially trained by the university career service and subsequently provided career guidance to their peers. The increased access to career-related guidance also helped to improve social mobility by overcoming instances where certain students felt too intimidated to approach university career advisors. We also know from the academic literature that social support can help individuals protect themselves from burnout during university studies and throughout their careers (Kim et al., 2018). However, peer mentoring requires significant resources to train and support mentors and evaluate mentorship's impacts against pre-determined objectives (Gunn et al., 2017). Peer mentoring should also not be viewed as a substitute for qualified mental health service provisions, and mentors should signpost mentees to such services where appropriate (Cage et al., 2021).

Embedding Employability Into the Curriculum

The increased prevalence of chance events and the need for individuals to navigate complex and evolving labor markets places additional emphasis on career counseling to support sustainable career development across the lifespan (Argyropoulou, 2021). University career counselors need to understand what matters to students and what support they need when entering higher education (Meehan & Howells, 2018). They also need to ensure they make the support on offer highly visible to students and focus on encouraging the development of career adaptability dimensions, including concern, control, curiosity, and confidence (Ma et al., 2022).

One approach to increasing sustainable career outcomes for university students is embedding employability and career counseling into the curriculum (Jakubik et al., 2023). Encouraging students to provide feedback at the end of the module can help to enhance curriculum design over time (Bell & Reed, 2021), leading to benefits for subsequent student cohorts (Bowman et al., 2021). Embedding employability into the curriculum can also foster social mobility by (i) accessing students who need the support the most, (ii) engaging students early and throughout their degree studies, (iii) utilizing the personal networks of academics to access alums and employers, and (iv) removing barriers to work experience opportunities by sourcing them as part of the degree course provision (Donald et al., 2018; 2022; McCafferty, 2022).

Embedding employability and career guidance into the curriculum also allows students to take ownership of their careers, embrace lifelong learning, and make more informed career decisions (Coetzee & Engelbrecht, 2020). The approach acknowledges that a university education can be an antecedent to a sustainable career (De Vos et al., 2020). The international nature of students participating in higher education also provides opportunities within the curriculum to embrace intercultural citizenship, which is critical for success within global labor markets (Baker & Fang, 2021) and for enhancing the university experience of international students (Fakunle, 2021). Moreover, initiating employability discussions between students can "act as a catalyst to identify what support mechanisms and types of human capital they require and how they can proactively secure access to such resources and opportunities" (Padgett & Donald, 2023, p. 10). When curriculum content is delivered effectively via flipped learning (Selvaratnam, 2021), active learning (Ward, 2020), and whole-person pedagogical approaches (Kim et al., 2021), universities can promote practical wisdom, subsequently enhancing the contribution of their graduates to the workplace and broader society (Jakubik, 2020).

However, there can be tension here if lecturers do not perceive enhancing students' employability as their responsibility and feel that trying to do so undermines the quality of their academic courses (Sin & Neave, 2016). To address this, universities must clearly articulate their priorities, encourage open dialogue, and frame the partnership between lecturers and university career advisors as a win-win outcome (Cheng et al., 2022).

Additional Partnerships and Resources

University career services often face a trade-off regarding the delivery and coverage of career advice. Either they can provide a wider range of services and offer tailored support to a subset of students, or they can offer a reduced range of services and more general career-related guidance to all students (AGCAS & Symplicity, 2022). Neither of these approaches is optimal, and whilst additional resources from the university would be helpful, it does not appear to be a pragmatic or forthcoming option for higher education institutions at this time. Yet, an interesting point of note comes from a study by Gallup and Purdue (2016), who found that graduates who had positive experiences with their career centers during their time at university were more likely to recommend and donate to their alma mater. Therefore, if initial funding can be secured in the short-term to provide high-quality career support, the increased donations from alums in the medium- to long-term could replace the internal funding requirement. However, if university career services cannot serve the needs of all of their students, it would make sense to focus the limited resources available on those students with the lowest levels of social capital and the least access to alternative support networks. Such a focused approach would need to be underpinned by data to a) identify the individuals who need the most support and b) assess the effectiveness of interventions over time to inform iterative improvements.

Three potential avenues exist (either as a stand-alone or integrated approach) to address the challenge of career service provision. One potential avenue is the large-scale use of technology, despite concerns that digitalization of learning can reduce the impact of learning outcomes (Hill & Fitzgerald, 2020). For example, Drewery et al. (2022) found that AI helped provide tactical feedback (e.g., highlighting spelling errors, overused and filler words, and poor formatting) on résumés but was less useful in providing strategic feedback (e.g., identifying strengths and interests, helping to share their career story, and tailoring content to a specific employer), with no influence on students' perceptions of the quality of the career service. Consequently, for a technologically-driven strategy to be effective, university career services should (i) focus on the quality of communications over quantity, (ii) involve students in the creation of content, and (iii) combine online resources with access to in-person or virtual one-to-one sessions to enable self-exploration of personal resources and potential career paths (Klein et al., 2022).

Another potential approach is to secure support from other career influencers to promote sustainable careers and the wellbeing of underrepresented students (Ho et al., 2023). We know that following the restrictions to our daily lives of the COVID-19 pandemic, students want access to counseling, mindfulness, opportunities to participate in student societies, flexible work and study options, as well as career guidance and peer interaction (Baik et al., 2019; Cage et al., 2021; Jackson & Donald, 2022). Within a sustainable career ecosystem, supporting actors can individually and cumulatively play a crucial role in engaging students and preparing them for the university-to-work transition (Donald & Hughes, 2023; Donald et al., 2022). For example, academics, student support services, friends, family, peers, mentors, alums, graduate recruitment agencies, and employers may each be able to contribute to increasing the likelihood of student engagement toward improving wellbeing and employability perceptions (Donald et al., 2018; 2023b). This approach acknowledges that careers and employability professional roles are much broader than individuals employed within university career services (Healy, Brown et al., 2022; Hughes et al., 2023).

The third potential avenue is for career services to put the competition of university league table rankings aside and consider collaborating with other institutions to optimize their resources. The approach seems the most logical of the three (especially when combined with either or both the aforementioned approaches). Yet, due to the ever-increasing neoliberalization of higher education, the approach also seems the least likely beyond ad-hoc events. Perhaps other actors within the career ecosystem, such as graduate recruitment agencies, employers, or national governments, may need to take the lead on this particular approach.

We revisit the challenges and opportunities for greater collaboration between actors within a sustainable career ecosystem later in the book (Chapters 8 and 9). However, having explored the challenges and engagement strategies, our focus in this chapter now moves to four lived experience insights related to student engagement initiatives.

LIVED EXPERIENCE INSIGHTS

Lived Experience Insight

Shared By Dinuka Gunaratne, University of Waterloo, Canada

The Challenge

Based on my experience as a career development practitioner who has worked across several Canadian postsecondary institutions, I have found that motivating students to take an active role in their career development can be tricky. Despite our efforts to provide resources such as orientations, websites, information sessions, and classroom announcements detailing our services, students remain primarily uninterested in engaging with career centers and career development practitioners on a regular basis. Instead, they usually turn to their informal networks, such as family, friends, and other close contacts, for career-related information, rather than seeking out expert sources within the institution.

The Context

Four primary factors contribute to this difficulty (i) time constraints, (ii) misunderstandings, (iii) a perceived lack of relevance, and (iv) information overload. Students are already busy with studying and their social lives, meaning they might not prioritize visiting the career center. Additionally, some students may assume that career centers only assist students who are close to graduating without realizing that career centers offer support and guidance to all students. There is also a perception that career services may not be useful to some students because of their particular major or career ambitions. These students believe that internships, good grades, and personal networks are enough to succeed. Finally, some other students find the sheer amount of information available overwhelming.

Action Taken

We worked on implementing a strong social media campaign that utilized student partnerships to create content, scripts, and assets. We recognized that many students are active on social media platforms, so we focused on engaging with our target audience through Instagram, TikTok, and LinkedIn. Our team produced entertaining videos related to career development, employment support, and other services offered by the career center. We ensured that all digital assets, messaging, and videos were designed with a sense of purpose and inclusivity. Using calls to action and live direct messaging support, we directed students who required just-in-time services to our career center.

The Outcome

Keeping things informative yet informal produced the best results. Our engaging content helped students feel less overwhelmed and intimidated by career development and dispelled the myth that services were only available for final-year students or those who needed specific services. We successfully engaged many students undertaking various degree courses. We were pleased that our career education efforts also reached beyond our postsecondary audience to prospective students, alums, and the broader community.

Lessons Learned and Advice

One important lesson we learned was the need to go to students rather than expecting them to come to us. The second lesson is to provide students with multiple levels of support. While traditional methods like information sessions, classroom presentations, drop-in appointments, and one-on-one meetings are still useful, a robust marketing and communications plan can make a big difference. Consistency is crucial, and enlisting students as content creators can be incredibly effective since they understand the needs and motivations of their peers. In today's digital age, we must take advantage of the available tools and resources to ensure everyone can make informed decisions to enhance their employability and prepare for the university-to-work transition.

Lived Experience Insight

Shared By Kaz Scattergood, University of Liverpool, UK

The Challenge

Student engagement is one of the top challenges faced by university career services. The students who could benefit from career guidance the most are often those least likely to seek it. Whilst the emphasis is partly on those students taking a more proactive approach, career services also need to do more to increase levels of engagement. A separate albeit related challenge comes from needing to innovate to deliver career-related support at scale. The COVID-19 pandemic has seen record numbers of students seek career support, yet career services often have limited resources to meet such demand. Consequently, the challenge we faced was to increase student engagement sustainably.

The Context

To address this challenge, we wanted to see how we could make more effective use of social media as a career service. Unfortunately, many career services view social media as a box-ticking exercise that is neither well-resourced nor strategized. Additionally, innovative approaches can initially prove controversial and be met with significant pushback from career professionals. The approach needed to overcome these barriers whilst simultaneously acknowledging that students decide whether to engage with university career services via social media based on the content provided by these channels.

Action Taken

Students at the university were approached and asked what social media content and interaction they wanted from the career service. Two clear themes emerged. First, students desired informative content that looks good and is delivered authentically (i.e., real-world insights from various voices). Subsequently, we pivoted from editorial and promotional material to offer more informative, educational content, which could enhance students' self-perceived employability. Second, students had a strong desire for peer-led content. In response, significant emphasis was placed on peer-led engagement whereby the Communications and Engagement team resourced social media content properly, lent into current trends, and created material alongside students and graduates to produce relatable and fun content that their students would like to see.

The Outcome

The action taken proved to be a great success. Before the intervention, content posted on Instagram received fewer than 10 likes and no saves. Now, these engagement metrics are considerably higher. A post advertising part-time job opportunities was saved 162 times, and a guide to formatting a cover letter was saved 148 times. We have also seen increased attendance at on-campus employability events, whereby social media has helped increase the careers service's visibility. Finally, the delivery of collaborative content via social media with the central University of Liverpool channel increased exposure to previously less-engaged students, who can often benefit the most from career guidance. A recent collaboration with this team led to a video receiving 18.5k views on Instagram. The approach has also improved rapport between the university and its student body whilst enhancing the reputation of the University of Liverpool as a pioneer of novel approaches to student engagement.

Lessons Learned and Advice

Creative, innovative, fun, and on-trend content from career services can improve student engagement and employability outcomes. The time has come to value the work of content creators in university career services to benefit students, graduates, the careers service, universities, organizations, and broader society.

Lived Experience Insight

Shared By Simon Howell, Griffith University, Australia

The Challenge

The Australian government uses the Graduate Outcomes Survey to report the percentage of graduates who have secured employment four to six months after graduation. However, the Graduate Outcomes metrics for our engineering students were lower than for other universities in our region. We needed to improve our Graduate Outcomes metrics and address employer feedback that engineering graduates across the sector need more prior exposure to engineering professional practice during their studies.

The Context

Griffith University is situated in Queensland, Australia, and offers engineering degrees via two campuses, one in Brisbane and one on the Gold Coast. Griffith University is a relatively young institution, and around 40% of the cohort are the first in their families to attend university.

Action Taken

In 2017, we redesigned our engineering degree and embedded a 'Professional Practice and Employability Skills' stream into the curriculum. The stream aimed to increase student exposure to industry and ensure that students have a career 'toolkit' consisting of items including a resume and cover letter. To do this, we took two key actions. Firstly, in one module per semester over the first three years of the four-year engineering degree, students undertook an assessed assignment relating to employability development, typically weighted at 10% of the overall mark for the specific module. Secondly, we deemed one week in the second term as ‘Employability Week’, whereby standard timetabled classes were replaced with an alternative program of guest lectures, site visits, and professional development sessions linked to the assessment items. We believed these actions would also help prepare students for their final year capstone project thesis, typically conducted in the industry.

The Outcome

We have seen some good improvements in our Graduate Outcomes metrics, but there is still room to grow. I have been really pleased with the positive feedback from students, with many commenting that they could use the resume and/or cover letter they had created as part of the module assessment task to secure interviews that led to internships or graduate roles. Some students also secured internships after a site visit. From an industry perspective, we made it easier for organizations to promote themselves to our students and source suitable intern and graduate talent.

Lessons Learned and Advice

My experiences with the ‘Professional Practice and Employability Skills’ stream have clarified that employability development is not a ‘bolt-on’ activity that can be dealt with in a single module, or solely offered as a co-curricular option whereby students have to seek career support proactively. I believe it must be embedded into the curriculum and supported with suitable assessment tasks to ensure engagement and maximize the potential benefits to students. Additionally, it is important to continually seek student feedback to ensure the provisions within the ‘Professional Practice and Employability Skills’ stream meet their needs. For example, students requested opportunities for interview practice, seemingly unaware of the services that were freely available through the central career office. Consequently, I added an assessment task where students develop their interview skills through an online training platform to raise awareness and increase engagement with the software that was already available. Finally, I would advise universities to look at strategies to link students with career services since I suspect many students are unaware that the department exists and/or the many ways it can support them.

Lived Experience Insight

Shared By Rebecca C. Padgett, University of Leeds, UK

The Challenge

The business school tasked us with designing a compulsory module for a one-year taught postgraduate program to ensure students understood the professional competencies required for non-linear graduate careers. The module design included career thinking and planning, fostering career agency, and reflective practice elements. Participants reported an increase in their self-perceived employability from 37.5% at the start of the module to 92.5% upon completion. The success of the compulsory module led to further calls by the business school to develop a co-curricular program of events. The challenge was to deliver the new program to a large cohort of students alongside a full-time postgraduate degree whilst navigating time and resource constraints for staff and students.

The Context

The program needed to enhance and enrich the student experience and help students signal their employability to prospective employers. We wanted to involve students in the program design to foster a sense of belonging and increase engagement. We also wanted to ensure that the program did not detract from the valuable work the careers service already did around career advice and guidance.

Action Taken

We established a team of 30 volunteer student ambassadors who demonstrated a desire to partner with us and gain valuable experience working with different stakeholders across departmental boundaries. We established a co-curricular program called 'Making a Difference', which ran during evenings and weekends. The program consisted of a series of short, non-credit bearing, professional courses such as 'The Essentials of Business Planning', 'Sales and Negotiation Bootcamp', 'The Sustainability Challenge' and 'The Entrepreneurship in Marketing Award', supported by a mentoring program and executive guest speaker series.

The Outcome

The program was overwhelmingly successful, with over 385 student engagements with activities. Student ambassadors helped to market, generate interest, and compile communications, which led to successful student engagement due to a fear of missing out. All programs were at total capacity and, in most cases, had a waiting list since participant numbers were limited by room size and staff availability. Overall, 99% of students were satisfied with the courses, 97% felt the courses were relevant to the job market, 96% would recommend the courses to a friend, and 84% said that their self-perceived confidence in their employability had increased from taking part in the program.

Lessons Learned and Advice

In an era where student engagement poses a significant challenge, it felt like various people were waiting for the initiative to fail. However, this made our small team of academic staff even more determined to succeed. Partnering with students to deliver a program with such a significant impact was extremely rewarding. However, it also required significant amounts of time, which must be accounted for in the workload allocations of academic staff for such programs to remain viable and sustainable. Higher education institutions should therefore ensure that curriculum and co-curriculum activities are adequately resourced to avoid staff burnout whilst offering meaningful benefits to students.

Reflection on Lived Experience Insights

The four lived experience insights from Australia, Canada, and the UK present valuable strategies for enhancing student engagement. A recurring theme is the positive impact students can have in encouraging their peers to engage proactively with career-related guidance and support. One effective strategy involves students as co-creators, where they contribute creative, informative, and inclusive peer-led content distributed through popular social media platforms like Instagram, LinkedIn, and TikTok. Another successful approach involves the utilization of volunteer student ambassadors to increase student engagement in co-curricular career-related activities.

Furthermore, embedding career-related content into the curriculum as an assessed component of a module across each year of study is highlighted as an impactful strategy to maximize student engagement. The insights also identify mentoring, guest speaking, and industry partnerships as effective engagement strategies, whether implemented as co-curricular activities or integrated within the curriculum.

In summary, providing multiple avenues for students to access career support is vital. Academics can also play a crucial role in delivering co-curricular content and providing dedicated capacity within the curriculum for career-related topics. Moreover, continuously seeking student feedback is critical to ensure that the content and delivery methods effectively meet their needs. Gathering student feedback can also help overcome resistance to innovative approaches for increasing student engagement by demonstrating an informed strategy and articulating positive outcomes.

CONCLUSION

In this chapter, we identified four interlinked challenges:

- A lack of student awareness and engagement
- A lack of institutional commitment
- Student demands for health and wellbeing support
- Issues promoting social mobility

Five engagement strategies were presented:

- Raising awareness and visibility
- Accessible, timely and tailored support
- Peer mentoring and alums mentoring
- Embedding employability into the curriculum
- Additional partnerships and resources

Four lived experience insights were also provided, offering examples of real-world challenges, strategic approaches, and outcomes related to the issue of student engagement.

If you are a university student, you might like to take this opportunity to reflect on how you could be more proactive in taking advantage of the career-related and wellbeing-related support offered by your university. Additionally, do not wait until your final year of study to seek such support. Students that seek support throughout their university degrees experience the greatest cumulative benefits due to increased opportunities to acquire employability capital and personal resources over time. If you are a first-generation student or a student from a disadvantaged background, then it is essential that you use your university career service to access networking opportunities and gain work experience. Finally, consider getting involved in a peer mentoring scheme at your university. If such a scheme does not currently exist, you might consider speaking to your university career service about setting one up.

If you are a career counselor either within a centralized university career service or based at the school or faculty level, you might like to share some of the strategic approaches discussed in this chapter with your team to see where they may help to overcome the main issue that career services face of poor levels of student engagement. You may also have thought of additional opportunities or strategies whilst reading this chapter, as those presented here are not meant to be all-encompassing. However, a lack of resources can be a significant challenge for university career advisors, so developing key partnerships with other actors operating within a sustainable career ecosystem is crucial. These partnerships include those with organizations and graduate recruiters, which we explore later in this book from the perspectives of challenges (Chapter 8) and opportunities (Chapter 9). Finally, please remember that you play a critical role in fostering social mobility and preparing students for sustainable careers. Your role and contribution matter more than you might know.

The next chapter now concludes Section Two of the book, which has focused on how the university career service and other actors within the university ecosystem can prepare their students for the university-to-work transition and sustainable graduate careers. Chapter 4 adopts a signaling theory framework to understand how students can signal their employability to prospective employers, enabling students to showcase their employability capital and resources, as well as increase their chances of securing employment.

REFERENCES

AGCAS & Symplicity. (2022). *The opportunities and challenges of student engagement in careers and employability provision*. AGCAS. https://www.agcas.org.uk/write/MediaUploads/Resources/Research%20and%20knowledge/Symp_22_Student_Engagement_Report_Final.pdf

Akkermans, J., Seibert, S. E., & Mol, S. (2018). Tales of the unexpected: Integrating career shocks in the contemporary careers' literature. *SA Journal of Industrial Psychology*, *44*, 1503. doi:10.4102ajip.v44i0.1503

Argyropoulou, K. (2021). Sustainable career development: A new challenge in career counselling in the modern era. *Advances in Social Sciences Research Journal*, *8*(12), 128–138. doi:10.14738/assrj.812.11393

Baik, C., Larcombe, W., & Brooker, A. (2019). How universities can enhance student mental wellbeing: The student perspective. *Higher Education Research & Development*, *38*(4), 674–687. doi:10.1080/07294360.2019.1576596

Baker, W., & Fang, F. G. (2021). So maybe I'm a global citizen: Developing intercultural citizenship in English medium education. *Language, Culture and Curriculum, 34*(1), 1–17. doi:10.1080/07908318.2020.1748045

Baruch, Y., Bhaskar, A. U., & Mishra, B. (2020). Career dynamics in India: A two-wave study of career orientations and employability of graduates. *Personnel Review, 49*(3), 825–845. doi:10.1108/PR-10-2018-0429

Bates, L., Hayes, H., Walker, S., & Marchesi, K. (2018). From employability to employment: A professional skills development course in a three-year bachelor program. *International Journal of Work-Integrated Learning, 19*(4), 413–423.

Bell, K., & Reed, M. (2021). The tree of participation: A new tool for engagers in participatory decision-making. *Community Development Journal: An International Forum, 2021*, 1–20. doi:10.1093/cdj/bsab018

Bell, R. (2019). Predicting entrepreneurial intention across the university. *Education + Training, 61*(7/8), 815–831. doi:10.1108/ET-05-2018-0117

Blokker, R., Akkermans, J., Tims, M., Jansen, P., & Khapova, S. (2019). Building a sustainable start: The role of career competencies, career success, and career shocks in young professionals' employability. *Journal of Vocational Behavior, 112*, 172–184. doi:10.1016/j.jvb.2019.02.013

Bowman, B., Bell, K., & Alexis-Martin, B. (2021). Youth, climate and environmentalism. In K. Bell (Ed.), *Diversity and Inclusion in Environmentalism* (pp. 195–210). Routledge. doi:10.4324/9781003099185-9

Bradley, A., Quigley, M., & Bailey, K. (2019). How well are students engaging with the careers services at university? *Studies in Higher Education, 46*(4), 663–676. doi:10.1080/03075079.2019.1647416

Britton, J., Deardon, L., Shephard, N., & Vignoles, A. (2019). Is improving access to university enough? Socio-economic gaps in the earnings of English graduates. *Oxford Bulletin of Economics and Statistics, 81*(2), 328–368. doi:10.1111/obes.12261

Bukodi, E. (2017). Cumulative inequalities over the life-course: Life-long learning and social mobility in Britain. *Journal of Social Policy, 46*(2), 367–404. doi:10.1017/S0047279416000635

Cage, E., Jones, E., Ryan, G., Hughes, G., & Spanner, L. (2021). Student mental health and transitions into, through and out of university: Student and staff perspectives. *Journal of Further and Higher Education, 45*(8), 1076–1089. doi:10.1080/0309877X.2021.1875203

Cheng, M., Adekola, O., Albia, J., & Cai, S. (2022). Employability in higher education: A review of key stakeholders' perspectives. *Higher Education. Evolution & Development*, *16*(1), 16–31. doi:10.1108/HEED-03-2021-0025

Clarke, M. (2018). Rethinking graduate employability: The role of capital, individual attributes and context. *Studies in Higher Education*, *43*(11), 1923–1937. doi:10.1080/03075079.2017.1294152

Coetzee, M., & Engelbrecht, L. (2020). How employability attributes mediate the link between knowledge workers' career adaption concerns and their self-perceived employability. *Psychological Reports*, *123*(4), 1005–1026. doi:10.1177/0033294119844981 PMID:31060459

De Vos, A., Van der Heijden, B. I. J. M., & Akkermans, J. (2020). Sustainable careers: Towards a conceptual model. *Journal of Vocational Behavior*, *117*, 103196. doi:10.1016/j.jvb.2018.06.011

Donald, W. E. (2017). *Students' Perceptions of Graduate Employability: A Sequential Explanatory Approach.* Doctoral Thesis, University of Southampton. https://eprints.soton.ac.uk/id/eprint/415935

Donald, W. E., Ashleigh, M. J., & Baruch, Y. (2018). Students' perceptions of education and employability: Facilitating career transition from higher education into the labor market. *Career Development International*, *23*(5), 513–540. doi:10.1108/CDI-09-2017-0171

Donald, W. E., Ashleigh, M. J., & Baruch, Y. (2022). The university-to-work transition: Responses of universities and organizations to the COVID-19 pandemic. *Personnel Review*, *51*(9), 2201–2221. doi:10.1108/PR-03-2021-0170

Donald, W. E., Baruch, Y., & Ashleigh, M. J. (2019). The undergraduate self-perception of employability: Human capital, careers advice and career ownership. *Studies in Higher Education*, *44*(4), 599–614. doi:10.1080/03075079.2017.1387107

Donald, W. E., Baruch, Y., & Ashleigh, M. J. (2020). Striving for sustainable graduate careers: Conceptualization via career ecosystems and the new psychological contract. *Career Development International*, *25*(2), 90–110. doi:10.1108/CDI-03-2019-0079

Donald, W. E., Baruch, Y., & Ashleigh, M. J. (2023a). Technological transformation and human resource development of early career talent: Insights from accounting, banking, and finance. *Human Resource Development Quarterly*, *34*(3), 329–348. doi:10.1002/hrdq.21491

Donald, W. E., Baruch, Y., & Ashleigh, M. J. (2023b). Construction and operationalisation of an Employability Capital Growth Model (ECGM) via A systematic literature review. *Studies in Higher Education*, 1–15. doi:10.1080/03075079.2023.2219270

Donald, W. E., & Ford, N. (2023). Fostering social mobility and employability: The case for peer learning. *Teaching in Higher Education, 28*(3), 672–678. doi:10.1080/13562517.2022.2145467

Donald, W. E., & Hughes, H. P. N. (2023). How academics can play a more influential role during a year-in-industry placement: A contemporary critique and call for action. *Industry and Higher Education.* doi:10.1177/09504222231162059

Donald, W. E., & Jackson, D. (2022). Subjective wellbeing among university students and recent graduates: Evidence from the United Kingdom. *International Journal of Environmental Research and Public Health, 19*(11), 6911. doi:10.3390/ijerph19116911 PMID:35682494

Donald, W. E., Jakubik, M., & Nimmi, P. M. (2023). Preparing university graduates for sustainable careers: Qualitative insights from the UK. In W. E. Donald (Ed.), *Handbook of Research on Sustainable Career Ecosystems for University Students and Graduates* (pp. 320–341). IGI Global. doi:10.4018/978-1-6684-7442-6.ch017

Donald, W. E., & Scattergood, K. (2023). *Fostering student social mobility via social media: Opportunities for university career services.* Times Higher Education. doi:10.13140/RG.2.2.34483.71204

Donald, W. E., Van der Heijden, B. I. J. M., & Manville, G. (2023). *Sustainable Careers and Organisations: Development of a Conceptual Framework and Future Research Agenda.* British Academy of Management Conference 2023.

Drewery, D., Woodside, J., & Eppel, K. (2022). Artificial intelligence and résumé critique experiences. *Canadian Journal of Career Development, 21*(2), 28–39. doi:10.53379/cjcd.2022.338

Evans, S., Alkan, E., Bhangoo, J. K., Tenenbaum, H., & Ng-Knight, T. (2020). Effects of the COVID-19 lockdown on mental health, wellbeing, sleep, and alcohol use in a UK student sample. *Psychiatry Research, 298*, 33640864. doi:10.1016/j.psychres.2021.113819 PMID:33640864

Fakunle, O. (2021). International students' perspectives on developing employability during study abroad. *Higher Education Quarterly, 75*(4), 575–590. doi:10.1111/hequ.12308

Forrier, A., De Cuyper, N., & Akkermans, J. (2018). The winner takes it all, the loser has to fall: Provoking the agency perspective in employability research. *Human Resource Management Journal, 28*(4), 511–523. doi:10.1111/1748-8583.12206

Friedman, S., & Laurison, D. (2019). *The Class Ceiling: Why It Pays To Be Privileged.* Policy Press.

Gallup & Purdue. (2016). *Gallup-Purdue Index Report 2016.* Gallup and Purdue. https://news.gallup.com/reports/199229/gallup-purdue-index-report-2016.aspx

Gradleaders (2022). *16 biggest challenges every career center faces today.* GradLeaders. https://www.gradleaders.com/career-services-challenges

Gunn, F., Lee, S. H. M., & Steed, M. (2017). Students perceptions of benefits and challenges of peer mentoring programs: Divergent perspectives from mentors and mentees. *Marketing Education Review, 27*(1), 15–26. doi:10.1080/10528008.2016.1255560

Haelermans, C., Korthals, R., Jacobs, M., de Leeuw, S., Vermeulen, S., Van Vugt, L., Aarts, B., Prokic-Breuer, T., Van der Velden, R., Van Wetten, S., & de Wolf, I. (2022). Sharp increase in inequality in education in times of the COVID-19-Pandemic. *PLoS One, 17*(2), e0261114. doi:10.1371/journal.pone.0261114 PMID:35108273

Healy, M., Brown, J. L., & Ho, C. (2022). Graduate employability as a professional proto-jurisdiction in higher education. *Higher Education, 83*(5), 1125–1142. doi:10.100710734-021-00733-4

Higher Ed Partners. (2021). *University Career Services: A Critical Tool in A Competitive Climate.* Higher Ed. Partners. https://higheredpartners.co.uk/university-career-services-a-critical-tool-in-a-competitive-climate/

Hill, K., & Fitzgerald, R. (2020). Students' perspectives on the impact of the COVID-19 on learning. *All Ireland Journal of Teaching and Learning in Higher Education, 12*(2), 1-9. https://ojs.aishe.org/index.php/aishe-j/article/view/459

Ho, C., Stewart-Smith, C., & Gunaratne, D. (2023). How career influencers can promote sustainable careers and wellbeing of underrepresented students. In W. E. Donald (Ed.), *Handbook of Research on Sustainable Career Ecosystems for University Students and Graduates* (pp. 407–427). IGI Global. doi:10.4018/978-1-6684-7442-6.ch021

Hughes, H. P. N., Mouratidou, M., & Donald, W. E. (2023). *Exploring the impact of an industrial placement year on students' competency development: A three-cohort, longitudinal study. Higher Education, Skills and Work-Based Learning*. Advanced Online Publication. doi:10.1108/HESWBL-02-2023-0044

Jakubik, M. (2020). Enhancing human capital beyond university boundaries. *Higher Education. Skills and Work-Based Learning, 10*(2), 434–446. doi:10.1108/HESWBL-06-2019-0074

Jakubik, M., Beke, J., & Shtaltovna, Y. (2023). The roles of universities: Enhancing students' capabilities for work and life. In W. E. Donald (Ed.), *Handbook of Research on Sustainable Career Ecosystems for University Students and Graduates* (pp. 15–37). IGI Global. doi:10.4018/978-1-6684-7442-6.ch002

Kim, B., Jee, S., Lee, J., An, S., & Lee, S. M. (2018). Relationships between social support and burnout: A meta-analytic approach. *Stress and Health, 34*(1), 127–134. doi:10.1002mi.2771 PMID:28639354

Kim, D., Wortham, S., Borowiec, K., Yatsu, D. K., Ha, S., Carroll, S., Wang, L., & Kim, J. (2021). Formative education online: Teaching the whole person during the global COVID-19 pandemic. *AERA Open, 7*. Advance Online publication. doi:10.1177/23328584211015229

Klein, L., Phillips, P., Duran, D. F., Tierney, D., Loby, M. G., Murphy, N., Orgias, O., & Carcione, C. (2022). Students' opinions on their experience of university career services: Suggestions for post-COVID-19 Ireland. *All Ireland Journal of Teaching and Learning in Higher Education, 14*(1), 1-13. https://ojs.aishe.org/index.php/aishe-j/article/view/589

Ma, Y., Bennett, D., & Chen, S.-C. (2022). Perceived organisational support and university students' career exploration: The mediation role of career adaptability. *Higher Education Research & Development, 42*(4), 903–919. doi:10.1080/07294360.2022.2115983

McCafferty, H. (2022). An unjust balance: A systematic review of the employability perceptions of UK undergraduates from disadvantaged socio-economic backgrounds. *Research in Post-Compulsory Education, 27*(4), 570–593. doi:10.1080/13596748.2022.2110774

Meehan, C., & Howells, K. (2018). 'What really matters to freshers?': Evaluation of first year student experience of transition into university. *Journal of Further and Higher Education, 42*(7), 893–907. doi:10.1080/0309877X.2017.1323194

Nadya, A., & Farozin, M. (2021). Career guidance conceptualization to improve career adaptability for generation Z. *Journal of Professionals in Guidance and Counselling*, *2*(1), 20–26. doi:10.21831/progcouns.v2i1.39906

Padgett, R. C., & Donald, W. E. (2023). Preparing graduates for sustainable careers: A case of 'The Global Marketing Professional' module. *Higher Education, Skills, and Work-Based Learning*, *13*(1), 22–35. doi:10.1108/HESWBL-03-2022-0073

Plewes, J. (2022). *Analysis: The Rise in Mental Health Demand*. NHS Confed. https://www.nhsconfed.org/articles/analysis-rise-mental-health-demand

Redekopp, D. E., & Huston, M. (2020). *Strengthening Mental Health Through Effective Career Development*. CERIC.

Rickmann, J., Perez-Encinas, A., & Fernadez-de-Pinedo, N. (2020). Addressing career services' internationalisation challenges through transnational consortia. In A. Curaj, L. Deca, & R. Pricopie (Eds.), *European Higher Education Area: Challenges for a New Decade* (pp. 53-65). Springer. doi:10.1007/978-3-030-56316-5_4

Scattergood, K. & Donald, W. E. (2023). Using social media to enhance student engagement and employability outcomes. *Career Matters, 11*(3), 28-29. doi:10.13140/RG.2.2.16401.40802

Sin, C., & Neave, G. (2016). Employability deconstructed: Perceptions of Bologna stakeholders. *Studies in Higher Education*, *41*(8), 1447–1462. doi:10.1080/03075079.2014.977859

The Daily. (2023). *Racialized Canadians are Less Likely to Find as Good Jobs as Their Non-Racialized and Non-Indigenous Counterparts Early in Their Careers*. The Daily. https://www150.statcan.gc.ca/n1/daily-quotidien/230118/dq230118b-eng.htm

Tomlinson, M. (2017). Forms of graduate capital and their relationship to graduate employability. *Education + Training*, *59*(4), 338–352. doi:10.1108/ET-05-2016-0090

Van der Heijden, B. I. J. M. (2005). No one has ever promised you a rose garden. *On shared responsibility and employability enhancing strategies throughout careers. Heerlen: Open University of the Netherlands*. Van Gorcum.

Van der Heijden, B. I. J. M., & De Vos, A. (2015). Sustainable careers: Introductory chapter. In A. De Vos & B. I. J. M. Van der Heijden (Eds.), *Handbook of Research on Sustainable Careers* (pp. 1–19). Edward Elgar. doi:10.4337/9781782547037.00006

Ward, R. (2020). *Personalised Learning for the Learning Person*. Emerald Publishing. doi:10.1108/9781789731477

Wright, E., & Mulvey, B. (2021). Internships and the graduate labour market: How upper-middle-class students 'get ahead'. *British Journal of Sociology of Education, 42*(3), 339–356. doi:10.1080/01425692.2021.1886051

Xiong, J., Lipsitz, O., Nasri, F., Lui, L. M. W., Gill, H., Phan, L., Chen-Li, D., Lacobucci, M., Ho, R., Majeed, A., & McIntyre, R. S. (2020). Impact of the COVID-19 pandemic on mental health in the general population: A systematic review. *Journal of Affective Disorders, 277*(1), 55–64. doi:10.1016/j.jad.2020.08.001 PMID:32799105

ADDITIONAL READING

Bradley, A., Priego-Hernández, J., & Quigley, M. (2022). Evaluating the efficacy of embedding employability into a second-year undergraduate module. *Studies in Higher Education, 47*(11), 2161–2173. doi:10.1080/03075079.2021.2020748

Cranmer, S. (2006). Enhancing graduate employability: Best intentions and mixed outcomes. *Studies in Higher Education, 31*(2), 169–184. doi:10.1080/03075070600572041

Inceoglu, I., Selenko, E., McDowall, A., & Schlachter, S. (2019). (How) do work placements work? Scrutinizing the quantitative evidence for a theory-driven future research agenda. *Journal of Vocational Behavior, 110*, 317–337. doi:10.1016/j.jvb.2018.09.002

Jorre de St Jorre, T., & Oliver, B. (2018). Want students to engage? Contextualise graduate learning outcomes and assess for employability. *Higher Education Research & Development, 37*(1), 44–57. doi:10.1080/07294360.2017.1339183

Kornelakis, A., & Petrakaki, D. (2020). Embedding employability skills in UK higher education: Between digitalization and marketization. *Industry and Higher Education, 34*(5), 290–297. doi:10.1177/0950422220902978

Ma, Y., Huang, G., & Autin, K. L. (2021). Linking decent work with academic engagement and satisfaction among first-generation college students: A psychology of working perspective. *Journal of Career Assessment, 29*(1), 148–163. doi:10.1177/1069072720943153

Park, C. K. (2015). Student factors on employment of engineering graduates: A Korean university case. *Asian Journal of Innovation and Policy, 4*(3), 288–306. doi:10.7545/ajip.2015.4.288

Peters, M., & Romero, M. (2019). Lifelong learning ecologies in online higher education: Students' engagement in the continuum between formal and informal learning. *British Journal of Educational Technology*, *50*(4), 1729–1743. doi:10.1111/bjet.12803

Williams, K. E., Hutchings, P. B., & Phelps, C. (2022). Beyond learning in higher education: An evaluation of the 'Life Design' initiative to improve student employability. *Studies in Higher Education*, *47*(6), 1184–1198. doi:10.1080/03075079.2020.1870946

Zahid, G., Hooley, T., & Neary, S. (2020). Careers work in higher education in Pakistan: Current practice and options for the future. *British Journal of Guidance & Counselling*, *48*(4), 443–453. doi:10.1080/03069885.2019.1576030

Chapter 4
Signaling Employability:
Branding, Metaphors, and Narratives

ABSTRACT

This chapter concludes section two of the book (chapters two-four) by delving into the topic of how university career services and additional actors can assist students in signaling their employability to potential employers. The chapter begins with an overview of signaling theory and the possibility of its integration with other career theories, including Social Exchange Theory (SET), Conservation of Resources (CoR) theory, Job Demands-Resources (JD-R) theory, Career Construction Theory (CCT), the New Psychological Contract (NPC), Career Ecosystems Theory (CET), and Sustainable Career Theory (SCT). Next, the authors consider why students must develop strategies for communicating their employability in preparation for the university-to-work transition, and how career advisors can play a pivotal role in supporting this process. Three themes are then presented for developing and operationalizing one's employability: personal branding, career metaphors, and career narratives. The chapter concludes with four lived experience insights to bridge theory and practice.

INTRODUCTION

Section Two of the book has thus far focused on the need for students to acquire various forms of employability capital (Chapter 2) and offered strategies to enhance student engagement with career-related support (Chapter 3). To conclude Section Two, our focus now shifts to exploring how university students can develop and operationalize their employability capital via effective signaling strategies to

DOI: 10.4018/978-1-6684-9827-9.ch004

prospective employers. The approach captures the interlinked nature of signals and capitals when preparing for the university-to-work transition (Tomlinson & Anderson, 2021). Consequently, this chapter aims to introduce signaling theory, explore three ways that students can develop and signal their employability via (i) personal branding, (ii) career metaphors, and (iii) career narratives, and present four lived experience insights related to these themes.

SIGNALING EMPLOYABILITY

Signaling theory (Spence, 1973; 1978) explores the interplay of *signalers*, *signals*, and *receivers* to address information asymmetry. Spence positions candidates as *signalers* who use their credentials during the application and selection process to *signal* their suitability for employment to an agent acting on behalf of the organization. The agent, as the *receiver,* then decodes the *signal* to assess the person-organization fit. Interestingly, despite overlapping agendas, the vocational behavior and human resource management literature streams have tended to develop in parallel with limited interaction. However, there is an emergent interest in bridging these two literature streams and integrating the various underlying career theories within the context of early career talent (Akkermans et al., 2023; Donald, 2021; Tomlinson & Anderson, 2021).

For example, Social Exchange Theory (SET) (Blau, 1964) captures how exchanging beneficial resources between actors increases the quality of the exchange relationship resulting in productive behaviors. The notion of resources draws on the Conservation of Resources (CoR) theory (Hobfoll, 1989), whereby an individual seeks to acquire personal resources while safeguarding against the loss of existing resources. Subsequently, the Job Demands-Resources (JD-R) model (Bakker & Demerouti, 2007) explains how stress and burnout can occur if the demands of a job regularly exceed one's personal resources. The CoR and JD-R theories also link to Career Construction Theory (CCT, Savickas, 2005) since deciding which resources to acquire and which job roles to undertake is driven by how the individual gives meaning to their life. Akkermans et al. (2023) examine the interaction between signaling and social exchange theories in the context of early career talent. They observe how the notion of reciprocity is central to both theories capturing the interdependent and interactive dimensions of graduate employability. Donald (2021) refers to these interactions as *signals* and *counter signals* to establish and maintain person-organization fit across the attraction, selection, and employment processes (please see Chapter 7 for an extensive discussion of person-organization fit). Concurrently, the integration of the New Psychological Contract (NPC) (Rousseau, 1995) and Career Ecosystem Theory (CET) (Baruch, 2015) captures the need for mutually beneficial relationships for the sustainability of career ecosystems (Baruch & Rousseau, 2019; Donald & Jackson, 2023; Donald et al., 2020). In other words, (prospective) employees and (prospective) employers are interdependent and interconnected actors (Baruch, 2015), relying on mutual and reciprocal obligations via written and unwritten contracts (Rousseau, 1995) to maintain talent flow and acquisition at the interface between higher education and industry (Baruch et al., 2023). Psychological contracts have also been shown to shape graduate experiences, further highlighting opportunities for theory integration (Clarke & Scurry, 2020). However, the main challenge for bridging these literature streams and theories into integrated frameworks stems from researchers continuing to operate in silos and journals favoring particular theories, thus reducing their readers' exposure to alternatives.

Shifting our focus to the practical perspective of early career talent, the application and selection phases are prominent signaling opportunities (Celani & Singh, 2011), whereby applicants and employers can benefit from signals and counter signals to overcome information asymmetry and assess person-organization fit (Donald, 2021). One way that this has been presented is the notion of applicants learning to become "players" (Brown & Hesketh, 2004, p. 115) in a "signaling game" (Spence, 1973, p. 356). The approach involves consideration of how regional contexts and employment sectors can influence employability norms and processes, capturing the person and context dimensions of a sustainable career (Van der Heijden & De Vos, 2015). For example, Tang and Jang (2023) believe that providing career support can help international students to differentiate their employability capital and signal their unique contributions to potential employers (e.g., being bilingual or having lived experience of different cultures). However, Ugiagbe-Green (2023) calls for students to be informed of the risks associated with institutional and cultural reproduction. In such cases, the assessment of person-organization fit (e.g., culture, behaviors, and values) from the organization's perspective relies on the interpretation by the receiver of specific signals (e.g., race, age, gender, accents and aesthetics). Yet, engaging in behavior modification to self-regulate identity can be harmful by creating a significant cognitive load. Thus, students should embrace a sense of agency to decide whether to mask specific behaviors or present their authentic selves when seeking employment (Pham & Soltani, 2021; Ugiagbe-Green, 2023), perhaps engaging in mindfulness practices to support authentic functioning (Choi et al., 2022).

Moreover, university career services can also support their students by helping them to define career goals, identify growth opportunities, enhance their CV to navigate applicant tracking systems, optimize their LinkedIn profile, and perfect their interviewing skills (Higher Ed Partners, 2021; Michael Page, 2022). The ability to signal one's employability is crucial since 36% of UK graduates are over-qualified for the job role they secure when undertaking the university-to-work transition, leading to lower job and life satisfaction levels than their peers (Chartered Institute of Personnel and Development (CIPD), 2022). The need to signal employability has also seen students turn to third-party 'helper apps' offering "online-test practice sessions, templated careers advice, and other methods for gaming the recruitment process" (Handley & den Outer, 2022, p. 1). However, these 'helper apps' can risk overemphasizing performance at the expense of substance or authenticity and overlook the contextual determinants for signaling employability.

Consequently, the optimal approach appears to involve using 'helper apps' to enhance one's performance *AND* using the university career service to identify resources and operationalize one's employability by tailoring signals to specific contexts. Therefore, university career services must help students deduce which signals are most powerful for a given situation and subsequently craft ways to showcase relevant signals during the application and selection processes (Handley & den Outer, 2022). Acquiring different forms of employability capital, as presented in the Employability Capital Growth Model in Chapter 2 (Donald et al., 2023), can help students to ensure that they develop the necessary personal resources on which to draw (Hobfoll, 1989) and avoid an over-emphasis on academic achievements (Graduate Coach, 2020) when operationalizing their employability via signals. We now consider three opportunities for career counselors to support their students in developing strategies to process information and take action to enhance and signal their employability: (ii) personal branding, (ii) career metaphors, and (iii) career narratives.

PERSONAL BRANDING

Personal branding involves individuals marketing themselves as a brand to enhance their employment opportunities and career sustainability (Lair et al., 2005). It entails capturing and promoting one's strengths and uniqueness to a target audience (Labrecque et al., 2011), whereby a group of people identify a set of associations with the individual (Parmentier et al., 2013). In the context of graduates, Khedher (2019) suggests that personal branding represents an act of agency whereby individuals invest in themselves during their university studies and subsequently gain benefits in the labor market, reflecting CCT (Savickas, 2005). These perspectives of personal branding are underpinned by Bourdieu's (1983) 'Forms of Capital' which posits that personal brands are underpinned by field-specific social capital and cultural capital. An individual's network, status, and reputation help them to be noticed, whilst acquiring doxa (understanding of norms, values, attitudes, and behaviors of a particular social group) enables them to 'fit in' by understanding and conforming to the rules of a particular industry, employer, or occupation (Parmentier et al., 2013).

Personal branding can also be framed as acquiring personal resources (Hobfoll, 1989) in a targeted manner to signal employability (Spence, 1973). Enhancing one's personal brand can thus increase access to employment opportunities and help navigate application and selection processes.

Moreover, Nolan (2020) observes how career motivations are linked to identity. Consequently, during their time at university, students can shape and develop their personal brand (identity) to showcase (signal) their employability to potential employers during the university-to-work transition and increase the likelihood of a sustainable career. Chan (2023) suggests that building a brand can help an individual access job opportunities because (i) they are seen as an expert, (ii) potential employers know more about them, (iii) they are seen as an asset to the company, (iv) they will attract the right job opportunities, and (v) it gives them confidence. Subsequently, during the application and assessment stages, organizations and individuals can assess person-environment fit (Schneider, 1987), specifically person-organization fit (Cable & Judge, 1996), informed by institutional and personal brands (e.g., culture, behaviors, and values). The two-way exchange of knowledge reflects SET (Blau, 1964) and the establishment of NPCs (Rousseau, 1995) as captured by CET (Baruch, 2015) via the interconnected and interdependent nature of the relationships between actors (Baruch & Rousseau, 2019; Donald et al., 2020).

As a life and performance coach, I have worked with many students and graduates to help them establish and develop their personal brands. Based on my experiences and an excellent opinion piece by Caroline Green (2023), here are five dimensions and associated questions for career counselors to facilitate students to develop a personal brand.

1. **Unique Value Proposition**: What are your values, background, strengths, skills, and unique attributes? What sets you apart from your peers? What do you want your personal brand to be? What industry or job are you interested in? How do you want people to view you? How do you want people to remember you? How can you consistently signal your personal brand to others authentically? What really matters to me?
2. **Online Presence**: Have you set up a LinkedIn profile? Do you have a professional headshot? Have you used a compelling headline to increase the visibility of your profile to recruiters? Have you clearly articulated your unique value proposition in the summary section? Are you keeping your profile up to date? Who is your target audience? Which social media platforms can help you access your target audience? How can you balance personal and professional aspects online? Have you conducted a Google Search of your name in Incognito mode to see what recruiters or other people will see when they do the same?

3. **Knowledge Sharing and Expertise**: Do you regularly post valuable social media content? Are you engaging with other people's posts in a respectful way that adds value to the conversation? Are you writing blog posts or contributing to relevant publications in your field of interest? What other ways can you share your knowledge and demonstrate expertise?
4. **Networking**: What steps are you taking to network with people in-person and online? Are you attending industry events? What about participating in online communities? Can people in your existing network introduce you to other people in their network? Are you making a concerted effort to establish and maintain these relationships over time? Can your network provide you with access to the hidden job market to provide you with a competitive advantage when applying for jobs? How can you increase your visibility and reputation, so others advocate for you when you are not in the room? Pham (2022) also advocates for *quality* over *quantity* when networking and advises that industry professionals and mentors can offer significant value to enhancing one's social capital.
5. **Building a Portfolio**: Do you have a portfolio of your work to showcase your skills and accomplishments? Are there gaps in your portfolio that you would like to address? How can you address these gaps (e.g., volunteering, internships, freelancing, student societies, etc.)? How can you use your portfolio to signal your employability to prospective employers (e.g., cover letter, CV, verbal pitch) as part of your marketing materials that help you showcase your personal brand?

I have also worked with Professor Ray Sylvester to develop his Personal Brand V.A.L.U.E. Career Development Tool to bridge personal branding and career theory literature, which we have detailed elsewhere (Sylvester & Donald, 2023). The tool offers five questions that enable students and clients to establish an authentic career development plan by focusing on intra-Personal and inter-Personal Brand V.A.L.U.E.:

1. What is your **V**ision? (Purpose and direction).
2. What is your **A**bility? (Competence to perform a task effectively and efficiently).
3. What do you **L**ove? (Deep emotional attachment towards a particular career path).
4. What is your industry **U**nderstanding? (Knowledge of the job and industry you are interested in).
5. What is the employment **E**cosystem? (Pragmatic integration of the various aspects of one's brand).

To summarize, building a personal brand takes time and requires sustained effort. Authenticity is key, so be prepared to refine and evolve your brand as you grow your career.

CAREER METAPHORS

Building on the notion of a personal brand, our attention now shifts to how university career counselors can support their students to develop and operationalize their employability through the use of career metaphors.

"The metaphorical conceptualization of lived experiences, social situations, and self-identity involves a subjective yet deeply personal meaning-making process" (Creed, 2023, p. 40). In other words, metaphors can enable individuals to make sense of their careers as they evolve over time (Inkson et al., 2015) by framing one's future career as a mental object for exploration and reflection (Creed & Nacey, 2021). The traditional career was often represented as a career ladder whereby an individual's progress from one role to another followed a linear upward fashion. Success was determined by job title and remuneration (Strauss, 1962). The ladder metaphor was subsequently advanced to capture lateral movement between ladders reflecting the notion of a dual career path whereby technical workers had the same hierarchical opportunities for career progression as managerial workers (Allen & Katz, 1986). However, the career ladder metaphor in isolation no longer fits the purpose when discussing contemporary careers. One could argue that the notion of the traditional career and a 'job for life' was never actually as prevalent as portrayed, particularly in countries such as the UK, once accounting for World Wars, a lack of workers' rights, technological advancement, and closures of factories or mines requiring reskilling of local labor.

Consequently, new metaphors can help university students understand how contemporary careers unfold over more than forty years, with the potential for movement across various organizations, sectors, and locations. Inkson and Amundson (2002) summarize ten archetypal metaphors, including the career as (i) a journey, (ii) an inheritance, (iii) fit, (iv) a sequence of seasons, (v) growth, (vi) a creative work, (vii) a network, (viii) a resource, (ix) a story, and (x) a cultural artifact (pp. 103-105). Other prominent metaphors include games (Pryor & Bright, 2009), bridges, cycles, stages, and patterns (as summarized by McIlveen & Creed, 2020). However, in this chapter, I would like to focus on the 'Weather as a Career' Metaphor (WCM) that I recently developed (Donald, 2022) before considering how university career counselors can use career metaphors to help students unlock career narratives to develop and signal employability.

The WCM is underpinned by Sustainable Career Theory (SCT) (Van der Heijden & De Vos, 2015) and CoR theory (Hobfoll, 1989), complemented by over a decade of my experience providing mentoring and career coaching to university students and graduates. The WCM offers a versatile tool as part of a more comprehensive tool kit that university career counselors (and other individuals providing career-related support) can use to help clients prepare for sustainable careers. Specifically, the WCM can help individuals foster a sense of agency and identify/acquire personal resources to manage the university-to-work transition and navigate contemporary labor markets. Table 1 offers illustrative examples of ten weather elements.

Table 1. Ten weather elements

ID	Element	Represents
1	Sun	Intrinsically rewarding employment
2	Rain	Personal growth through the acquisition of resources
3	Drought	Career stagnation
4	Thunder and Lightening	Visible conflicts with other people
5	Ice	Hidden challenges that cannot always be seen
6	Fog	Uncertainty and an inability to see ahead
7	Tailwind	Support mechanisms for career progression
8	Headwind	Barriers to career progression
9	Tornado	Negative outcome of a career shock or a chance event
10	Rainbow	Positive outcome of a career shock or a chance event

Source: Donald (2022, p. 4).

Career counselors may wish to introduce these ten weather elements and then encourage clients to think of additional elements and representations. Alternatively, the notion of weather as a career metaphor could be introduced before clients identify their own set of weather elements and representations based on their specific circumstances. The approach could be beneficial if students or recent graduates live in countries or locations where certain weather elements are more prevalent than those listed in Table 1 (e.g., tropical cyclones, hurricanes, sand storms, etc.). Additional benefits come from a more holistic and integrated approach that enables students to consider a broader array of factors and potential actions. Such an approach can also overcome concerns that the narrow focus of existing metaphors can unintentionally mislead clients by obscuring nuances or distorting perceptions (Inkson, 2006).

SCT posits three dimensions: person, context, and time (Van der Heijden & De Vos, 2015). Let us consider the WCM from the *person* dimension. The acquisition of resources in one's resource caravan enables the individual to prepare an array of responses to new or recurring situations and *contexts* as they occur over *time*. If we consider the WCM from the *context* dimension

on a hot day, we might wear suncream, a hat, and sunglasses, whereas when it is raining, we might wear a coat or carry an umbrella. Each of these resources is useful in a specific circumstance, yet is of less use in the context of different weather elements. Furthermore, we might run out of suncream or need to replace an old coat in the same way that one needs to constantly refresh their skills via a commitment to lifelong learning to remain relevant to the evolving needs of the workplace and broader labour market. (Donald, 2022, p. 8)

Then, if we consider the WCM from the *time* dimension, sustainable careers can be represented by seasons, whereby an individual

either moves from spring to summer, to autumn, and to winter from the point of entry to the point of exit from the labour market (e.g., student, early-stage, mid-stage, or late-stage career), or one moves iteratively through these seasons multiple times across their career. (Donald, 2022, p. 8)

Additionally, a student (*person*) preparing to undertake the university-to-work transition may lack the lived experience (*time*) of navigating career shocks (*context*). Career advisors could simulate specific scenarios and ask students to consider what resources they need and how they would navigate the situation. The process enables students to practice articulating responses to interview-style questions (*signals*) whilst presenting an opportunity for the career counselor to provide feedback (*counter signals*), including alternative approaches that the student might not have considered. The insights gained from these sessions can help students signal to prospective employers how they have taken proactive steps to acquire personal resources and prepare for a sustainable career. The student can also use the selection phase to overcome information asymmetry and evaluate person-organization fit. For example, by asking prospective employers (i) What opportunities exist to acquire specific personal resources (identified via the WCM process as significant for career sustainability)? and (ii) How will the organization facilitate the operationalization of one's resource caravan via resource passageways?

CAREER NARRATIVES

Our focus now shifts to how career metaphors can help university students unlock career narratives to (i) construct and (ii) operationalize their personal brand and employability.

Career narratives can help students identify and align their purpose, significance, and meaning in life (Bruner, 1986; Martela & Steger, 2016), and form their professional identity (Tomlinson & Jackson, 2021). The approach, underpinned by CCT, enables an individual's vocational identity to be presented as a structured story that explains "how the self of yesterday became the self of today and will become the self of tomorrow" (Savickas, 2005, p. 58). Career counselors can encourage students to use metaphors such as the WCM to reflect on experiences and consider their future needs. Subsequently, by identifying potential/relevant career options, students can explore what resources they currently possess and what resources they need to acquire to meet the demands of their preferred job(s). The implications also apply to their personal brand, ensuring it is targeted to the correct audience to increase the chances of securing a desired role following graduation. The approach combines CoR Theory (Hobfoll, 1989), the JD-R Model (Bakker & Demerouti, 2007), and SET (Blau, 1964) by capturing how students can preemptively plan via career agency for the exchange of beneficial resources between actors.

Career counselors can also introduce the Employability Capital Growth (ECG) model (Chapter 2) to help students consider what forms of capital would be most beneficial and how to put a strategy in place to acquire these personal resources. Additionally, Blaquière et al. (2019) observe how experiential learning can present students with an authentic and challenging problem or issue to address. Subsequently, students can develop solutions in teams and undertake self-reflection to gain awareness of the employability skills they have acquired and to develop career narratives to share these insights with prospective employers. The approach can be particularly compelling since narratives can provide convincing examples of one's employability during the application and selection stages of the recruitment process. The view is complemented by Le Rossignol and Kelly's (2023) perspective of how career narratives can facilitate "changing perspectives so that graduates are able not only to identify and reflect on their own individual behaviors and attributes, but are able to empathize and/or imagine other perspectives" (p. 166). Consequently, career narratives can help individuals prepare for (and adjust to) challenges and career transitions (including the university-to-work transition) by creating a cohesive and stable identity upon which to build in the future (Del Corso & Rehfuss, 2011; McMahon & Watson, 2013). The approach captures the SCT's person, context, and time dimensions and desired outcomes of health, happiness, and productivity (De Vos et al., 2020; Van der Heijden & De Vos, 2015).

Furthermore, storytelling as a form of career narrative can be an extremely powerful tool to develop and operationalize one's personal brand and associated employability (Tomlinson & Anderson, 2021). Storytelling involves "using concrete examples that reframe a moment by personifying human consequences" (Grenny, 2017, Online, Paragraph 1), with the potential to increase levels of self-esteem and positive perceptions of employment opportunities (Alchin et al., 2018). Initially, alums could be invited to university campuses to share their career narratives, experiences, and insights with current students. The approach could be particularly valuable for increasing the diversity of applicants since university students have previously reported concerns regarding the notion that 'you cannot be what you cannot see' (Donald et al., 2018). Additionally, such sessions (particularly when combined with the WCM) may encourage students to develop career narratives that can help them to explore the hiring process, gain a better understanding of what employers are looking for, and articulate how they can meet these requirements in preparation for the application and selection phases of the recruitment process (Flat & Drewery, 2023; Sjolander & Dodd, 2022). Career counselors may also benefit from listening to the career narratives of alums and current students to identify opportunities to inform and/or improve higher education policies and practices for preparing students for the university-to-work transition (Higdon, 2016).

By helping students know their worth and make it known to others, career narratives can help their brand resonate with a target audience to form connections by consistently demonstrating values, strengths, and experiences. The strategy is particularly effective 'to stand out from the crowd' in competitive labor markets since other people cannot authentically replicate the same stories in the same way. Thus, career narratives can enhance the visibility of one's personal brand leading to increased access to job opportunities via networks and social capital. Subsequently, career narratives can help to signal employability to employers (Gorbatov et al., 2021) and demonstrate the value an individual can bring to the workplace (Maree, 2020).

Moreover, career narratives can capture the notion of reciprocity and the need for mutually beneficial relationships central to signaling theory, SET, CET, and NPC (Akkermans et al., 2023; Baruch & Rousseau, 2019; Donald & Jackson, 2023; Donald et al., 2020). Specifically, students can create engaging career-based stories to signal their employability to employers (Le Rossignol & Kelly, 2023). The responses by the employer via counter signals (Donald, 2021) enable the applicant to assess POF (discussed further in Chapter 7) and to gather insights into the unwritten and unspoken rules that form the NPC within sustainable career ecosystems (Rousseau, 1995; Baruch & Rousseau, 2019; Donald et al., 2020).

Four lived experience insights are now presented to offer practical applications of the themes discussed in this chapter.

LIVED EXPERIENCE INSIGHTS

Lived Experience Insight

Shared By Candy Ho, University of Fraser Valley, Canada

The Challenge

For over a decade, I have taught a career course to undergraduate students in their final year of study. The course facilitates opportunities for them to reflect on their education and life experiences; identify attributes, skills, and knowledge they have to offer future employers; and develop strategies and supports for lifelong career management. A consistent challenge students face is how to signal their relevant skills and experience to potential employers. The gap is especially evident in individuals who do not have (or do not perceive themselves as having) significant work experiences, such as stay-at-home parents and international students.

The Context

Higher education institutions in Canada often task university career services with offering career courses to students as part of co-curricular education. However, the 'Career Capstone' course provides an exciting opportunity to integrate career education meaningfully into the academic curriculum. Furthermore, most students undertaking the Career Capstone course are first-generation learners: the first in their families to attend post-secondary education. These students often lack social capital compared to their peers. However, their experiences are valuable to their employability through evidencing resourcefulness and taking the initiative.

Action Taken

I adopted a two-prong approach. First, within the course, initial discussions focused on notions of employability, skills, and frameworks (e.g., institutional learning outcomes and the 'Canada's Skills for Success' framework). Students consider how they already develop these employability skills through their lived experiences. As the course develops, students practice telling stories of their lived experiences to highlight skills development and signal employability to potential employers. Second, outside the course, I collaborate with course instructors and employers to share my students' views and help other actors to understand how they can contribute to student career development.

The Outcome

Students complete a survey at the end of each course to evidence their perceived development. In the 2021 Winter Semester, 106 students completed the survey. Forty-six students (44%) 'Strongly Agreed' or 'Agreed' with the statement, "Before this course, I believed I could effectively articulate my skills, experience, and strengths to future employers, schools, and organizations." However, 106 students (100%) 'Strongly Agreed' or 'Agreed' with the statement, "After this course, I believe I can effectively articulate my skills, experience, and strengths to future employers, schools, and organizations." Additional testimonials from graduates of the benefits of the course to attaining career goals and success support these self-reported, positive outcomes.

Lessons Learned And Advice

Post-secondary institutions can play a crucial role in helping students understand the value of education, knowledge, and skills to enable them to articulate their value to potential employers effectively. While career service departments are primarily responsible for providing career services and programs for all students, my doctoral research shows that not all students take (or have) the time to benefit from these initiatives. Those students subsequently miss opportunities to minimize their skill-awareness gap or to learn how to signal the value of their experiences to employers. Hence, an immense opportunity exists to embed career education into the academic curriculum to enhance student learning, employability, and lifelong success.

Lived Experience Insight

Shared By Michael Healy, careerED, Australia

The Challenge

As a university careers and employability educator at a large university, I supported hundreds of nursing students in their graduate employment applications. I noticed that they all focused on the same basic claims in their documents and mock interviews: "I am a (soon to be) qualified and competent nurse". This is a redundant claim, given that they had almost completed an accredited degree, rendering their applications largely indistinguishable from each other. Their resumes and interviews were well presented and articulate, but they were dull and uninspiring, with few standing out as particularly unique or memorable.

The Context

The students did not understand the actual priorities of the graduate recruiters, who took qualifications and basic competence for granted, having screened for them in the earliest stages of the online application process. Instead, recruiters were looking for those qualities broadly recognized as "employability capitals": strong interpersonal and self-management skills; attitudes such as proactivity, resilience, and adaptability; and interesting formative work and life experiences. Recruiters also were attentive to applicants' knowledge of and alignment with their particular organization's mission and values, and their ability to articulate their professional purpose and career goals.

Action Taken

In response, I revised the graduate application workshops and resources we provided to nursing students. I reduced the focus on basic elements of quality applications, such as design and formatting. Instead, I focused on two critical questions that I knew recruiters cared about:

1. What experiences and skills do you have that are unique to you?
2. Why did you decide to become a nurse, and why did you choose your preferred employer?

I designed interactive workshops in which students explored their study, work, and life histories, reflected on their values, and started to express their professional purpose. I coached the students to tell stories rather than recite lists.

The Outcome

As a result, student applications became more diverse and unique, expressing more interesting employability narratives rather than lists of credentials and skills. Some examples include:

- A student who could speak four languages commonly spoken in her community.
- A student who managed a McDonalds in a notorious nightlife area, regularly dealing with drunk and drug-affected customers.
- A student who was the first responder to a cardiac arrest during a placement, receiving a commendation for her professionalism.
- A mature-age student who maintained a perfect academic record while working and parenting.

Students were also better at explaining why they chose nursing as a profession, why they preferred a particular employer, and what they hoped to achieve in their careers.

Lessons Learned and Advice

This experience underlined for me the importance of thinking carefully about what graduate recruiters care most about. Often, the basics of qualification and competence can be taken for granted to some extent - of course, they should never be ignored - leaving room for other elements that are more unique and interesting. Most important among those other things is the employability narrative of how and why the applicant came to be at this point, and their future direction of travel. Qualifications and skill sets will often be common among applicants, but their employability narratives will be theirs alone.

Lived Experience Insight

Shared By Karen Le Rossignol, Deakin University, Australia

The Challenge

The creative writing undergraduate degree, an industry-leading program at Deakin University for 30 years, has shifted from a models-centered design to greater contextuality with the writing and publishing industry. Concurrently, penultimate and final-year students are constantly asking how to get a foot in the door concerning writing, editing and publishing opportunities. These students are just-in-time learners, whereby assessment tasks often represent tick-box exercises rather than learning opportunities. This practical/pragmatic approach has contributed to a lack of confidence in their transfer of knowledge and skills within a workplace environment.

The Context

Tensions between the pragmatic learning approach of 'time-poor' students and their expectations of gaining employment following graduation have been exacerbated by external pressures—for example, lockdowns during the COVID-19 pandemic and increasing freelance or micro-business adaptations across the industry sector. Therefore, Deakin University has moved further towards the professionalization of the writing degree, integrating work-oriented experiences such as internships, career hubs, and industry projects into the curriculum. Concurrently, there has been a greater push to deliver programs online, requiring a strategic pedagogical approach that embeds digital resources and engages learners via industry-relevant content.

Action Taken

Using my digital storymaking experience in industry-oriented scenarios for immersive learning, I established digital 'micro-businesses' to provide context for the industry-related assessment tasks. The two industry areas with a strong technological basis, digital publishing and writing for videogames, became *Digi-Anth Publishing* and *Bunyip Studios*, web-based entities, aligned with rapidly changing industry practices, providing a 'safe space' testing ground for applying skills and knowledge. *Digi-Anth Publishing* is based on the Australian and New Zealand Institute of Professional Editors Ltd standards, contextualizing the small group anthologies developed from a callout across the writing degree. *Bunyip Studios,* an indie videogame developer, asks students to pitch their prototypes incorporating industry-standard required documentation, and imaginative/innovative game concepts.

The Outcome

These two digital entities were integrated into the curriculum to provide processes and outputs demonstrating industry skills and knowledge, such as editorial and production skills, videogames conceptualization and pitching. Industry digital publishing and indie games studios seek creative self-starters prepared to make decisions and create opportunities in rapidly changing environments. Learners became more confident in developing small business or freelancing options, or finding ways through back door entry points such as digital production or reviewing games. Their group processes and outputs also helped them signal their employability to employers through e-portfolio presentations and narratives demonstrating industry-specific skills.

Lessons Learned And Advice

Previous iterations of digital scenarios had encompassed visuals, audio, mini-websites and complex storylines/characters. Although immersive, they were complex and time-consuming to produce whilst frustrating learners who were not game/play-oriented. Instead, the digital entities are deliberately simple platforms, flexible and easy to maintain, for up-to-date industry linkages. Visuals such as a business logo or open-access photos are sufficient to create believability, and learners engage to the depth they individually require to understand the industry. The ‘micro-businesses’, incorporated seamlessly with the tasks, also encourage a developmental transition towards industry standards and expectations.

Lived Experience Insight

Shared By Ray Sylvester, Professor, Coach, and Consultant, USA and UK

The Challenge

A final-year student was involved with a pirate radio station in Manchester. Theoretically, the operation of an unlicensed radio station is illegal in the UK. However, things are never that simple, so due to the station’s reach and popularity, the local police force opted to use it to make important public information announcements. When the British Broadcasting Corporation (BBC) identified and decided to create a legal national station aimed at the same market as the existing regional pirate station communities, the final-year student decided to investigate and try to secure employment at BBC Radio 1Xtra. The challenge was to signal their employability and demonstrate their person-organization fit.

The Context

The BBC decided to launch a new radio station called ‘BBC Radio 1Xtra’ as a sister station to ‘BBC Radio 1’ in August 2002. BBC Radio 1Xtra aimed to broadcast music created, produced, or inspired by Black people or people of African and Caribbean descent and music genres of the global Black diaspora. The target audience was people aged between fifteen and thirty.

Action Taken

The final-year student was very aware of the British radio market segments. They were completing a final-year dissertation about the efficacy of a broadcast station that would offer the same music genre mix and operational broadcast culture of prevailing UK pirate station networks in cities across the UK. They also knew the importance of presenting an authentic personal brand that could signal their employability to the BBC. During the application phase, they shared their experience with pirate radio show broadcasts, their audience segmentation, targeting and positioning knowledge, insight about their dissertation, and references from their educational and industry network. During the interview phase, they explained how the aim of BBC Radio 1Xtra aligned with the many pirate stations building and serving their brand community of loyal listeners. They also agreed with the Radio 1Xtra station's vision of becoming a legitimate (pirate-like) music station that had the potential to establish a national network.

The Outcome

The graduate secured a job at BBC Radio 1Xtra, turned their passion into a legitimate job, and now has a music business career of over twenty years. They secured the role through a strong and critical integration of lived experience in real-life and classroom settings.

Lessons Learned and Advice

Developing authentic knowledge about one's personal brand requires sustained reflection (What happened?) and reflexion (What was experienced?). This process takes effort over time. However, it is worth it, as when you know who you are, you can leverage it for desirable outcomes (e.g., employment, happiness, passion, etc.). Your intentional personal brand and its affiliate network of contacts can produce a distinctiveness. This can signal the all-important competitive edge that allows you to stand out from the crowd in an increasingly competitive employability ecosystem. The strategy can be particularly effective in creative industries where the supply of graduates exceeds labor market demand.

Reflection on Lived Experience Insights

The four lived experience insights covering Australia, Canada, and the UK evidence valuable opportunities for students to signal their employability to potential employers when undertaking the university-to-work transition. University career services lack the capacity to provide adequate support to their entire student body. Consequently, students also rely on academics to use the curriculum to enhance their learning, employability, and lifelong success. For example, using digital storymaking and real-world simulations can help students develop industry-related skills and increase their confidence. The approach can also enable students to develop an e-portfolio to help them signal their employability via presentations and narratives.

Using narratives is essential since applicants often have similar qualifications and skills, whereas authentic narratives are unique to the individual. Workshops can provide an opportunity for self-reflection whereby one can consider personal responses to questions such as 'What makes you unique?' and 'What motivates you to join a specific industry, organization or role?'. The notion of authenticity also applies to one's personal brand, which, when combined with professional networks, can offer a significant competitive advantage, particularly in creative industries.

Finally, adopting a holistic and lifewide approach to learning can enable students to draw on classroom and non-classroom-based experiences, providing metrics and rich narratives to signal passion for a specific employment opportunity.

CONCLUSION

Section Two of this book consisted of three chapters. In Chapter 2, we explored the need for university students to acquire various forms of employability capital to enhance their graduate employability by introducing the 'Employability Capital Growth (ECG) model' (Donald et al., 2023). We also observed a need for proactive behaviors to operationalize strengths and overcome challenges (Pham, 2020; Tang, 2022) by combining individual resources, agency, and an understanding of local labor markets (Pham & Jackson, 2020).

In Chapter 3, we considered strategic opportunities for how university career services and other actors within universities could enhance student engagement, recognizing that student engagement is the number one issue that university career services currently face (Gradleaders, 2022). We explored four interlinked challenges:

- A lack of student awareness and engagement
- A lack of resources for career advisors
- Student demands for health and wellbeing support
- Issues promoting social mobility

Five engagement strategies were then presented:

- Raising awareness and visibility
- Accessible, timely and tailored support
- Peer mentoring and alums mentoring
- Embedding employability into the curriculum
- Additional partnerships and resources

Chapter 4 then acknowledged that whilst engaging with career support services and enhancing one's employability is beneficial to students, they also need to be capable of signaling their employability to prospective employers (Anderson & Tomlinson, 2021). Three approaches to helping students to develop and signal their employability were then presented. These encompassed:

- Personal branding effects on employability (Gorbatov et al., 2021; Khedher, 2019)
- Career metaphors, including 'Weather as a Career Metaphor' (Donald, 2022)
- Career narratives (storytelling) "using concrete examples that reframe a moment by personifying Human consequences" (Grenny, 2017, Online, Paragraph 1)

Each chapter was complemented by four lived experience insights to help bridge theory and practice.

At this point in the book, you might like to take some time to reflect on Section Two and consider what pragmatic steps you can take to enhance the sustainability of the career ecosystem. For example, if you are a student, perhaps you might think about:

- Where you could access career support,
- How you can develop your personal brand,
- What personal resources do you need to acquire to enhance your employability capital,
- How you can signal your employability to prospective employers in preparation for the university-to-work transition.

Suppose you are part of a university career service. In that case, you might consider:

- New approaches to engage students at your university,
- Opportunities for working in partnership with other actors (e.g., lecturers, alums),
- Using the 'Employability Capital Growth (ECG) model' (Donald et al., 2023) and the 'Weather as a Career Metaphor' (Donald, 2022) as additional tools to complement storytelling and personal branding to prepare your students for entry into the labor market.

If you are a lecturer, how can you contact:

- Your university career service,
- Alums,
- Your personal networks to work together to embed employability into the curriculum (e.g., guest lectures, real-world case studies, authentic assessment approaches, etc.)?

If you are an employer, Section 2 has hopefully provided you with additional insights into the university perspective of the career ecosystem. Section 3 of the book now shifts our focus to the employer perspective before Section 4 considers the challenges and opportunities for increased collaboration via pragmatic strategies to bridge the university-employer divide before the book concludes with some thoughts about future workplace trends and their implications.

REFERENCES

Akkermans, J., Tomlinson, M., & Anderson, V. (2023). Initial employability development: Introducing a conceptual model integrating signalling and social exchange mechanisms. *European Journal of Work and Organizational Psychology*, 1–13. doi:10.1080/1359432X.2023.2186783

Alchin, C., McIlveen, P., & Perera, H. N. (2018). Negative career outlook and the working alliance in career counseling. *The Career Development Quarterly*, *66*(3), 279–284. doi:10.1002/cdq.12149

Allen, T. J., & Katz, R. (1986). The dual ladder: Motivational solution or managerial delusion? *R & D Management*, *16*(2), 185–197. doi:10.1111/j.1467-9310.1986.tb01171.x

Anderson, V., & Tomlinson, M. (2021). Signaling standout graduate employability: The employer perspective. *Human Resource Management Journal*, *31*(3), 675–693. doi:10.1111/1748-8583.12334

Bakker, A. B., & Demerouti, E. (2007). The Job Demands-Resources model: State of the art. *Journal of Managerial Psychology*, *22*(3), 309–328. doi:10.1108/02683940710733115

Baruch, Y. (2015). Organizational and labor market as career eco-system. In A. De Vos & B. I. J. M. Van der Heijden (Eds.), *Handbook of Research on Sustainable Careers* (pp. 164–180). Edward Elgar. doi:10.4337/9781782547037.00029

Baruch, Y., Ashleigh, M. J., & Donald, W. E. (2023). A sustainable career ecosystem perspective of talent flow and acquisition: The interface between higher education and industry. In W. E. Donald (Ed.), *Handbook of Research on Sustainable Career Ecosystems for University Students and Graduates* (pp. 177–194). IGI Global. doi:10.4018/978-1-6684-7442-6.ch010

Baruch, Y., & Rousseau, D. M. (2019). Integrating psychological contracts and ecosystems in career studies and management. *The Academy of Management Annals, 13*(1), 84–111. doi:10.5465/annals.2016.0103

Blau, P. (1964). *Exchange and Power in Social Life*. Wiley.

Bourdieu, P. (1983). The Forms of Capital. In J. G. Richardson (Ed.), *Handbook of Theory and Research for the Sociology of Education* (pp. 241–258). Greenwood Press.

Brown, P., & Hesketh, A. (2004). *The Mismanagement of Talent*. Oxford University Press. doi:10.1093/acprof:oso/9780199269532.001.0001

Bruner, J. (1986). *Actual Minds, Possible Worlds*. Harvard University Press. doi:10.4159/9780674029019

Cable, D. M., & Judge, T. A. (1996). Person-organization fit, job decisions, and organizational entry. *Organizational Behavior and Human Decision Processes, 67*(3), 294–311. doi:10.1006/obhd.1996.0081

Celani, A., & Singh, P. (2011). Signaling theory and applicant attraction outcomes. *Personnel Review*, *40*(2), 222–238. doi:10.1108/00483481111106093

Chan, G. (2023). 5 Reasons Why Building Your Personal Brand Will Land Your Next Job. *Forbes*. https://www.forbes.com/sites/goldiechan/2023/01/17/5-reasons-why-building-your-personal-brand-will-land-your-next-job/

Chartered Institute of Personnel and Development. (2022). *Growing proportion of UK graduates ending up in low-skills jobs, where they experience lower levels of job and life satisfaction*. CIPD. https://www.cipd.co.uk/about/media/press/041122-graduate-overqualification-cipd-report#gref

Choi, E., Leroy, H., Johnson, A., & Nguyen, H. (2022). Flaws and all: How mindfulness reduces error hiding by enhancing authentic functioning. *Journal of Occupational Health Psychology*, *27*(5), 451–469. doi:10.1037/ocp0000327 PMID:35549505

Clarke, M., & Scurry, T. (2020). The role of the psychological contract in shaping graduate experiences: A study of public sector talent management programmes in the UK and Australia. *International Journal of Human Resource Management, 31*(8), 965–991. doi:10.1080/09585192.2017.1396545

Creed, A. (2023). Development of the 'Transition Is A Becoming' metaphor: The perspectives of international students. In W. E. Donald (Ed.), *Handbook of Research on Sustainable Career Ecosystems for University Students and Graduates* (pp. 38–57). IGI Global. doi:10.4018/978-1-6684-7442-6.ch003

Creed, A., & Nacey, S. (2021). Qualitative and quantitative examination of metaphorical language use in career-life preparedness. In W. Murphy & J. Tosti-Kharas (Eds.), *Handbook of Research Methods in Careers* (pp. 283–298). Elgar. doi:10.4337/9781788976725.00023

de Blaquière, G., Nolan, J. E., & Wray, K. (2019). Joining up the dots: Telling the story of skills: How can students in Higher Education be supported to better understand and articulate their employability? *Journal of Teaching and Learning for Graduate Employability*, *10*(2), 15–35. doi:10.21153/jtlge2019vol10no2art699

Del Corso, J., & Rehfuss, M. C. (2011). The role of narrative in career construction theory. *Journal of Vocational Behavior*, *79*(2), 334–339. doi:10.1016/j.jvb.2011.04.003

Donald, W. E. (2021). *Conceptualisation of a new 'Early Careers Talent Pipeline' Framework: Enhancing Organisational Sustainability via Feedback-Seeking Behaviour.* Graduate Recruitment Bureau. doi:10.13140/RG.2.2.28278.47684

Donald, W. E. (2022). The Conceptualisation of Weather as a Career Metaphor. *Sustainability (Basel)*, *14*(14), 8856. doi:10.3390u14148856

Donald, W. E., Ashleigh, M. J., & Baruch, Y. (2018). Students' perceptions of education and employability: Facilitating career transition from higher education into the labor market. *Career Development International*, *23*(5), 513–540. doi:10.1108/CDI-09-2017-0171

Donald, W. E., Baruch, Y., & Ashleigh, M. J. (2020). Striving for sustainable graduate careers: Conceptualization via career ecosystems and the new psychological contract. *Career Development International*, *25*(2), 90–110. doi:10.1108/CDI-03-2019-0079

Donald, W. E., Baruch, Y., & Ashleigh, M. J. (2023). Construction and operationalisation of an Employability Capital Growth Model (ECGM) via a systematic literature review (2016-2022). *Studies in Higher Education*, 1–15. doi:10.1080/03075079.2023.2219270

Donald, W. E., & Jackson, D. (2023). Sustainable career ecosystems: Setting the scene. In W. E. Donald (Ed.), *Handbook of Research on Sustainable Career Ecosystems for University Students and Graduates* (pp. 1–13). IGI Global., doi:10.4018/978-1-6684-7442-6.ch001

Flat, A., & Drewery, D. (2023). How career development professionals can close the gap between human resources and Gen Z: The creation of sustainable relationships. In W. E. Donald (Ed.), *Handbook of Research on Sustainable Career Ecosystems for University Students and Graduates* (pp. 195–213). IGI Global., doi:10.4018/978-1-6684-7442-6.ch011

Gorbatov, S., Khapova, S. N., Oostrom, J. K., & Lysova, E. I. (2021). Personal brand equity: Scale development and validation. *Personnel Psychology*, *74*(3), 505–542. doi:10.1111/peps.12412

Gradleaders. (2022). *16 biggest challenges every career center faces today*. GradeLeaders. https://www.gradleaders.com/career-services-challenges

Graduate Coach. (2020). *6 top graduate employability issues.* Graduate Coach. https://graduatecoach.co.uk/blog/graduate-employability-issues/

Green, C. (2023). *How to Communicate About Your Career*. Browning York. https://www.browningyork.com/how-to-communicate-about-your-career/

Grenny, J. (2017). *Great Storytelling Connects Employees to Their Work.* HBR. https://hbr.org/2017/09/great-storytelling-connects-employees-to-their-work

Handley, K., & den Outer, B. (2022). Learning to signal graduate employability: An exploratory study of UK students' experiences of online recruitment process. *Journal of Youth Studies*, 1–19. doi:10.1080/13676261.2022.2157252

Higdon, R. D. (2016). Employability: The missing voice: How student and graduate views could be used to develop future higher education policy and inform curricula. *Power and Education*, *8*(2), 176–195. doi:10.1177/1757743816653151

Higher Ed Partners. (2021). *University career services: A critical tool in a competitive climate*. Higher Ed Partners. https://higheredpartners.co.uk/university-career-services-a-critical-tool-in-a-competitive-climate/

Hobfoll, S. E. (1989). Conservation of resources: A new attempt at conceptualizing stress. *The American Psychologist*, *44*(3), 513–524. doi:10.1037/0003-066X.44.3.513 PMID:2648906

Inkson, K. (2006). Protean and boundaryless career metaphors. *Journal of Vocational Behavior*, *69*(1), 48–63. doi:10.1016/j.jvb.2005.09.004

Inkson, K., & Amundson, N. E. (2002). Career metaphors and their application in theory and counseling practice. *Journal of Employment Counseling*, *39*(3), 98–108. doi:10.1002/j.2161-1920.2002.tb00841.x

Inkson, K., Dries, N., & Arnold, J. (2015). *Understanding Careers: Metaphors of Working Lives* (2nd ed.). Sage.

Khedher, M. (2019). Conceptualizing and researching personal branding effects on employability. *Journal of Brand Management*, *26*(2), 99–109. doi:10.105741262-018-0117-1

Labrecque, L. I., Markos, E., & Milne, G. R. (2011). Online personal branding: Processes, challenges, and implications. *Journal of Interactive Marketing*, *25*(1), 37–50. doi:10.1016/j.intmar.2010.09.002

Lair, D. L., Sullivan, K., & Cheney, G. (2005). Marketization and recasting of the professional self: The rhetoric and ethics of personal branding. *Management Communication Quarterly*, *18*(3), 307–343. doi:10.1177/0893318904270744

Le Rossignol, K., & Kelly, M. (2023). A career ecosystem approach to developing student agency through digital storymaking. In W. E. Donald (Ed.), *Handbook of Research on Sustainable Career Ecosystems for University Students and Graduates* (pp. 158–175). IGI Global. doi:10.4018/978-1-6684-7442-6.ch009

Maree, J. G. (2020). How global change necessitates innovation in career counseling: Linking economic, industrial, psychology, and career counseling waves. In J. G. Maree (Ed.), *Innovating Counseling for Self- and Career Construction: Connecting Conscious Knowledge with Subconscious Thought* (pp. 67–84). Springer. doi:10.1007/978-3-030-48648-8_4

Martela, F., & Steger, M. F. (2016). The three meanings of meaning in life: Distinguishing, coherence, purpose, and significance. *The Journal of Positive Psychology*, *11*(5), 531–545. doi:10.1080/17439760.2015.1137623

McIlveen, P., & Creed, A. (2020). La conversation, métaphore de l'approche narrative du counseling d'orientation. In Masdonati, J., Massoudi, K. & Rossier, J. (Eds.) *Landmarks for Career Counseling (Repères pour l'orientation), Antipodes in Actualités Psychologiques Collection* (pp. 361-383). Lausanne, Suisse: Éditions Antipodes.

McMahon, M., & Watson, M. (2013). Story telling: Crafting identities. *British Journal of Guidance & Counselling*, *41*(3), 277–286. doi:10.1080/03069885.2013.789824 PMID:24009405

Michael Page. (2022). *Career Development Toolkit: Maximising your professional value*. Michael Page. https://www.michaelpage.co.uk/career-development-toolkit-maximise-professional-value

Nolan, J. E. (2020). *Narrating Employability from English Studies: An Ethnographic Study*. Doctoral Thesis, Newcastle University. https://theses.ncl.ac.uk/jspui/handle/10443/4940

Parmentier, M. A., Fischer, E., & Reuber, A. R. (2013). Positioning person brands in establishing organizational fields. *Journal of the Academy of Marketing Science*, *41*(3), 373–387. doi:10.100711747-012-0309-2

Pham, T. (2020). Reconceptualising employability of returnees: What really matters and strategic navigating approaches. *Higher Education*, *81*(6), 1329–1345. doi:10.100710734-020-00614-2

Pham, T. (2022). Preparing graduates for cross-country labor markets: What do we know about human and social capital work in Australia and Vietnam? In W. Lee, P. Brown, A. Goodwin, & A. Green (Eds.), *International Handbook on Educational Development in Asia-Pacific* (pp. 1–17). Springer.

Pham, T., & Jackson, D. (2020). Employability and determinants of employment outcomes. In N. Tran, T. Pham, M. Tomlinson, K. Medica, & C. Thompson (Eds.), Developing and utilizing employability capitals: Graduates' strategies across labour markets (pp. 237–255). Routledge. 10.4324/9781003004660-17

Pham, T., & Sultani, B. (2021). *Enhancing Student Education Transitions and Employability: From Theory to Practice*. Routledge. doi:10.4324/9781003168737

Pryor, R. G. L., & Bright, J. E. H. (2009). Game as a career metaphor: A chaos theory career counselling application. *British Journal of Guidance & Counselling*, *37*(1), 39–50. doi:10.1080/03069880802534070

Rousseau, D. M. (1995). Psychological Contracts in Organizations: Understanding Written and Unwritten Agreements. *Sage (Atlanta, Ga.)*. doi:10.4135/9781452231594

Savickas, M. L. (2005). The theory and practice of career construction. In S. D. Brown & R. W. Lent (Eds.), *Career Development and Counseling: Putting Theory and Research to Work* (pp. 42-70). Wiley.

Schneider, B. (1987). The People Make The Place. *Personnel Psychology*, *40*(3), 437–453. doi:10.1111/j.1744-6570.1987.tb00609.x

Sjolander, C., & Dodd, J. S. (2022). *Career Centre Resources, Services and Metrics: A Pan-Canadian Benchmarking Survey*. Canadian Association of Career Educators and Employers.

Spence, M. (1973). Job market signalling. *The Quarterly Journal of Economics*, *87*(3), 355–374. doi:10.2307/1882010

Spence, M. (1978). Job market signaling. In P. Diamond & M. Rothschild (Eds.), *Understanding in Economics* (pp. 281–306). Academic Press. doi:10.1016/B978-0-12-214850-7.50025-5

Strauss, A. (1962). Transformation of identity. In A. M. Rose (Ed.), *Human Behaviour and Social Processes: An Interactionist Approach* (pp. 63–85). Routledge & Kegan Paul.

Sylvester, R., & Donald, W. E. (2023). The Personal Brand V.A.L.U.E. Career Development Tool: A multi-perspective and interdisciplinary framework. In W. E. Donald (Ed.), *Handbook of Research on Sustainable Career Ecosystems for University Students and Graduates* (pp. 238–257). IGI Global. doi:10.4018/978-1-6684-7442-6.ch013

Tang, M. (2022). Challenges Associated with Employability Capitals Facing Chinese International Graduates in Australia. In B. Ng (Ed.), *Graduate Employability and Workplace-Based Learning Development: Insights from Sociocultural Perspectives* (pp. 83–99). Springer Nature Singapore. doi:10.1007/978-981-19-5622-5_6

Tang, M., & Jiang, W. (2023). Chinese international graduates in the Australian labor market: Employability capitals and wellbeing. In W. E. Donald (Ed.), *Handbook of Research on Sustainable Career Ecosystems for University Students and Graduates* (pp. 214–237). IGI Global. doi:10.4018/978-1-6684-7442-6.ch012

Tomlinson, M., & Anderson, V. (2021). Employers and graduates: The mediating role of signals and capitals. *Journal of Higher Education Policy and Management*, *43*(4), 384–399. doi:10.1080/1360080X.2020.1833126

Tomlinson, M., & Jackson, D. (2021). Professional identity formation in contemporary higher education students. *Studies in Higher Education*, *46*(4), 885–900. doi:10.1080/03075079.2019.1659763

Ugiagbe-Green, I. (2023). Identity regulation through the whiteness of "Right Fit": Mitigating racism in graduate recruitment. In W. E. Donald (Ed.), *Handbook of Research on Sustainable Career Ecosystems for University Students and Graduates* (pp. 278–299). IGI Global. doi:10.4018/978-1-6684-7442-6.ch015

Van der Heijden, B. I. J. M., & De Vos, A. (2015). Sustainable careers: Introductory chapter. In A. De Vos & B. I. J. M. Van der Heijden (Eds.), *Handbook of Research on Sustainable Careers* (pp. 1–19). Edward Elgar. doi:10.4337/9781782547037.00006

ADDITIONAL READING

Amundson, N. E. (2015). Using metaphor in career intervention. In P. J. Hartung, M. L. Savickas, & W. B. Walsh (Eds.), *APA Handbook of Career Intervention, Vol. 2. Applications* (pp. 293–304). American Psychological Association. doi:10.1037/14439-022

Connelly, B. L., Certo, S. T., Ireland, R. D., & Reutzel, C. R. (2011). Signaling theory: A review and assessment. *Journal of Management, 37*(1), 39–67. doi:10.1177/0149206310388419

Creed, A., & McIlveen, P. (2018). Metaphor identification as a research method for the study of career. *International Journal for Educational and Vocational Guidance, 18*(1), 27–44. doi:10.100710775-017-9345-2

Cropanzo, R., & Mitchell, M. S. (2005). Social exchange theory: An interdisciplinary review. *Journal of Management, 31*(6), 874–900. doi:10.1177/0149206305279602

Guest, D. E., Sanders, K., Rodrigues, R., & Oliveira, T. (2021). Signaling theory as a framework for analysing human resource management processes and integrating human resource attribution theories: A conceptual analysis and empirical validation. *Human Resource Management Journal, 31*(3), 796–818. doi:10.1111/1748-8583.12326

Inkson, K. (2007). *Understanding careers: The metaphors of working lives*. SAGE Publications, Inc., doi:10.4135/9781483328867

McIlveen, P., & Patton, W. (2007). Narrative career counselling: Theory and exemplars of practice. *Australian Psychologist, 42*(3), 226–235. doi:10.1080/00050060701405592

Mutanen, H., Korhonen, M., & Siivonen, P. (2023). Employability as self-branding in job search games: A case of Finnish business graduates. In P. Siivonen, U. Isopahkala-Bouret, M. Tomlinson, & N. Haltia (Eds.), *Rethinking Graduate Employability in Context* (pp. 319–339). Springer Link. doi:10.1007/978-3-031-20653-5_15

Rochat, S., & Borgen, W. A. (2021). Career life as a game: An overlooked metaphor for successful career transitions. *British Journal of Guidance & Counselling, 51*(2), 298–309. doi:10.1080/03069885.2021.1940844 PMID:37313007

Spence, M. (2002). Signaling in retrospect and the informational structure of markets. *The American Economic Review, 92*(3), 434–459. doi:10.1257/00028280260136200

Section 3
Graduate Recruiters

Chapter 5
Attracting Early Career Talent

ABSTRACT

This chapter focuses on attracting early career talent, which is essential for organizational and career ecosystem sustainability. The chapter begins with an overview of Generation Z and Industry 4.0, including consideration of graduate migration patterns and holistic identity formation. Next, the authors explore the challenges of attracting early career talent, including (i) war for talent and skills shortages, (ii) attracting diverse applicants, (iii) mental health, wellbeing, and flexible working, and (iv) corporate citizenship via social and environmental impacts. Then, opportunities for attracting early career talent are presented, comprising (i) early and ongoing engagement, (ii) authentic branding, values, and culture, and (iii) compensation, benefits, and development opportunities. The chapter concludes with four lived experience insights highlighting challenges to attracting early career talent and pragmatic strategies to address them.

INTRODUCTION

Section One of the book set the scene by introducing university career advisors, graduate recruiters, and sustainable graduate careers. In Section Two, our focus shifted to the role of university career advisors in helping their students prepare for successful and sustainable careers. In Section Three, our attention now turns to the role of in-house graduate recruiters and other individuals working as agents of an organization via recruitment agencies. This chapter focuses on the challenges and opportunities concerning attracting early career talent. Chapter 6 discusses how to

DOI: 10.4018/978-1-6684-9827-9.ch005

prepare students for undertaking the university-to-work transition. Subsequently, Chapter 7 considers how to establish and maintain Person-Organization Fit (POF) in the context of attracting, selecting, and retaining graduate talent.

Generation Z and Industry 4.0

Generation Z

The Pew Research Centre (2018) proposes that Generation Z refers to individuals born between 1997 and 2012, although they are keen to state that an exact cut-off date has not yet been determined. Subsequently, Generation Z individuals enter tertiary education between 2015 and 2030, undertaking the university-to-work transition between 2018 and 2033 (assuming they enter tertiary education at age 18 and undertake a 3-year undergraduate degree). Consequently, the needs and preferences of Generation Z must inform attraction and retention strategies for the next decade (Careers2032 Project, 2022).

As the first generation to grow up with the internet and portable technology from a young age, Generation Z individuals are considered digital natives, although they also appreciate human connection (Khanna & Dutta, 2023). Compared to previous generations, Generation Z (i) consumes less alcohol, (ii) has lower levels of teenage pregnancies, (iii) cares more about examination grades, and (iv) has higher levels of stress, anxiety, and depression (The Economist, 2019). Generation Z has also experienced the COVID-19 pandemic during at least one and potentially two of primary, secondary or tertiary education or in the early years of their transition from education to work. Like other individuals, the lockdown restrictions related to the COVID-19 pandemic gave Generation Z a chance to reflect on what they truly want from life (Afshari & Nasab, 2021). A study by Pandita (2022) conducting 21 interviews with HR leads, managers, and consultants in India on the topic of branding for Generation Z found

Gen Z has high career aspirations, working styles, attributes, education preferences and has an innovative mindset. This demands the flexibility of being independent and confident. They prefer diversity not just through race and gender but also through identity and orientation. Most important, money is not the only priority for them when it comes to their career development. They also want themselves to be associated with a workplace exhibiting community support. They are driven by an innovative mindset where they resort to creative means to achieve their goals. (p. 556)

The findings are supported by other research worldwide, showing that Generation Z seeks meaning and social impact in their work (Chillakuri, 2020; Green, 2020). Generation Z also values flexible work arrangements, a healthy work-life balance, and wants to be judged on their own merits rather than the performance of a wider team (Barhate & Dirani, 2021). We also know that Generation Z uses social media to gain insight into company culture but is less likely to use social media to find job opportunities (Hawes, 2022). Therefore, organizations must consider the content *AND* the means of dissemination for different aspects of their attraction strategy.

Having provided a brief overview of Generation Z, our attention now shifts to consider the migration patterns of graduates before introducing Industry 4.0.

Graduate Migration Patterns

Understanding graduate migration patterns is essential to inform strategic approaches to attract early career talent to an organization.

Ball (2021) looked at data collected from 2017/2018 graduates 15 months after completing their studies. He found that 66% of graduates worked in the region where they lived before attending university, and 54% worked in the region where they went to university. The data has remained relatively consistent over the last two decades. However, Ball (2023) notes that the increase in remote or hybrid working opportunities following the lockdown restrictions of the COVID-19 pandemic might erode previous links between work locations and employers. For example, organizations in less attractive locations may be able to increase their attractiveness if individuals can live elsewhere. A related aspect to consider is that the 2017/2018 graduates were the first cohort of Generation Z to undertake the university-to-work transition. The UK's departure from the EU on 31st January 2020 also placed additional restrictions on the free movement of people between the UK and other EU countries. The ongoing cost of living crisis and looming recession could also influence decision-making processes. Consequently, it will be interesting to see if graduate migration patterns change in the years ahead.

The international migration of students and graduates has also been explored in the USA and Australia. Grimm (2019) observes how visa schemes that allow individuals to remain in a country following graduation from a domestic institution encourage students to move abroad to study. Grimm claims that higher education institutions must be considered "not only as a temporary home for globally mobile student sojourners but as a starting point for transnational talent on complex migration journeys" (p. 235). Moreover, Pham (2021) observes how international graduates in Australia need more than credentials to navigate the host labor market. Pham advocates for universities and employers to help students acquire social capital by establishing meaningful connections, recognizing that acquiring social capital takes time. Tang and Jiang (2023), based on qualitative interviews with Chinese international graduates in Australia, also found that social capital played a prominent role in determining one's self-perceived wellbeing. These observations suggest that employers who provide opportunities for students to develop social capital and signal a commitment to promoting employee wellbeing may be viewed as attractive workplaces by international graduates.

Industry 4.0

The first three Industrial Revolutions were driven respectively by (i) mechanization via steam and water power, (ii) electricity and mass production via assembly lines, and (iii) computers and preliminary automation (Marr, 2018). The Fourth Industrial Revolution (often referred to as Industry 4.0 or 4IR) is defined by Mc Kinsey & Company (2022) as "the next phase in the digitization of the manufacturing sector, driven by disruptive trends including the rise of data and connectivity, analytics, human-machine interaction, and improvements in robotics" (Online, Paragraph One). Consequently, Industry 4.0 combines technological advancement with an increased demand for skilled workers (Črešnar & Nedelko, 2020) in areas such as data analysis, AI, and robotics to enable businesses to automate processes, increase productivity, and reduce costs (World Economic Forum, 2018). The McKinsey Global Institute (2017) predicts that up to 375 million workers will have to acquire new skills or switch occupations by 2030, accounting for 14 per cent of the global workforce. The same article reported that whilst less than 5 per cent of occupations consist of activities that could be fully automated, in around 60 per cent of occupations, this figure increases to around 60 per cent. We explore future workplace trends further in the final chapter of this book.

In the context of early career talent, the Association of Graduate Careers Advisory Services (AGCAS), the Institute of Student Employers (ISE), WONKHE, and Handshake led an industry research project looking at the role technology could play in facilitating human connections and what the careers sector might look like over the next decade (Careers2032 Project, 2022). Their key findings from the perspective of 159 graduate employers in the UK included:

- 86% feel technology can open careers to more people from an inclusivity perspective.
- 85% feel technology can improve social mobility.
- 81% believe that in a decade, they will be recruiting for jobs that do not exist today.
- 78% believe engaging students earlier in their educational journey (e.g., during primary and secondary school) would be beneficial.

- 76% believe that technology will facilitate ongoing interaction between employers and students moving beyond ad-hoc communication or contact at pre-set times (such as career events).
- 75% believe that technology will help to automate the provision of information and advice.
- 72% believe technology will make sharing information about career paths and opportunities easier.
- 68% list the attraction of talent via Equality, Diversity, and Inclusion (EDI) initiatives as a business priority.
- 56% list preventing successful applicants from reneging on job offers as a business priority.

These observations suggest an increased significance in attracting talent, preparing students for entry into the labor market (discussed in Chapter 6), and assessing person-organization fit via streamlined and effective selection processes (discussed in Chapter 7).

We now shift our attention to consider the need for holistic identity formation to foster sustainable career ecosystems at the intersection of Generation Z and Industry 4.0.

Holistic Identity Formation

King et al. (2021) offer a framework of holistic identity formation at the individual (micro), organizational (meso) and professional (macro) levels. The micro level refers to an individual's traits, needs and motivations. The meso level captures the organization's culture, HRM policies, and workspace expectations (e.g., office-based, hybrid, or virtual working). The macro level refers to a profession's industry image, educational programs, and comparisons with alternative industries or sectors. Their framework suggests that for the sustainability of various actors operating within a career ecosystem, there is a need for open and authentic sharing of information to overcome information asymmetry (Spence, 1973; 1978). The perspective also aligns with the views of Baruch et al. (2023), who suggest sustainable career ecosystems can facilitate the integration of research areas, including "career counseling, career development, graduate employability, graduate recruitment, human resource development, human resource management, organizational behavior, organizational change, sustainable careers, vocational behavior, and vocational psychology" (p. 185).

From the meso-level employer's perspective, attracting and retaining diverse early career talent is critical for organizational sustainability (Careers2032 Project, 2022). The view is supported by Clark-Ambrosini et al. (2023), who observe how early career talent pipelines must help an organization meet its aims and enable graduates to align with its identity. Consequently, organizations must attract and retain early career talent by balancing opportunities for employees to develop and showcase their strengths with structure and direction so that both parties can benefit from the relationship (Nurjanah & Indawati, 2021). The perspective captures the relevance of the NPC (Rousseau, 1995) and its integration with CET (Baruch, 2015) and SCT (Van der Heijden & De Vos, 2015) to offer sustainable career ecosystems (Donald, 2023a), as previously discussed in Chapter 4.

A related dimension of holistic identity formation comes from comparing different generations. Zaharee et al. (2018) looked at technical workers and found little difference in workplace preferences between Millennials and earlier generations. My own research also found minimal variance between Generation Z and Millennial graduates, other than over time, their preference shifts from office-based to a greater desire for hybrid or virtual working (Donald, 2023b). However, we are currently in the emerging stages of Industry 4.0, and the entry of Generation Z graduates into the workforce. Therefore, a divergence of views between Millennials and Generation Z may become more apparent in the years ahead.

Having set the scene via a discussion of Generation Z, graduate migration patterns, Industry 4.0, and holistic identity formation, our focus now shifts to the challenges of attracting early career talent. The challenges capture the micro, meso, and macro levels of the holistic identity formation framework (King et al., 2021), albeit framed from the organizational (meso) perspective.

Challenges Of Attracting Early Career Talent

War for Talent and Skill Shortages

Hawes (2022) suggests that talent shortages in the graduate labor market will persist for at least a decade. The view is supported by the Graduate Employer Priorities 2023 report, which identifies the war for talent and skills shortages as significant challenges for organizations (Handshake, 2023). Yet, organizations often make the situation worse due to their decision-making processes. For example, Ball (2023) highlights the limited number of graduates each year with an upper second or first class degree classification in a specific subject area from Oxbridge or Russell Group universities. Ball explains how applying these criteria artificially shrinks the pool of talent available, a situation that worsens based on the number of employers applying such criteria. Consequently, Ball argues that removing requirements such as an upper second or first class degree classification enhances diversity and the potential to meet organizational headcount needs without compromising applicant quality. Somewhat encouragingly, recent trends indicate that some organizations are moving away from such restrictive criteria, perhaps recognizing the importance of diverse and sustainable talent pipelines for long-term growth and success (McCracken et al., 2016).

To develop and maintain talent pipelines, organizations must differentiate themselves and gain a competitive advantage via employment branding (Donald, 2021). However, Alexander et al. (2019) reported significant discrepancies between recruiters and job seekers concerning the use of social media, indicating a failure to overcome information asymmetry during the attraction phase. Additionally, a lack of authenticity when advertising jobs can lead to a mismatch between applicants and the job role, playing out as a perceived lack of quality of applicants or high turnover rates due to a misalignment in person-organization fit (Pohl et al., 2022). These recent findings are concerning given that for nearly 50 years, researchers have advocated for organizations to provide realistic job previews that encompass appealing and less appealing aspects, suggesting that the initial stages of the organization-applicant relationship are pivotal for fostering loyalty and commitment (e.g., Wanous, 1975).

Attracting Diverse Applicants

According to a report by Handshake (2023), one of the top priorities for graduate employers is to build a more diverse workforce. However, the increasing reliance on social networks, such as recommending candidates or filling roles through informal channels, tends to favor individuals with higher levels of social capital, reducing the diversity of hires (Donald et al., 2023). Another concerning finding by Hawes (2022) is that only 9.5% of human resource professionals come from an ethnic minority background. This lack of diversity limits the opportunities to address personal biases during the attraction and selection phases of recruitment. It also acts as a barrier for students and graduates who point out the challenges of aspiring to roles without seeing recruiters or role models with whom they can identify (Donald, 2017; Donald et al., 2018). Moreover, claims made during the attraction phase about company culture, such as inclusivity, often do not align with the actual lived experiences of the organization's employees. The lack of authenticity in promoting inclusivity leads to lower retention rates among diverse hires (Pohl et al., 2022).

A further concern for attracting diverse applicants relates to ChatGPT. Table 1 was produced by two data scientists at Develop Diverse who wanted to answer the question, 'Can ChatGPT be used to write job descriptions?'. They randomly selected over 7,000 publicly available, human-written job advertisements spanning 15 industries and then prompted ChatGPT to create a job advertisement for each position based on the job titles. Subsequently, proprietary software allocated each advertisement an inclusivity score from 0 to 100, whereby 0 is entirely non-inclusive, and a score above 90 is considered inclusive. Concerningly, the average ChatGPT job advertisement inclusivity score was 39 versus the average human-written score of 65. Therefore, using ChatGPT to write job advertisements in its current form is likely to decrease the inclusivity of the applicant pool and should thus be avoided. As a side note, even when ChatGPT is instructed to write an inclusive job advertisement, the output often only varies by adding a statement about the company's commitment to inclusivity rather than making any additional changes to the advertisement.

Table 1. Inclusivity scores for job advertisements written by humans and ChatGPT

Category	Inclusivity Score: Human Written Ads	Inclusivity Score: ChatGPT Written Ads	ChatGPT Bias Increase (v) Human Written Ads
	Inclusivity Score		
Total	65	39	40%
Male	92	84	9%
Female	66	39	41%
Nonconforming *	68	42	38%
Privileged Ethnic Groups	77	57	26%
Marginalized Ethnic Groups **	65	38	42%
Young	76	54	29%
Old	67	42	37%
Abled	76	54	29%
Disabled	63	37	41%
Neurotypical	76	54	29%
Neurodivergent	63	37	41%

Notes provided by the table's creators: * Nonconforming includes anyone who does not fit into gender norms, such as nonbinary people and other LGBTQ+ people. Gender norms are built on a binary worldview, with biological sex and heterosexuality as the expectation. ** Marginalized Ethnic Groups are underprivileged or underrepresented in the society they are in.

Source: English Translation of the Danish version from Kamil and Amann (2023).

Mental Health, Wellbeing, and Flexible Working

Higher education institutions have faced longstanding challenges in managing mental health issues among their students (White & McCallum, 2021). Additionally, two recent factors have exacerbated this challenge. First, the impacts of the COVID-19 pandemic have highlighted the urgent need for mental health support globally (Liu et al., 2020). Second, Gen Z is experiencing higher mental illness rates than previous generations (Russo, 2019). Consequently, students and recent graduates are prioritizing their mental health and wellbeing (Donald & Jackson, 2022), meaning organizations must communicate effectively and authentically how they support these aspects to differentiate themselves from competitors (Sánchez-Hernández et al., 2019). Failure to offer pre-emptive mental health support and flexible working conditions will negatively impact an organization's attraction and retention rates (Stumpf & Fielding, 2023).

Organizations should also consider a blend of approaches and acknowledge their workforce's differing needs and preferences. For example, organizations should consider the pros and cons of mandating in-person, virtual, or hybrid approaches to prospective employees during the attraction phase (Handshake, 2023). Virtual or hybrid approaches may increase the available talent pool by removing accessibility barriers for disabled workers or reducing the constraint of living within a reasonable commuting distance of a physical office location (Donald et al., 2023). Reducing time spent commuting may also increase opportunities to participate in serious leisure activities that have been shown to help graduate employees manage stress, acquire and replenish resources, and increase workplace wellbeing (Nimmi & Donald, 2023). Conversely, an entirely virtual approach might increase feelings of isolation and loneliness while also acting as a barrier to inclusion due to digital poverty or a lack of space to work if living in shared housing (Hawes, 2022). Therefore, organizations must balance flexible approaches that offer employees autonomy while ensuring the needs of the business are met.

Corporate Citizenship: Social And Environmental Impacts

Hawes (2022) also discusses how Generation Z has a strong desire for organizations to be socially and environmentally responsible (i.e., to act as good corporate citizens). A survey of over 1,000 graduates supports this view, revealing that 86% of participants believe it is vital for organizations to have a positive environmental impact, while 85% believe it is vital for organizations to have sustainable practices (Semencuka, 2022). However, Keppeler & Papenfuß (2021) found that relying solely on promoting an organization's social and environmental impacts is not an effective branding strategy in competitive labor markets. Effective communication of these commitments and achievements can also be challenging, especially for lesser-known organizations or those lacking a strong brand presence.

Furthermore, organizations that make false claims about their corporate citizenship (e.g., greenwashing) can face significant consequences. In the context of consumer branding, De Jong et al. (2018) discovered that "greenwashing has only limited benefits (perceived environmental performance), poses a major threat (perceived integrity), and has no true competitive advantage (purchase interest)" (p. 77). When it comes to attracting early career talent, Speckemeier and Tsivrikos (2022) found that *a firm's perceived green identity can either benefit or harm its overall reputation depending on whether the firm's sustainability claims are considered genuine or misleading. The negative effects of providing misleading information are found to have significant impact on job pursuit intentions. (p. 23)*

Additionally, regarding activism and retention of early career talent, Semencuka (2022) reported that if graduates discover an organization has made false claims during the attraction phase, 71% will raise the issue with management, while 28% will look for a new job. This highlights the importance of authenticity, openness, and a genuine commitment to the issues an organization claims to value during the attraction phase to establish and maintain trust.

Opportunities For Attracting Early Career Talent

Early And Ongoing Engagement

The Careers2032 Project (2022) reveals that as students progress through primary and secondary school, their confidence in self-perceived employability declines, highlighting the importance for employers of accessing talent at an early stage. This aligns with the findings of interviews that I conducted with university students, which emphasized the need for employers to actively engage with students in primary and secondary education, presenting diverse role models and job roles to challenge stereotypes (Donald et al., 2018). For the effective attraction of early career talent, Forbes (2019) proposes several strategies. These include partnering with schools and colleges, sponsoring or organizing competitions, and building relationships with primary and secondary school students to position your organization as an attractive place for them to seek employment after their education. Engaging family members and friends is also beneficial since Generation Z highly values their opinions (Goh & Okumus, 2020). Similarly, Sanctuary Graduates (2017) report that students trust recommendations from peers and academics more than if they came across the same information shared directly by organizations through websites or job advertisements.

Ongoing engagement by employers with students throughout their university studies is also crucial. This is because self-perceived employability among undergraduate students decreases between the penultimate and final year of study due to external market factors such as competition for jobs, location constraints, and rejection decisions (Donald et al., 2018). Organizations can also adopt specific approaches in sectors such as hospitality, where attracting Generation Z graduate talent is challenging. Providing a visual pathway that illustrates opportunities for career advancement, emphasizing the sector's benefits, and establishing mentorship or buddy programs can nurture and inspire potential talent (Goh & Okumus, 2020).

Authentic Branding, Values, and Culture

Authentic branding is crucial in attracting top talent by effectively communicating corporate goals, outcomes, and intentions (Hiltrop, 1999). To establish an authentic brand image, organizations should showcase meaningful work, a mission-driven approach, and a positive impact on the community (Locke et al., 2022). Research in Australia and the United Kingdom has shown that potential applicants to the accounting, banking, and finance sector value (i) positive societal impact, (ii) a positive workplace culture, (iii) work-life balance, (iv) flexibility in hours and location, and (v) a strong employer brand image and reputation (Jackson et al., 2022; Donald, 2023b). In industries with talent shortages, it may be necessary to implement industry-level branding efforts to attract talent (Wallace et al., 2012). For example, in the hospitality sector, organizations can focus on travel opportunities, host open days to showcase hospitality work, and share success stories or testimonials (Goh & Okumus, 2020). Additionally, organizations should allocate sufficient resources to develop talent and address skills shortages (Holland et al., 2007), which requires integrating the literature on graduate recruitment and organizational change (Kriener & Fischer, 2022).

To effectively communicate values and culture, organizations can leverage social media, maintain a positive public relations image, and offer high-quality paid internships (Forbes, 2019; Sanctuary Graduates, 2017) to send clear signals to potential applicants (Keppeler & Papenfuß, 2021). Optimizing job boards can also help by improving the relevance of search results, providing company metrics, and facilitating communication between individuals and organizations (Donald & Pychtin, 2022). Seeking feedback from interns and graduates can provide unique insights that marketing and branding teams may overlook (Donald, 2021). Moreover, increasing the representation of women in middle and senior management enhances financial performance (Joo et al., 2023) and makes the organization more appealing to graduates (Donald et al., 2018). Lastly, removing requirements such as upper second or first-class degree classifications can enhance diversity and meet organizational headcount needs without compromising applicant quality (Ball, 2023).

Compensation, Benefits, and Development Opportunities

Organizations can utilize compensation, benefits, and development opportunities to attract graduate talent. Competitive salaries and financial benefits are critical to enticing candidates (Donald, 2023b). Transparent pay structures, such as disclosing salary information in job advertisements, can provide clarity and attract graduate applicants (Goh & Okumus, 2020). However, offering more than just monetary rewards is crucial. Organizations should demonstrate ongoing development opportunities, including structured programs and career pathways (Donald, 2023b; Forbes, 2019). Graduates value learning and growth, seeking opportunities to acquire new skills and knowledge (Jackson et al., 2022). Additionally, graduates appreciate benefits like healthcare coverage, retirement plans with matching contributions from employers, and comprehensive professional development plans (Zaharee et al., 2018). The same study also found that early career professionals prioritize quick rotations through projects and roles, continuous feedback, and generous paid time off. Similarly, a survey of 475 accounting and finance students in Australia found that 35% desired structured graduate programs of defined length with possible rotations, which provide opportunities for learning from others, continuous learning, and career advancement (Jackson et al., 2022). These students also emphasized the importance of a sense of challenge, autonomy, responsibility, and professional fulfilment.

Interestingly, the attraction strategies mentioned in this section also reflect discussions with engineering students over a decade ago. Wallace et al. (2012) found that the five most important factors for attracting graduates were (i) the opportunity to work on interesting projects, (ii) having a good relationship with the team, (iii) gaining experience to support career progression, (iv) an attractive employment package (e.g., travel, allowances, etc.), and (v) competitive salary.

Our attention now turns to four lived experience insights exploring some of the challenges and opportunities presented in this chapter across four unique real-world settings.

LIVED EXPERIENCE INSIGHTS

Lived Experience Insight

Shared By Lilah Brook Nash, Media And Entertainment Company, UK

The Challenge

In the age of digital and decision fatigue, it can be difficult for an organization to stand out from their competitors in the war for graduate talent. Generation Z wants to know a clear description of what the role entails, understand the compensation on offer, and work for an organization whose views on environmental and mental health issues align with their own. Organizations that are not clear on these aspects will fail to attract graduate talent. Organizations that are not open about these aspects will fail to retain graduate talent.

The Context

Working in a role tasked with attracting and recruiting early career talent is very different from other types of recruitment. Applicants are effectively applying for their first full-time role after completing university studies. Many graduates will have developed incredible skills and knowledge during their time in education. Still, we need to give them the confidence (i) to apply for roles and (ii) to apply to our organization.

Action Taken

Our organization adopted a six-point approach to attract (and subsequently retain) early career talent.

1. Transparency. We are open and honest about what each role entails, whether it is office-based, hybrid, or fully remote, and what the salary is.
2. Prioritize values. We would rather hire an individual who shares the values of our organization but lacks some of the technical skills. We can teach technical skills, but a lack of person-organization fit is more challenging to overcome.
3. Authentic branding. We ensure that our attraction materials are an accurate reflection of our organization. If we try and pretend to be something different, turnover rates will be high when graduates experience the reality of working for us.
4. Think outside the box. Attention spans are decreasing with the rise of instant gratification. Rather than competing with other organizations solely on salary or benefits, we try innovative approaches (e.g., short TikTok videos) to communicate our values and brand.
5. Engage with schools and universities. We aim to provide career support and advice in educational settings to establish our brand and communicate our values. Showing young people what their future can hold can inspire them to work for us.
6. Social corporate responsibility. We know young people are worried about the climate emergency and that the pandemic has worsened mental health and financial issues from the cost of living crisis. We show that we are aware of these factors and listen to young people to learn how to support them best.

The Outcome

Implementing the six-point approach has improved the application quality and diversity of applicants. Each of these approaches works individually and cumulatively to achieve this goal. Interestingly, we found that listing the salary on job adverts increased the quality and diversity of our applicants. Individuals from lower socio-economic backgrounds do not have the luxury or privilege to take a role 'just for the experience', so they are less likely to apply if the salary is not provided. In a tough labor market, our organization has continued to fill our graduate vacancies, meet the needs of our business, and retain talent to become future leaders of the organization.

Lessons Learned and Advice

To summarize, when advertising roles to our early career audience, we want to be transparent, authentic, and show alliance with social issues that matter to young people. We have learned that this approach increases the quality and diversity of applicants, increases person-organization fit, and ultimately has a positive cost-benefit return due to long-term talent retention.

Lived Experience Insight

Shared By Claire House-Norman, Fundraising Academy Via Bournemouth University, UK

The Challenge

Fundraising is not recognized as a potential career by many students in the UK, despite charities of all sizes experiencing a skills shortage. It is often seen as a voluntary pastime rather than a career with good promotion opportunities. We wanted to trial a Fundraising Academy with undergraduate placement students to see if we could change their mindset, and produce a cohort of employment-ready graduates interested in a career in fundraising. The Fundraising Academy was designed to be experiential rather than academic, although it did include some theory-based modules.

The Context

The UK and other countries face a shortage of experienced fundraisers. Consequently, an overreliance on the same individuals leads to personal burnout and a lack of realized income for vital charity work. New fundraisers often lack the socio-emotional skills and resilience to succeed in a competitive industry. Additionally, there are few training courses on vital topics (such as donor dominance and working with Royal Patrons). Therefore, employing an inexperienced fundraiser can be resource-intensive for charities, and a reluctance to take the risk further diminishes the pipeline of applicants.

Action Taken

Bournemouth University ran a pilot Fundraising Academy for two years (the third year was paused owing to the COVID-19 pandemic), with a total of nine undergraduate students in their placement year. Each student was partnered with a local charity to fundraise in the community, attended theory sessions with the Bournemouth University fundraising team, and undertook group consultancy work. At the end of the year, they had completed the curriculum and had been intensively trained as fundraisers. The theory sessions were wide-ranging, including charity law, psychology, copywriting, accountancy, and personal skills development.

The Outcome

After participating in the Fundraising Academy, the students returned to the university for the final year of their undergraduate degree. On graduating, five of the nine students secured fundraising or similar positions; three went on to further study, and one launched his own business. The Fundraising Academy was hailed as a huge success by the partner charities, the volunteers who supported the curriculum, and the placement students. Bournemouth University's Fundraising Director ran the Fundraising Academy on top of her 'day job', significantly burdening her work and family life. This setup was necessary as a 'proof of concept' but was not viable or sustainable in the long term.

Lessons Learned and Advice

The personal skills greatly in demand in fundraising can be taught or brought out in appropriate individuals. It takes time and dedication, but the Fundraising Academy model results in new graduates ready to enter the fundraising career pipeline – essential for the profession's sustainability. Since the Fundraising Academy finished, some graduates have been head-hunted away from the charity sector into the commercial sector. This reflects a broader challenge for the charity sector and also highlights that the skills necessary to be a good fundraiser are valued by many other industries. The Fundraising Academy offers a 'proof of concept' for attracting talent, but such an approach needs adequate backing and resources to be sustainable.

Lived Experience Insight

Shared By Michal Kasprzak and Samantha Chang, University of Toronto, Canada

The Challenge

Attracting, recruiting and mentoring graduate students from different disciplinary backgrounds and with various teaching experiences into educational development work at a teaching and learning centre can be challenging. Graduate students often hope to be introduced to, explore, and leverage such complex curriculum development work (e.g., design and facilitation of training programs, teaching dossier reviews, in-class observation, microteaching workshops, resource creation, etc.) for a range of academic, alt-academic, and non-academic career pathways. Some are also recruited as permanent staff, researchers and/or project coordinators to support faculty and graduate student teaching advancement.

The Context

The Teaching Assistants' Training Program (TATP), housed at the University of Toronto's main teaching and learning centre (Centre for Teaching Support & Innovation), is a peer-based program (rooted in the 'Students as Partners' framework) that annually hires 16 Graduate Educational Developers (GEDs) to facilitate mandatory paid teacher training and professional development certificates for thousands of graduate students. The GEDs, typically senior doctoral students from various disciplinary backgrounds, aim to acquire curriculum development experience for various career options (in and out of academia). Typically, about half are interested in using the experience as a springboard into a career in educational development (or instructional design) either in higher education or the non-profit sector.

Action Taken

A wide-ranging communications strategy across the institution ensures that a high number of candidates from across different disciplinary backgrounds apply for GED roles at the TATP annually. Some potential GEDs connect with TATP through mandatory paid training and/or professional development certificates, others through their interest in teaching and learning in higher education. About a quarter of GED contract hours are devoted to training to prepare staff for diverse areas of educational development work. They are also involved in the program planning cycle, committee work, working groups, special projects and initiatives, instructional design, and Scholarship of Teaching and Learning (SoTL). Throughout each academic cycle, they are offered professional development, mentoring, and networking opportunities. The objective is to help GEDs document and articulate their educational development work at the TATP for various careers and to identify those who may want to join the Centre for Teaching Support & Innovation (as well as other faculty advancement offices) as permanent staff.

The Outcome

The TATP program has become a gateway for graduate students to discover educational development work for various career pathways (especially educational development), which they otherwise may not have explored. Since it offers extensive training, direct experience across different dimensions of educational development work, and career-focused mentoring, it attracts graduate students from various disciplinary backgrounds. Many hired to work at the TATP, continue as GEDs for several years. This allows them to position the experience as educational leadership (for academic roles) or as an early career educational development (for alt-academic or non-academic roles). It also creates a pool of talent for permanent positions in faculty advancement roles across the institution (and beyond).

Lessons Learned and Advice

Peer-based programs, when structured for genuine experiential (i.e., work-integrated) opportunities rooted in training and mentoring, can become both a way to engage graduate students in a conversation about a range of career options (in and out of academia) and a way to recruit early career talent (in our case, into educational development). Effective training and professional development become key to orienting students from different disciplinary backgrounds (and with varying degrees of teaching experience) to a common ground of curriculum design and teaching advancement. The 'Students as Partners' framework, which allows for genuine collaboration and immersion in the work, builds graduate students' confidence in doing the work and allows them to acquire the skills and expertise to pursue a career in educational development.

Lived Experience Insight

Shared by Kristina C. Noble, Aviation Industry, USA

The Challenge

An aviation company announced a competitive summer internship to be filled by an undergraduate student. The internship focused on learning with the Chief Operations Executive and on the following tasks: planning and supervising the overall operations strategy, setting priorities and managing projects to create and work within the operations budget, developing quality assurance programs, and ensuring everyone completed their tasks on schedule. The internship aimed to bridge the knowledge students gained at university with the operational activities at every level of a company. The only requirement for the trainee was excellent written and verbal communication skills.

The Context

The Chief Operations Executive of the aviation company contacted the student club of a local university to give a presentation as a keynote speaker to attract talented students for the internship. The event had the full participation of all undergraduate classes and was a success. Students were given the opportunity to write a summary of what they learned from the event as part of their class assignments, and they were all highly impressed with the talk. The keynote speaker talked about the real challenges of his job as Chief Operations Executive. Women were strongly encouraged to apply for the internship. However, the student interest in the talk did not translate to applications for the internship.

Action Taken

Subsequently, the company asked for the help of the careers office at the university to convince students to apply to the aviation company summer internship. A member of the careers office organized a new meeting with a group of students who signed up for more information about the specific summer internship. However, the aviation company did not send any of their employees or agents to the meeting because they thought they had a unique opportunity with their summer internship. The company did not take any further action to attract students to apply.

The Outcome

The recruitment effort at the event failed, and the aviation company did not receive any applications for their summer internship role. Although students were impressed with the talk by the Chief Operations Executive, they felt the internship was too complicated and stressful. Most undergraduate and non-executive MBA students had never worked in a corporate environment, and the only jobs they ever had were at retail shops or in their family businesses. Other companies (e.g. those in the beverages sector) were in direct competition, offering internships that aligned more closely with students' identities and experiences. The aviation company was disappointed with the outcome but did not take any further investigation to understand the failure of its attraction strategy.

Lessons Learned and Advice

The Chief Operations Executive should have focused on the specific student profile and discussed their mentorship program. Instead, he focused on the challenges of his job at the aviation company, which were extremely demanding. Taking into account other companies competing for talent for their internships, it is also necessary to build reassuring relationships by having a company employee present at meetings to make students feel comfortable, protected, and engaged in the next step of their lives. In sum, the aviation company did not know the students' work identity and how to approach them to market the opportunities of such a challenging internship. Consequently, their attraction strategy failed.

Reflection on Lived Experience Insights

The four lived experience insights covering Canada, the UK, and the USA evidence some challenges and opportunities around attracting early career talent. The second and last insights highlight the difficulties of attracting applicants to the fundraising sector and the aviation industry. The first and last insights provide contrasting examples of effective and ineffective attraction strategies.

For instance, in the first insight, the media and entertainment company increased the quality and diversity of applicants via a multi-dimension attraction strategy focusing on (i) transparency, (ii) values, (iii) authentic branding, (iv) thinking outside the box with the use of social media, (v) engaging with schools and universities, and (vi) a commitment to corporate social responsibility.

The last insight shows the disastrous consequences of an attraction approach whereby an organization does not (i) understand the work identity and values of potential applicants, (ii) engagingly communicate opportunities, and (iii) send a variety of people from different levels of the organization to engage students and encourage them to apply. The second and third insights also highlight additional challenges, such as (i) a lack of resources, (ii) a mismatch between the skills required and the skills students possess, and (iii) attracting individuals from different disciplinary programs.

We also see in the second and third insights examples of how the university could support the attraction process for specific sectors by (i) providing tailored training courses, and (ii) acting as a gateway to discovering career pathways that students might not otherwise have considered.

CONCLUSION

In this chapter, we (i) provided an overview of Generation Z and Industry 4.0, (ii) explored the challenges of attracting early career talent, (iii) offered opportunities for attracting early career talent, and (iv) presented four lived experience insights.

If you are a student reading this book, you might like to consider the following questions:

- Are there opportunities here for you to take practical steps to attend certain attraction events?
- Could attending such events enhance your knowledge of specific industries or organizations?
- Are there opportunities for you to develop a professional network and increase your visibility in preparation for applying for graduate roles?
- Perhaps you can think of other events that would be useful and have not been mentioned in this chapter. If so, can you communicate these to your university career service and help to put such opportunities in place for the benefit of you and your peers?

If you are a graduate recruiter reading this book, you might like to follow up by reading some of the practitioner reports cited throughout this chapter. You might like to consider the following questions:

- What opportunities exist to partner with other organizations or universities to increase the visibility and attractiveness of your organization?

- Do you feel there is sufficient integration between your role acting as an agent of the organization and the broader organizational objectives and business needs? Perhaps there could be greater alignment between the marketing/ branding and recruitment teams to deliver a cohesive message to potential applicants.
- Does online, in-person, or a blend of both approaches give your organization the best opportunity to enhance its appeal to students?
- Do you have strategies in place to deal with the challenges of talent attraction?

Keep these thoughts in the front of your mind as we move through the two remaining chapters of Section Three, which discuss how graduate recruiters can prepare students for undertaking the university-to-work transition (Chapter 6), as well as establish and maintain the Person-Organization Fit (POF) of early career talent (Chapter 7). Taken together, these three chapters offer a platform for graduate recruiters to consider innovative ways to establish and maintain talent pipelines necessary for the sustainability of organizations and career ecosystems.

REFERENCES

Afshari, L., & Nasab, A. H. (2021). Enhancing Organizational Learning Capability Through Managing Talent: Mediation Effect Of Intellectual Capital. *Human Resource Development International*, *24*(1), 48–64. doi:10.1080/13678868.2020.1727239

Alexander, E. C., Mader, D. R. D., & Mader, F. H. (2019). Using social media during the hiring process: A comparison between recruiters and job seekers. *Journal of Global Scholars of Marketing*, *29*(1), 78–87. doi:10.1080/21639159.2018.1552530

Ball, C. (2021). *Graduate Migration Patterns in the UK.* Luminate. https://luminate.prospects.ac.uk/graduate-migration-patterns-in-the-uk

Ball, C. (2023). *3 Ways to Build A Deeper Graduate Talent Pool.* InSights. https://insights.ise.org.uk/attraction-and-marketing/blog-3-ways-to-build-a-deeper-graduate-talent-pool/

Barhate, B., & Dirani, K. M. (2021). Career aspirations of Generation Z: A systematic literature review. *European Journal of Training and Development*, *46*(1/2), 139–157. doi:10.1108/EJTD-07-2020-0124

Baruch, Y. (2015). Organizational and labor market as career eco-system. In A. De Vos & B. I. J. M. Van der Heijden (Eds.), *Handbook of Research on Sustainable Careers* (pp. 164–180). Edward Elgar. doi:10.4337/9781782547037.00029

Baruch, Y., Ashleigh, M. J., & Donald, W. E. (2023). A sustainable career ecosystem perspective of talent flow and acquisition: The interface between higher education and industry. In W. E. Donald (Ed.), *Handbook of Research on Sustainable Career Ecosystems for University Students and Graduates* (pp. 177–194). IGI Global., doi:10.4018/978-1-6684-7442-6.ch010

Cappelli, P. (1999). *The New Deal at Work*. Harvard Business School Press.

Careers2032 Project. (2022). *An industry research project co-produced by AGCAS, ISE, Wonkhe and Handshake, looking at the careers sector of 2032 and the role technology could play in facilitating human connections*. Handshake. https://joinhandshake.co.uk/careers2032

Chillakuri, B. (2020). Understanding Generation Z expectations for effective onboarding. *Journal of Organizational Change Management*, *33*(7), 1277–1296. doi:10.1108/JOCM-02-2020-0058

Clark-Ambrosini, J. L., Ashleigh, M. J., Higgs, M., & Baruch, Y. (2023). Quid pro quo? The future for graduate development programmes through the lens of talent management. *International Journal of Human Resource Management*, *34*(17), 3253–3276. doi:10.1080/09585192.2022.2117991

Črešnar, R., & Nedelko, Z. (2020). Understanding future leaders: How are personal values of generations Y and Z tailored to leadership in industry 4.0? *Sustainability (Basel)*, *12*(11), 4417. doi:10.3390u12114417

De Jong, M. D., Harkink, K. M., & Barth, S. (2018). Making green stuff? Effects of corporate greenwashing on consumers. *Journal of Business and Technical Communication*, *31*(1), 77–112. doi:10.1177/1050651917729863 PMID:30034204

Donald, W. E. (2017). *Students' perceptions of graduate employability: A sequential explanatory approach*. Doctoral Thesis, University of Southampton. https://eprints.soton.ac.uk/id/eprint/415935

Donald, W. E. (2021). *Conceptualisation of a new 'Early Careers Talent Pipeline' Framework: Enhancing Organisational Sustainability via Feedback-Seeking Behaviour*. Graduate Recruitment Bureau. doi:10.13140/RG.2.2.28278.47684

Donald, W. E. (2023a). Preface. In W. E. Donald (Ed.), *Handbook of Research on Sustainable Career Ecosystems for University Students and Graduates*, (Preface). IGI Global. doi:10.4018/978-1-6684-7442-6

Donald, W. E. (2023b). Sustainable talent pipelines and person-organisation fit: Strategic insights from UK graduates. *Career Development International*, *28*(2), 234–249. doi:10.1108/CDI-10-2022-0285

Donald, W. E., Ashleigh, M. J., & Baruch, Y. (2018). Students' perceptions of education and employability: Facilitating career transition from higher education into the labor market. *Career Development International*, *23*(5), 513–540. doi:10.1108/CDI-09-2017-0171

Donald, W. E., Baruch, Y., & Ashleigh, M. J. (2023). Technological transformation and human resource development of early career talent: Insights from accounting, banking, and finance. *Human Resource Development Quarterly*, *34*(3), 329–348. doi:10.1002/hrdq.21491

Donald, W. E., & Jackson, D. (2022). Subjective wellbeing among university students and recent graduates: Evidence from the United Kingdom. *International Journal of Environmental Research and Public Health*, *19*(11), a,6911. doi:10.3390/ijerph19116911

Donald, W. E., & Pychtin, P. (2022). Optimization of job boards and the graduate recruitment process: Advancing HRM strategies for the acquisition of early career talent. In D. Mentor (Ed.), *Handbook of Research on New Media, Training, and Skill Development for the Modern Workplace* (pp. 47–66). IGI Global., doi:10.4018/978-1-6684-3996-8.ch003

Forbes. (2019). *10 Ways Employers Can Attract Top Graduate Talent*. Forbes. https://www.forbes.com/sites/forbeshumanresourcescouncil/2019/05/31/10-ways-employers-can-attract-top-grad-talent/?sh=354715d64094

Goh, E., & Okumus, F. (2020). Avoiding the hospitality workforce bubble: Strategies to attract and retain generation Z talent in the hospitality workforce. *Tourism Management Perspectives*, *33*, 100603. doi:10.1016/j.tmp.2019.100603

Green, G. (2020). *Attracting and Retaining Graduate Talent with Local Opportunities*. Luminate. https://luminate.prospects.ac.uk/attracting-and-retaining-graduate-talent-with-local-opportunities

Grimm, A. (2019). Studying to stay: Understanding graduate visa policy content and context in the United States and Australia. *International Migration (Geneva, Switzerland)*, *57*(5), 235–251. doi:10.1111/imig.12561

Handshake. (2022). *Graduate employer priorities 2023*. Handshake. www.handshake.co.uk/gep

Hawes, D. (2022). *ISE Conference 2022 Roundup*. GRB. https://www.grb.uk.com/employer-services/blog/ise-conference-2022-roundup

Hiltrop, J.-M. (1999). The quest for the best: Human resources practices to attract and retain talent. *European Management Journal*, *17*(4), 422–430. doi:10.1016/S0263-2373(99)00022-5

Holland, P., Sheehan, C., & De Cieri, H. (2007). Attracting and retaining talent: Exploring human resources development trends in Australia. *Human Resource Development International*, *10*(3), 247–262. doi:10.1080/13678860701515158

Jackson, D., Richardson, J., Michelson, G., & Munir, R. (2022). Attracting accounting and finance graduate talent – beyond the Big Four. *Accounting and Finance*, *62*(3), 3761–3790. doi:10.1111/acfi.12904

Joo, M.-K., Lee, J.-Y., Kong, D. T., & Jolly, P. M. (2023). Gender diversity advantage at middle management: Implications for high performance work system improvement and organizational performance. *Human Resource Management*, *62*(5), 765–785. doi:10.1002/hrm.22159

Kamil, J., & Amann, J. (2023). *Drop ChatGPT if you Care About Inclusion*. Develop Diverse. https://bootstrapping.dk/ny-forskning-drop-chatgpt-hvis-i-bekymrer-jer-om-inklusion/

Keppeler, F., & Papenfuß, U. (2021). Employer branding and recruitment: Social media field experiments targeting future public employees. *Public Administration Review*, *81*(4), 763–775. doi:10.1111/puar.13324

Khanna, P., & Dutta, R. (2023). Designing Gen Z careers: A design thinking approach to sustainable careers. In W. E. Donald (Ed.), *Handbook of Research on Sustainable Career Ecosystems for University Students and Graduates* (pp. 428–449). IGI Global. doi:10.4018/978-1-6684-7442-6.ch022

King, C., Madera, J. M., Lee, L., Murillo, E., Bauum, T., & Solnet, D. (2021). Reimagining attraction and retention of hospitality management talent – A multilevel identity perspective. *Journal of Business Research*, *136*, 251–262. doi:10.1016/j.jbusres.2021.07.044

Kriener, F., & Fischer, S. (2022). Hiring during change: A dynamic consideration of person-environment fit. *Academy of Management Proceedings, 2022*(1), doi:10.5465/AMBPP.2022.17171abstract

Liu, C. H., Pinder-Amaker, S., Hahm, H., & Chen, J. A. (2020). Priorities for addressing the impact of the COVID-19 pandemic on student mental health. *Journal of American College Health*, *70*(5), 1356–1358. doi:10.1080/07448481.2020.1803882 PMID:33048654

Locke, R., McGinty, M., Guerrero Ramirez, G., & Sellers, K. (2022). Attracting new talent to the government public health workforce: Strategies for improved recruitment of public health graduates. *Journal of Public Health Management and Practice*, *28*(1), 235–243. doi:10.1097/PHH.0000000000001336 PMID:33570871

Marr, B. (2018). *What is Industry 4.0? Here's A Super Easy Explanation for Anyone*. Forbes. https://www.forbes.com/sites/bernardmarr/2018/09/02/what-is-industry-4-0-heres-a-super-easy-explanation-for-anyone/?sh=41167f7d9788

McCracken, M., Currie, D., & Harrison, J. (2016). Understanding graduate recruitment, development and retention for the enhancement of talent management: Sharpening 'the edge' of graduate talent. *International Journal of Human Resource Management*, *27*(22), 2727–2752. doi:10.1080/09585192.2015.1102159

McKinsey & Company. (2022). *What are Industry 4.0, the Fourth Industrial Revolution, and 4IR?* McKinsey & Company. https://www.mckinsey.com/featured-insights/mckinsey-explainers/what-are-industry-4-0-the-fourth-industrial-revolution-and-4ir

McKinsey Global Institute. (2017). *Jobs Lost, Jobs Gained: What the Future of Work will Mean for Jobs, Skills and Wages*. McKinsey. https://www.mckinsey.com/featured-insights/future-of-work/jobs-lost-jobs-gained-what-the-future-of-work-will-mean-for-jobs-skills-and-wages

Nimmi, P. M., & Donald, W. E. (2023). Modelling the Interaction Between Serious Leisure, Self-Perceived Employability, Stress, and Workplace Well-being: Empirical Insights from Graduates in India. *Personnel Review*, *54*(1), 272–287. doi:10.1108/PR-04-2021-0305

Nurjanah, D., & Indawati, N. (2021). Effect of emotional intelligence on employee engagement and job satisfaction with work-life balance as intervening variables in the Generation Z in Surabaya. [IJEMBIS]. *International Journal of Economics, Management, Business, And Social Science*, *1*(3), 316–328.

Pandita, D. (2022). Innovation in talent management practices: Creating an innovative employer branding strategy to attract generation Z. *International Journal of Innovation Science*, *14*(3/4), 556–569. doi:10.1108/IJIS-10-2020-0217

Pew Research Center. (2018). *Defining Generations: Where Millennials End And Generation Z Begins*. Pew Research. https://www.pewresearch.org/short-reads/2019/01/17/where-millennials-end-and-generation-z-begins/

Pham, T. (2021). *Navigating the Host Labour Market: International Graduates Need More Than Credentials*. Centre for Global Higher Education, Department of Education, University of Oxford.

Pohl, E., Ajadi, T., Soucy, T., Carroll, H., Earl, J., Verduyn, C., & Connolly, M. (2022). "Knowing nothing about EDI:" A collaborative autoethnography exploring how an anti-racist project was created, publicized, and silenced. *International Journal for Students as Partners*, *6*(1), 30–46. doi:10.15173/ijsap.v6i1.4882

Rousseau, D. M. (1995). *Psychological Contracts in Organizations: Understanding Written and Unwritten Agreements*. Sage (Atlanta, Ga.). doi:10.4135/9781452231594

Russo, M. (2019). Gen Z is coming. Is your firm prepared? *ARCHITECT*, *108*(8), 68–70.

Sánchez-Hernández, M. I., González-López, Ó. R., Buenadicha-Mateos, M., & Tato-Jiménez, J. L. (2019). Work-life balance in great companies and pending issues for engaging new generations at work. *International Journal of Environmental Research and Public Health*, *16*(24), 5122. doi:10.3390/ijerph16245122 PMID:31847460

Sanctuary Graduates. (2017). *The Top 10 Ways to Attract Graduates Without Having to Go Onto Campus Yourself*. Sanctuary Graduates. https://sanctuarygraduates.co.uk/top-10-ways-attract-graduates-without-going-onto-campus/

Semencuka, M. (2022). How Do Sustainable Practices Impact Graduate Attraction and Retention? *Insights*.https://insights.ise.org.uk/attraction-and-marketing/blog-how-do-sustainable-practices-impact-graduate-attraction-and-retention/

Speckemeier, L., & Tsivrikos, D. (2022). Evidence of greenwashing in talent attraction: Is deceptive marketing an effective recruitment strategy? *European Journal of Business and Management*, *7*(3), 14–25. doi:10.24018/ejbmr.2022.7.3.1406

Spence, M. (1973). Job market signalling. *The Quarterly Journal of Economics*, *87*(3), 355–374. doi:10.2307/1882010

Spence, M. (1978). Job market signaling. In P. Diamond & M. Rothschild (Eds.), *Understanding in Economics* (pp. 281–306). Academic Press. doi:10.1016/B978-0-12-214850-7.50025-5

Stumpf, A. M., & Fielding, R. (2023). Fulfilling Gen Z's needs and expectations of Industry 4.0: Attracting and retaining early career talent. In W. E. Donald (Ed.), *Handbook of Researchn on Sustainable Career Ecosystems for University Students and Graduates* (pp. 258–277). IGI Global. doi:10.4018/978-1-6684-7442-6.ch014

Tang, M., & Jiang, W. (2023). Chinese international graduates in the Australian labor market: Employability capitals and wellbeing. In W. E. Donald (Ed.), *Handbook of Research on Sustainable Career Ecosystems for University Students and Graduates* (pp. 214–237). IGI Global. doi:10.4018/978-1-6684-7442-6.ch012

The Economist. (2019). Generation Z is stressed, depressed, and exam-obsessed. *The Economist.* https://www.economist. com/graphic-detail/2019/02/27/generation-z-is-stressed-depressed-and-exam-obsessed

Van der Heijden, B. I. J. M., & De Vos, A. (2015). Sustainable careers: Introductory chapter. In A. De Vos & B. I. J. M. Van der Heijden (Eds.), *Handbook of Research on Sustainable Careers* (pp. 1–19). Edward Elgar. doi:10.4337/9781782547037.00006

Wallace, M., Lings, I., & Cameron, R. (2012). Industry branding: Attracting talent to weaker profile industries. *Asia Pacific Journal of Human Resources, 50*(4), 483–502. doi:10.1111/j.1744-7941.2012.00040.x

Wanous, J. P. (1975). Organizational entry: Newcomers moving from outside to inside. *Psychological Bulletin, 84*(4), 601–618. doi:10.1037/0033-2909.84.4.601

White, M., & McCallum, F. (2021). Crisis or Catalyst? Examining COVID-19's implications for wellbeing and resilience education. In M. White & F. McCallum (Eds.), *Wellbeing and Resilience Education: COVID-19 and Its Impact on Education*. Routledge. doi:10.4324/9781003134190-1

World Economic Forum. (2018). *Machines Will Do More Tasks Than Humans by 2025 but Robot Revolution Will Still Create 58 Million Net New Jobs in Next Five Years.* WEF. https://www.weforum.org/press/2018/09/machines-will-do-more-tasks-than-humans-by-2025-but-robot-revolution-will-still-create-58-million-net-new-jobs-in-next-five-years/

Zaharee, M., Lipkie, T., Mehlman, S. K., & Neylon, S. K. (2018). Recruitment and retention of early-career technical talent. *Research Technology Management, 61*(5), 51–61. doi:10.1080/08956308.2018.1495966

ADDITIONAL READING

Aljbour, A., French, E., & Ali, M. (2022). An evidence-based multilevel framework of talent management: A systematic review. *International Journal of Productivity and Performance Management*, *71*(8), 3348–3376. doi:10.1108/IJPPM-02-2020-0065

Benítez-Márquez, M. D., Sánchez-Teba, E. M., Bermúdez-Gonález, G., & Núñez-Rydman, E. S. (2022). Generation Z within the workforce and the workplace: A bibliometric analysis. *Frontiers in Psychology*, *12*, 736820. doi:10.3389/fpsyg.2021.736820 PMID:35178005

DeIuliis, E. D., & Saylor, E. (2021). Bridging the gap: Three strategies to optimize professional relationships with generation Y and Z. *The Open Journal of Occupational Therapy*, *9*(1), 1–13. doi:10.15453/2168-6408.1748

Gaidhani, S., Arora, L., & Sharma, B. K. (2019). Understanding the attitude of generation Z towards the workplace. *International Journal of Management. Technology and Engineering*, *9*(1), 2804–2812.

Grow, J. M., & Yang, S. (2018). Generation-Z enters the advertising workplace: Expectations through a gendered lens. *Journal of Advertising Education*, *22*(1), 7–22. doi:10.1177/1098048218768595

Jooss, M., McDonnel, A., & Conroy, K. (2021). Flexible global working arrangements: An integrative review and future research agenda. *Human Resource Management Review*, *31*(4), 100780. doi:10.1016/j.hrmr.2020.100780

Kautish, P., Hameed, A., Kour, P., & Walia, S. (2020). Career beliefs, self-efficacy and VUCA skills: A study among generation Z female students of tourism and hospitality. *Journal of Hospitality, Leisure, Sport and Tourism Education*, *30*, 100340. doi:10.1016/j.jhlste.2021.100340

McKinsey Global Institute. (2023). *Performance Through People: Transforming Human Capital into Competitive Advantage.* McKinsey. https://www.mckinsey.com/mgi/our-research/performance-through-people-transforming-human-capital-into-competitive-advantage

Schroth, H. (2019). Are you ready for Gen Z in the workplace? *California Management Review*, *61*(3), 5–18. doi:10.1177/0008125619841006

Sehra, S. (2023). *Unlocking the Secrets to Recruiting and Retaining Today's Young Workers*. Talent Mgmt. https://www.talentmgt.com/articles/2023/04/19/unlocking-the-secrets-to-recruiting-and-retaining-todays-young-workers/?utm_source=bambu&utm_medium=social&blaid=4527090

Chapter 6
Preparing Students for the University-to-Work Transition

ABSTRACT

This chapter focuses on preparing students for the university-to-work transition, predominantly from the perspectives of graduate recruiters and recruitment agency representatives acting on behalf of organizations. First, the university-to-work transition is defined, and the benefits organizations can expect from hiring graduates are considered. Next, the Graduate Recruitment Attraction Matrix (GRAM) is introduced, encompassing twenty-five activities to enhance talent attraction efforts and prepare students for undertaking the university-to-work transition. The four quadrants that form the GRAM are subsequently explored, followed by the activities grouped into six themes: (i) careers fairs, (ii) presentations and panel events, (iii) sponsorship and ambassador roles, (iv) networking and mentoring, (v) experience opportunities, and (vi) diversity-focused events. The chapter concludes with four lived experience insights offering real-world examples of the challenges and opportunities associated with preparing students for the university-to-work transition.

INTRODUCTION

In Section Two of this book, we explored graduate employability and employability capital (Chapter 2), strategies to encourage students to utilize their university career services (Chapter 3), and how university career services can assist students in signaling their employability to potential employers (Chapter 4). Now, we will revisit some of those themes. However, this chapter aims to explore how graduate recruiters and

DOI: 10.4018/978-1-6684-9827-9.ch006

recruitment agency representatives who act on behalf of organizations can prepare students for the transition from university to the professional world. This builds upon and complements previously discussed talent attraction strategies (Chapter 5).

Examining the topic of preparing students for the university-to-work transition from the perspectives of graduate recruiters and recruitment agency representatives is particularly relevant. Healy, Hammer et al. (2022) analyzed the direct citation networks among 4,068 journal articles focused on graduate employability and career development. They discovered that "despite clear alignment of research concerns and educational goals, there has been limited theoretical or practical exchange between the two fields" (p. 799). We begin to address the research gap in this chapter, with further exploration in Chapters 8 and 9, which delve into the challenges and opportunities for collaboration among various actors operating within a sustainable career ecosystem (Donald, 2023).

The current chapter is structured as follows. Initially, the university-to-work transition is defined, and the benefits organizations can expect from hiring graduates are considered. Next, the Graduate Recruitment Attraction Matrix (GRAM) is introduced, encompassing twenty-five activities mapped across four quadrants that organizations can use to attract talent and prepare students for the university-to-work transition. The four quadrants that form the GRAM are subsequently explored, along with the twenty-five activities grouped by six themes. The chapter concludes with four lived experience insights, offering examples of real-world challenges, strategic approaches, and outcomes related to the issue of preparing students for the university-to-work transition.

THE UNIVERSITY-TO-WORK TRANSITION

The university-to-work transition refers to the period when individuals move from academic to professional life, typically after graduation (Ng & Feldman, 2007). It can be a challenging phase as individuals navigate the job market, adjust to new work environments, and take on new routines and responsibilities. From a sustainable career perspective, the university-to-work transition is seen as "the intersection of education and work, shaped by the individual (i.e., person) operating in different contexts (i.e., educational, organizational, and societal) over time (i.e., a career transition process)" (Blokker et al., 2023, p. 243). Properly preparing students for this transition is crucial because a successful transition increases the likelihood of career sustainability, while an unsuccessful transition can have negative consequences throughout an individual's career and lifespan (Akkermans, Blokker et al., 2021; Zacher & Froidevaux, 2021).

Preparing students for the university-to-work transition not only enhances their employability and post-graduation employment prospects but also positively impacts organizations (Buckholtz & Donald, 2022). The unique perspectives, skills, and knowledge of graduates enhance the ability of organizations to adapt, compete, and thrive in a dynamic business landscape (The Graduate Project, 2023). Therefore, recruiters and representatives from recruitment agencies recognize the significance of attracting high-quality applicants from diverse backgrounds to their organizations (Ab Wahab & Tatoglu, 2020).

Additionally, hiring graduates offers a cost-effective talent management strategy, as they often have lower salary expectations compared to individuals with similar skill sets but more labor market experience (Graduate Recruitment Bureau, 2023). As a result, organizations can invest the money they save on wages to provide graduates with training opportunities and foster growth to develop them into future leaders. This investment cultivates specific organizational capital or firm-specific knowledge and skills (Wright et al., 2014), whereby organizational investment in human capital pays dividends over time (Rodrigues et al., 2020). Consequently, organizations can gain a sustainable competitive advantage by preparing students for the university-to-work transition, hiring graduates, and retaining graduate talent (D'Armagnac et al., 2022; Donald et al., 2020).

However, as identified in Chapter 5, organizations face challenges in attracting early career talent, including:

- The war for talent and skill shortages
- Attracting diverse talent
- Mental health, wellbeing, and flexible working
- Corporate citizenship: Social and environmental impacts

In response, we previously explored some opportunities for attracting early career talent, including:

- Early and ongoing engagement
- Authentic branding, values, and culture
- Compensation, benefits, and development opportunities

Building on these opportunities from Chapter 5, our attention now turns to twenty-five activities mapped to a four-box matrix that organizations can use to attract talent and prepare students for the university-to-work transition.

THE GRADUATE RECRUITMENT ATTRACTION MATRIX (GRAM)

The Graduate Recruitment Attraction Matrix (GRAM) was developed based on interviews I carried out with university career advisors and graduate recruiters in the United Kingdom during the COVID-19 pandemic (Donald et al., 2023a). Figure 1 shows the GRAM, with twenty-five activities mapped to one or more quadrants. Some activities appear in multiple quadrants because they can be run in different formats. Subsequently, an overview of each quadrant is provided, and the activities are grouped by six themes.

Figure 1. Graduate Recruitment Attraction Matrix
(C) 2023 Donald, Baruch & Ashleigh. Used with permission.

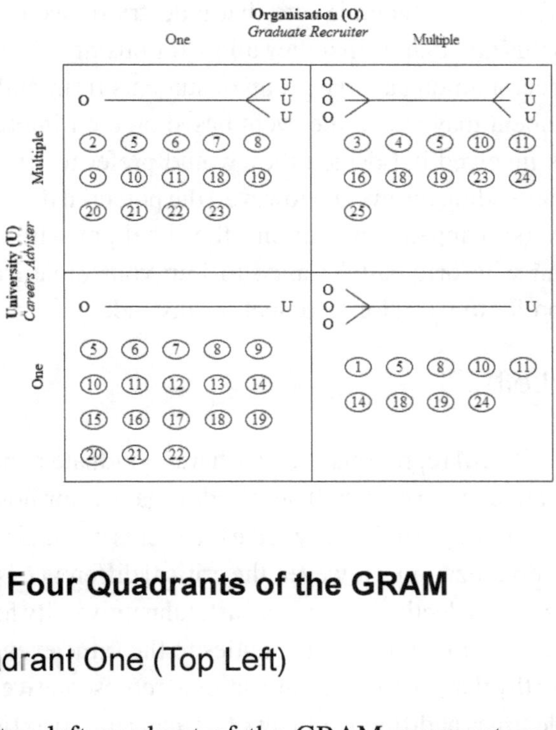

ID	Activity
1	University careers fair
2	Company careers fair
3	National careers fair
4	Regional careers fair
5	Industry focused presentations
6	Company focused presentations
7	Application process presentations
8	Skills based presentations
9	Mock assessment centres
10	Panel events
11	Networking events
12	Guest lectures
13	Sponsoring a course or module
14	Student society event
15	Sponsoring student society
16	Mentoring
17	Student ambassador scheme
18	Diversity focused event
19	Financial services event
20	Office visits
21	Virtual office tours
22	Virtual engagement days
23	University collaboration events
24	Organisation collaborative events
25	Graduate agency events

The Four Quadrants of the GRAM

Quadrant One (Top Left)

The top left quadrant of the GRAM represents events where a single graduate recruiter or recruitment agency representative, who works on behalf of a particular organization, organizes an event inviting students from multiple universities. While multiple organizations may hold similar events, each event is conducted separately by their respective representatives. These events aim to promote a specific organization and assist students from various universities in transitioning from their academic life to that organization. The advantage of organizing events in this quadrant is that it saves time and money by hosting a single event for students from multiple universities. It also helps to showcase your organization without having to share the exposure from the event with other employers. However, the drawback is that you have to offer more generic content because you cannot tailor the event to the needs of students from a single university. This could pose a challenge if the attending students from different universities have distinct perspectives, experiences, and needs.

Quadrant Two (Top Right)

The top right quadrant of the GRAM represents events where multiple graduate recruiters or recruitment agency representatives acting on behalf of different organizations jointly arrange an event and invite students from various universities. These events aim to promote a specific industry or sector and prepare students from different universities to transition from academia into that industry or sector. The advantage of hosting events in this quadrant is that they allow for raising awareness about a particular industry or sector among a large group of students from multiple universities. Additionally, a student may attend the event based on their interest in one of the other organizations involved but decide they would prefer to work for your organization instead after attending the event. However, the potential downside of these events is that the reverse happens and sharing the limelight with other organizations means that talent who originally wanted to join your organization now decides that they would prefer to work for a competitor instead.

Quadrant Three (Bottom Left)

The bottom left quadrant of the GRAM represents events where a graduate recruiter or recruitment agency representative acting on behalf of a single organization hosts an event exclusively for students from a single university. Like the events in Quadrant 1, the aim is to promote a specific organization. However, the critical difference is that the representative of the organization selectively targets a particular university for the event rather than inviting students from multiple universities to the same event at a single point in time. It is noteworthy that the same organizational representative may conduct the same event multiple times at different universities, catering specifically to the students of each university. The advantage of organizing events in this quadrant is that the agent of the organization can create a more personalized experience since each event can be tailored slightly differently to cater to the students of a specific university. This targeted approach can make the event feel more intimate and relevant to the attendees. On the downside, running the same event multiple times for students from different universities requires additional time and incurs extra costs to the organization. This is the opposite of the benefit provided by events in Quadrant 1, where hosting a single event for students from multiple universities saves time and money. Consequently, a representative from an organization may choose to host events at a limited number of universities one at a time (Quadrant 3) but also opt to run the event for students from all universities (Quadrant 1) in an attempt to strike a balance between the advantages and disadvantages of both approaches.

Quadrant Four (Bottom Right)

The bottom right quadrant of the GRAM represents events where multiple graduate recruiters or recruitment agency representatives acting on behalf of different organizations host an event exclusively for students from a specific university. Like those events in Quadrant 2, the focus is on promoting an industry or sector with the hope that students will also consider joining the specific organization the agent is representing at the event. The critical distinction between Quadrant 2 and Quadrant 4 is that in Quadrant 4, the events are conducted for students from one university at a time. However, the same representatives may organize the same event multiple times at various universities, explicitly targeting the students of each university. The benefits of events in Quadrant 4 are similar to those in Quadrant 2, as they raise awareness about a particular industry. Additionally, events in Quadrant 4 share the advantage of Quadrant 3, as they can be tailored to cater to the students from a specific university. However, there are downsides similar to Quadrant 3, such as the additional time and cost required to run multiple events. Additionally, like Quadrant 2, attendees might prefer a competitor over your organization after attending the event.

Student Attraction and Preparation Activities

The twenty-five activities in the GRAM are now grouped into six themes which are subsequently explored:

(i) Careers fairs
(ii) Presentations and panel events
(iii) Sponsorship and ambassador roles
(iv) Networking and mentoring
(v) Experience opportunities
(vi) Diversity-focused events

Theme One: Careers Fairs

University career fairs traditionally entail representatives from multiple employers traveling to various universities for one or two days at a time (Quadrant 4 of the GRAM). These events provide opportunities for recruiters and employees to network with students, showcase their organizations as desirable workplaces, and allow all parties to assess person-organization fit (an aspect we will explore further when discussing the selection process in Chapter 7). However, over the last five to ten years, employers have observed a steady decline in student engagement when attending university career fairs (Donald et al., 2022). Students have also raised concerns that the fees universities charge organizations to attend their career fairs mean that multinational corporations are overrepresented, whilst small and medium-sized enterprises (SMEs) and other organizations offering local employment opportunities are underrepresented (Donald et al., 2022). Concurrently, increased competition for diverse talent and technological advancements fueled by social restrictions during the COVID-19 pandemic have seen employers begin to favor company, national, and regional career fairs over university career fairs (Donald et al., 2023a).

Company career fairs predominantly involve a single employer meeting students from multiple universities (Quadrant 1 of the GRAM). These events tend to occur at an organization's corporate offices, a neutral off-campus venue, or virtually. National and regional career fairs engage multiple employers and students from various universities simultaneously (Quadrant 2 of the GRAM). These events are often held at convention centers, at a venue provided by a sponsor (e.g. an organization's corporate offices or university campus), or run virtually. The increased prevalence of national and regional career fairs acknowledges that "employability is characterised by the local structural conditions, demographic features and socio-economic norms" (Tran et al., 2022, p. 1). These alternative formats save organizations time and money compared to university career fairs since their representatives no longer have to travel to individual universities on different days. Consequently, organizations can use the time and money they save for strategic planning, marketing, and other events to prepare students for the university-to-work transition (Donald et al., 2022).

Theme Two: Presentations and Panel Events

This theme covers an extensive array of activities, such as:

- Industry-focused presentations
- Company-focused presentations
- Application process presentations
- Skills-based presentations

- Panel events
- Guest lectures
- Student society events

These activities, which sit across multiple GRAM quadrants because of the various ways they can be run, can also be delivered in-person, hybrid, virtually or made available as pre-recorded resources for students.

They serve three core purposes for organizations:

- To raise awareness of the industry and their specific organization
- To provide access to potential early career talent ahead of competitors
- To inform students how to prepare for the university-to-work transition.

In today's dynamic job market, individuals must take ownership of actively shaping their careers (Rudolph et al., 2019). A proactive personality increases the chances of a successful transition from university to the workforce (Zhou et al., 2018), whilst career competencies significantly influence career success (Lo Presti et al., 2022). Activities such as presentations and panel events can assist students in developing career competencies, defined as the "knowledge, skills, and abilities central to career development, which can be influenced and developed by the individual" (Akkermans et al., 2013, p. 249). These competencies involve actively reflecting on and constructing one's career (Tims & Akkermans, 2020). By understanding their personal qualities and motivations, students can establish a solid foundation for sustainable careers by enhancing their adaptability (Blokker et al., 2019; Savickas & Porfeli, 2012).

Furthermore, there is an ongoing discrepancy between the expectations of organizations and graduates (Jackson, 2020). A study conducted in Australia discovered that measures of Graduate Skills (GSS) and Graduate Qualities (GQS) only demonstrated minimal predictive value in terms of employment outcomes (Brown et al., 2021). One possible explanation for these findings is that students may possess the necessary skills but cannot adequately apply them in different contexts (Moore & Morton, 2017). Consequently, universities must adapt to provide a learning environment that effectively equips students and graduates with the requisite skills and the ability to apply them in the workplace (Shtaltovna & Muzzu, 2021). Unfortunately, students who need career support the most are often the least likely to seek it proactively (Donald et al., 2018). Therefore, incorporating employability-focused events into the curriculum can be instrumental in supporting these students to construct their careers via the acquisition of career competencies (Lo Presti et al., 2022).

Another significant advantage of presentations and panel events is their flexibility in terms of format and delivery, allowing employers to tailor their approach to specific groups of students. As a result, employers can become valuable partners in developing employability initiatives and providing proactive, tailored, and timely scaffolding to prepare students for the university-to-work transition (O'Regan et al., 2022). Presentation and panel events also serve as a means to raise awareness among students of contextual factors beyond their agency (Forrier et al., 2018). This exposure helps them develop more realistic expectations and emphasizes the value of psychological capital to navigate setbacks, such as rejection decisions (Zucker, 2019). Encouraging the acquisition of psychological capital can also lead to additional benefits of increased self-perceived employability and enhanced wellbeing outcomes (e.g., Baluku et al., 2021; Donald, 2017; Donald et al., 2019; Nimmi, Kuriakose et al., 2021; Nimmi et al., 2022).

Theme Three: Sponsorship and Ambassador Roles

University campuses offer various sponsorship opportunities, including support for student societies, specific degree courses or modules, or prizes related to performance. In these arrangements, an employer provides sponsorship through financial assistance or other benefits, expecting to promote their brand and company logo through various means (e.g., clothing, posters, flyers, and websites). The primary objective is to raise brand awareness on campus and differentiate themselves from competitors. However, another important objective can be to target specific groups of students to try and increase the diversity of an early career talent pipeline (Bright Network, 2022). By sponsoring specific initiatives, organizations can effectively leverage the marketing efforts of 100 to 200 students (Davies, 2014). However, the trade-off of a high volume of students is that promotion is often done passively. Therefore, to maximize the benefits, organizations should consider combining sponsorship opportunities with the involvement of campus ambassadors, who can actively and engagingly represent the organization on campus.

Being a student ambassador offers a unique employment opportunity characterized by part-time work, flexible hours, and compensation in the form of an hourly rate or a monthly stipend (Miao, 2021). Unlike many other job options, this arrangement effectively balances students' study and work commitments. The involvement of student ambassadors can benefit the organization, the student ambassador, and fellow students on campus. From an employer perspective, it provides valuable exposure to potential early career talent. Research conducted in the USA on consumer behavior has shown that micro-influencers (non-celebrity influencers such as peers) are perceived as more credible, believable, and knowledgeable than the general population (Berger & Keller Fay Group, 2016). The same report found that 82% of consumers are likely to follow a recommendation from a micro-influencer. Additionally, student ambassadors gain valuable insights into the organization's culture and marketing techniques, as well as access to networking opportunities with employees, the graduate recruitment team, and fellow students on campus (Violet, 2019). Finally, from the perspective of fellow students on campus, engaging with student ambassadors enables them to ask questions they might feel uncomfortable posing to graduate recruiters or other organization representatives. These interactions help students assess their compatibility with the organization's values, understand the necessary skills an organization is looking for, and gain insight into the various stages of the selection process.

Theme Four: Networking and Mentoring

Graduate recruiters and recruitment agency representatives, acting on behalf of organizations, can play a crucial role in providing students with valuable access to networking and mentoring opportunities. These approaches allow students to connect with industry professionals, stay up-to-date with emerging technologies, and gain valuable insights about specific industries and organizations (Hawes, 2023). Alums can offer significant value by providing networking and mentoring opportunities to students. Drawing from their firsthand experiences as former students, applicants, and current employees, they offer relevant insights in a relatable and accessible manner (Donald et al., 2018). The benefits of networking and mentoring are further enhanced through peer learning. As students engage with organization representatives, they acquire valuable insights they can share with their peers, fostering a collaborative learning environment, and enhancing employability and social mobility outcomes (Donald & Ford, 2023). Peer learning also complements formal mentoring by empowering students to exchange knowledge and experiences, enriching the learning process.

Moreover, engaging in networking activities has been shown to increase the likelihood of a successful university-to-work transition (Okay-Somerville et al., 2022). Similarly, mentoring opportunities can positively impact career behaviors and enable individuals to identify areas for self-improvement (Ogbuanya & Chukwuedo, 2017). By providing access to networking and mentoring opportunities, employers can assist students in exploring diverse career options (Green et al., 2020) and making well-informed career decisions (Xin et al., 2020). This support facilitates the development of essential career competencies (Zhou et al., 2018) and various forms of employability capital (Donald et al., 2019; 2023). By understanding their personal qualities and motivations, students can establish a solid foundation for sustainable careers by enhancing their adaptability (Blokker et al., 2019; Savickas & Porfeli,

2012). Therefore, access to networking and mentoring opportunities addresses the immediate challenge of preparing students for the university-to-work transition and equips them with valuable skills and attributes for their future career growth.

Theme Five: Experience Opportunities

Mock assessment centers are a helpful preparation tool for students about to undergo assessment centers as part of the selection process. During my time in industry as a graduate recruiter, I observed numerous candidates dropping out of the process during this stage. Many candidates believed that remaining silent and allowing other applicants to engage in heated discussions was their best strategy. However, this was based on the flawed assumption that everyone started with maximum points and gradually lost points as the activity progressed, which was the opposite of how it worked. As a result, these candidates scored no points because they did not contribute anything. Participating in mock assessment centers would have been extremely valuable for them as they could have received this feedback and modified their behavior accordingly. It could also increase confidence levels in students due to greater familiarity and direct experience with the assessment center process.

Another dimension of the 'experience opportunities' theme encompasses office tours, internships, and placements. These activities offer invaluable opportunities for students to immerse themselves in a professional work environment and engage with employees of the organization. Graduate recruiters and agency representatives play a pivotal role in effectively communicating the value of work experience. They must also facilitate opportunities for students to gain practical exposure through internships, placements, and other programs. Based on an extensive literature review, Jackson and Cook (2023) observed the following benefits for students of participating in work-based learning:

- Improved academic outcomes
- Developing discipline-related skills and knowledge
- Developing professional capabilities
- Career self-management
- Professional identity development
- Perceived employability
- Employment outcomes
- Wellbeing

The researchers also raised concerns about relying solely on self-reported data whilst acknowledging that not all students participating in work-integrated learning will experience all of the mentioned benefits. In the UK, empirical research by Hughes

(2020) and Hughes et al. (2023) supported these views. Hughes et al. (2023) found that the impact of undertaking a placement on competency development varied significantly among students, while students' self-reported competency scores were lower than those reported by their line managers. The researchers noted that "the value of undertaking a placement is often poorly measured (e.g. satisfaction) rather than competency-based outcomes, which can lead to conclusions that are overly simplistic and difficult to use in practice" (p. 1). Consequently, they urge employers to design placement schemes that empower students "to acquire personal resources and signal these to prospective employers as an antecedent to career sustainability" (p. 1).

Theme Six: Diversity-Focused Events

The final theme acknowledges the difficulties employers encounter when trying to develop diverse talent pipelines for early career positions (Careers2032 Project, 2022). While talent exists everywhere, not all applicants from underrepresented groups have equal access to opportunities (LaunchPad, 2022), emphasizing the importance of considering diversity and social mobility when designing and delivering events to prepare students for the university-to-work transition (Trendence, 2020). For instance, access to networking and mentoring opportunities is crucial for underrepresented students who typically, compared to their peers, face resource limitations and lack professional networks (Hawes, 2023). A study in Canada also found that international students seek opportunities to network with employers and call for employers to "be more open-minded about hiring people with international experience and see the benefits of a diverse workforce" (Arthur & Flynn, 2013, p. 28). Another study in the UK also saw international students call for greater opportunities to develop their employability while studying abroad (Fakunle, 2021). Furthermore, employers should ensure that internship and placement opportunities are paid, as students from disadvantaged backgrounds may otherwise be unable to pursue them (Social Mobility Commission, 2017). Excluding talented individuals from accessing such opportunities can be particularly problematic when an organization predominantly or entirely fills their graduate roles from this talent pipeline (Donald et al., 2022).

Additionally, the timing of running events to prepare students for the university-to-work transition is a crucial factor to consider. Some employers start their application process 9-12 months before the potential start date, making it essential to engage talent well in advance. Waiting until the final year of undergraduate study is too late. Instead, employers should aim to access and engage diverse talent during primary and secondary school, as well as through all years of university study (Donald et al., 2018). Supporting diverse student groups has become even more important in the aftermath of the COVID-19 pandemic, as students have shown an increased demand for career-related support (Donald et al., 2021). Graduate recruitment agencies can play a significant role in this regard since as the level of perceived agency support increases, the relationship between positivity and self-perceived employability becomes stronger (Consiglio et al., 2021). In the study, an agency's role was assessed on:

- Providing needed information
- Supporting individuals to deal with difficult occurrences (e.g., rejection decisions)
- Developing an individualized/tailored plan
- Facilitating the development of professional skills.

Providing these services to underrepresented students is critical since performing job search activities systematically rather than haphazardly can improve employment outcomes that determine wellbeing and influence career development trajectories (Van Hooft et al., 2020).

Summary

Generation Z is projected to become the most educated generation in history (Parker & Igielnik, 2020). However, organizations have a crucial role to play in fostering a comprehensive learning approach known as lifewide learning. While lifelong learning emphasizes continuous learning throughout one's life, lifewide learning involves embracing diverse learning opportunities at a particular moment in time (Cole & Donald, 2022). The GRAM categorizes twenty-five activities, mapped into four quadrants and subsequently grouped into six themes, demonstrating how organizations can utilize different activities to support students' lifewide learning and address their own talent acquisition needs. However, it is essential to note that these activities and themes are not exhaustive, and the most suitable ones for any specific organization will depend upon their specific circumstances and goals. Moreover, the six themes suggest there may be a critical need for and benefit of formal partnerships between different actors operating within a sustainable career ecosystem. We explore this idea further from the perspective of challenges and opportunities for bridging the university-employer divide in Chapters 8 and 9, respectively.

Our attention now turns to four lived experience insights offering real-world examples of the challenges and opportunities associated with preparing students for the university-to-work transition.

LIVED EXPERIENCE INSIGHTS

Lived Experience Insight

Shared By Tonia Galati, TG Consulting Ltd, UK

The Challenge

There are many ongoing discussions with higher education institutions about getting students ready for the world of work. Many of the students we support come from backgrounds where they may not have anyone to talk to about the assessment process. So when they come to do assessment centers, the process and setup are a surprise. We aim to provide a safe environment where students come and participate; if they fail, it does not matter. It is the fact that they have tried. The idea is to expose them to a situation they might go through during the recruitment process, enabling them to prepare themselves and build confidence. Our approach is also another way to engage students since not all of them access their university career service.

The Context

Our business is focused on partnerships with our clients. We recognize that all universities are different, and their students have different needs. To provide a meaningful experience, we want to understand their specific barriers. Since the aim is to build confidence, we want students to feel like they belong in that situation and to provide them with reassurance and confidence. For some students, turning up is a massive step, so we want to ensure they get from the day what they need as individuals regardless of where they are on their journey.

Action Taken

We work with each university client to tailor our mock assessment center sessions to provide a bespoke offering and ensure that students get what they need from the experience. For example, whilst we offer presentations, interviews, and group sessions, we are open to switching an aspect out and replacing it with something else if the university client identifies different needs. Once we have these conversations, we start to operationalize the assessment center. Typically, students are allocated into groups and attend either a morning or an afternoon assessment. Upon completion of the mock assessment center, each student is provided with general feedback and a report that identifies areas where they performed well and areas they can reflect upon to help shape their preparation for the real-world assessment centers.

The Outcome

By working in partnership with universities to ensure the assessment centers are timetabled, we get over 80% attendance at the assessment centers, which is really high for such events. We also find the feedback from students is really positive in terms of enhanced confidence in their career aspirations, confidence in themselves, and also this buzz where they have surprised themselves. For example, some students experience initial anxiety around giving presentations but then know what to expect and become more confident. The excellent feedback from students about their experience also means institutions continue to partner with us to prepare their future student cohorts.

Lessons Learned and Advice

My advice would be to tailor the mock assessment center to the audience. Yes, you want a real-world experience that should be maintained throughout. However, because it is a mock assessment center, there is some flexibility to do things slightly differently and break down barriers for students. We set up pre-preparation sessions to allow students to ask questions before the day. We also have an open dialogue with institutions where we each provide input to set up the sessions to provide the best outcomes for their students. We also reflect and review as a team after each session to see what can be improved and keep an eye on how the labor market is evolving. This ensures we remain agile and relevant to the needs of students, universities, and employers.

Lived Experience Insight

Shared By Robert Szabó, Learnship, Germany

The Challenge

Learnship, as a growing international organization, has a series of projects that need overseeing from conceptualization to delivery. These projects may be temporary in nature and require a certain level of expertise in a given area. There are multiple ways to approach the challenge, including hiring freelance employees or employees on fixed-term contracts. However, in Germany, another path exists, collaboration with "werkstudenten" or "working students".

The Context

According to the Munich Business School (2022),

A working student is a student who, in addition to their full-time studies at a university or a state-accredited university of applied science, is employed by a company on a more-than-marginal basis. A student must meet two specific preconditions to qualify as a working student and benefit from the privileges it entails, based on the overarching assumption is always that the student's primary focus is their studies, and work is a secondary priority. Therefore, a working student 1. must be a matriculated student on a full-time program at a university, and 2. must not usually work more than 20 hours per week. Working student status is suspended during semester breaks. (Online)

Action Taken

Over my eight years of working with Learnship, I have managed and collaborated with many working students in my own department and others. Specific projects allocated to these students have included work around 'translation', 'content research', 'business administration', and 'business intelligence'. Working students form part of the team, attend internal meetings, are given company email addresses, and integrate into daily workflows.

The Outcome

On the whole, the system works well. There are some administrative elements to keep in mind. Working students cannot work more than 20 hours per week in any form of employment as they must attend classes on the days they are not at work. Working students are paid the minimum wage (currently 12 Euros per hour) and receive paid annual leave (pro-rata based on the hours worked compared to full-time employees). Line managers must be prepared for specific challenges that students may face, such as exams and the rhythms of the university year. Some students will be more motivated than others. Some will be more apt for the role. Generally, this scheme has been of great benefit to our company and the students alike. Several working students have been offered full-time employment after their studies concluded.

Lessons Learned and Advice

Working students develop in-work skills, such as interdisciplinary collaboration, effective communication, taking ownership of work, providing updates, defending a point of view, and many other aspects of project and task management. The working student model can also benefit employers, per Munich Business School (2022)

As working students usually spend longer at a company than most interns, hiring working students present a useful opportunity for companies to keep an eye out for the talented, up-and-coming professionals of the future. Students bring with them some expertise gained at university, which means they can be integrated more closely into projects. Their fresh perspective and the results they deliver offer genuine added value for the company. The working student model therefore opens doors for both parties – the student and their employer. (Online)

Lived Experience Insight

Shared by Judit Beke and Craig V. Johnson, GiLE Foundation, Hungary

The Challenge

The global war for talent emphasizes the need for higher education institutions to produce highly-skilled graduates ready for the world of work. Unfortunately, a mismatch remains between employers' expectations and the graduates that universities produce. Moreover, universities are struggling to meet the demands of their students for career guidance and support, threatening social mobility opportunities. Subsequently, young people can remain unaware of the need to develop various forms of employability capital, experiences, and personal values during their time spent in education. Additionally, there are insufficient mentors to serve students as agents for positive social change.

The Context

University students in Hungary often fail to equip themselves with critical human skills, hindering their success in life. Human skills are essential because, unlike technical skills, there is less risk of roles requiring these skills being replaced by robots or automation. Part of the problem is that Hungarian and international students often lack the opportunities to develop the necessary personal skills that can act as the foundation for a sustainable career. Consequently, we founded the

Global Institute for Lifelong Empowerment (GiLE Foundation) with the mission to support young people's pursuit of a successful and meaningful life by developing their competencies, and through research and advocacy.

Action Taken

The GiLE Foundation is composed of three pillars: (i) GiLE Academy, (ii) GiLE Advocacy, and (iii) GiLE Journal. The Foundation offers free or subsidized workshops and training sessions to help young people develop vital skills and competencies. The GiLE Journal offers free publication opportunities and helps establish research-based collaborations for young researchers from all fields of study. The GiLE4Youth annual conference addresses three focus areas of the Foundation: (i) career planning, (ii) character building, and (iii) communication skills. The Changemakers Youth Forum (CYF) provides a space for young changemakers and innovators to interact and network with each other and with academics, practitioners, and decision-makers.

The Outcome

Over 150 students have attended one or more of the GiLE Foundation's training sessions, while many more have accessed the blogs and podcasts. Our two international online conferences addressed the skills gap young people face and promoted interdisciplinary synergy between academia, trainers and the corporate sector. GiLE Advocacy has seen the development of the CYF via partnerships with five student/youth organizations. The CYF has provided a youth-led ecosystem to facilitate knowledge sharing, skills development, capacity building, cross-sector collaborations, and networking opportunities for young changemakers. Finally, five issues of our scientific journal, the GiLE Journal of Skills Development, have been published, along with a conference proceedings book.

Lessons Learned and Advice

The GiLE Foundation is continuously evaluating its programs and initiatives to ensure the Foundation adapts to the evolving needs of young people, employers, and society. We learnt that collaboration with other student/youth organizations is beneficial since we can share our knowledge and resources. Our advice would be to think of innovative ways to motivate young people to take responsibility for enhancing their employability and broader personal development. Such an approach can prepare them to undertake sustainable careers and live fulfilling and meaningful lives. Finally, motivated volunteers are essential to helping the GiLE Foundation to attract, engage, and inform as many young people as possible.

Lived Experience Insight

Shared By Rebecca Fielding, Gradconsult Ltd, UK

The Challenge

Preparing students and graduates for the university-to-work transition is a perennial challenge. While universities and employers have made considerable strides in this area, an enormous amount must be taught outside the traditional confines of the academic environment. Indeed, I am tempted to argue that the skills and behaviors encouraged and rewarded within academia are sometimes directly counter to those skills and behaviors which help students succeed at work. One example is the 'quest for perfection' pursued within education, with students encouraged to invest as much time and effort as possible in an assignment to achieve the highest grade. Contrarily, in the work environment, it is the 'quest for efficiency' which is crucial. In work, perfection is oft the enemy of done.

The Context

A new graduate joined my consultancy team. Early in their role, they were asked to complete a piece of research to support a more senior consultant. The brief was simple; to seek out examples of best practices across the sector on a particular topic and provide some sources/links/examples. The senior consultant required the findings in a report by the following week. The graduate in question was keen to demonstrate their expertise and produce high-quality work to impress. They dedicated the following week to scouring websites, reading journals, and producing a beautifully crafted, academically referenced, 8,000-word report. Unfortunately, it was structured and read like an academic assignment. The senior consultant and I were horrified. Not only was it an entirely disproportionate and wasteful use of time (and therefore money), but it also meant that a raft of other important (but less high profile/interesting) priorities had been neglected.

Action Taken

We recognized immediately that we needed to be more explicit in our brief. The graduate in question had approached the work precisely as they had been trained to do so throughout their academic career. We provided feedback and coaching to the person in question, using the 80:20 Pareto principle, and agreed that in the future, all new graduate hires should be:

- Shown an example of 'what good looks like' in terms of output (a short PowerPoint deck would have sufficed).
- Provided clear guidance on how much time to invest in the task and how it stacked up against other priorities/work that week.
- Given a 'check-in' shortly after starting the work to ensure they were on the right track.

The Outcome

The graduate in question was very open to the feedback and quickly able to adapt their style and approach once provided with clear guidance, advice and support. By adopting this approach with other early career hires (students, interns and graduates), we have had far fewer instances of work being 'over-delivered'.

Lessons Learned and Advice

It is easy to underestimate the transition from education into employment, not least the behaviors and mindset within the two different contexts. One's desire for perfection versus the quest for efficiency is one example, but there are many others. Taking the time to set expectations, demonstrate what good work looks like, offering regular work progress check-ins (and early course corrections where necessary), providing coaching, and offering feedback are all critical to helping a new graduate quickly perform well in the role. It is rarely the case that new graduates lack the desire or skills or are willfully inefficient – but rather that we, as line managers and employers, are not doing enough to let them know what they are striving for in this new context.

Reflection on Lived Experience Insights

The four lived experience insights from Germany, Hungary, and the UK present valuable strategies for preparing students for the university-to-work transition. The dominant theme is that more than a degree is needed, and a gap still exists between the needs of employers and what graduates can offer. Students should have opportunities alongside their degrees to develop the skills employers seek. They should also learn how to navigate the job application and selection process, as well as how to adapt to the norms of the workplace.

Employers can directly provide these opportunities to students or work with other organizations that support student development. Approaches adopted successfully in one country (such as the example in Germany) may also be of interest to trial in other countries. These opportunities must be available to all students and provided in a safe environment where individuals can learn from their mistakes. Access to professional networks is vital for students from disadvantaged backgrounds, as it can help them overcome some barriers to accessing workplace opportunities and employment.

The insights also suggest that employers must help new graduate hires adjust to the workplace environment and to understand expectations. Giving ongoing feedback and communicating the needs and norms of the organization can assist graduates in learning on the job and adapting accordingly. Employers should also be aware of the challenges of preparing students for the university-to-work transition during their degree, such as conflicting time pressures around coursework deadlines and exam periods. However, integrating students into the workplace while they are still studying can help organizations secure 'work-ready' graduate talent ahead of competitors, offering a strategic advantage. Being prepared to support and develop new hires also results in a larger pool of talent to choose from, increasing opportunities for diverse talent pipelines.

CONCLUSION

This chapter defined the university-to-work transition and presented benefits to organizations from hiring graduate talent. The GRAM was then introduced, encompassing twenty-five activities to enhance talent attraction efforts and prepare students for undertaking the university-to-work transition. The four quadrants that form the GRAM were subsequently explored, followed by the twenty-five activities grouped by six themes:

(i) Careers fairs
(ii) Presentations and panel events
(iii) Sponsorship and ambassador roles
(iv) Networking and mentoring
(v) Experience opportunities
(vi) Diversity-focused events

Finally, four lived experience insights were provided, offering examples of real-world challenges, strategic approaches, and outcomes related to the issue of preparing students for the university-to-work transition.

If you are a university student, consider taking a moment to think about how ready you feel for the transition from university to the professional world. There may be certain areas where you could use some extra support. If so, consider attending events organized by employers or recruitment agencies. You can refer back to the Employability Capital Growth (ECG) model in Chapter 2 and use this alongside the GRAM in this chapter to inform which events to attend based on your specific needs. These events can allow you to ask questions, gain valuable insights, and receive the support you need. To find these events, you can visit specific employers' websites or social media pages or contact your university career service for a list of upcoming employer events.

If you work as a graduate recruiter or as a recruitment agency representative, consider taking a moment to think about the specific challenges faced by the organization(s) you recruit for. This is an excellent opportunity to assess the effectiveness of your current strategies and interventions. The GRAM, including the quadrants and activities grouped by themes, can be a starting point for discussing alternative approaches with team members. By addressing existing challenges and considering previously overlooked approaches, you can better prepare students to transition from university into the workplace. Consequently, the organization(s) you recruit for can gain a competitive advantage by identifying, developing, and hiring talented graduates. We revisit the topic of preparing students for the university-to-work transition in Chapters 8 and 9 to discuss the challenges and opportunities for collaboration with representatives from other organizations or universities to offer strategic opportunities for bridging the university-employer divide.

The next chapter concludes section three of the book, which has focused on the organizational perspective to consider strategies for attracting early career talent (Chapter 5) and preparing students for the university-to-work transition (Chapter 6) by examining the process of establishing and maintaining Person-Organization Fit (POF) of early career talent.

REFERENCES

Ab Wahab, M., & Tatoglu, E. (2020). Chasing productivity demands, worker well-being, and firm performance: The moderating effects of HR support and flexible work arrangement. *Personnel Review*, *49*(9), 1823–1843. doi:10.1108/PR-01-2019-0026

Akkermans, J., Blokker, R., Buers, C., Van der Heijden, B. I. J. M., & De Vos, A. (2021). Ready, set, go! In A. Marshall & J. Symonds (Eds.), *Adult Development at the School-to-Work Transition: International Pathways and Processes* (pp. 77–103). Oxford University Press. doi:10.1093/oso/9780190941512.003.0004

Akkermans, J., Brenninkmeijer, V., Huibers, M., & Blonk, R. W. B. (2013). Competencies for the contemporary career: Development and preliminary validation of the career competencies questionnaire. *Journal of Career Development*, *40*(3), 245–267. doi:10.1177/0894845312467501

Arthur, N., & Flynn, S. (2013). International students' views of transition to employment and immigration. *Canadian Journal of Career Development, 12*(1), 28–37.

Baluku, M. M., Mugabi, E. N., Nansamba, J., Matagi, L., Onderi, P., & Otto, K. (2021). Psychological capital and career outcomes among final year university students: The mediating role of career engagement and perceived employability. *International Journal of Applied Positive Psychology, 6*(1), 55–80. doi:10.100741042-020-00040-w

Berger, J., & the Keller Fay Group. (2016). *Research Shows Micro-Influencers Have More Impact Than Average Consumers*. Experticity. https://go2.experticity.com/rs/288-AZS-731/images/Experticity-Keller FaySurveySummary_.pdf

Blokker, R., Akkermans, J., Marciniak, J., Jansen, P. G. W., & Khapova, S. N. (2023). Organizing school-to-work transition research from a sustainable career perspective: A review and research agenda. *Work, Aging and Retirement, 9*(3), 239–261. doi:10.1093/workar/waad012

Blokker, R., Akkermans, J., Tims, M., Jansen, P. G. W., & Khapova, S. N. (2019). Building a sustainable start: The role of career competencies, career success, and career shocks in young professionals' employability. *Journal of Vocational Behavior, 112*, 172–184. doi:10.1016/j.jvb.2019.02.013

Bright Network. (2022). *What do graduates want? 2022/23*. Bright Network. https://employers.brightnetwork.co.uk/what-do-graduates-want-report-and-video

Brown, J. L., Hammer, S. J., Perera, H. N., & McIlveen, P. (2021). Relations between graduates' learning experiences and employment outcomes: A cautionary note for institutional performance indicators. *International Journal for Educational and Vocational Guidance, 22*(1), 137–156. doi:10.100710775-021-09477-0

Buckholtz, T. J., & Donald, W. E. (2022). Direct outcomes and win-win relationships between university careers advisors and graduate recruiters. *GiLE Journal of Skills Development, 2*(1), 9–25. doi:10.52398/gjsd.2022.v2.i1.pp9-25

Careers2032 Project. (2022). *An industry research project co-produced by AGCAS, ISE, Wonkhe and Handshake, looking at the careers sector of 2032 and the role technology could play in facilitating human connections*. Handshake. https://joinhandshake.co.uk/careers2032

Cole, D., & Donald, W. E. (2022). Shifting the narrative: Towards a more holistic approach to learning. *GiLE Journal of Skills Development, 2*(11), 3–4. doi:10.52398/gjsd.2022.v2.i1.pp3-4

Consiglio, C., Menatta, P., Borgogni, L., Alessandri, G., Valente, L., & Caprara, G. V. (2021). How youth may find jobs: The role of positivity, perceived employability, and support from employment agencies. *Sustainability (Basel), 13*(16), 9468. doi:10 3390u13169468

D'Armagnac, S., Al Ariss, A., & N'Cho, J. (2022). Talent management in turbulent times: Selection, negotiation, and exploration of strategies for talent management in aeronautics and space industries. *International Journal of Human Resource Management, 33*(13), 2767–2799. doi:10.1080/09585192.2021.1879205

Davies, H. (2014). *A Quick Guide to Society Sponsorship: Help Your Club and Your Career*. https:// careersblog.enterprise.co.uk/a-quick-guide-to-society-sponsorship-help-your-club-and-your-career/

Donald, W. E. (2017). Students' perceptions of graduate employability: A sequential explanatory approach. Doctoral Thesis, University of Southampton. https://eprints.soton.ac.uk/id/eprint/415935

Donald, W. E. (2023). *Handbook of Research on Sustainable Career Ecosystems for University Students and Graduates*. IGI Global., doi:10.4018/978-1-6684-7442-6

Donald, W. E., Ashleigh, M. J., & Baruch, Y. (2018). Students' perceptions of education and employability: Facilitating career transition from higher education into the labor market. *Career Development International, 23*(5), 513–540. doi:10.1108/CDI-09-2017-0171

Donald, W. E., Ashleigh, M. J., & Baruch, Y. (2022). The university-to-work transition: Responses of universities and organizations to the COVID-19 pandemic. *Personnel Review, 51*(9), 2201–2221. doi:10.1108/PR-03-2021-0170

Donald, W. E., Baruch, Y., & Ashleigh, M. J. (2019). The undergraduate self-perception of employability: Human capital, careers advance and career ownership. *Studies in Higher Education, 44*(4), 599–614. doi:10.1080/03075079.2017.1387107

Donald, W. E., Baruch, Y., & Ashleigh, M. J. (2020). Striving for sustainable careers: Conceptualization via career ecosystems and the new psychological contract. *Career Development International, 25*(2), 90–110. doi:10.1108/CDI-03-2019-0079

Donald, W. E., Baruch, Y., & Ashleigh, M. J. (2023a). Technological transformation and human resource development of early career talent: Insights from accounting, banking, and finance. *Human Resource Development Quarterly, 34*(3), 329–348. doi:10.1002/hrdq.21491

Donald, W. E., Baruch, Y., & Ashleigh, M. J. (2023b). Construction and operationalisation of an Employability Capital Growth Model (ECGM) via a systematic literature review (2016-2022). *Studies in Higher Education*, 1–15. Advance Online Publication. doi:10.1080/03075079.2023.2219270

Donald, W. E., & Ford, N. (2023). Fostering social mobility and employability: The case for peer learning. *Teaching in Higher Education*, *28*(3), 672–678. doi:10.1080/13562517.2022.2145467

Fakunle, O. (2021). International students' perspective on developing employability during study abroad. *Higher Education Quarterly*, *75*(4), 575–590. doi:10.1111/hequ.12308

Forrier, A., De Cuyper, N., & Akkermans, J. (2018). The winner takes it all, the loser has to fall: Provoking the agency perspective in employability research. *Human Resource Management Journal*, *28*(4), 511–523. doi:10.1111/1748-8583.12206

Graduate Recruitment Bureau. (2023). *The 7 Benefits of Hiring Graduates*. GRB. https://www.grb.uk.com/recruiter-research/7-benefits-of-hiring-graduates

Green, Z. A., Noor, U., & Hashemi, M. N. (2020). Furthering proactivity and career adaptability among university students: Test of intervention. *Journal of Career Assessment*, *28*(3), 402–424. doi:10.1177/1069072719870739

Hawes, D. (2023). Navigating graduate recruitment in 2023: Diversity, skills shortages, AI and more. *Career Matters*, *11*(3), 42–43.

Healy, M., Hammer, S., & McIllveen, P. (2022). Mapping graduate employability and career development in higher education research: A citation network analysis. *Studies in Higher Education*, *47*(4), 799–811. doi:10.1080/03075079.2020.1804851

Hughes, H. P. N. (2020). *Understanding the Value of Internships*. University of Leeds. https://business. leeds.ac.uk/downloads/download/202/understanding_the_value_of_work_placements

Hughes, H. P. N., Mouratidou, M., & Donald, W. E. (2023). Exploring the impact of an industrial placement year on students' competency development: A three-cohort, longitudinal study. *Higher Education, Skills and Work-Based Learning*. Advanced Online Publication. doi:10.1108/HESWBL-02-2023-0044

Jackson, D. (2020). The changing nature of graduate roles and the value of the degree. *Journal of Higher Education Policy and Management*, *43*(2), 182–197. doi:10.1080/1360080X.2020.1777634

Jackson, D., & Cook, E. J. (2023). Benefits of work-integrated learning for students. In K. E. Zegwaard & T. J. Pretti (Eds.), *The International Handbook for Work-Integrated Learning*. Routledge / Taylor & Francis. doi:10.4324/9781003156420-8

LaunchPad. (2022). *Key challenges in recruitment include expensive graduate schemes*. Launchpad. https://launchpadrecruits.com/insight-articles/grad-recruitment-strategies-and-challenges

Lo Presti, A. L., Capone, V., Aversano, A., & Akkermans, J. (2022). Career competencies and career success: On the roles of employability activities and academic satisfaction during the school-to-work transition. *Journal of Career Development*, *49*(1), 107–125. doi:10.1177/0894845321992536

Miao, H. (2021). *College Students and Getting Valuable Career Experience Working as Brand Ambassadors for Companies like TikTok and Bumble*. CNBC. https://www.cnbc.com/2021/04/24/tiktok-bumble-others-are-hiring-college-students-as-brand-ambassadors.html

Moore, T., & Morton, J. (2017). The myth of job readiness? Written communication, employability, and the 'skills gap' in higher education. *Studies in Higher Education*, *42*(3), 591–609. doi:10.1080/03075079.2015.1067602

Munich Business School. (2022). *What is a "Working Student"?* Munich Business School. https://www.munich-business-school.de/insights/en/2022/what-is-a-working-student/

Ng, T. W., & Feldman, D. C. (2007). The school-to-work transition: A role identity perspective. *Journal of Vocational Behavior*, *71*(1), 114–134. doi:10.1016/j.jvb.2007.04.004

Nimmi, P. M., Joseph, G., & Donald, W. E. (2022). Is it all about perception? A sustainability viewpoint on psychological capital and life wellbeing of management graduates. *Higher Education. Skills and Work-Based Learning*, *12*(2), 384–398. doi:10.1108/HESWBL-01-2021-0004

Nimmi, P. M., Kuriakose, V., Donald, W. E., & Nowfal, M. (2021). HERO elements of psychological capital: Fostering career sustainability via resource caravans. *Australian Journal of Career Development*, *30*(3), 199–210. doi:10.1177/10384162211066378

O'Regan, M., Carthy, A., McGuiness, C., & Owende, P. (2022). Employer collaboration in developing graduate employability: A pilot study in Ireland. *Education + Training*, *65*(10), 1–13. doi:10.1108/ET-03-2022-0081

Ogbuanya, T. C., & Chukwuedo, S. O. (2017). Career-training mentorship intervention via the Dreyfus model: Implications for career behaviors and practical skills acquisition in vocational electronic technology. *Journal of Vocational Behavior*, *103*, 88–105. doi:10.1016/j.jvb.2017.09.002

Okay-Somerville, B., & Scholarios, D. (2022). Focused for some, exploratory for others: Job search strategies and successful university-to-work transitions in the context of labor market ambiguity. *Journal of Career Development*, *49*(1), 126–143. doi:10.1177/08948453211016058

Parker, K., & Igielnik, R. (2020). *On the cusp of adulthood and facing an uncertain future: What we know about Gen Z so far*. Pew Research. https://www.pewresearch.org/social-trends/2020/05/14/on-the-cusp-of-adulthood-and-facing-an-uncertain-future-what-we-know-about-gen-z-so-far-2/

Rodrigues, R., Butler, C. L., & Guest, D. (2020). Evaluating the employability paradox: When does organizational investment in human capital pay off? *International Journal of Human Resource Management*, *31*(9), 1134–1156. doi:10.1080/09585192.2019.1704825

Rudolph, C. W., Zacher, H., & Hirschi, A. (2019). Empirical developments in career construction theory. *Journal of Vocational Behavior*, *111*(1), 1–6. doi:10.1016/j.jvb.2018.12.003

Savickas, M., & Porfeli, E. J. (2012). Career adapt-abilities scale: Construction, reliability, and measurement equivalence across 13 countries. *Journal of Vocational Behavior*, *80*(3), 661–673. doi:10.1016/j.jvb.2012.01.011

Shtaltovna, Y., & Muzzu, C. (2021). Enhancing students' digital competencies within the Employability module of the University of Europe's skills-based curricula. In Proceedings of the first GiLE4Youth International Conference: The Development of Competencies for Employability (pp. 71-89). *GiLE Journal of Skills Development*. 10.56611/conf.proc.2021.1.71-89

Social Mobility Commission. (2017). *Unpaid Internships are Damaging to Social Mobility*. Social Mobility Commission. https://www.gov.uk/government/news/unpaid-internships-are-damaging-to-social-mobility

The Graduate Project. (2023). *The Benefits of Hiring Graduates*. The Graduate Project. https://www.thegraduateproject.co.uk/news/2023/04/the-benefits-of-hiring-graduates/112

Tims, M., & Akkermans, J. (2020). Job and career crafting to fulfill individual career pathways. In J. W. Hedge & G. W. Carter (Eds.), *Career Pathways: From School to Retirement* (pp. 165–190). Oxford University Press. doi:10.1093/oso/9780190907785.003.0010

Tran, L. T., Ngo, N. T. H., Nguyen, H. T. M., Le, T. T. T., & Ho, T. T. H. (2022). "Employability in context": Graduate employability attributes expected by employers in regional Vietnam and implications for career guidance. *International Journal for Educational and Vocational Guidance*. doi:10.100710775-022-09560-0 PMID:35910080

Trendence. (2020). *Black Lives Matter Infographic: Racial Justice in the Workplace.* Trendence. https://trendence.co.uk/thoughtleadership/reports

Van Hooft, E. A. J., Kammeyer-Muller, J. D., Wanberg, C. R., Kanfer, R., & Basburg, G. (2020). Job search and unemployment success: A quantitative review and future research agenda. *The Journal of Applied Psychology*, *106*(5), 674–713. doi:10.1037/apl0000675 PMID:32658493

Violet. (2019). *What are the Advantages of Working as a Law Firm Campus Ambassador?* Violet. https://www.lawcareers.net/Explore/BlogPost/Violet/What-are-the-advantages-of-working-as-a-law-firm-campus-ambassador

Wright, P. M., Coff, R., & Moliterno, T. P. (2014). Strategic human capital crossing the great divide. *Journal of Management*, *40*(2), 353–370. doi:10.1177/0149206313518437

Zacher, H., & Froidevaux, A. (2021). Life stage, lifespan, and life course perspectives on vocational behavior and development: A theoretical framework, review, and research agenda. *Journal of Vocational Behavior*, *126*, 103476. doi:10.1016/j.jvb.2020.103476

Zhou, W., Li, M., Xin, L., & Zhu, J. (2018). The interactive effect of proactive personality and career exploration on graduating students' well-being in school-to-work transition. *International Journal of Mental Health Promotion*, *20*(2), 41–54. doi:10.32604/IJMHP.2018.010737

Zucker, R. (2019). *How to manage the emotional roller coaster of a job search.* HBR. https://hbr.org/2019/10/how-to-manage-the-emotional-roller-coaster-of-a-job-search

ADDITIONAL READING

Grosemans, I., Hannes, K., Neyens, J., & Kyndt, E. (2020). Emerging adults embarking on their careers: Job and identity explorations in the transition to work. *Youth & Society*, *52*(5), 795–819. doi:10.1177/0044118X18772695

Kuron, L. K. J., Lyons, S. T., Schweitzer, L., & Ng, E. S. W. (2015). Millennials' work values: Differences across the school to work transition. *Personnel Review*, *44*(6), 991–1009. doi:10.1108/PR-01-2014-0024

Liu, S., Huang, J. L., & Wang, M. (2014). Effectiveness of job search interventions: A meta-analytic review. *Psychological Bulletin*, *140*(4), 1009–1041. doi:10.1037/a0035923 PMID:24588365

Ma, Y., Yue, Y., & Hou, L. (2021). The impact of proactive personality and clinical learning environment on nursing college students' perceived employability. *Nurse Education in Practice*, *56*, 103213. doi:10.1016/j.nepr.2021.103213 PMID:34597862

Monteiro, S., Almeida, L., & García-Aracil, A. (2021). "It's a very different world": Work transition and employability of higher education graduates. *Higher Education. Skills and Work-Based Learning*, *11*(1), 164–181. doi:10.1108/HESWBL-10-2019-0141

Okay-Somerville, B., & Scholarios, D. (2017). Position, possession or process? Understanding objective and subjective employability during university-to-work transitions. *Studies in Higher Education*, *42*(7), 1275–1291. doi:10.1080/03075079.2015.1091813

Pastore, F., Quintano, C., & Rocca, A. (2023). Stuck at a crossroads? The duration of the Italian school-to-work transition. *International Journal of Manpower*, *42*(3), 442–469. doi:10.1108/IJM-05-2020-0199

Peeters, E. R., Akkermans, J., & De Cuyper, N. (2020). The only constant is change? Movement capital and perceived employability. *Journal of Career Assessment*, *28*(4), 674–692. doi:10.1177/1069072720918195

Schoon, I. (2020). Navigating an uncertain labor market in the UK: The role of structure and agency in the transition from school to work. *The Annals of the American Academy of Political and Social Science*, *688*(1), 77–92. doi:10.1177/0002716220905569

Xin, L., Tang, F., Li, M., & Zhou, W. (2020). From school to work: Improving graduates' career decision-making self-efficacy. *Sustainability (Basel)*, *12*(3), 804. doi:10.3390u12030804

Chapter 7
Establishing and Maintaining Person-Organization Fit

ABSTRACT

This chapter provides an overview of the Person-Environment Fit (PEF) theory and its application in the workplace through the Person-Organization Fit (POF) theory. The Graduate Recruitment Selection Process (GRSP) model outlines a typical selection process, followed by a discussion of sustainable talent pipelines and the Early Career Talent Pipeline (ECTP) conceptual framework. Next, the chapter addresses challenges and strategies in assessing POF, focusing on four themes: (i) volume of applicants, (ii) selection stage choices, (iii) use of technology, and (iv) bias in the selection process. The chapter also examines how POF can evolve over time from either the employee perspective, the employer perspective, or both, by introducing the Early Career Attraction and Retention (ECAR) model and the POF Assessment Matrix (POFAM). The chapter concludes with four lived experience insights that offer real-world examples of assessing POF during the selection process for early career talent.

INTRODUCTION

Section Three of the book has thus far covered two main topics: attracting early career talent (Chapter 5) and preparing students for the university-to-work transition (Chapter 6). To conclude Section Three, our attention now turns to establishing and maintaining Person-Organization Fit (POF) to attract, select, and retain graduate talent. This chapter introduces Person-Environment Fit (PEF) theory and its application through the POF theory in the workplace. Next, the chapter provides an overview

DOI: 10.4018/978-1-6684-9827-9.ch007

of a typical graduate recruitment selection process, emphasizes the significance to organizations of developing sustainable talent pipelines, and discusses the challenges and strategies involved in assessing POF. The chapter also considers how POF can evolve from individual, organizational, or both perspectives. The chapter then concludes with four lived experience insights evidencing the challenges various organizations face and their actions to ensure alignment of POF during the attraction and selection process.

PERSON-ENVIRONMENT FIT (PEF) AND PERSON-ORGANIZATION FIT (POF)

PEF theory explores the dynamic interaction between individuals and their environments, recognizing that individuals can influence their surroundings while the environment can impact their motivation, behavior, and overall wellbeing (Schneider, 1987). Specifically, PEF theory suggests that "people have an innate need to fit their environments and seek out environments that match their own characteristics" (Van Vianen, 2018, p. 77). When applied to the workplace, this concept is known as POF theory (Cable & Judge, 1996). POF offers an example of supplementary fit, whereby strong POF exists when the individual's attributes or values match those of the organization (Gander et al., 2020). Employers (providing the environment via the organization) and job applicants (as individuals) utilize the attraction and selection process to assess the alignment of POF by considering supplementary fit. As Anderson and Tomlinson (2021) observe,

employers frame and decode signals of standout employability from graduates' narrations of experientially referenced skilful social action. These form the dramaturgical backdrop from which employers infer unique personal brand assets and qualities they associate with standout employability. (p. 675)

Job applicants consider both intrinsic and extrinsic factors to achieve career sustainability, which benefits the employer by providing a strategic competitive advantage (Jackson, Richardson et al., 2022). A study by Bright Network (2022) reveals that students consider various factors when deciding where to apply for employment, including organizational culture, reputation, job role characteristics, and remuneration. Moreover, 89% of students consider an employer's commitment to diversity and inclusion, while 91% prioritize the commitment to the mental wellbeing of employees. The COVID-19 pandemic has also influenced 20% of students to change their career sector of interest.

Adapting to changing landscapes is crucial for recruiting, developing, and retaining talent (McCracken et al., 2016). For example, the impact of the COVID-19 social distancing restrictions accelerated technological advancement (Amankwah-Amoah et al., 2021; Donald et al., 2023a), a theme we will explore later in this chapter. Given the evolving nature of work and the impact of the pandemic, there is a need for a new psychological contract that focuses on career agility and aligns with individual values (Coetzee et al., 2022). Breaching this psychological contract can lead to increased staff turnover, reduced commitment, and negative impacts on job satisfaction and performance (Dhir et al., 2020; Griep et al., 2020; Grobler & Rensburg, 2019; Ma et al., 2019). Collaborating with university career services can help employers to get accurate information about students whilst offering students access to information about the company and employment opportunities (Bol et al., 2019; Donald & Mouratidou, 2022). We will delve deeper into the challenges and opportunities for collaboration between these actors in Chapters 8 and 9.

Lack of POF poses a significant concern for organizations as low retention rates result in a loss of investment in developing early career talent and the loss of strategic advantage to competitors (Rodrigues et al., 2020). However, opting not to allocate resources for training, job design, and career management to try and safeguard against such losses also hinders POF and risks losing talented individuals (Borg & Scott-Young, 2022). In sectors with high demand for early career talent, replacing an employee who leaves due to a lack of POF can be challenging, time-consuming, and may require offering a higher salary and better benefits to attract a replacement hire to leave their existing employer. According to Zaharee et al. (2018), organizations should provide rotation-based roles, continuous feedback, learning and development programs, professional qualifications, and attractive employee benefits beyond the base salary to retain early career talent.

Having introduced PEF and POF theories, our focus now shifts to providing an overview of the graduate selection process and highlighting the significance of sustainable talent pipelines before exploring some of the challenges and strategies associated with assessing POF.

THE GRADUATE RECRUITMENT SELECTION PROCESS

Before the COVID-19 pandemic, multinational organizations had begun to adopt digital selection procedures, such as online applications, psychometric testing, digital interviews, and gamified assessments (Woods et al., 2020). However, the later stages of the selection process still relied on in-person interactions (Cheng & Hackett, 2021). When the pandemic hit and social distancing measures were implemented, technological investment was significantly increased, particularly for the latter stages of the selection process (Soto-Acosta, 2020). The recruitment of early career talent underwent a rapid digital transformation, equivalent to five years of progress in just four months (Donald et al., 2022). However, Small and Medium-Sized Enterprises (SMEs) faced significant challenges because they were less likely to have invested in technology for the selection process before the pandemic since it was cost-prohibitive relative to the number of people they were hiring (Tarofder, 2017). Therefore, many SMEs had to rely on video conferencing tools such as Teams or Zoom as a temporary measure to conduct their interviews during the social distancing restriction periods of the pandemic.

During the COVID-19 pandemic, I had the opportunity to interview graduate recruiters from the banking, finance, and accounting sectors. These recruiters were either working in-house or as agents for organizations through recruitment agencies. Drawing from these interviews and my previous experience as a graduate recruiter for an Investment Bank in London, our research team developed a Graduate Recruitment Selection Process (GRSP) model (Donald et al., 2023a). The GRSP model consists of thirteen stages. Stages 1-5 had already undergone a technological transformation in larger organizations before the pandemic, while stages 6-13 were primarily conducted in person (Schlogl et al., 2021). Figure 1 illustrates the GRSP model.

Figure 1. Graduate Recruitment Selection Process (GRSP) model
(C) 2023 Donald, Baruch & Ashleigh. Used with permission.

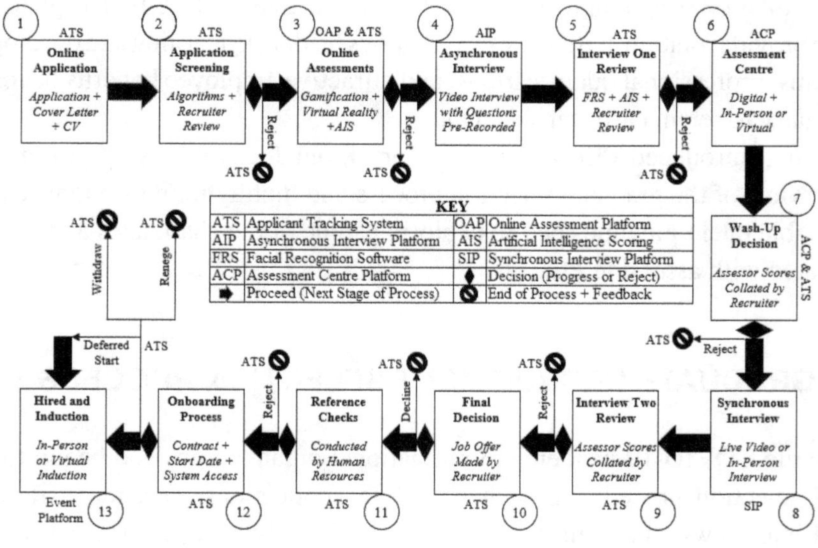

Different organizations may use different approaches to selecting early career talent. For instance, some organizations may have additional stages not shown in the GRSP, while others may use fewer stages. However, the shared objective is to assess POF efficiently whilst ensuring an excellent candidate experience and reducing the risk of bias. Consequently, organizations can use the selection process to develop sustainable talent pipelines by hiring suitable talent to meet existing and future business demands.

SUSTAINABLE TALENT PIPELINES

Organizations vary in their cultures, values, and approaches to achieving objectives. When recruiting new employees, assessing how well they will fit into the organization is crucial, as failing to do so can have serious consequences. For instance, hiring someone with poor POF can disrupt the entire team, leading to lower workplace satisfaction and reduced productivity. Therefore, effective talent management is vital for gaining a competitive advantage and ensuring the long-term success of an organization (Ab Wahab & Ekrem, 2020; Illes et al., 2010). One specific aspect of talent management is identifying and hiring the most employable graduates, enabling an employer to establish and sustain competitive advantage and success (Petruzziello et al., 2022). Consequently, organizations continue to look for innovative approaches to talent management, which take on increased relevance due to the disruptive impacts of the COVID-19 pandemic as a global chance event (Akkermans et al., 2020).

One effective approach to talent management is feedback-seeking behavior through counter signals, which enhances the overall signaling process (Taj, 2016). In Section Two (Chapter 4), we discussed signaling theory (Spence, 1973; 1978) and how it applied to Human Resource Management (HRM). Scholars in HRM have explored how organizations can leverage signaling in their brand marketing to enhance talent management strategies (Gutpa et al., 2019; Pernkopf et al., 2021). Counter signals build upon the concept of signaling theory, where the recipient of a signal provides feedback to the sender. Additionally, creating an environment that encourages and embraces feedback-seeking behavior is crucial, as it has been found to moderate the benefits of the counter signals in employer branding research (Srivastava, 2001). However, despite evidence showing that 90% of candidates are willing to provide feedback if asked, only 25% have been asked for feedback on their experiences of the attraction and selection process (Bach, 2021).

Figure 2 demonstrates how the early careers recruitment team (individuals involved in attracting and selecting talent for an organization) can indicate their openness to receiving feedback from individuals through counter signals (Donald, 2021). These counter signals are vital in informing strategic decision-making for future recruitment cycles.

Figure 2. Early Career Talent Pipeline (ECTP) conceptual framework
(C) 2021 Donald. Used with permission.

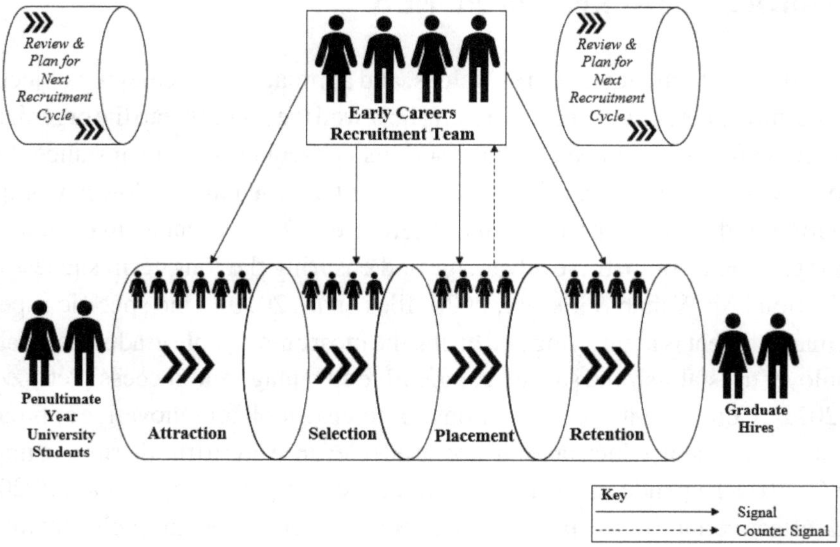

Figure 2 provides an example of penultimate-year university students experiencing an organization's attraction and selection process before undertaking a placement (e.g., a 2-4 week micro placement, summer internship, or year-in-industry placement). Each individual and the organization continue to assess their POF during the placement. Additionally, the early careers recruitment team can seek feedback from these individuals on their experiences of the attraction and selection process. The figure also acknowledges the significance of retention, referring to so-called 'keep-warm activities' in this particular context. The objective of the organization is to ensure that if an individual is offered and accepts a graduate employment contract upon completion of a placement, the individual subsequently joins the organization after their final year of study rather than reneging and opting to join an alternative employer instead (Rodrigues et al., 2020).

The feedback provided through counter signals to the early careers recruitment team can be supplemented with feedback from other sources to make informed strategic decisions. This additional feedback can include data from the Applicant Tracking System (ATS), which covers the application, selection, and retention phases (Holt-White & Montacute, 2021). Furthermore, input from managers who oversee interns and graduates can also contribute valuable insights (Hughes et al., 2023). By combining feedback from multiple sources, organizations can identify strategies to cultivate sustainable talent pipelines, including promoting positive outcomes for candidates from underrepresented and diverse backgrounds (Lee et al., 2022).

ASSESSING PERSON-ORGANIZATION FIT: CHALLENGES & STRATEGIES

Our attention now turns to briefly considering some challenges and strategies in assessing POF when selecting early career talent. Four themes are explored, including the:

(i) Volume of applicants
(ii) Selection stage choices
(iii) Use of technology
(iv) Bias in the selection process

Volume of Applicants

Challenge

Organizations often face challenges related to the number of applicants they receive. These challenges can be due to an extremely high or very low volume of applicants (Donald, 2021). This reflects the external factors of supply and demand of graduates, which is beyond an individual's agency (Donald et al., 2023b). When there is a high volume of applicants, the time it takes from the initial application to a job offer increases. In such cases, competitors who shorten this timeframe gain a competitive advantage by securing the most employable graduates (Petruzziello et al., 2022). This is because highly employable applicants often receive multiple job offers, and their experience with the attraction and selection process influences their decision on which offer to accept (Shivoro et al., 2018). Additionally, many applicants may not clearly understand the organization's culture and values, making it difficult for them to demonstrate alignment, which also hampers the assessment of the fit between the organization and the applicant. On the other hand, when there is a low volume of applicants, it becomes challenging for organizations to fill vacant roles. As a result, they may have to settle for lower-quality graduates or compromise on the POF (Donald, 2021). Multinational organizations typically face a high volume of applicants, while SMEs struggle more with a lower volume of applicants, although there are also variances by sector and geographical location (Donald et al., 2022).

Strategy

Donald and Pychtin (2022) emphasize the importance of organizational transparency in job advertisements. They recommend clearly stating which requirements are essential and which are optional, as well as providing salary information for the specific roles. This transparency helps individuals to make informed decisions about whether to apply, reducing the overall volume of applicants without compromising the quality of the talent pipeline. Another effective strategy is to convert micro placement, summer internship, or year-in-industry participants into graduate hires. This approach allows the organization and the individual to assess POF to a greater extent than solely via the selection process and make better-informed decisions (Smith & Green, 2021). Investing in promoting the organization more effectively may be necessary for organizations facing challenges with a low volume of applicants. This can involve partnering with graduate recruitment agencies or establishing regional collaborations with local universities to raise student awareness about available employment opportunities and access to talent (Donald et al., 2022).

Selection Stage Choices

Challenge

When hiring graduate talent, organizations must carefully consider the stages in the selection process to establish POF most efficiently. It is crucial to strike a balance because having too many stages can discourage talented applicants from investing their time, leading them to drop out of the process (LaunchPad, 2022). Conversely, having too few stages allows unqualified candidates to advance to later stages, which can be resource-intensive for organizations (Linos & Riesch, 2019). Furthermore, more stages in the recruitment process mean a longer timeframe from application to job offer (LaunchPad, 2022). This further highlights how the experience of the attraction and selection process plays a significant role in an individual's decision regarding which job offer to accept (Shivoro et al., 2018). It also underscores the interconnectedness of these various challenges in assessing POF when selecting early career talent.

Strategy

Donald and Pychtin (2022) propose optimizing the recruitment process by eliminating unnecessary stages, which reduces the time required for both applicants and assessors. They also emphasize the importance of providing timely and constructive feedback to applicants. This feedback not only helps attract more applicants by demonstrating an organization's commitment to providing feedback and personal development but also positively impacts the organization's reputation (LaunchPad, 2022). Another effective approach is to allow candidates to complete multiple assessment stages on the same day. Research has shown that this practice leads to higher-quality hires (Linos & Riesch, 2019). Furthermore, organizations can better understand a candidate's POF by incorporating multiple assessment methods such as interviews, case studies, and behavioral assessments. Using gamified assessment in the recruitment process can also help identify candidates' human skills and psychometric properties (Georgiou et al., 2019). This holistic view subsequently enhances the effectiveness of the selection process and the determinant of POF.

Use of Technology

Challenge

The COVID-19 pandemic accelerated digital transformation in the workplace (Schlogl et al., 2021). As Black and Van Esch (2020) observe, "recent and near-future advances in AI-enabled recruiting have improved recruiting efficiency to the point that managers ignore them or procrastinate their utilization at their own peril" (p. 215). However, graduate recruiters faced challenges during the COVID-19 pandemic's social distancing restrictions. They found it difficult to make well-informed hiring decisions regarding POF without at least one face-to-face meeting during the selection process (Donald et al., 2023a). This was primarily due to technology-driven assessments struggling to capture nuances and nonverbal cues compared to in-person methods. Candidates also encountered technical issues, a poor user experience, and a lack of familiarity with assessment technologies, leading some to drop out of the process. Candidates and assessors also reported experiencing emotional and cognitive exhaustion when using or evaluating automated job interviews (Jaser et al., 2022). Furthermore, Donald et al. (2023a) identified issues with bias in the recruitment process, which we will discuss in more detail shortly. Moreover, the same study found that organizations faced difficulties conducting virtual onboarding, leading some organizations to defer start dates or rescind offers during the social restriction periods of the COVID-19 pandemic.

Strategy

Organizations must communicate clearly to university students that while an ATS can filter applicants, the recruiter determines the parameters for filtering, such as keywords (Indeed, 2023). This helps prevent an excessive focus on making a CV 'ATS compliant' at the expense of tailoring it to showcase one's abilities, potential, and motivations effectively. Additionally, organizations must ensure students understand the selection processes and are prepared to utilize digital technologies (Donald & Mouratidou, 2022). A blended approach that combines technology-based and in-person methods is considered the most favorable option. Technology can be deployed more extensively in the early stages of the selection process to manage a high volume of applicants. However, face-to-face assessments are preferred in the later stages to inform POF and hiring decisions (Donald et al., 2023a). The study also suggests keeping assessment centers in a digital format but conducting them in person, where candidates gather at a central location. This approach leverages technology to reduce the need for printing materials, contributing to the organization's efforts to reduce its carbon footprint in response to the challenge of climate change (Faulconbridge et al., 2020). Organizations should regularly review and validate their technology-driven recruitment processes to ensure fairness and effectiveness, prioritizing transparency and clear communication, as well as continuously monitoring for biases and ethical implications (Donald, 2023a). Achieving a balance between technology and human involvement and incorporating feedback can create a more comprehensive and equitable graduate recruitment selection process. Consequently, there are emerging calls in the literature to explore human-technology intersections in the context of talent management and careers (Kim et al., 2022).

Bias in the Selection Process

Challenge

Another challenge organizations face is the risk of bias in the selection process, which further emphasizes the interconnected nature of these various themes. As Heaslip (2022) observes, when recruiters have to process a large volume of applicants, they often "get screened based on how similar or recognizable their background is to the recruiter or the existing employee pool, using heuristics like education, extracurriculars, or professional associations" (Online). Applicants often come from diverse educational backgrounds, which poses another challenge in assessing POF, as it is objectively difficult to compare applicants due to the absence of a standardized evaluation system. Interestingly, the use of technology can risk either replicating or exacerbating human bias if these biases are embedded into the algorithms and applied to all applicants. This was seen in the accounting, banking, and finance sector during the COVID-19 pandemic, whereby algorithm bias led to some of the least diverse cohorts of graduate hires in recent years (Donald et al., 2023a). Additionally, technology can present barriers for individuals experiencing digital poverty or those lacking a quiet space to complete assessments (Donald et al., 2022). Furthermore, the diversity of a talent pipeline during the selection process tends to reduce with each subsequent stage of the application process (Linos & Riesch, 2019). This links to the challenge of ensuring that diverse applicants do not feel alienated from applying in the first place due to the language used in the attraction phase or job descriptions. For instance, Wynn and Correll (2018) found that "gender-imbalanced presenter roles, geek culture references, overt use of gender stereotypes, and other gender speech and actions" (p. 149) by USA-based technology companies resulted in women opting to apply to alternative employers.

Strategy

Donald (2017) and Donald et al. (2018) propose several recommendations to address diversity and inclusion in the attraction and selection process. These include providing suitable role models during the attraction phase, implementing 'blind screening' where the recruiter does not know the applicant's name, providing diversity training for hiring managers, and ensuring diverse representation among assessors and decision-makers. Linos and Riesch (2019) also observed that simplifying the recruitment process for the Los Angeles Police Department (LAPD) reduced voluntary drop-offs in police recruitment. Furthermore, insights from interviews I conducted with graduate recruiters and university career advisors during the COVID-19 pandemic offered valuable information regarding promoting inclusivity in the selection process (Donald et al., 2022; 2023a). For instance, using inclusive language in the attraction and selection process, covering travel costs related to attending selection stages (preferably upfront as some students may not have the means to cover travel costs, even if they are reimbursed later), and making feasible adjustments to ensure inclusivity and accessibility. Suppose candidates lack a private space, a stable internet connection, or a suitable device like a laptop or tablet. In that case, organizations should arrange to provide these resources for undertaking the selection process, aiming to reduce the impact of digital poverty. Lastly, the attraction and selection process should accurately reflect the company culture. Failure to do so may result in a high turnover of diverse talent who experience a lack of POF after joining the organization, undermining the efforts made in the attraction and selection process to develop diverse and sustainable talent pipelines.

THE EVOLUTION OF PERSON-ORGANIZATION FIT OVER TIME

The COVID-19 pandemic has prompted individuals to search for a greater sense of purpose and meaning in their lives (Afshari, 2023), marking a departure from the traditional belief that an employee will only opt to leave their existing employer as a *strategy of last resort* rather than proactively seeking other employment opportunities (Follmer et al., 2018). The shift in employee attitudes is reflected in results from a survey of 107 employers which revealed that graduate retention rates in the UK hit a record low of 71% in 2022, the lowest since records began in 2011 (Institute of Student Employers, 2022). Another study involving 159 UK employers found that 71% identified retaining early career talent as their top challenge for the next decade (Careers2032 Project, 2022). These findings support that POF evolves over time (Vleugels et al., 2019).

To examine the difficulties associated with retaining early career talent and the changes in POF over time, I conducted interviews with two groups of individuals: those who graduated in 2008 during the 2007-2008 Global Financial Crisis and those who graduated in 2020 amidst the COVID-19 pandemic (Donald, 2023b). The findings from these interviews are summarized in Figure 3, which presents the Early Career Attraction and Retention (ECAR) model, depicting the main themes and sub-themes identified.

Figure 3. Early Career Attraction And Retention (ECAR) model
(C) 2023 Donald. Used with permission.

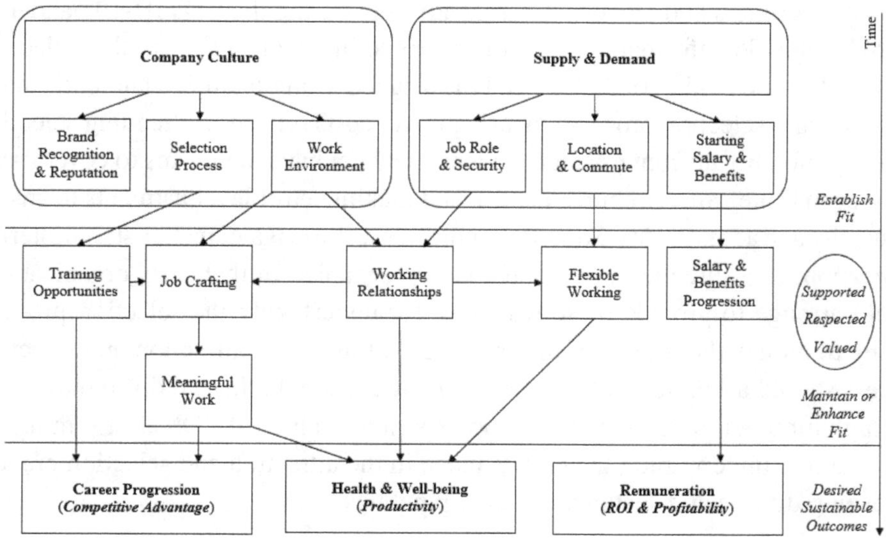

Moreover, the findings revealed a significant alignment between the themes and sub-themes identified from interviews with individuals who graduated in 2008 or 2020. The key difference I found from the interviews was "the prioritisation of factors, whereby 2020 graduates prioritise job roles and job security, whereas 2008 graduates prioritise job location and commute duration" (Donald, 2023b, p. 245). This supports the view that differences between these groups are often overstated and tend to be more subtle (Zaharee et al., 2018). The themes from these interviews also aligned with previous research conducted by the Chartered Institute of Personnel Development (2022b, pp. 3-4), that offered seven dimensions of 'Good Work':

1. Pay and benefits
2. Contracts
3. Work-life balance
4. Job design and the nature of work
5. Relationships at work
6. Employee voice
7. Health and wellbeing

However, the emphasis on learning and progression opportunities in Figure 3 extends these seven dimensions, supporting previous conceptual work (Donald et al., 2020). Additionally, the inclusion of learning as a critical dimension in Figure 3 aligns with existing scholarly perspectives that recognize the role of lifewide and lifelong learning in fostering career agency (Cole & Coulson, 2022; Cole & Donald, 2022). Furthermore, the desire for career progression reflects a growing willingness by individuals to explore inter- and intra-organizational mobility across the career span (Baruch & Sullivan, 2022).

The interviews with graduates also shed light on how a person representing an employee and an organization representing the employer could have similar or evolving expectations over time (Donald, 2023b). Figure 4 offers the Person-Organization Fit Assessment Matrix (POFAM), which visually represents the four quadrants and the corresponding effects on the alignment or divergence of POF.

Notably, the matrix provides empirical evidence supporting an emerging perspective in the literature that, under certain circumstances, retaining employees can have negative consequences (Boswell et al., 2017). Furthermore, the findings support the idea that employer branding acts as a precursor to retention (Bharadwaj et al., 2022) by influencing an individual's choice of employer through their assessment of POF (Huang, 2022). Additionally, the recruitment process is crucial in establishing POF from individual and organizational perspectives (Jackson, Riebe et al., 2022), highlighting the interdependent and interconnected nature of different actors operating within a sustainable career ecosystem (Donald, 2023a).

Figure 4. Person-Organization Fit Assessment Matrix (POFAM)
(C) 2023 Donald. Used with permission.

Person \ Organization	Remains The Same	Evolves
Remains The Same	1a) If good fit based on attraction and selection process, then **initial fit remains good** 1b) If bad fit based on attraction and selection process, then **initial fit remains bad**	2a) If good initial fit, then **fit worsens** 2b) If bad initial fit, then either (i) **fit remains bad** or (ii) **fit improves**
Evolves	3a) If good initial fit, then **fit worsens** 3b) If bad initial fit, then either (i) **fit remains bad** or (ii) **fit improves**	4a) If good initial fit, then either (i) **fit remains good** or (ii) **fit worsens** 4b) If bad initial fit, then either (i) **fit remains bad** or (ii) **fit improves**

Movement between quadrants over time

ID	Notes
1a	Retention: But risk of stagnation
1b	Turnover: Beneficial to both parties
2a	Turnover: Benefits organisation more
2bi	Turnover: Beneficial to both parties
2bii	Retention: Beneficial to both parties
3a	Turnover: Benefits the person more
3bi	Turnover: Beneficial to both parties
3bii	Retention: Beneficial to both parties
4ai	Retention: Beneficial to both parties
4aii	Turnover: Beneficial to both parties
4bi	Turnover: Beneficial to both parties
4bii	Retention: Beneficial to both parties

Our focus now shifts to exploring four lived experience insights that offer real-world examples of assessing POF during the selection process for recruiting early career talent.

LIVED EXPERIENCE INSIGHTS

Lived Experience Insight

Shared By Sophie Zdenkowski, Facto, Australia

The Challenge

The challenge I encountered upon joining Facto to enhance their graduate program was a disconnect between what the leadership team were seeking in early career hires and whom they were attracting and hiring through their existing recruitment processes. The hires had relevant degrees and experience but were difficult to manage due to attitude problems and misaligned expectations.

The Context

Facto is a start-up tech consulting firm transitioning from a small to a medium enterprise. Consequently, more processes, systems, policies, operations, and specialized hires are needed to support this growth. Currently, 60% of hires are contractors, and 40% are permanent. Facto wants to bring in more permanent junior talent that we can shape and develop in line with our consulting standards. The Chief Executive Officer passionately believes that a positive attitude to work and learning is more important than qualifications or previous experience. Their vision is to make hiring decisions based on a candidate's attitude and the potential for skill development, subsequently providing experiential training and client placement opportunities to develop the required skills and experience.

Action Taken

A survey I conducted with leadership team members confirmed they did not believe in the need for set qualifications when hiring early career talent. Consequently, we decided to re-style our Graduate Program to an Early and Emerging Career Program, allowing people to join us from high school, university, or other educational or work experience routes. We also offered an initial two-year contract to align with industry standards, diversify our talent pool, and reduce risk if the hires proved to have a weak POF. I also developed an assessment matrix for use during assessment centers to ensure alignment between the attitudes we sought in candidates and what we were assessing. I also communicated the attitudes we sought in candidates to the assessors, ensuring a transparent process and the ability to provide appropriate post-interview feedback to candidates.

The Outcome

It is early days, as we have only had one cohort join us since implementing these changes, but we have seen an increase in the diversity of hires. For example, we have hired four international graduates and two people seeking career changes. Candidates have provided positive feedback on the recruitment process and felt the communication was clear regarding expectations and that they felt supported throughout the process. We have since had the opportunity to get to know our new hires via a three-week intensive professional skills development induction program. We also provide regular feedback about our expectations, where the new hires excel, and where development opportunities exist.

Lessons Learned and Advice

Assessment matrixes are a great way to make leaders accountable for aligning hiring decisions with the qualities that they desire in applicants. Feedback from hiring each cohort also helps us to iteratively improve the assessment matrix, ensuring that activities during the selection process suitably assess the desired qualities that we seek. Moreover, regular communication with candidates and new hires is crucial to managing expectations and providing timely feedback. This enables us to capture and address minor problems early in the selection process or, in the case of new hires, before it impacts the program's reputation with managers or clients. The approach also helps us monitor POF, modify the assessment process, or provide training where needed.

Lived Experience Insight

Shared By Zsolt Ábrahám, Case Solvers, Hungary

The Challenge

A case method is an active form of instruction whereby students are presented with real-world scenarios from the past and tasked with identifying issues and offering solutions. As part of experiential learning and work-based simulations, the case method helps employers engage talent and build a visible employer brand. The approach also helps to reduce information asymmetry between students (as potential applicants) and employers. However, case competitions and case-based education were limited to top-tier business schools and not widely available to other students, resulting in a skills gap and a reduced opportunity for both parties to assess POF.

The Context

In 2012, Zsolt Ábrahám, a former case competitor from Corvinus University of Budapest, started to blog about case solving and co-founded Case Solvers, a Budapest-based start-up company. Case Solvers' vision was to train problem solvers and produce high-quality talent worldwide. Since 2012, the company has held case competitions in more than 30 countries and developed more than 30,000 young professionals. The case method is particularly valuable in preparing students to enter complex and evolving labor markets since it enables them to think critically and innovatively.

Action Taken

Case Solvers took three main approaches to decrease the skills gap and improve the assessment of POF:

1. **Case competitions for everyone:** Case Solvers organized case competitions at national and international levels. These competitions were available to high school students, university students (e.g., Mastercard Case Challenge, Central European Case Competitions), and professionals (e.g., Telekom Slovenije)
2. **Interview training for job seekers**: Case Solvers provided case interview training for candidates willing to apply for management, consulting, and investment banking positions. These events involved practical training where participants practiced case solving, learned more about the industry and the application process at different companies, and had the opportunity to network with peers and industry professionals.
3. **Spartafy**: Case Solvers developed a case-based skill assessment tool called Spartafy to map candidates' problem-solving skills.

The Outcome

Since 2012, more than 30,000 professionals have been supported by Case Solvers. Employers report that the approach has helped decrease the skills gap and improve the POF of applicants because individuals have a greater understanding of the industry, organization, and role they are applying for. Employers also report how access to talent has given them a competitive advantage, whilst individuals report how participation helped to support their career decision-making and personal development.

Lessons Learned and Advice

We learned that the case method as a teaching and development approach could benefit individuals and organizations in three main ways:

1. **Engaging talent**: Case Solvers used live cases for skill development and assessment, which helped to engage individuals (potential applicants and future talent for organizations).
2. **Decreased information asymmetry**: The cases simulated real-life situations and provided additional information about the job and the working culture.

The method also enabled skill assessment, which gave relevant insights about the individuals to themselves and employers.

3. **Better decision-making**: Based on the unique learning experience, individuals and organizations made more informed decisions leading to enhanced POF. For example, the approach helped individuals decide where to apply and which job offer to accept. Employers could better understand a candidate because the candidate could signal their employability more clearly, increasing the likelihood of the right hiring decision for both parties.

Lived Experience Insight

Shared By Peter Pychtin, GradSift, Australia

The Challenge

A leading Australian government agency wanted to broaden the diversity of its graduate hires. They had performed their own analysis, which showed the profile of their hires was skewed heavily to dual degree graduates from the country's top universities. While their graduate program was popular and the selection process was highly competitive, they saw an opportunity to broaden the diversity of their intake, both socio-economically and geographically.

The Context

The agency runs a two-year graduate program and welcomes candidates from a broad range of backgrounds. That includes fresh graduates from university to those with several years of professional experience. Previously, the agency initially screened applicants using a cognitive ability assessment. However, they realized that was problematic, especially with respect to applicants from a lower socio-economic background. They also wanted greater control to screen applicants on the attributes and experiences that the agency valued. Moreover, they wanted an efficient mechanism to proactively consider applicants from regional universities who lacked the reputational capital associated with attending more prestigious universities. Naturally, the solution had to involve blind screening and objective assessment of each applicant.

Action Taken

They chose to use the GradSift screening and shortlisting platform, which assesses applicants across multiple criteria. It applies Artificial Intelligence (AI) to interpret an applicant's background across academic, work experience and extra-curricular interests while evaluating interpersonal skills and fit for the organization and role. The agency could modify the algorithm based on their input criteria to tailor the recommendations to their specific needs. Applicants were then screened and ranked by AI before being reviewed by a recruiter, making it simple for the agency to identify the stronger applicants. The platform also made it easy to identify the best applicants from regional universities. This meant they could ensure an appropriate proportion of their shortlisted candidates were from diverse backgrounds, both socio-economically and geographically. The agency rationalized that once shortlisted, it was up to those regional candidates to perform over the balance of the assessment stages.

The Outcome

At the conclusion of the graduate recruitment process, the agency undertook a comprehensive review. Specifically, their analysis focused on the diversity of applicants progressing to each stage of the assessment process. The findings showed that using the GradSift platform, there was greater diversity among the shortlisted candidates and at every subsequent stage of the selection process. The agency had achieved its objective and increased the diversity of its hires.

Lessons Learned and Advice

One of the common challenges in graduate recruitment is managing the high volume of applicants and their data. In the past, employers have resorted to a waterfall assessment approach, rejecting significant numbers of applicants based on a single or narrow set of attributes. That has been efficient and cost-effective for employers but has led to the rejection of otherwise strong applicants, including those from a lower socio-economic background. Innovations in technology and assessments enable employers to manage large volumes of data efficiently, assess applicants across multiple criteria, and offer diverse hiring decisions with strong POF.

Lived Experience Insight

Shared By Jenny Surridge, Health and Beauty Industry, UK

The Challenge

Throughout my 15 years in recruitment across different sectors, a consistent theme has been the high volume of applicants compared to the limited number of roles available. My current employer receives 300,000+ applications each year. Engaging with our candidates is crucial to evaluate their fit with the organization, provide a positive candidate experience, and ensure an equitable recruitment process, all within the constraints of a low-cost recruitment model. However, the high volume of applicants meant we needed to make our recruitment process more efficient without impacting the quality of our hiring decisions.

The Context

Handling a large number of applicants becomes particularly critical when recruiting for a major-volume, low-cost retailer. Qualifications and technical skills are less relevant when recruiting for sales advisor roles in our retail stores. What truly matters is the candidate's ability to approach and engage with customers, a desire to maintain a presentable store environment, and the passion to ensure positive outcomes for our customers and their team. Therefore, a holistic evaluation allows us to identify individuals best suited to our retail environment's unique challenges and requirements.

Action Taken

In our quest to streamline the selection process, we explored various potential options. Unfortunately, most of these were not viable due to their high costs and time requirements, which exceeded our available resources. Nevertheless, a thorough analysis of our teams' activities shed light on a significant time-consuming aspect: the processing of offers, contracts, and onboarding procedures. To tackle this challenge, we collaborated closely with our in-house robotics and technology team to develop an automated offer process.

The Outcome

Following successful initial testing, we proceeded to implement our automated offer process. This roll-out proved highly effective and saved our team over 500 work hours annually. By automating these tasks, we significantly improved our overall efficiency, allowing us to redirect our focus towards meaningful interactions with candidates. This shift empowered us to make better-informed hiring decisions. However, we decided that all offers should continue to be made verbally. This balance between automation and human interaction ensured that we optimized our recruitment process and upheld our commitment to providing a positive and engaging experience for all candidates. The significant time savings have also led us to consider if any additional administrative tasks are resource-heavy, where automation of these processes could save us additional time to re-direct to promoting a strong candidate experience and making more informed hiring decisions.

Lessons Learned and Advice

A one-size fits all approach to recruitment across different organizations or for different roles within the same organization is not feasible. A key piece of advice is to evaluate how to optimize the resources available during the design process and as part of an ongoing review of each recruitment cycle. Finally, it is essential to ensure that candidates have the best possible experience during the application and selection process since this can influence their decision whether or not to accept an offer of employment. The organization also benefits from increased engagement with candidates by hiring people with a strong person-organization fit, increasing the likelihood of talent retention and strategic competitiveness.

Reflection on Lived Experience Insights

The four lived experience insights from Australia, Hungary, and the UK shed light on the challenges and opportunities in assessing POF during the attraction and selection processes. One effective method to help potential candidates understand the industry, organization, and available roles is the use of case methods as a form of active instruction. This approach helps overcome information asymmetry, enabling applicants and organizations to evaluate their POF. However, being transparent about company culture and job expectations is critical to empower potential applicants to make informed career decisions.

Another prominent observation is the importance of carefully considering selection criteria. By doing so, an organization can broaden the available talent pool, enhance diversity, and make hiring decisions that align with business needs. Technology can play a valuable role in this process, allowing for the assessment of multiple criteria and efficient management of a high volume of applicants, thereby reducing costs and increasing efficiency. However, it is vital to continuously review each phase of the hiring process to ensure that the technology does not introduce unintended biases. Furthermore, implementing an assessment matrix for assessment centers can promote objective decision-making and provide candidates with explicit feedback on their performance.

The candidate's experience also holds significant weight in securing top talent, especially since highly sought-after candidates often receive multiple job offers. Therefore, streamlining the hiring process while providing ongoing and timely communication is crucial to assessing POF, creating a positive impression, and increasing the acceptance rate of job offers.

CONCLUSION

Section Three of this book consisted of three chapters exploring the role of in-house graduate recruiters and other individuals working as agents of an organization via recruitment agencies. Chapter 5 focused on the challenges and opportunities concerning attracting early career talent. Chapter 6 discussed how to prepare students for undertaking the university-to-work transition. Subsequently, Chapter 7 considered how to establish and maintain POF in the context of attracting, selecting, and retaining graduate talent. Each chapter was complemented by four lived experience insights to help bridge theory and practice.

At this point in the book, consider taking some time to reflect on Section Three and consider what pragmatic steps you can take to enhance the sustainability of the career ecosystem. For example, if you are a graduate recruiter acting on behalf of an employer, perhaps you might think about the following:

- How successful is your current strategy for attracting early career talent? Are there opportunities to enhance the strategy by incorporating additional activities or replacing existing ones?
- What are the most significant disparities between the organization's requirements and the performance of recent graduate hires? How can you address these gaps to prepare students for undertaking the university-to-work transition?
- How well does your current attraction and selection process accurately establish the extent to which POF exists?
- What measures are currently in place to sustain POF? Do these initiatives contribute to favorable retention rates? If not, what changes could be made?

If you are a university student preparing to undertake the university-to-work transition, you might wish to consider the following:

- What criteria do I prioritize when seeking an employer? How do I rank the importance of these various aspects? Which ones are non-negotiable?
- Which forms of employability capital should I focus on developing the most for the types of jobs that I am interested in doing?
- Am I actively seizing opportunities to engage with employers and building a network of industry contacts? If not, how can I initiate participation in such activities?
- Do I possess a clear understanding of the industries, companies, and jobs to which I am applying? What does the selection process entail for these jobs? What specific qualities are they seeking?

Additionally, as a candidate during the interview phase, you might consider asking some of the questions below to the interviewer to enable you to assess POF from your perspective since they provide insights into management styles, the role, and company culture:

- What are the three key personality traits necessary for success in this environment?
- Could you share an anecdote demonstrating your preferred team management approach?
- Within the past six months, can you recount and explain how you resolved a team conflict?
- How is performance assessed, and what measures are in place to support meeting performance expectations?
- What professional growth opportunities are available within this role and department?
- I acknowledge the significance of [company value] in this organization. Can you provide some instances of how it manifests on a daily basis?
- Who is the most accomplished individual you have recruited, and what actions did they take to achieve success?

If you are part of a university career service, Section 3 has hopefully provided you with additional insights into the employer perspective of the career ecosystem. Section 4 now considers the challenges and opportunities for increased collaboration via pragmatic strategies to bridge the university-employer divide before the book concludes with some thoughts about future workplace trends and their implications.

REFERENCES

Ab Wahab, N., & Ekrem, T. (2020). Chasing productivity demands, worker well-being, and firm performance: The moderating effects of HR support and flexible work arrangement. *Personnel Review*, *49*(9), 1823–1843. doi:10.1108/PR-01-2019-0026

Afshari, L. (2023). Identification through meaning-making: Identity enactment towards organizational commitment. *Human Resource Development International*, *26*(1), 7–28. doi:10.1080/13678868.2021.1996171

Akkermans, J., Richardson, J., & Kraimer, M. (2020). The Covid-19 crisis as a career shock: Implications for careers and vocational behavior. *Journal of Vocational Behavior, 119*, a.103434. doi:10.1016/j.jvb.2020.103434

Amankwah-Amoah, J., Khan, Z., Wood, G., & Knight, G. (2021). COVID-19 and digitalization: The great acceleration. *Journal of Business Research*, *136*(1), 602–611. doi:10.1016/j.jbusres.2021.08.011 PMID:34538980

Anderson, V., & Tomlinson, M. (2021). Signaling standout graduate employability: The employer perspective. *Human Resource Management Journal*, *31*(3), 675–693. doi:10.1111/1748-8583.12334

Bach, R. (2021). *Early Careers Recruitment Challenges and How to Overcome Them*. People Scout. https://peoplescout.passle.net/post/102gr41/early-careers-recruitment-challenges-and-how-to-overcome-them-blog-series-par

Baruch, Y., & Sullivan, S. E. (2022). The why, what and how of career research: A review and recommendations for future study. *Career Development International*, *27*(1), 135–159. doi:10.1108/CDI-10-2021-0251

Bharadwaj, S., Khan, N. A., & Yameen, M. (2022). Unbundling employer branding, job satisfaction, organizational identification and employee retention: A sequential mediation analysis. *Asia-Pacific Journal of Business Administration*, *14*(3), 309–334. doi:10.1108/APJBA-08-2020-0279

Black, J. S., & Van Esch, P. (2020). What is it and how should a manager use it? *Business Horizons*, *63*(2), 215–226. doi:10.1016/j.bushor.2019.12.001

Bol, T., Ciocca Eller, C., Van de Werfhorst, H. G., & DiPrete, T. A. (2019). School-to-work linkages, educational mismatches, and labor market outcomes. *American Sociological Review*, *84*(2), 275–307. doi:10.1177/0003122419836081

Borg, J., & Scott-Young, C. M. (2022). Contributing factors to turnover intentions of early career project management professionals in construction. *Construction Management and Economics*, *40*(10), 835–853. doi:10.1080/01446193.2022.2110602

Boswell, W. R., Gardner, R. G., & Wang, J. (2017). Is retention necessarily a win? Outcomes of searching and staying. *Journal of Vocational Behavior*, *98*, 163–172. doi:10.1016/j.jvb.2016.11.006

Bright Network. (2022). *What do Graduates Want?* Bright Network. https://employers.brightnetwork.co.uk/what-do-graduates-want-report-and-video

Cable, D. M., & Judge, T. A. (1996). Person-organization fit, job decisions, and organizational entry. *Organizational Behavior and Human Decision Processes*, *67*(3), 294–311. doi:10.1006/obhd.1996.0081

Careers2032 Project. (2022). *An industry research project co-produced by AGCAS, ISE, Wonkhe and Handshake, looking at the careers sector of 2032 and the role technology could play in facilitating human connections*. Handshake. https://joinhandshake.co.uk/careers2032

Chartered Institute of Personnel and Development. (2022b). *CIPD Good Work Index 2022*. CIPD. https://www.cipd.co.uk/Images/good-work-index-survey-report-2022_tcm18 -109896.pdf

Cheng, M. M., & Hackett, R. D. (2021). A critical review of algorithms in HRM: Definitions, theory, and practice. *Human Resource Management Review*, *31*(1), 100698. doi:10.1016/j.hrmr.2019.100698

Coetzee, M., Deas, A., Veldsman, D., & Dhliwayo, P. (2022). Career agility and career embeddedness as psychological needs of the value-oriented psychological contract. *South African Journal of Psychology. Suid-Afrikaanse Tydskrif vir Sielkunde*, *52*(3), 364–378. doi:10.1177/00812463221081341

Cole, D., & Coulson, B. (2022). Through and beyond COVID-19, promoting whole person, lifelong and lifewide learning. *Journal of Innovation in Polytechnic Education*, *4*(1), 81–90.

Cole, D., & Donald, W. E. (2022). Shifting the narrative: Towards a more holistic approach to learning. *GiLE Journal of Skills Development*, *2*(1), 3–4. doi:10.52398/gjsd.2022.v2.i1.pp3-4

Dhir, S., Dutta, T., & Ghost, P. (2020). Linking employee loyalty with job satisfaction using PLS-SEM modelling. *Personnel Review*, *49*(8), 1695–1711. doi:10.1108/PR-03-2019-0107

Donald, W. E. (2017). Students' perceptions of graduate employability: A sequential explanatory approach. Doctoral Thesis, University of Southampton. https://eprints.soton.ac.uk/id/eprint/415935

Donald, W. E. (2021). *Conceptualisation of a new 'Early Careers Talent Pipeline' Framework: Enhancing Organisational Sustainability via Feedback-Seeking Behaviour*. Graduate Recruitment Bureau. doi:10.13140/RG.2.2.28278.47684

Donald, W. E. (2023a). Preface. In W. E. Donald (Ed.), *Handbook of Research on Sustainable Career Ecosystems for University Students and Graduates*, (Preface). IGI Global. doi:10.4018/978-1-6684-7442-6

Donald, W. E. (2023b). Sustainable talent pipelines and person-organisation fit: Strategic insights from UK graduates. *Career Development International*, *28*(2), 234–249. doi:10.1108/CDI-10-2022-0285

Donald, W. E., Ashleigh, M. J., & Baruch, Y. (2018). Students' perceptions of education and employability: Facilitating career transition from higher education into the labour market. *Career Development International*, *23*(5), 513–540. doi:10.1108/CDI-09-2017-0171

Donald, W. E., Ashleigh, M. J., & Baruch, Y. (2022). The university-to-work transition: Responses of universities and organizations to the COVID-19 pandemic. *Personnel Review*, *51*(9), 2201–2221. doi:10.1108/PR-03-2021-0170

Donald, W. E., Baruch, Y., & Ashleigh, M. J. (2020). Striving for sustainable graduate careers: Conceptualization via career ecosystems and the new psychological contract. *Career Development International*, *25*(2), 90–110. doi:10.1108/CDI-03-2019-0079

Donald, W. E., Baruch, Y., & Ashleigh, M. J. (2023a). Technological transformation and human resource development of early career talent: Insights from accounting, banking, and finance. *Human Resource Development Quarterly*, *34*(3), 329–348. doi:10.1002/hrdq.21491

Donald, W. E., Baruch, Y., & Ashleigh, M. J. (2023b). Construction and operationalisation of an Employability Capital Growth Model (ECGM) via A systematic literature review. *Studies in Higher Education*, 1–15. doi:10.1080/03075079.2023.2219270

Donald, W. E., & Mouratidou, M. (2022). Preparing for a sustainable career: Challenges and opportunities. *GiLE Journal of Skills Development*, *2*(2), 3–5. doi:10.52398/gjsd.2022.v2.i2.pp3-5

Faulconbridge, J., Jones, I., Marsden, G., & Anable, J. (2020). Work, ICT and travel in multinational corporations: The synthetic work mobility situation. *New Technology, Work and Employment*, *35*(2), 195–214. doi:10.1111/ntwe.12162

Follmer, E. H., Talbot, D. L., Kristof-Brown, A. L., Astrove, S. L., & Billsberry, J. (2018). Resolution relief, and resignation: A qualitative study of misfit at work. *Academy of Management Journal*, *61*(2), 440–465. doi:10.5465/amj.2014.0566

Gander, G., Hofmann, J., & Ruch, W. (2020). Character strengths: Person-Environment fit and relationships with job and life satisfaction. *Frontiers in Psychology*, *11*, 1582. doi:10.3389/fpsyg.2020.01582 PMID:32793038

Georgiou, K., Gouras, A., & Nikolaou, I. (2019). Gamification in employee selection: The development of a gamified assessment. *International Journal of Selection and Assessment*, *27*(2), 91–103. doi:10.1111/ijsa.12240

Griep, Y., Vantilborgh, T., & Jones, S. K. (2020). The relationship between psychological contract breach and counterproductive work behavior in social enterprises: Do paid employees and volunteers differ? *Economic and Industrial Democracy*, *41*(3), 727–745. doi:10.1177/0143831X17744029

Grobler, A., & Rensburg, M. J. V. (2019). Organisational climate, person–organisation fit and turn over intention: A generational perspective within a South African Higher Education Institution. *Studies in Higher Education*, *44*(11), 2053–2065. doi:10.1080/03075079.2018.1492533

Gupta, B., Mittal, S., & Mittal, V. (2019). Employer branding and its relation with HR functions of employee recruitment and retention: A review of the literature. *The Marketing Review*, *19*(1-2), 85–105. doi:10.1362/146934719X15633618140792

Heaslip, E. (2022). *5 Reasons Why Hiring Diverse Candidates Is Still Hard in 2021*. Vervoe. https://vervoe.com/hiring-diverse-candidates/

Holt-White, E., & Montacute, R. (2020). *COVID-19 and Social Mobility Impact Brief #5: Graduate Recruitment and Access to the Workplace*. IOE. https://dera.ioe.ac.uk/36101/1/Access-to-the-Workplace-Impact-Brief.pdf

Huang, J.-C. (2022). Effects of person-organization fit objective feedback and subjective perception on organizational attractiveness in online recruitment. *Personnel Review*, *51*(4), 1262–1276. doi:10.1108/PR-06-2020-0449

Hughes, H. P. N., Mouratidou, M., & Donald, W. E. (2023). Exploring the impact of an industrial placement year on students' competency development: A three-cohort, longitudinal study. *Higher Education, Skills and Work-Based Learning*. Advanced Online Publication. doi:10.1108/HESWBL-02-2023-0044

Illes, P., Chuai, X., & Preece, D. (2010). Talent management and HRM in multinational companies in Beijing: Definitions, differences and drivers. *Journal of World Business*, *45*(2), 179–189. doi:10.1016/j.jwb.2009.09.014

Indeed. (2023). *What is a Recruiting ATS and How Does it Work? A Guide*. Indeed. https://uk.indeed.com/career-advice/career-development/recruiting-ats

Institute of Student Employers. (2022). *ISE Student Development Survey 2022*. ISE. https://ise.org.uk/page/graduate-job-vacancies-20-higher-than-pre-pandemic

Jackson, D., Richardson, J., Michelson, G., & Munir, R. (2022). Attracting accounting and finance graduate talent – beyond the Big Four. *Accounting and Finance*, *62*(3), 3761–3790. doi:10.1111/acfi.12904

Jackson, D., Riebe, L., & Macau, F. (2022). Determining factors in graduate recruitment and preparing students for success. *Education + Training*, *64*(5), 681–699. doi:10.1108/ET-11-2020-0348

Jaser, Z., Petrakaki, D., Starr, R., & Oyarbide-Magaña, E. (2022). *Where Automated Job Interviews Fall Short*. HBR. https://hbr.org/2022/01/where-automated-job-interviews-fall-short

Kim, S., Egan, T., & Akdere, M. (2022). Advancing social science standards and communities for the future of HRDQ and its impact. *Human Resource Development Quarterly*, *33*(1), 7–10. doi:10.1002/hrdq.21474

LaunchPad. (2022). *Key Challenges in Recruitment Include Expensive Graduate Schemes*. LaunchPad. https://launchpadrecruits.com/insight-articles/grad-recruitment-strategies-and-challenges

Lee, J., Waung, M., & Beatty, J. E. (2022). Internships and promises of diversity: How anticipatory psychological contracts shape employment intentions in the U.S. *International Journal of Human Resource Management*, *33*(17), 3560–3590. doi:10.1080/09585192.2021.1916775

Linos, E., & Riesch, N. (2020). Thick red tape and the thin blue line: A field study on reducing administrative burden in police recruitment. *Public Administration Review*, *80*(1), 92–103. doi:10.1111/puar.13115

Ma, B., Liu, S., Lassleben, H., & Ma, G. (2019). The relationships between job insecurity, psychological contract breach and counterproductive workplace behavior. *Personnel Review*, *48*(2), 595–610. doi:10.1108/PR-04-2018-0138

McCracken, M., Currie, D., & Harrison, J. (2016). Understanding graduate recruitment, development and retention for the enhancement of talent management: Sharpening 'the edge' of graduate talent. *International Journal of Human Resource Management, 27*(22), 2727–2752. doi:10.1080/09585192.2015.1102159

Pernkopf, K., Latzke, M., & Mayrhofer, W. (2021). Effects of mixed signals on employer attractiveness: A mixed-method study based on signalling and convention theory. *Human Resource Management Journal, 31*(2), 392–413. doi:10.1111/1748-8583.12313

Petruzziello, G., Chiesa, R., & Mariani, M. G. (2022). The storm Doesn't touch me!—The role of perceived employability of students and graduates in the pandemic era. *Sustainability (Basel), 14*(7), 4303. doi:10.3390u14074303

Rodrigues, R., Butler, C. L., & Guest, D. (2020). Evaluating the employability paradox: When does organizational investment in human capital pay off? *International Journal of Human Resource Management, 31*(9), 1134–1156. doi:10.1080/09585192.2019.1704825

Schlogl, L., Weiss, E., & Prainsack, B. (2021). Constructing the 'future of work': An analysis of the policy discourse. *New Technology, Work and Employment, 36*(3), 307–326. doi:10.1111/ntwe.12202

Schneider, B. (1987). The People Make The Place. *Personnel Psychology, 40*(3), 437–453. doi:10.1111/j.1744-6570.1987.tb00609.x

Shivoro, R., Shalyefu, R., & Kadhila, N. (2018). Perspectives on graduate employability attributes for management sciences graduates. *South African Journal of Higher Education, 32*(1), 216–232. doi:10.20853/32-1-1578

Smith, K. N., & Green, D. K. (2021). Employer internship recruiting on college campuses: 'the right pipeline for our funnel'. *Journal of Education and Work, 34*(4), 572–589. doi:10.1080/13639080.2021.1943333

Soto-Acosta, P. (2020). COVID-19 pandemic: Shifting digital transformation to a high-speed gear. *Information Systems Management, 37*(4), 260–266. doi:10.1080/10580530.2020.1814461

Spence, M. (1973). Job market signalling. *The Quarterly Journal of Economics, 87*(3), 355–374. doi:10.2307/1882010

Spence, M. (1978). Job market signaling. In P. Diamond & M. Rothschild (Eds.), *Understanding in Economics* (pp. 281–306). Academic Press. doi:10.1016/B978-0-12-214850-7.50025-5

Srivastava, J. (2001). The role of inferences in sequential bargaining with one-sided incomplete information: Some experimental evidence. *Organizational Behavior and Human Decision Processes*, *85*(1), 166–187. doi:10.1006/obhd.2000.2936 PMID:11341821

Taj, S. A. (2016). Application of signalling theory in management research: Addressing major gaps in theory. *European Management Journal*, *34*(4), 338–348. doi:10.1016/j.emj.2016.02.001

Tarofder, A. K., Azam, S. M. F., & Jalal, A. N. (2017). Operational or strategic benefits: Empirical investigation of internet adoption in supply chain management. *Management Research Review*, *40*(1), 28–52. doi:10.1108/MRR-10-2015-0225

Van Vianen, A. E. M. (2018). Person-environment fit: A review of its basic tenets. *Annual Review of Organizational Psychology and Organizational Behavior*, *5*(1), 75–101. doi:10.1146/annurev-orgpsych-032117-104702

Vleugels, W., Tierens, H., Billsberry, J., Verbruggen, M., & De Cooman, R. (2019). Profiles of fit and misfit: A repeated weekly measures study of perceived value congruence. *European Journal of Work and Organizational Psychology*, *28*(5), 616–630. doi:10.1080/1359432X.2019.1583279

Wood, S. A., Ahmed, S., Nikolaou, I., Costa, A. C., & Anderson, N. R. (2020). Personnel selection in the digital age: A review of validity and applicant reactions, and future research challenges. *European Journal of Work and Organizational Psychology*, *29*(1), 64–77. doi:10.1080/1359432X.2019.1681401

Wynn, A. T., & Correll, S. J. (2018). Puncturing the pipeline: Do technology companies alienate women in recruiting sessions? *Social Studies of Science*, *48*(1), 149–164. doi:10.1177/0306312718756766 PMID:29424284

Zaharee, M., Lipkie, T., Mehlman, S. K., & Neylon, S. K. (2018). Recruitment and Retention of Early-Career Technical Talent: What Young Employees Want From Employers. *Research Technology Management*, *61*(5), 51–61. doi:10.1080/08956308.2018.1495966

ADDITIONAL READING

Ahmad, B., Nasir, S., Hai, M., & Bilal, S. (2022). Do career adaptability and employee-employer fit relate to career resilience? A collaborative effort to depart from the state of "silos" to "mutuality" in academia. *Kybernetes*. Advance Online Publication. doi:10.1108/K-04-2022-0617

Cable, D. M., & DeRue, D. S. (2002). The convergent and discrimination validity of subjective fit perceptions. *The Journal of Applied Psychology*, *87*(5), 875–884. doi:10.1037/0021-9010.87.5.875 PMID:12395812

Carless, S. A. (2005). Person-job fit versus person-organization fit as predictors of organizational attraction and job acceptance intentions: A longitudinal study. *Journal of Occupational and Organizational Psychology*, *78*(3), 411–429. doi:10.1348/096317905X25995

Crucke, A., & Bockaert, H. (2023). Exploring the attractiveness of social enterprises to job seekers: The role of perceived value fit and prestige. *Annals of Public and Cooperative Economics*, *94*(2), 399–422. doi:10.1111/apce.12393

Hodder, A. (2020). New technology, work and employment in the era of COVID-19: Reflecting on legacies of research. *New Technology, Work and Employment*, *35*(3), 262–275. doi:10.1111/ntwe.12173 PMID:32836624

Judge, T. A., & Cable, D. M. (2006). Applicant personality, organizational culture, and organizational attraction. *Personnel Psychology*, *50*(2), 359–394. doi:10.1111/j.1744-6570.1997.tb00912.x

Ma, Y., Austin, K. L., & Ezema, G. N. (2023). Validation of the Chinese Decent Work Scale. *Journal of Career Development*, *50*(1), 37–51. doi:10.1177/08948453221080980

Malhotra, N., Sahadev, S., & Sharom, N. Q. (2022). Organisational justice, organisational identification and job involvement: The mediating role of psychological need satisfaction and the moderating role of person-organisation fit. *International Journal of Human Resource Management*, *33*(8), 1526–2561. doi:10.1080/09585192.2020.1757737

Schein, E. (2010). *Organizational Culture and Leadership* (4th ed.). John Wiley & Sons.

Treviño, L. J., Egri, C. P., Ralston, D. A., Naoumova, I., Li, Y., Darder, F. L., de la Garza Carranza, M. T., & Furrer, O. (2020). A cross-cultural examination of person-organization fit: Is P-O fit congruent with or contingent on societal values? *MIR. Management International Review*, *60*(2), 287–314. doi:10.100711575-020-00411-0

Section 4

Challenges, Opportunities, and Future Workplace Trends

Chapter 8
Challenges for Greater Collaboration Between Actors

ABSTRACT

This chapter considers the challenges for greater collaboration between actors operating within a career ecosystem. First, five challenges for university career advisors are presented, including: (i) resource constraints, (ii) range of employers, (iii) alignment of goals and objectives, (iv) league table rankings, and (v) recruitment agencies. Next, five challenges for graduate recruiters are considered, including: (i) resource constraints, (ii) targeting universities, (iii) cultural differences, (iv) compliance approval, and (v) evolving business demands. The challenges faced by five additional actors are then briefly considered, including (i) students, (ii) lecturers, (iii) alums, (iv) professional bodies, and (v) national governments. The chapter concludes with four lived experience insights offering real-world examples of the challenges for greater collaboration between actors.

INTRODUCTION

Section One of the book set the scene (Chapter one) by introducing university career advisors, graduate recruiters, and sustainable graduate careers. Section Two of the book was framed from the university career advisor perspective and explored graduate employability and employability capital (Chapter two), student engagement strategies (Chapter three) and signaling employability (Chapter four). Section Three of the book was framed from the graduate recruiter perspective and covered attracting early career talent (Chapter five), preparing students for the university-to-work transition (Chapter six), and establishing and maintaining Person-Organization Fit

DOI: 10.4018/978-1-6684-9827-9.ch008

(Chapter seven). In the final section of the book (Section Four), our focus shifts to challenges and opportunities for collaboration between actors and a consideration of what the future of work might hold in store. This chapter focuses on the challenges for greater collaboration between actors. Chapter nine subsequently discusses the opportunities for greater collaboration before Chapter ten considers the future of work and provides some final thoughts to conclude the book.

THE CHALLENGES FOR UNIVERSITY CAREER ADVISORS

We begin by considering five challenges that university career advisors face when seeking to collaborate with graduate recruiters, including:

(i) Resource constraints
(ii) Range of employers
(iii) Alignment of goals and objectives
(iv) League table rankings
(v) Recruitment agencies

Resource Constraints

During the 2021/2022 academic year in the USA, the National Association of Colleges and Employers (2022) discovered an alarming shortage of career professionals, with just one professional available for every 2,263 students on average. This understaffing was further exacerbated by the fact that 60% of their time was dedicated to students, leaving only 40% for employers and other university-focused tasks. Similarly, Donald and Jackson (2022) noted an unprecedented demand for wellbeing and career-related support among university students in the UK due to the COVID-19 pandemic, which has strained existing resources. Unfortunately, many career counsellors lack the resources to support their student population adequately (Donald et al., 2022), emphasizing the importance of establishing win-win partnerships with employers or other institutions (Buckholtz & Donald, 2022). However, such collaborations often occur through informal channels, leading to sporadic efforts and a need for integrated strategic direction (Galan-Muros & Davey, 2019). Cooperation between universities and organizations, according to Orazbayeva et al. (2019), remains weak and fragmented, whereby most research into this area “is undertaken around specific elements, rather than as an encompassing, overarching and interconnected system” (p. 1311).

To illustrate the impact of resource constraints, including time and budget limitations, a personal anecdote from the 2020/2021 academic year is telling. During the COVID-19 pandemic, I prepared and freely shared a pre-recorded presentation with several universities across the UK, highlighting the support that university career services offer and encouraging students to use such services throughout their university studies. While most universities I contacted added the presentation to their career service websites, two institutions declined to use it due to concerns about overwhelming their already limited career service capacities. One university, with a student population exceeding 20,000, had only two full-time and two part-time career advisors. My observations are supported by Fisher (2023), who found that career services are struggling due to their low capacity to serve students' needs adequately.

Range of Employers

The Institute of Student Employers (2023) has highlighted a significant issue regarding the mismatch between the employment opportunities offered by university career services and the job preferences of students. This mismatch encompasses various aspects, including sectors, job locations, and employer sizes. My own research, which involved interviewing university career advisors during the COVID-19 pandemic, further supports this observation. It revealed that students were increasingly seeking job opportunities with local employers and small to medium-sized enterprises (SMEs) rather than solely focusing on large multinational organizations represented on campus (Donald et al., 2022). Interestingly, academic literature has advocated for university career advisors to diversify their employer partners for several years (e.g., Minocha et al., 2017).

However, responding to this call for a more diverse mix of employer partners faces three main barriers (Donald et al., 2022). Firstly, organizations often seek exclusive relationships with universities, especially when direct competitors are involved. This exclusivity can limit the range of employers and job opportunities available to students. Secondly, the turnover of graduate recruiters is relatively high, making it challenging to establish and maintain relationships at the individual level. This turnover can lead to losing ad-hoc relationships between specific universities and organizations. Finally, on-campus employer events are often seen as revenue-generating opportunities for universities (although less so during the COVID-19 pandemic!). The costs involved in having a presence on campus can be off-putting to SMEs because the low volume of jobs they are hiring for does not offer a suitable return on such investment.

Alignment of Goals and Objectives

CFE Research (2023) explored the challenges and complexities surrounding effective collaboration between university career services and employers. The interaction between these two actors is critical because their perspectives on work readiness vary based on their own contexts and interests (Winterton & Turner, 2019). A key obstacle to successful collaboration is the lack of communication between career advisors and graduate recruiters. This communication gap can result in misunderstandings and missed opportunities for collaboration. For example, career advisors may not have access to the latest industry trends and changes, limiting their ability to provide relevant advice to students.

Another related challenge is the limited availability of feedback and evaluation mechanisms. Evaluating the effectiveness of collaboration initiatives and obtaining feedback from students and employers is essential for identifying areas of improvement and demonstrating the impact of collaboration to facilitate talent flow and acquisition between higher education and industry (Baruch et al., 2023). However, resource constraints and competing goals, objectives, and priorities may hinder the establishment of robust evaluation processes. The differing needs of university career advisors and graduate recruiters also create tension and misunderstandings (CFE Research, 2023). University career services concentrate on supporting students in their career development and job market preparation to strive towards helping students to find fulfilling careers. At the same time, recruiters prioritize finding candidates that meet their specific needs. Bridging this gap requires effective communication and coordination between the two actors, but often, they operate independently, resulting in missed opportunities for students and employers (Buckholtz & Donald, 2022).

Practical challenges exist as well, such as differences in recruitment timelines. Career services may provide continuous support to students throughout their academic journey, while recruiters may have specific recruitment periods that do not align with the academic calendar. This discrepancy can make it challenging to coordinate recruitment activities and ensure that students are aware of available opportunities (Donald et al., 2018). Additionally, geographic distance can create further obstacles to collaboration. In some cases, graduate recruiters may be located in different regions than the university career services, making it challenging to establish regular communication and coordination for recruitment events and initiatives (Donald et al., 2022).

League Table Rankings

A further challenge for collaboration between actors operating within a career ecosystem is the role of university league table rankings, which can significantly influence future student numbers and associated revenue. The Complete University Guide (2023) states on their website

Our league tables rank the best universities in the UK, overall and in 74 subject areas. Knowing how best to choose your future university can be tough. Our league tables can help by showing you the top universities in the UK and allowing you to sort them by what's important to you. See the university rankings for your chosen subject and then filter by region, entry standards, student satisfaction, graduate prospects, and more. By comparing universities using our filters and your chosen metrics, you can start to get a clear picture of which one is the right one for you. (Online)

Consequently, many universities strive to enhance their rankings and closely examine how they compare to other universities at the local, national, and international levels (Hazelkorn 2019).

Therefore, universities face a challenging dilemma. Collaborating and sharing resources with other institutions seems logical, as their common goal is to produce employable graduates (Donald et al., 2022). However, university competition often hinders collaboration (QS Employer Insights, 2020). The fear stems from the fact that graduate employability measures significantly influence university league table rankings (Hora, 2020), which, in turn, impacts attracting future students and their tuition fees (Oliver, 2020). Additionally, universities may be hesitant to share insights with employers, fearing that the employer might pass those insights on to competing university career services that they partner with. As a result, this competitive environment, driven by university league table rankings, can ultimately harm students' employability prospects. *As a side note here, practitioners in Canada inform me that there is active collaboration between universities supported by numerous professional associations. Nevertheless, they experience a disconnect between career development professionals and work-integrated learning professionals.*

Recruitment Agencies

During my interviews with university career advisors, a significant challenge in the career ecosystem collaboration came to light. Many university career advisors expressed concerns about the potential threat posed by graduate recruitment agencies to their role in supporting university students (Donald et al., 2022). They feared these agencies might replace university career services as the primary link between organizations and students, putting their positions at risk. Another worry was the perception that recruitment agencies might prioritize their client's needs, which may not always align with the best interests of university students.

However, when speaking to graduate recruiters working for recruitment agencies, it became evident that they perceived their roles differently. They view their role as facilitators, aiming to connect organizations and universities by understanding and communicating the distinct needs of each actor (Donald et al., 2022). Interestingly, the representatives from recruitment agencies acknowledged the value of university career services, recognizing that university career advisors possess a deeper understanding of their specific students' needs, enabling tailored support. These findings underscore the importance of fostering open dialogue among the various actors within the career ecosystem (Buckholtz & Donald, 2022). Promoting communication and collaboration between university career advisors and recruitment agencies can address potential conflicts, leading to more effective support for university students.

THE CHALLENGES FOR GRADUATE RECRUITERS

Now that we have considered the challenges to collaboration from the university career advisor perspective, our attention shifts to considering five challenges from the graduate recruiter perspective, including:

(i) Resource constraints
(ii) Targeting universities
(iii) Cultural differences
(iv) Compliance approval
(v) Evolving business demands

Resource Constraints

Limited resources emerge as a prominent obstacle for graduate recruiters. For instance, a report by the Graduate Recruitment Bureau (2022) revealed that 27% of respondents identified the scarcity of resources within their recruitment teams as a significant issue. The report identified resource constraints to include various aspects such as lack of staff, insufficient budget, and time pressures. Limited staffing and high staff turnover can hinder recruiters' engagement with university career services, as they lack dedicated personnel to nurture and sustain these relationships

(Hogarth et al., 2007). Collaboration with multiple universities also becomes costly and time-consuming, placing significant demands on resource-limited graduate recruiters (Hogarth et al., 2007).

Moreover, the Careers2032 Project (2022) highlighted the impact of resource constraints on smaller businesses. As these companies often lack name recognition and financial resources, they face additional challenges in attracting top talent from universities. The resource disparity between large corporations and Small and Medium-sized Enterprises (SMEs) can create an uneven playing field in the competition for talented graduates. Investing in technology for attraction and selection further exacerbates the resource gap between larger organizations and SMEs (Donald et al., 2023a). Larger corporations with more significant hiring volumes can make cost-effective technology investments, streamlining their recruitment process. In contrast, resource-limited SMEs may find it challenging to adopt cutting-edge technology, meaning they miss out on time-saving opportunities, hindering their ability to collaborate effectively with university career services.

Targeting Universities

In January 2023, High Fliers conducted its annual research into the graduate labor market. Their findings are based on *The Times Top 100 Graduate Employers* for 2022 based on the views of 12,432 final-year students at UK-based universities. According to High Fliers (2023), the ten most targeted universities in the UK were "Manchester, Nottingham, Birmingham, Bristol, Warwick, Leeds, University College London, Cambridge, Durham and Southampton" (p. 6). The report observes how "it is interesting that this list of universities bears little resemblance to The Times & Sunday Times Good University Guide 2023" (p. 24). This is particularly relevant given our earlier discussions in this chapter around the influence of university league table rankings as a challenge to greater collaboration between actors operating within a career ecosystem. High Fliers (2023) also reported that employers targeted, on average, 27 universities in the 2022-2023 academic year, up from 21 universities in the 2020-2021 academic year. Table 1 shows the number of universities targeted by top employers in the 2022-2023 academic year.

However, it should be noted that the organizations featured in this survey are predominantly multinational corporations that hire large volumes of graduates each year and often have significantly higher recruitment budgets than SMEs. Nevertheless, multinational organizations also face issues. A study on internship recruiting in the USA found two significant challenges *identifying target institutions* and *establishing campus connection points* (Smith & Green, 2021). Therefore, university career services need to look for opportunities to engage with employers and showcase what their students can offer specific organizations to establish relationships and make their university an attractive option as a target institution.

Table 1. Number of universities targeted by top employers in 2022-2023

Number of Universities	%
More than 35	17
31-35	16
26-30	9
21-25	18
16-20	15
11-15	8
1-10	9
0	8

Source: Based on Chart 4.4 by High Fliers (2023, p. 24).

Cultural Differences

Michel-Schneider (2021) states that "the primary challenges for Academia and Industry remain access to funding, however, also the tackling of contrary mindsets and missions as well as overcoming organisational and cultural differences create serious barriers to a successful cooperation" (p. 47). Differences in perceptions of time can further complicate cooperation (de Wit-de Vries et al., 2019). My own transition from industry to higher education revealed disparities in decision-making approaches. Academia tends to exhibit greater resistance to change, risk aversion, bureaucratic decision-making, and more hierarchical structures than the industry's more adaptive and risk-tolerant nature (although exceptions exist in both cases). SMEs, in particular, encounter difficulties in collaborating with universities, as they often have limited resources, lack HR departments, and face challenges in aligning their goals with other actors (Bertello et al., 2022). These difficulties and cultural differences can lead to reluctance from SMEs to share knowledge and intellectual property, impacting students' learning opportunities (Bikard et al., 2019).

An interesting observation to consider when thinking about cultural differences is the notion of isolation versus collaboration. While an individual actor's approach may serve their immediate needs, more sustainable strategies may exist for the entire career ecosystem. Graduate recruiters may not fully understand the culture and values of universities, which can limit their ability to collaborate effectively with university career advisors and students. Thus, adopting a holistic view and encouraging collaboration between all stakeholders becomes necessary. Again, open and ongoing dialogue between actors is essential to overcome differences in language usage (de Wit-de Vries et al., 2019).

Compliance Approval

Graduate recruiters, especially those acting as agents for multinational organizations, face a challenge in obtaining approval from the compliance team for their marketing, attraction, and selection strategies. The compliance team tends to be cautious and seeks to safeguard the organization's reputation regarding content, delivery, and partnerships. A common theme emerged in interviews that I conducted with graduate recruiters, emphasizing how "organizations must consider the risk versus reward of sharing resources and strategies whilst competing for early career talent" (Donald et al., 2022, p. 2213). In Chapter 5, we explored the significance of effective talent management in gaining a competitive edge and ensuring long-term organizational success (Ab Wahab & Ekrem, 2020; Illes et al., 2010). We also observed that hiring the most employable graduates contributes to establishing and maintaining a competitive advantage for organizations (Petruzziello et al., 2022), while an organization's culture and reputation significantly influence student applications (Bright Network, 2022). Consequently, graduate recruiters may be prohibited by the organization's compliance team from collaborating with specific organizations or universities to maintain a competitive edge. This can result in a reluctance to share information or resources that could benefit their competitors. Similarly, the effectiveness of collaboration initiatives with university career advisors can be hampered if organizations do not openly share data or information about their recruitment needs or processes.

On a related topic, while gathering lived experience insights for this book, I encountered a noticeable difference in the ease of obtaining insights from university career advisors compared to industry professionals. Despite having a strong network of contacts in both areas, securing insights from individuals in the industry required significantly more effort. I discovered that many individual employees were willing to share their experiences, but their employers, through the compliance team, often vetoed such occurrences. Instead of seeing it as an opportunity to showcase the organization's achievements, there was a prevailing concern about potential reputational risks and the fear of giving away strategic insights to competitors. However, what I found somewhat strange about the approach adopted by various compliance teams was that many organizations already share such information in public forums when competing for industry, regional or national awards.

Evolving Business Demands

Graduate recruiters face a significant challenge in preparing students for the future of work and navigating potential organizational challenges arising from evolving business demands. Izzo et al. (2022) emphasize that this becomes even more difficult if recruiters only have partial and incomplete perceptions about possible futures. For instance, the impact of the COVID-19 pandemic as a global level chance event has transformed the workforce, with individuals now prioritizing work-life balance, flexible work arrangements, and healthy lifestyle choices to a greater extent (Donald, 2020; Donald et al., 2022). This shift, combined with the scarcity of graduates with specialized degrees, has implications for organizations seeking to fill specific roles (Graduate Recruitment Bureau, 2022). The ongoing debate about the mismatch between employer-demanded skills and the skills developed in students by universities adds further complexity to the recruitment process (Römgens et al., 2020). Moreover, the existence of a skills gap can be influenced by factors such as gender and geographical location (Institute of Student Employers, 2023).

A tailored approach to talent attraction has become crucial in response to these challenges, as the conventional one-size-fits-all method has proven ineffective (Ng et al., 2022). Career advisors are pivotal in helping organizations develop personalized recruitment strategies that cater to diverse student populations with varying skill sets and preferences. The pandemic has also exacerbated existing disparities in the labor market (Ho, 2023), highlighting the importance of inclusive hiring practices to address persistent inequalities and ensure equal opportunities for all students preparing for the university-to-work transition. Therefore, successful collaboration between organizations and university career advisors requires navigating challenges associated with uncertain futures, skills mismatch, work-life balance preferences, persistent inequalities, and tailored attraction strategies. By working together, both parties can bridge the gap between academia and the job market, equipping graduates with the necessary skills and knowledge to thrive in an ever-evolving workplace landscape.

THE CHALLENGES FOR ADDITIONAL ACTORS

Having considered the challenges to collaboration for university career advisors and graduate recruiters, our attention now shifts to considering the challenges of five additional actors, including:

(i) Students
(ii) Lecturers

(iii) Alums
(iv) Professional bodies
(v) National governments

Students

In semester two of the academic year 2016/2017, I interviewed 38 final-year university students in the UK as part of a mixed-methods study (Donald et al., 2018). We had previously collected self-reported survey data in two waves at the beginning of the 2015/2016 and 2016/2017 academic years (Donald et al., 2019). The interviews focused on how the students perceived changes in their employability throughout their university years. From a personal standpoint, the students felt that their employability had increased with each subsequent year of their undergraduate study. These perceptions align with the Employability Capital Growth (ECG) model discussed in Chapter 2, which includes dimensions such as social capital, cultural capital, psychological capital, personal identity capital, health capital, scholastic capital, market-value capital, career identity capital, and economic capital (Donald et al., 2023a). On the other hand, when considering market factors, the students reported that their perceived employability had declined between the penultimate and final years of their undergraduate study. They attributed this decline to factors such as the "volume of graduates, the lack of jobs available, and receiving rejections from job applications" (Donald et al., 2018, p. 529). These market-related aspects correspond to the external factors presented in the ECG model in Chapter 2. These challenges also resonate with the findings of Greaves (2021), who identified difficulties for students in finding opportunities and staying motivated during the job-hunting stage. Additionally, Akkermans, Collings et al. (2021) highlight that career development and employability learning can be traumatic due to factors like career shocks or application rejections.

Another focus of the interviews was to identify the various actors in the career ecosystem who could support students in enhancing their employability during their time at university (Donald et al., 2018). Students mentioned university career advisors, lecturers, graduate recruiters, and alums as potential sources of support. However, as discussed in Chapter 3, the students expressed dissatisfaction with the engagement strategies employed by university career advisors. They pointed out issues such as limited provision beyond the main university campus and a lack of representation of different organizations on campus. Additionally, students believed there should be more collaboration between university career advisors, lecturers, graduate recruiters, and alums, as each actor has different objectives and priorities. Furthermore, students raised concerns about the relevance of the university curriculum to the needs of employers. These challenges are likely to have been exacerbated by the impact of the COVID-19 pandemic on education and work experience opportunities, leaving students ill-prepared to enter the labor market and needing additional support (Donald & Mouratidou, 2022).

Lecturers

The involvement of lecturers in developing the employability of university students remains a contested area. Over a decade ago, Blackmore and Kandiko (2012) observed,

Some staff in universities question whether employability should be a concern of universities, because they believe either that universities exist for the disinterested pursuit of knowledge or that, in successful universities, graduates are likely to be highly employable anyway. (p. 6)

More recently, Daubney (2022) also highlighted the need to address negative perceptions held by some academics, including:

- Whatever it is, employability is not academic knowledge
- Employability is the responsibility or "job" of the careers service, not the academic
- Employability is not about knowing, it is about doing (p. 95).

Lecturers dedicated to integrating opportunities to enhance students' employability into the curriculum still encounter additional challenges. For example, when incorporating authentic assessment, Manville et al. (2022) acknowledge several issues, including a lack of training and support, increased paperwork, and more teaching hours. Additionally, they point out that an authentic assessment approach may pose a risk to student feedback evaluations of the module, particularly if students do not fully embrace it or feel that it demands too much time compared to other modules (Thurab-Nkhosi et al., 2018). Furthermore, utilizing peer learning also comes with its own set of concerns. These include the potential risks associated with an increased workload, power dynamics between students, and a perceived lack of instructor availability (Adachi & Dawson, 2018; Brewer & Movahedazarhouligh, 2018; Donald & Ford, 2022).

The use of student evaluations of modules and lecturers presents further challenges. Chávez and Mitchell (2020) observed that students tend to give higher satisfaction scores to white male lecturers compared to other lecturers. To address this problem, the authors support calls by Martin (2016) for academia to develop better measures of teaching effectiveness instead of expecting individual lecturers to change their behaviors to fit better into the current performance metrics system.

Consequently, national governments need to consider all actors operating within a career ecosystem when implementing top-down policy decisions to ensure that student evaluations or university league table rankings do not negatively impact the sustainability of the ecosystem.

Alums

University students believe alums can provide valuable links between universities and organizations (Donald et al., 2018). However, Kinash et al. (2018) discovered in their interviews with various actors within a career ecosystem that alums perceived a disconnect between academia and industry concerning performance assessment. Universities were found to emphasize exams and report writing, while industry prioritized human skills. Interestingly, the study revealed that when discussing graduate employability, alums, students, and employers were less likely to mention curriculum-based assessment as a dominant theme. In contrast, lecturers explicitly connected assessment and graduate employability. Kinash and colleagues suggest that developing professional networks is crucial to enhancing graduate employability in university students and call for alums to play a more integral role in facilitating such opportunities.

A further challenge to understanding differing actors' perspectives is the need for more evidence from industry alums regarding the effectiveness of employability strategies (Bilsland et al., 2019). Studies involving alums have tended to focus more on philanthropic activities or gathering testimonials for marketing purposes (English et al., 2021). Nevertheless, there has been an emerging interest in exploring the role of alums in informing university strategies and enhancing student employability. For example, Zhao & Cox (2022) investigated the views of alums in the context of Chinese students studying in the UK and their employability. Similarly, Donald (2023b) recently explored the perspectives of alums who graduated in 2008 and 2020 to inform university strategies to enhance students' employability.

However, the use of alums to support university students to enhance their employability also presents some additional challenges and potential conflicts of interest, including:

- Alums may not have sufficient time or availability to provide ongoing career guidance to students.
- While alums may be knowledgeable about their own industries or career paths, they may lack expertise in other areas. Their advice may not always be applicable or relevant to all students.

- The advice from alums can be influenced by biases or personal opinions, which can limit students' exposure to different career options or lead them in directions that are not a good fit.
- Alums may not adequately reflect the diversity of the student body at a specific university, limiting students' exposure to diverse perspectives and career paths.
- Alums involved in recruiting or hiring may face conflicts of interest when providing career guidance to students, potentially favoring their employer or industry and consequently restricting students' exposure to other opportunities.

Professional Bodies

An affiliation with a professional body, whether as an organization or an individual, implies adhering to specific standards, best practices, and benchmarks. In a sustainable career ecosystem, professional bodies serve as intermediaries between individuals, organizations, and national governments (Donald, 2023a). They gather ongoing feedback to understand the changing needs of these actors (Arnold et al., 2021). As a result, professional bodies can tailor their formal training programs to help individuals meet organizations' present and future requirements.

Moreover, many professional bodies provide student affiliation options for those pursuing university studies. Notable benefits of student membership in a professional body include:

- Access to information and sector-specific resources
- Access to relevant certification or professional qualifications
- Lobbying for interests within the sector
- Professional advice
- Work experience and job opportunities
- Events and networking (Pearson, 2021, Online).

Nevertheless, various challenges are related to professional bodies' involvement and collaboration with other actors in the career ecosystem. Some examples of such challenges include:

- Students may lack awareness regarding the significance of professional bodies and the benefits of becoming a member, resulting in a lack of engagement and limited participation in professional development opportunities.

- Due to limited resources, professional bodies might face constraints investing in comprehensive career development programs, internships, and experiential learning initiatives. Consequently, their capacity to support students in gaining practical skills and experience could be restricted.
- The absence of well-established connections with diverse employers may hinder the professional bodies' ability to facilitate work-integrated learning opportunities and offer student placements.
- Insufficient understanding of the specific skills and competencies required by employers may limit a professional body's capacity to design effective programs that adequately prepare students for the labor market upon graduation.
- The existing standards and accreditation requirements may not always align with employers' needs or keep up-to-date with evolving labor market needs. This leads to a disconnect between what students learn in their academic programs and what employers seek in candidates.

National Governments

The Triple Helix model (Etzkowitz & Leydesdorff, 1995) highlights the intertwined relationship between universities, employers, and national governments to foster knowledge-based economic development. According to Pitan (2023), the Triple Helix model "transforms the interaction between the university, industry, and government to produce knowledgeable, innovative, and employable workers for the 21st century" (p. 86). While this current book primarily focuses on the role of universities and employers, it is essential to recognize the significant impact of national governments through their policies, particularly in the context of neoliberal agendas and funding allocations. Additionally, Jackson (2018) emphasizes the need to "open up, constructively, the meaning of what it is to be employable and encourage people to think beyond the acquisition of generic skills to more holistic ways of knowing, being and performing in the world of highly situated and contextualised learning" (p. 5). However, this requires a shift in how national governments perceive and measure employability since "only when there is mutual understanding between stakeholders can we truly say that we are working effectively towards the shared goal of developing lifelong and lifewide learners" (Cole & Hallett, 2019, p. 126). It is also crucial to focus on developing relationships and strategies that are forward-looking and applicable for the next 10-20 years rather than relying on approaches that may have been suitable in the past or are unlikely to remain effective in the medium-to-long term.

Several challenges arise when involving national governments as an actor operating within a career ecosystem when attempting to promote graduate employability:

- The process of coordinating government departments, universities, and industry partners can be time-consuming, leading to delays and inefficiencies in implementing programs that support graduate employability.
- Differences in priorities between governments, universities, and industry partners may hinder effective collaboration. Governments focus on job creation and economic growth, while universities may prioritize research and student learning.
- A limited understanding of industry needs may prevent government officials from designing effective programs that align with employers' skill requirements.
- The constantly changing job market challenges governments to develop relevant career development programs that adequately prepare students for emerging employment opportunities.
- Government budget limitations may restrict investment in initiatives that prepare students for the labor market, resulting in a lack of resources for career development programs and experiential learning opportunities.
- Restricted access to a diverse range of employers can limit the government's ability to facilitate work-integrated learning opportunities and job placements for students.
- Some students may not fully embrace government-led initiatives, which can limit the overall effectiveness of employability programs.
- National governments tend to serve limited terms in office, whereby a newly elected government may have different economic and policy priorities or different strategies to graduate employability.

Now that we have considered the challenges for greater collaboration from the perspectives of various actors operating within a career ecosystem, our attention now turns to providing four lived experience insights. Subsequently, Chapter 9 offers some strategic opportunities to address the challenges discussed in Chapter 8.

LIVED EXPERIENCE INSIGHTS

Lived Experience Insight

Shared By Marina Boz, Anglia Ruskin University, UK

The Challenge

Underrepresented students face barriers such as time constraints, a lack of financial resources, and caring responsibilities when seeking to engage in extracurricular activities offered by career services. These barriers can also prevent students from accessing and participating in internships or placements, which may limit their graduate employment outcomes due to a lack of work experience. The challenge of unequal access to employability development opportunities was the main driver for the Live Briefs Programme at Anglia Ruskin University.

The Context

The Active Curriculum underpins Anglia Ruskin University's education strategy. This bold and comprehensive curriculum framework provides a distinctive approach to course design, pedagogy and an enhanced student experience. The framework's eight dimensions include, among others: students as co-creators, authentic 'real-world' learning and assessment, and inclusivity. Accordingly, the Live Briefs Programme is an ambitious, innovative, curriculum-based strategy to integrate the inclusive provision of work-integrated learning opportunities for students into the curriculum.

Action Taken

The Live Briefs Programme offers an opportunity for students to work on a real-world challenge set by professional partners that aligns learning outcomes with the partners' objectives. Partners collaborate with the academic employability consultants and faculty to ensure these objectives are integrated into the assessment design of compulsory modules. In response, students produce agreed deliverables aligned with the partners' professional objectives, such as marketing plans, media assets, or analysis of data sets. In turn, the partner provides detailed professional feedback to each student on their performance.

The Outcome

In the first three years of the Live Briefs Programme, faculties across the university delivered 205 Live Briefs supported by 210 professional partnerships, enabling over 12,600 students to develop their professional-mindedness, skills, and confidence through work-integrated learning. Students reported increased self-perceived employability via skill development, real-world experience, and examples to share during interviews to signal their suitability for a role. Additionally, professional partners highlighted the benefits of enabling students to perform professional tasks and better understand industry-specific challenges while also having the opportunity to inspire future talent.

Lessons Learned and Advice

From the outset, the professional partnership development to support the Live Briefs Programme was considered our main obstacle due to the range and scale of actors involved. We created a governance structure to coordinate the business engagement activity across different services supporting the Live Briefs Programme. This was required to ensure that the different service teams, who typically had their own specific aims when developing professional partnerships, would share a common vision when approaching partners to ensure the success of the Live Briefs Programme. Despite the significant progress in developing professional partnerships collaboratively, we acknowledge that managing these relationships in a sustainable manner remains our greatest challenge. As part of our Live Briefs Programme meetings, we continuously discuss ways to improve our working practices to this aim, including how to empower academics to take ownership in managing professional partnerships for curriculum enhancement to improve students' authentic learning experiences.

Lived Experience Insight

Shared by Paul L. Rainey, Career Professional, USA

The Challenge

Towards the conclusion of my postgraduate degree in counseling, I took up a position as the head of a small careers service at a regional university in Louisiana, USA. During my on-campus job interview, the Vice President of Student Affairs indicated that the careers service had been unsuccessful in engaging the wider campus community and had failed to achieve the impact-related objectives that internal and external stakeholders had hoped for. The Vice President made it explicitly clear that I was being considered for the role due to the belief that I could address these issues.

The Context

A few months after accepting the job, I once again found myself in the office of the Vice President. They had been speaking to various stakeholders across the campus community to understand their desires and ideas for action. It quickly became clear that the stakeholders cared deeply about the potential for the careers service to support students and work collaboratively within the broader university ecosystem. However, the fragmented visions from the various stakeholder groups showed the need for a unified point of reference concerning the strategic direction of the careers service.

Action Taken

Typically, new leaders re-write an organization's mission, vision, and values statements as a symbolic gesture to make their mark and act as their legacy. However, having built up trust with key representatives of the various stakeholder groups over the first few months in my role, I decided to use this activity to unify them. I invited these individuals to an initial 45-minute meeting, asking them to help re-write the career service's mission, vision, and value statements. During the meeting, I asked each person to send me a draft document describing what they wanted the careers service to accomplish. Subsequently, I integrated the ideas into a single document that underwent several rounds of revisions before receiving stakeholder approval.

The Outcome

The new mission, vision, and value statements subsequently informed the career service's strategic plan. The collaborative approach to their development also enhanced the influence of the careers service on campus since it was easier to obtain institutional support for initiatives after demonstrating that I had listened to these various stakeholders. By the time I left the university, we had achieved most of the aims and objectives, and the careers service was fully integrated into the broader university ecosystem.

Lessons Learned and Advice

I remember telling the Vice President of Student Affairs how nervous I had felt during that initial 45-minute meeting with the representatives of the various stakeholder groups. They replied that feeling nervous was a good indicator since it showed my emotional investment and desire to enter dialogue with these representatives in a dignified and respectful manner. My advice is to engage different actors operating within a university ecosystem to facilitate knowledge sharing and execute shared governance. This approach is more effective than making strategic decisions in isolation and ignoring the expertise of individuals familiar with existing systems.

Lived Experience Insight

Shared By Michal Kasprzak and Samantha Chang, University of Toronto, Canada

The Challenge

Can 66 project team members from five partner institutions create an open-access series of four 60-minute self-paced asynchronous modules in 38 weeks? The short answer is 'yes!' but not without challenges. Communication and coordination require careful considerations in cross-institutional, inter-unit collaborations between actors from various academic disciplines (humanities, social sciences, and sciences) with different professional roles (graduate students, postdoctoral fellows, faculty members, educational developers, career educators, administrative staff, and industry professionals). In our context, the diverse experiences and voices of the 66-member team generated an open-access series that was truly collaborative, learner-driven, and digital by design.

The Context

Between April 2021 and January 2022, our cross-institutional, inter-unit collaborative team co-developed the open-access series "Developing Your Teaching Dossier" with funding from the Government of Ontario and through eCampusOntario's support of the 'Virtual Learning Strategy'. The series of four customizable interactive asynchronous modules—consisting of 260 elements, including 17 H5P interactive books, 41 YouTube videos, and 89 Pressbooks files—is designed for graduate students and postdoctoral fellows exploring strategies to reflect on their teaching and develop their teaching dossier. This adaptable series can be reused, retained, revised, remixed, and redistributed in various learning management ecosystems for diverse teaching, training, and learning contexts. The compressed project timeline with a firm deadline required thoughtful communication and coordination to support the work of the 66 project members.

Action Taken

Communication modes and coordination support promoted transparency and relationship building between actors (project members) across five institutions throughout the five development phases. The team members maintained communication synchronously and asynchronously. The entire project team met once a month, while smaller meetings supported specific tasks or subteams. The weekly Monday preview emails (i) listed weekly goals, (ii) provided digital notebooks documenting meeting notes and project status observations, and (iii) included survey links to collect feedback and provide ongoing asynchronous check-ins and project transparency. Coordination of resources such as templates and trackers (e.g., storyboards; photo, video, resource copyrights; and feedback forms) facilitated analysis, design, and development. The mock-up modules translating the resources and templates into a draft helped early implementation and evaluation—flagging early issues of transferability and adaptability of the content.

The Outcome

Transparent communication and relational coordination fostered a safe and meaningful collaborative space that ultimately led to the successful and on-time completion of the "Developing Your Teaching Dossier" series. The various forms of communication and coordination strengthened each team member's sense of ownership, agency, and accomplishment. Within the 66-member team, early career talents such as graduate students and postdoctoral fellows comprised 50% of the project membership. Including and promoting early career talent contributions throughout every step of the development process, from ideating to defining, prototyping, and testing, was essential as the open-access series is a resource made by and for graduate students and postdoctoral fellows.

Lessons Learned and Advice

In addition to transparent communication and relational coordination, there was intentional grouping and pairing of folks into four subteams (each working on a distinct module) from across institutions and roles to encourage greater collaboration. Each of the four subteams included at least one graduate student partnered with a staff member from their institution. The pairing ensured that the graduate student had direct access to their home institutional resources. Each subteam coordinated meetings and facilitated reciprocal processes that best supported their collaboration. While the non-hierarchical team structures worked well, opportunities still existed to enhance the student-partner experience. For example, ongoing opportunities for graduate student team members to gather for peer check-ins would facilitate discussions about the collaboration experience, further promoting transparency and relationship-building, and enhancing communication and coordination between actors.

Lived Experience Insight

Shared By Kelly Pfeffer, Financial Services Industry, Australia

The Challenge

Individuals undertaking the university-to-work transition often require significant support from their employer, particularly if the graduate has limited work experience or it is their first full-time job. A major challenge for the graduate-employer relationship is the employee's ability to reset their 'student' schedule and adjust to performing at their best during specific times and days of the week.

The Context

Graduates have experienced three or more years in a university environment, offering them a flexible and self-managed student experience. They have often balanced their studies and participation in student societies alongside casual or part-time employment (potentially involving irregular hours). The move to a hybrid model for certain classes gave them the flexibility to choose in-person or virtual participation (or even watch a recording at a time and day that best suited them). However, while many workplaces have moved towards (or retained) some opportunities for flexible ways of working, a mandate often remains for work tasks to be undertaken during core business hours and on specific days of the week.

Action Taken

Part of the onboarding process for new graduates into our business requires them to undertake significant learning and upskilling, especially concerning our business, customers, systems, and working methods. This means there is a high potential for cognitive overload during their first few weeks of employment. Consequently, we decided to embed wellbeing elements into our onboarding program to support graduates in resetting their natural circadian rhythm (e.g. setting a routine, using notifications/alarms to stay on track, coming into the office full-time, etc.) and helping them perform at their best. We also redesigned our onboarding program to deliver content in short bursts (a maximum of 1 hour at a time) with no more than four sessions per week for the first five weeks to increase absorption and retention of the information.

The Outcome

In a recent feedback survey of our onboarding program, we received positive feedback on all elements with an overall rating of 4.5 (out of 5) from sixty responses (80% of the cohort). Additionally, qualitative feedback via open-ended survey questions showed us that graduates felt we understood their feelings and provided them with the time and resources needed to adjust from university to working life. Graduates were particularly grateful for this since they underestimated the difficulty of the transition to 'normal' working hours.

Lessons Learned and Advice

When hiring graduates, the selection process can sometimes give the impression that they are high performing and competent in all areas of their life. In most cases, the perception is accurate, but even graduates do not know what they do not know. Until they are in the position of undertaking the university-to-work transition, it is difficult for them to pre-empt how long it will take them to adapt and what that process entails. I recommend discussing this transition with students when visiting university campuses or providing workshops. Additionally, once an individual accepts an offer of employment, provide them with information and tips for proactive steps to prepare for transitioning into the workplace.

Reflection on Lived Experience Insights

The four lived experience insights from Australia, Canada, the UK, and the USA highlight challenges when seeking greater collaboration between actors. One common theme is that actors within a career ecosystem often have different goals and agendas. Therefore, involving these different actors at various stages is essential, such as during the planning, implementation, and evaluation processes. By incorporating diverse perspectives and fostering buy-in, practitioners can create an environment that promotes knowledge sharing and acts as a common reference point for collaboration.

However, establishing and maintaining relationships among these actors can be difficult due to the time involved and high staff turnover. In projects involving multiple actors across different departments or institutions, additional challenges arise regarding transparent communication, building relationships, and coordinating resources. These challenges pose significant risks to the success and long-term sustainability of initiatives.

Moreover, transitioning from university life into the workplace can be challenging for graduates, with potential negative impacts on their wellbeing when onboarding programs lead to cognitive overload. To address this, employers should share their lessons with current students, helping them better prepare for the transition. Unfortunately, underrepresented students often face barriers in accessing career support through their university career service. This suggests that employers should directly engage with these students on campus and collaborate with other actors to promote the sustainability of career ecosystems and ensure a more inclusive approach to supporting student career development.

Some of the strategies suggested here to manage and overcome the challenges of collaboration between actors will be explored further in the next chapter.

CONCLUSION

In this chapter, we discussed various challenges related to collaboration faced by university career advisors, graduate recruiters, and five other actors. We also provided four insights based on real-life experiences to bridge the gap between theory and practice.

If you are a university career advisor or a graduate recruiter reading this book, you may like to reflect on the following five questions:

- How does each of the five themes mentioned in this chapter affect you or your team?
- Among the given themes, which one has the most significant impact?
- What additional challenges does your team face regarding collaboration with other actors?
- How can you address some of these challenges?
- Which individuals or stakeholders do you need buy-in from to address these challenges effectively?

If you are a student or one of the other additional actors discussed in this chapter, you might like to consider the following five questions:

- How do the challenges other actors face in the career ecosystem impact you?
- Do you have any suggestions for additional challenges that different actors might face?
- Can you propose any ideas on how these actors can address their challenges?

Having considered the challenges related to collaboration between actors, the next chapter of the book continues Section 4 by exploring opportunities for collaboration to enhance sustainability within a career ecosystem.

REFERENCES

Ab Wahab, N., & Ekrem, T. (2020). Chasing productivity demands, worker well-being, and firm performance: The moderating effects of HR support and flexible work arrangement. *Personnel Review*, *49*(9), 1823–1843. doi:10.1108/PR-01-2019-0026

Adachi, C., Tai, J. H.-M., & Dawson, P. (2018). Academics' perceptions of the benefits and challenges of self and peer assessment in higher education. *Assessment & Evaluation in Higher Education*, *43*(2), 294–306. doi:10.1080/02602938.2017.1339775

Akkermans, J., Collings, D. G., da Motta Veiga, S. P., Post, C., & Seibert, S. (2021). Towards a broader understanding of career shocks: Exploring interdisciplinary connections with research on job search, human resource management, entrepreneurship, and diversity. *Journal of Vocational Behavior*, *126*(1), 103563. doi:10.1016/j.jvb.2021.103563

Arnold, L., Mohamed-Ghouse, Z. S., & Wheeler, T. (2021). Role of the professional body in a pandemic. In A. Rajabifard, G. Foliente, & D. Paez (Eds.), *COVID-19 Pandemic, Geospatial Information, and Community Resilience* (pp. 161–169). Routledge. doi:10.1201/9781003181590-14

Baruch, Y., Ashleigh, M. J., & Donald, W. E. (2023). A sustainable career ecosystem perspective of talent flow and acquisition: The interface between higher education and industry. In W. E. Donald (Ed.), *Handbook of Research on Sustainable Career Ecosystems for University Students and Graduates* (pp. 177–194). IGI Global. doi:10.4018/978-1-6684-7442-6.ch010

Becker, K. L. (2021). We want connection and we do not mean wi-fi: Examining the impacts of Covid-19 on Gen Z's work and employment outcomes. *Management Research Review*, *45*(5), 684–699. doi:10.1108/MRR-01-2021-0052

Bertello, A., Ferraris, A., De Bernardi, P., & Bertoldi, B. (2022). Challenges to open innovation in traditional SMEs: An analysis of pre-competitive projects in university-industry-government collaboration. *The International Entrepreneurship and Management Journal*, *18*(1), 89–104. doi:10.100711365-020-00727-1

Bikard, M., Vakili, K., & Teodoridis, F. (2019). When collaboration bridges institutions: The impact of university-industry collaboration on academic productivity. *Organization Science*, *30*(2), 426–445. doi:10.1287/orsc.2018.1235

Bilsland, C., Carter, L., & Wood, L. (2019). Work integrated learning internships in transnational education. *Education + Training*, *61*(3), 359–373. doi:10.1108/ET-07-2017-0094

Blackmore, P., & Kandiko, C. (2012). *Strategic Curriculum Change*. Routledge.

Brewer, R., & Movahedazarhouligh, S. (2018). Successful stories and conflicts: A literature review on the effectiveness of flipped learning in higher education. *Journal of Computer Assisted Learning, 34*(4), 409–416. doi:10.1111/jcal.12250

Bright Network. (2022). *What do graduates want? 2022/23*. Bright Network. https://employers.brightnetwork.co.uk/what-do-graduates-want-report-and-video

Buckholtz, T., & Donald, W. E. (2022). Direct outcomes and win-win relationships between university careers advisors and graduate recruiters. *GiLE Journal of Skills Development, 2*(1), 9–25. doi:10.52398/gjsd.2022.v2.i1.pp9-25

Careers2032 Project. (2022). *An industry research project co-produced by AGCAS, ISE, Wonkhe and Handshake, looking at the careers sector of 2032 and the role technology could play in facilitating human connections*. Handshake. https://joinhandshake.co.uk/careers2032

CFE Research (2023). *The Benefits of And Barriers to Collaborative Access Activity by Higher Education Providers*. The Office for Students. https://www.officeforstudents.org.uk/publications/benefits-of-and-barriers-to-collaborative-access-activity/

Chávez, K., & Mitchell, K. (2020). Exploring bias in student evaluations: Gender, race, and ethnicity. *PS, Political Science & Politics, 53*(2), 270–274. doi:10.1017/S1049096519001744

Cole, D., & Hallett, R. (2019). The language of employability. In J. Higgs, G. Crisp, & W. Letts (Eds.), *Education for Employability* (pp. 119-130). Brill. doi:10.1163/9789004400832_010

Daubney, K. (2022). "Teaching employability is not my job!": Redefining embedded employability from within the higher education curriculum. *Higher Education: Skills and Work-Based Learning, 12*(1), 92–106. doi:10.1108/HESWBL-07-2020-0165

de Wit-de Vries, E., Dolfsma, W. A., Van der Windt, H. J., & Gerkema, M. P. (2019). Knowledge transfer in university-industry research partnerships: A review. *The Journal of Technology Transfer, 44*(4), 1236–1255. doi:10.100710961-018-9660-x

Donald, W. E. (2020). *Viewpoint: COVID-19 and the Future of Careers*. Graduate Recruitment Bureau. doi:10.13140/RG.2.2.19306.13760

Donald, W. E. (2023a). Application of career ecosystems theory and the new psychological contract to the field of project management: Toward a conceptual model. *Project Management Journal, 54*(1), 7–18. doi:10.1177/87569728221118873

Donald, W. E. (2023b). Sustainable talent pipelines and person-organisation fit: Strategic insights from UK graduates. *Career Development International*, *28*(2), 234–249. doi:10.1108/CDI-10-2022-0285

Donald, W. E., Ashleigh, M. J., & Baruch, Y. (2018). Students' perceptions of education and employability: Facilitating career transition from higher education into the labour market. *Career Development International*, *23*(5), 513–540. doi:10.1108/CDI-09-2017-0171

Donald, W. E., Ashleigh, M. J., & Baruch, Y. (2022). The university-to-work transition: Responses of universities and organizations to the COVID-19 pandemic. *Personnel Review*, *51*(9), 2201–2221. doi:10.1108/PR-03-2021-0170

Donald, W. E., Baruch, Y., & Ashleigh, M. J. (2019). The undergraduate self-perception of employability: Human capital, careers advice and career ownership. *Studies in Higher Education*, *44*(4), 599–614. doi:10.1080/03075079.2017.1387107

Donald, W. E., Baruch, Y., & Ashleigh, M. J. (2023a). Technological transformation and human resource development of early career talent: Insights from accounting, banking, and finance. *Human Resource Development Quarterly*, *34*(3), 329–348. doi:10.1002/hrdq.21491

Donald, W. E., Baruch, Y., & Ashleigh, M. J. (2023b). Construction and operationalisation of an Employability Capital Growth Model (ECGM) via A systematic literature review. *Studies in Higher Education*, 1–15. Advance online publication. doi:10.1080/03075079.2023.2219270

Donald, W. E., & Ford, N. (2023). Fostering social mobility and employability: The case for peer learning. *Teaching in Higher Education*, *28*(3), 672–678. doi:10.1080/13562517.2022.2145467

Donald, W. E., & Jackson, D. (2022). Subjective Wellbeing among University Students and Recent Graduates: Evidence from the United Kingdom. *International Journal of Environmental Research and Public Health*, *19*(11), 6911. doi:10.3390/ijerph19116911 PMID:35682494

Donald, W. E., & Mouratidou, M. (2022). Preparing for a Sustainable Career: Challenges and Opportunities. *GiLE Journal of Skills Development*, *2*(2), 3–5. doi:10.52398/gjsd.2022.v2.i2.pp3-5

Employer Insights, Q. S. (2020). *QS Employer Insights Report 2020*. Employer Insights. https://www.qs.com/portfolio-items/qs-employer-insights-report-2020/

English, P., de Villiers Scheepers, M. J., Fleischman, D., Burgess, J., & Crimmins, G. (2021). Developing professional networks: The missing link to graduate employability. *Education + Training*, *63*(4), 647–661. doi:10.1108/ET-10-2020-0309

Etzkowitz, H., & Leydesdorff, L. (1995). The Triple Helix: University-Industry-Government relations: A laboratory for knowledge based economic development. *EASST Review*, *14*(1), 14–19.

Fisher, J. F. (2023). *College Career Services Are Ailing-Networks Are the Cure*. Workshift. https://workshift.opencampusmedia.org/college-career-services-are-ailing-networks-are-the-cure/

Galan-Muros, V., & Davey, T. (2019). The UBC ecosystem: Putting together a comprehensive framework for university-business cooperation. *The Journal of Technology Transfer*, *44*(4), 1311–1346. doi:10.100710961-017-9562-3

Graduate Recruitment Bureau. (2022). *What are the Biggest Challenges Recruiting Graduates?* Graduate Recruitment Bureau. https://www.grb.uk.com/employer-services/graduate-recruiter-faq/what-are-the-biggest-challenges-recruiting-graduates

Greaves, L. (2021). *5 Student and Graduate Job-Hunting Pain Points*. Luminate. https://luminate.prospects.ac.uk/5-student-and-graduate-job-hunting-pain-points

HazelkornE. (2019). University Rankings: There is room for error and "malpractice". *Elephant in the Lab*. doi:10.5281/zenodo.2592196

Healy, M. (2023). Careers and employability learning: Pedagogical principles for higher education. *Studies in Higher Education*, *48*(8), 1301–1314. doi:10.1080/03075079.2023.2196997

High Fliers. (2023). *The Graduate Market in 2023*. High Fliers. https://www.highfliers.co.uk/download/2023/graduate_market/GMReport23.pdf

Ho, C. (2023). How Strong Career Development Can Lead to a Decent Work Future. *The Future Economy*. https://thefutureeconomy.ca/op-eds/career-development-decent-work-candy-ho-ceric/

Hogarth, T., Winterbotham, M., Hasluck, C., Carter, K., Daniel, W. W., Green, A. E., & Morrison, J. (2007). *Employer and University Engagement in the Use and Development of Graduate Level Skills*. Department for Education and Skills.

Hora, M. T. (2020). Hiring as cultural gatekeeping into occupational communities: Implications for higher education and student employability. *Higher Education*, *79*(1), 307–324. doi:10.100710734-019-00411-6

Illes, P., Chuai, X., & Preece, D. (2010). Talent management and HRM in multinational companies in Beijing: Definitions, differences and drivers. *Journal of World Business*, *45*(2), 179–189. doi:10.1016/j.jwb.2009.09.014

Institute of Student Employers. (2023). *Where Should Universities Focus Employer Engagement to Support Their Unique Student Population?* Insights. https://insights.ise.org.uk/attraction-and-marketing/blog-where-should-universities-focus-employer-engagement-to-support-their-unique-student-population/

Izzo, F., Mele, S., & Mustilli, M. (2022). University to work transition: A literature review. *International Journal of Manpower*, *43*(7), 1502–1515. doi:10.1108/IJM-07-2021-0398

Jackson, N. J. (2018). Ecological perspectives on learning to practice in the arts in health and arts therapies fields. In C. Holmwood & J. Taylor (Eds.), *Learning as a Creative and Developmental Process in Higher Education: A Therapeutic Arts Approach and its Wider Application*. Routledge. doi:10.4324/9781315142142-18

Kinash, S., McGillivray, L., & Crane, L. (2018). Do university students, alumni, educators and employers link assessment and graduate employability? *Higher Education Research & Development*, *37*(2), 301–315. doi:10.1080/07294360.2017.1370439

Manville, G., Donald, W. E., & Eves, A. (2022). Can Embedding Authentic Assessment Into the Curriculum Enhance the Employability of Business School Students? *GiLE Journal of Skills Development*, *2*(2), 73–87. doi:10.52398/gjsd.2022.v2.i2.pp73-87

Martin, L. L. (2016). Gender, teaching evaluations, and professional success in political science. *PS, Political Science & Politics*, *49*(2), 313–319. doi:10.1017/S1049096516000275

Michel-Schneider, U. (2021). *Challenges for University-Industry Collaboration – A Stakeholder View*. 12th Business & Management Virtual Conference, Prague. doi:10.20472/BMC.2021.012.007

Minocha, S., Hristov, D., & Reynolds, M. (2017). From graduate employability to employment: Policy and practice in UK higher education. *International Journal of Training and Development*, *21*(3), 235–248. doi:10.1111/ijtd.12105

National Association of Colleges and Employers. (2022). *NACE 2021-22 Career Services Benchmarks Survey Report*. NACE. https://www.naceweb.org/store/2022/career-services-benchmark-and-compensation

Ng, E. S., Posch, A., Köllen, T., Kraiczy, N., & Thom, N. (2022). Do "one-size" employment policies fit all young workers? Heterogeneity in work attribute preferences among the Millennial generation. *Business Research Quarterly*. doi:10.1177/23409444221085587

Oliver, C. (2020). *The Complete University Guide: University and Subject League Tables Methodology*. https://www.thecompleteuniversityguide.co.uk/sector/insights/university-andsubject-league-tables-methodology

Orazbayeva, B., Plewa, C., Davey, T., & Muros, V. G. (2019). The future of university-business cooperation: Research and practice priorities. *Journal of Engineering and Technology Management*, *54*, 67–80. doi:10.1016/j.jengtecman.2019.10.001

Pearson. (2021). *Six Benefits of Professional Body Membership*. Pearson. https://www.pearson.com/uk/educators/fe-college-educators/btec-blog/2021/09/six-benefits-of-professional-body-membership.html

Petruzziello, G., Chiesa, R., & Mariani, M. G. (2022). The storm Doesn't touch me!—The role of perceived employability of students and graduates in the pandemic era. *Sustainability (Basel)*, *14*(7), 4303. doi:10.3390u14074303

Pitan, O. S. (2023). Leveraging the triple helix system for effective employability delivery in Nigerian universities. In W. E. Donald (Ed.), *Handbook of Research on Sustainable Career Ecosystems for University Students and Graduates* (pp. 77–96). IGI Global. doi:10.4018/978-1-6684-7442-6.ch005

Römgens, I., Scoupe, R., & Beausaert, S. (2020). Unraveling the concept of employability: Bringing together research on employability in higher education and the workplace. *Studies in Higher Education*, *45*(12), 2588–2603. doi:10.1080/03075079.2019.1623770

Smith, K. N., & Green, D. K. (2021). Employer internship recruiting on college campuses: 'the right pipeline for our funnel'. *Journal of Education and Work*, *34*(4), 572–589. doi:10.1080/13639080.2021.1943333

The Complete University Guide. (2023). *University League Tables 2024*. https://www.thecompleteuniversityguide.co.uk/league-tables/rankings

Thurab-Nkhosi, D., Williams, G., & Mason-Roberts, M. (2018). Achieving confidence in competencies through authentic assessment. *Journal of Management Development*, *37*(8), 652–662. doi:10.1108/JMD-12-2017-0413

Winterton, J., & Turner, J. J. (2019). Preparing graduates for work readiness: An overview and agenda. *Education + Training*, *61*(5), 536–551. doi:10.1108/ET-03-2019-0044

Zhao, X., & Cox, A. (2022). Chinese students' study in the UK and employability: The views of Chinese employers, students and alumni, and UK teachers. *Journal of Education and Work*, *35*(4), 422–440. doi:10.1080/13639080.2022.2073339

ADDITIONAL READING

Ankrah, S. N., Burgess, T. F., Grimshaw, P., & Shaw, N. E. (2013). Asking both university and industry actors about their engagement in knowledge transfer: What single-group studies of motives omit. *Technovation*, *33*(2-3), 50–65. doi:10.1016/j.technovation.2012.11.001

Boden, R., & Nedeva, M. (2010). Employing discourse: Universities and graduate 'employability'. *Journal of Education Policy*, *25*(1), 37–54. doi:10.1080/02680930903349489

Etzkowitz, H., & Leydesdorff, L. (2000). The dynamics of innovation: From National Systems and "Mode 2" to a Triple Helix of university-industry-government relations. *Research Policy*, *29*(2), 109–123. doi:10.1016/S0048-7333(99)00055-4

Moeliodihardjo, B. Y., Soemardi, B. W., Brodjonegoro, S. S., & Hatakenaka, S. (2012). University, industry, and government partnerships: Its present and future challenges in Indonesia. *Procedia: Social and Behavioral Sciences*, *52*, 307–316. doi:10.1016/j.sbspro.2012.09.468

Perkmann, M., King, Z., & Pavelin, S. (2011). Engaging excellence? Effects of faculty quality on university engagement with industry. *Research Policy*, *40*(4), 539–552. doi:10.1016/j.respol.2011.01.007

Suleman, F., Videira, P., & Araújo, E. (2021). Higher education and employability skills: Barriers and facilitators of employer engagement at the local level. *Education Sciences*, *11*(2), 51. doi:10.3390/educsci11020051

Thomas, N. (2022). Harnessing the employer perspective. *Phoenix*, 166, 20-21.

Tomlinson, M. (2012). Graduate employability: A review of conceptual and empirical themes. *Higher Education Policy*, *25*(4), 407–431. doi:10.1057/hep.2011.26

Chapter 9
Opportunities for Greater Collaboration Between Actors

ABSTRACT

This chapter considers the opportunities for greater collaboration among the various actors operating within a career ecosystem. The chapter begins by advocating for greater collaboration between university career advisors and graduate recruiters before introducing the State Progress Checklist (SPC), which consists of nine themes grouped into three endeavor elements of potential, agendas, and effects. Next, the chapter presents fifty questions for university career advisors and graduate recruiters to consider. Each actor can initially consider these questions separately before being discussed further in a meeting with both actors present. Additionally, the chapter explores the opportunities for five additional actors to operate collaboratively for the sustainability of the career ecosystem, including (i) students, (ii) lecturers, (iii) alums, (iv) professional bodies, and (v) national governments. Finally, the chapter concludes with four lived experience insights, providing concrete examples illustrating the opportunities for enhanced collaboration among the various actors.

INTRODUCTION

Chapter eight outlined the challenges for greater collaboration between actors operating within a career ecosystem. In this chapter, our focus moves to the opportunities. Our initial focus is on cementing the case for collaboration between university career advisors and graduate recruiters with a specific interest in open dialogue and the optimization of resources. The next part of the chapter provides an overview of the State Progress Checklist (SPC), developed by Thomas Buckholtz

DOI: 10.4018/978-1-6684-9827-9.ch009

(2011) in his book *Create Crucial Insight: Use Direct Outcomes Checklists. Think Well. Do Great.* The chapter then continues by offering fifty questions that Buckholtz and I developed (Buckholtz & Donald, 2022), whereby university career advisors and graduate recruiters would initially work through the fifty questions separately and then work through them again together. The aim is to foster an open dialogue and look for opportunities to optimize resources, providing benefits for everyone operating within a sustainable career ecosystem. The chapter subsequently continues by considering opportunities for five additional actors operating within a career ecosystem to do so collaboratively and sustainably. The chapter concludes with the final set of four lived experience insights.

THE CASE FOR COLLABORATION

Universities and employers are critical actors within a career ecosystem (Baruch, 2015; Jakubik, 2017), relying on each other to achieve the best possible outcomes (Barnett, 2022). By working together, universities can produce global citizens and enhance human capital beyond university boundaries (Jakubik, 2020), contributing to regional and/or national economic growth (Blackmore et al., 2015). Furthermore, universities can enhance their reputation and league table rankings by improving graduate employment rates (Minocha et al., 2017). This increases the likelihood that students' perceived benefits of participation in higher education outweigh the costs (Donald et al., 2018). Similarly, collaboration offers organizations solutions to talent-related difficulties, such as filling roles, finding high-quality candidates, and establishing a diverse talent pool (Blackmore et al., 2015). Through partnerships with career development professionals, organizations can lay the groundwork for quality employment and decent work (Ho, 2023). They can achieve this by facilitating opportunities for work-integrated learning and mentorship (Ferns et al., 2019), influencing university curricula, and introducing innovative approaches that better prepare students for undertaking the university-to-work transition (Jakubik, 2022). Ultimately, such efforts can promote career development and wellbeing (Branicki et al., 2019), enhance organizational performance, productivity, and competitive advantage (Ybema et al., 2020), and contribute to sustainable economic growth (Ferns et al., 2019).

To continue to build the case for the collaboration between university career advisors (as agents of universities) and graduate recruiters (as agents of organizations), we now discuss two central themes: (i) open dialogue and (ii) optimization of resources.

Open Dialogue

Arranz et al. (2022) analyzed data from the *Flash Eurobarometer of the European Commission*, which focused on understanding how employers perceive the employability of graduates. The study encompassed responses from 7,036 companies located in Europe. The findings underscored the significance of establishing collaborations between university career advisors and graduate recruiters. These collaborations, characterized by breadth and depth, were found to enhance the employment outcomes of graduates. However, the lack of communication between these two groups, as Baruch et al. (2023) observe, leads to missed opportunities for adequately preparing students for the transition from university to the workplace. This issue, as framed by Buckholtz and Donald (2022), stems from the absence of open dialogue, which hampers the ability of both actors to understand each other's needs and resources. The importance of fostering open dialogue becomes even more pronounced due to the need for organizations to rethink their talent management strategies in the aftermath of the COVID-19 pandemic (Cooke et al., 2021). As Donald (2020) noted, businesses that balance profit, ethics, and compassion are better poised to thrive in the post-pandemic economy. Given these circumstances, Izzo et al. (2022) argue that there should be increased attention towards advancing our understanding of the university-to-work transition theme.

Several other academics share the view of Izzo and colleagues. For instance, Cole and Hallett (2019) suggest that,

Instead of seeing university provision as shortsightedly "deficient" of value for industry we might instead concentrate on what universities and learning journeys actually provide – flexible and creative thinking, multiple cultures and audience encounters, adaptable project work, civic engagement – all the things that modern employees need for their futures. (p. 122)

Similarly, Buckholtz and Donald (2022) emphasize the need for win-win outcomes, while Clark-Ambrosini et al. (2023) advocate for a more adaptable mindset among university career advisors and graduate recruiters. They propose collaborative efforts to identify ways to support the sustainable careers of graduates and sustainably improve talent management practices. Moreover, by focusing on shared objectives such as providing diverse support, timely interventions during degree programs, promoting social mobility, and supporting international students, both actors can enhance their strategies for guiding students through the transition into the workforce (Argent, 2016; Rickmann et al., 2020).

A shared vision, well-defined governance structures, and commitment from all actors underscore the necessity of ongoing dialogue between university career advisors and graduate recruiters (CFE Research, 2023). This communication is critical for cultivating a talent pool that aligns with the present and future needs of the industry (Aliu & Aigbayboa, 2021). For instance, this collaboration enables universities to understand the demands of the labor market (Jakubik, 2022; Okolie et al., 2019) and shape the evolution of university curricula (Reilly, 2021). Clear communication and collaboration between career services and graduate recruiters are paramount to accomplishing these objectives. Regular meetings, collaborative projects, and shared events facilitate the exchange of information and opportunities (Arranz et al., 2022). Infrastructure, such as shared databases or online platforms, can further support these efforts, which aid in effective coordination (Arranz et al., 2022).

Optimization of Resources

According to Awwad and Bose (2023), "the career service is a critical element in students' success and needs to be properly integrated to provide them with the career support they need to flourish post-graduation" (Online, Paragraph One). However, as previously discussed, many university career services lack the necessary resources (Donald et al., 2022). Subsequently, collaboration between university career advisors and graduate recruiters becomes crucial, especially when either party lacks the required resources or skillsets (Stevenson et al., 2017). Collaborative efforts can help eliminate redundancy, optimize the use of available resources, and identify specific areas requiring targeted assistance (CFE Research, 2023).

To accurately assess the impacts of interventions, it is essential to measure students' self-perceived employability (or any other desired metrics) before and after the intervention (Padgett & Donald, 2023). The presence of a control group that has not received the intervention is vital to gauge its effectiveness accurately (Koen et al., 2012). Recruitment agencies can also help enhance student engagement and offer valuable metrics for assessing the effectiveness of interventions (Gradleaders, 2022). Additionally, feedback from other sources, like managers during placements, is valuable since a study in the UK found that students often rate their competencies and self-perceptions of employability lower than when these same aspects are rated by their managers (Hughes et al., 2023).

Moreover, studies exploring the impacts of collaborative use of resources have shown positive outcomes. For instance, in Ireland, O'Regan et al. (2022) demonstrate the benefits of tailored employability workshops focusing on socio-emotional skills (also called human skills). Similarly, Aliu and Aigbavboa (2021) highlight how mentoring and relevant training improve employability and job market prospects in South African students, while Jakubik (2017; 2020) stresses the advantages of internships and work-based learning opportunities for providing real-world experience. Additionally, Blokker et al. (2019) emphasize the need for students to be provided with a sustainable start to their careers and ensure they are prepared to manage career shocks and navigate volatile labor markets. Consequently, addressing individual students' unique needs through personalized support is crucial, especially when seeking diverse talent pipelines through the flow of talent between universities and organizations (Baruch et al., 2023). However, as discussed in Chapter 8, this might require policy adjustments at the national level to mitigate the risk of negative impacts on league table rankings from acting as a deterrent to resource sharing among institutions (Donald et al., 2022).

With the importance of collaboration established and emphasized through two themes of open dialogue and resource optimization, our attention now turns to providing an overview of the State Progress Checklist.

THE STATE PROGRESS CHECKLIST

The State Progress Checklist (SPC) is underpinned by Direct Outcomes Theory (DOT), popularized by Buckholtz (2011) in their book *Create Crucial Insight: Use Direct Outcomes Checklists. Think Well. Do Great.* Direct outcomes theory (Buckholtz, 1995; 1996) provides individuals with a tool to enable them to develop insights, make decisions and implement these decisions effectively. Checklists facilitate the development of goals and plans, identifying and acquiring relevant resources, and the ability to 'think well' and 'do great'. The notion of 'thinking well' refers to the use – by resources, such as people and systems – of data, assumptions, and intuition to develop and evaluate possible goals, scenarios and plans (Buckholtz, 2011). The notion of 'doing great' refers to using resources and plans to achieve fruitful results and potential for application to broader purposes (Buckholtz, 2011).

Direct outcomes have broad applicability in both business and non-business settings, from individual to societal levels. Unlike rigid checklists such as those used by airline pilots, direct outcomes checklists are flexible and encourage innovative thinking tailored to specific circumstances. They serve as a valuable tool for addressing inquiries like "Have we sufficiently considered a diverse range of options?" or "Have we taken into account a diverse range of information?" and "Are we prepared to make an informed decision?" These outcomes encompass opportunities to enhance effectiveness (e.g., achieve more significant impact), improve efficiency (e.g., save time), and cultivate patterns of productive thinking and action (e.g., thinking critically and performing exceptionally). Direct outcomes prove particularly beneficial in contexts where work or collaboration is disorganized and unstructured because it provides a shared platform for spontaneous and systematic thinking, enabling individuals to develop or optimize new frameworks. This fosters constructive discussions, facilitates reflection, enables mutual understanding, garners support from diverse stakeholders, and establishes criteria for identifying successful outcomes.

Buckholtz and Donald (2022) applied DOT to a new context of the university-to-work transition to help university career advisors and graduate recruiters to achieve shared goals and adopt broader perspectives. They believe that DOT can address the challenges to collaboration discussed in Chapter 8 by "offering synergy effects via enhancing mutual understanding, sharing resources, and providing an audit trail to facilitate the continuity of a shared strategic vision over time" (p. 12). Specifically, they used Buckholtz's (2011, p. 98) State Progress Checklist (SPC), which can either be applied from a 'bottom-up' approach or a 'top-down approach'. In this chapter, the 'bottom-up approach' is adopted, per Buckholtz and Donald (2022). Figure 1 presents the SPC.

Figure 1. State Progress Checklist
(c) 2011 Buckholtz. Used with permission.

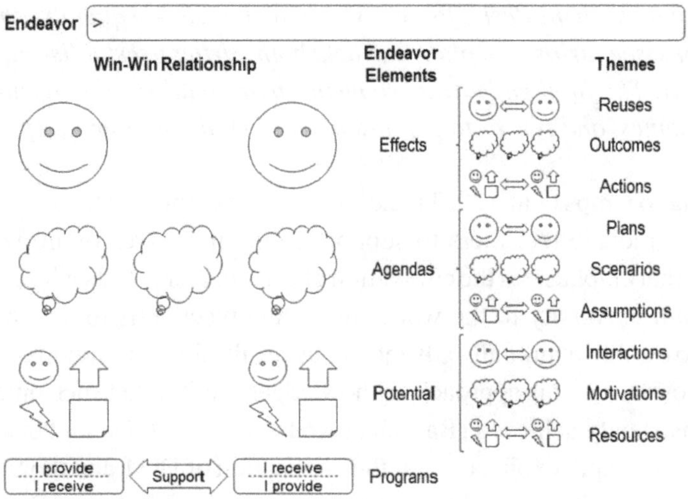

The 'bottom-up' approach progresses through nine themes grouped by three endeavor elements:

Endeavor Element One: Potential

- (i) Resources
- (ii) Motivations
- (iii) Interactions

Endeavor Element Two: Agendas

- (iv) Assumptions
- (v) Scenarios
- (vi) Plans

Endeavor Element Three: Effects

- (vii) Actions
- (viii) Outcomes
- (ix) Reuses

As Buckholtz and Donald (2022) state

The initial focus on resources, motivations, and interactions helps UCAs [University Career Advisors] and GRs [Graduate Recruiters] to collaborate and identify the potential benefits of adopting the state progress checklist. These include optimising limited resources and proactive strategic approaches to address pre-existing and future challenges with the desire for win-win outcomes. Subsequently, an awareness of assumptions, scenarios, and plans can help both parties to establish clear agendas and think well. The final endeavour element operationalises the agendas through actions, outcomes, and reuses to capture the notion of doing great. (p. 20)

According to Craps et al. (2021), the SPC can be employed by university career advisors and graduate recruiters to support policy initiatives by utilizing precise terminology that emphasizes the cultivation of early career talents who can smoothly transition from university to the workforce. The objective is to leverage the SPC framework to establish mutually advantageous results for all individuals involved in the career ecosystem. This approach acknowledges the fact that such outcomes have yet to be consistently achieved (Baruch & Rousseau, 2019; Donald et al., 2022).

For a more in-depth explanation of the application of DOT and the SPC to a new context of the university-to-work transition, please see Buckholtz and Donald (2022).

OPERATIONALIZATION OF THE STATE PROGRESS CHECKLIST

For the purpose of this chapter, here are some potential questions for each of the nine themes across the three endeavor elements (per Buckholtz & Donald, 2022, pp. 24-25). These example questions are not meant to be an exhaustive list. Their purpose is to act as a starting point for discussion and action. University career advisors and graduate recruiters could initially work through these questions separately before working through the questions a second time collaboratively. Please note that whilst the nine themes are presented sequentially, they can be applied iteratively as subsequent questions and ideas emerge. The aim is to offer strategic opportunities for bridging the university-employer divide through the use of the SPC.

Endeavor Element One: Potential

Theme One: Resources

1. What resources do we currently have?
2. What resources do we currently lack?
3. What resources does the other party have that could improve our situation?
4. What resources do we have to help the other party improve their situation?
5. What resources exist beyond the dyadic relationship?
6. How can both parties make the best use of the available resources?

Theme Two: Motivations

7. What are the motivations for collaboration?
8. What are the motivational issues that need to be addressed?
9. What help is required from the other party?
10. What support can be provided to the other party?
11. How do their respective motivations align?

Theme Three: Interactions

12. How regularly should interaction take place between the two parties?
13. What are feasible and reasonable response times?
14. What are the preferred methods for communication?

15. Who is responsible for scheduling meetings and writing minutes?
16. How can existing levels of interaction be optimized or enhanced?
17. How can documentation help manage the challenges of high personnel turnover rates?

Endeavor Element Two: Agendas (Think Well)

Theme 4: Assumptions

18. What are the existing issues in the dyadic relationship?
19. Have these issues been communicated to the other party?
20. Is the other party aware of the challenges being experienced?
21. Have working assumptions been clearly articulated?
22. What actions can be taken to address untoward pre-existing assumptions or to capitalize on applicable mutual assumptions?

Theme 5: Scenarios

23. What are the current challenges faced?
24. What are possible future challenges that may occur?
25. What steps can be taken to minimize the negative impacts of these challenges?
26. What opportunities exist for proactive and strategic planning to reduce the reliance on reactive behaviors?
27. Has an adequately diverse set of options been considered?
28. Has an adequately diverse set of information been considered?
29. Can an informed decision now be made?

Theme 6: Plans

30. What documentation is required?
31. How often should this documentation be updated?
32. Who is responsible for updating each section of the document?
33. What is the process for agreeing on metrics to measure successful outcomes?
34. Who is accountable for signing off the plans?
35. Who is accountable for monitoring the plans?
36. How can continuity of the plans be maintained?
37. What events should automatically trigger all parties to re-visit the plans at the earliest opportunity?

Endeavor Element III: Effects (Do Great)

Theme 7: Actions

38. What resources are needed to operationalize the plan?
39. Who is accountable for implementing each part of the plan?
40. When does each of the actions need to be taken?
41. How will progress be communicated between the two parties?
42. Who has overall accountability for the operationalization of the plan?

Theme 8: Outcomes

43. Have the results been realized?
44. What benefits have occurred?
45. Has there been a win-win focus for both parties?
46. Were the methods for recognizing and measuring outcomes appropriate?
47. What learning opportunities exist for future process improvement?
48. Where would funding and time be best invested in the future?

Theme 9: Reuses

49. What actions were taken, and what outcomes were achieved using the state progress checklist?
50. What other opportunities exist to create new insights using direct outcomes to foster win-win scenarios?

Source: © 2022 Buckholtz & Donald. Used with permission.

THE OPPORTUNITIES FOR ADDITIONAL ACTORS

This chapter has emphasized the significance of enhancing collaboration between university career advisors and graduate recruiters, whether they work within an organization or through a recruitment agency. Additionally, the concept of the SPC has been introduced and operationalized via a comprehensive list of fifty questions to support strategic opportunities for bridging the university-employer divide. Our attention now shifts to exploring the opportunities for additional actors to operate collaboratively for the sustainability of the career ecosystem (Donald, 2023a, Donald & Jackson, 2023).

The Actor Synergies for Preparing Early Career Talent (ASPECT) model, illustrated in Figure 2, was developed in partnership with Professor Yehuda Baruch and Associate Professor Melanie Ashleigh based on interviews conducted with graduate recruiters (Donald et al., 2022, p. 2210). The arrows in the ASPECT model depict how various actors can interact, highlighting the reciprocal nature of information sharing and its positive impact on enhancing the sustainability of the career ecosystem.

Figure 2. Actor Synergies For Preparing Early Career Talent (ASPECT) model
Source: © 2022 Emerald Group Publishing Limited. Used with permission. Creators: Donald, Ashleigh & Baruch (2022).

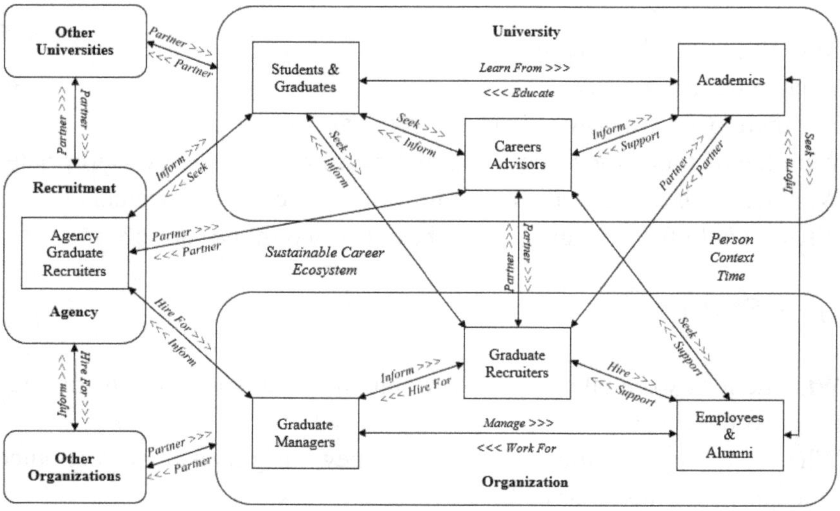

This chapter continues by considering three additional actors from the ASPECT model: (i) students, (ii) lecturers (academics), and (iii) alums (alumni). You will notice that graduate managers also feature in the ASPECT model. However, in this book, we primarily present the perspectives of graduate managers through the lens of graduate recruiters, specifically in the context of preparing individuals to undertake the university-to-work transition. There is also potential overlap between graduate managers and alums since an individual can perform both roles within the ecosystem. Additionally, this chapter advances the ASPECT model by considering two other actors that were not explicitly mentioned during interviews with graduate recruiters, including (iv) professional bodies (Donald, 2023b) and (v) national governments (Pitan, 2023). This extension enriches the ASPECT model and provides a comprehensive understanding of collaborative dynamics within a sustainable career ecosystem.

Students

In Chapter 2 of this book, we observed the emergence of different highly-cited employability capital models (e.g., Clarke, 2018; Donald, 2017; Donald et al., 2019; Tomlinson, 2017) and the integration of these and other models into the Employability Capital Growth (ECG) model (Donald et al., 2023). We also discussed the need to balance individual agency against contextual factors, recognizing that a sustainable career has three dimensions of person, context, and time (Van der Heijden & De Vos, 2015), and three indicators of health, happiness, and productivity (Van der Heijden, 2005). Additionally, in Chapter 3, we considered strategies for university career services to engage with students (Donald et al., 2022), while in Chapter 4, the theme was signaling employability (Tomlinson & Anderson, 2021). From the employer perspective, Chapter 6 addressed preparing students for the university-to-work transition (Jackson et al., 2022), while Chapter 7 focused on person-organization fit (Cable & Judge, 1996). Throughout these chapters, we observed the need for buy-in from students, positioning them as influential in facilitating collaboration between actors and determining the sustainability of the career ecosystem.

Other studies also support this view. For instance, Apa et al. (2021) emphasize the advantages of involving students in establishing partnerships between universities and employers, particularly SMEs. Similarly, Jackson et al. (2022) highlight in Australia how "work-based internships/placements were considered important for identifying graduate talent and developing strong industry–educator partnerships, needed for building networks between students and employers" (p. 681). Additionally, Jakubik (2018) and De Wit-de Vries et al. (2019) highlight that internship and thesis projects contribute to students' growth and foster a beneficial exchange of insights between universities and SMEs. The exchange of insights was also highlighted in Chapter 7, whereby employers can gain feedback from students concerning the attraction and selection process through counter signals during placements (Donald, 2021).

Lecturers

Creed et al. (2023) emphasize the importance of directly integrating career provision into the academic framework, positioning career services and lecturers as crucial for enhancing student success. Similarly, Kozhuk (2023) regards university career services as pivotal in driving broader employability initiatives across campus. Consequently, there is a growing consensus that lecturers should collaborate with university career services and employers to assist students in cultivating essential career management skills (Ho, 2023). The involvement of lecturers in offering support can significantly contribute to fostering greater student engagement with career-related pursuits (Petruzziello et al., 2022). Moreover, Borah et al. (2021) found that university-industry collaborations increased students' employability competencies when embedded into the curriculum.

There is also a growing emphasis on reshaping the notion of employability within the academic curriculum. Daubney (2022) evidences how the *extracted employability concept*, where lecturers emphasize the employability aspects of the curriculum to students, has the following benefits:

- Preserves academic excellence by integrating employability considerations into the curriculum without compromising rigor or integrity.
- Enhances relevance, particularly for students pursuing generalist degrees, by establishing meaningful connections between the curriculum content and the skills that employers actively seek.
- Elevates learning outcomes of modules by incorporating industry-relevant language and skills that align with the needs of the job market to bridge the university-employer divide effectively.
- Boosts engagement and social mobility by integrating employability as a fundamental aspect of the curriculum.

Several other published articles have put forth suggestions aimed at helping lecturers enhance the employability of their students. For example, the embedding of authentic assessment into the curriculum (Manville et al., 2022), taking a more proactive role during year-in-industry placements (Donald & Hughes, 2023), promoting peer learning to foster social mobility and employability (Donald & Ford, 2023; Donald & Scattergood, 2023), or promoting leisure activities to develop psychological resources (Kelly et al., 2020).

Alums

Alums are another actor with the potential to influence career ecosystems. These individuals possess recent first-hand knowledge of university life and, combined with their experience in the labor market as graduates, positions them uniquely to bridge the university-employer divide. To illustrate, they can establish mentoring programs to support disadvantaged students (Dollinger et al., 2019) or facilitate networking and deliver guest lectures, thereby expanding students' access to opportunities that contribute to developing social capital (Donald et al., 2018; 2023). Additionally, alums can contribute financial donations to their alma mater, which can be utilized to sustainably support initiatives that enhance students' employability (Gallo, 2018). This resonates with the long-held perspective that alum engagement and student experience are interrelated (Pearson, 1999).

Professional Bodies

During my interviews with graduate recruiters, it was interesting that they tended not to explicitly mention professional bodies as actors that can help students enhance their employability (Donald et al., 2022). An earlier study by Ferns et al. (2019) revealed that professional bodies were often perceived as burdensome regarding regulations, time, and resources required to foster such partnerships. On a more positive note, their findings indicated that forming partnerships with professional bodies could benefit universities and students. This potential for mutual benefit was also emphasized by Donald (2023b), who recently highlighted the significance of professional bodies as influential actors within a sustainable career ecosystem by looking at the careers of project managers. When we consider the works of Ferns et al. and Donald collectively, they present a clear set of potential advantages that professional bodies can bring by facilitating partnerships between universities and employers. These include:

- Enhancing university curricula to align with industry needs.
- Providing specialized training and development tailored to specific industries.
- Supporting students via career guidance and counseling to prepare for undertaking the university-to-work transition.
- Offering mentoring and networking opportunities to enhance students' social capital.
- Helping students understand and meet professional competencies and standards.
- Granting access to job postings and employment opportunities.
- Ensuring and upholding the professional reputation and trustworthiness of the field or industry on regional, national, and international scales.

National Governments

National governments can play a crucial role in enhancing graduates' employability by adopting a multifaceted strategy that considers individual needs, labor market trends, and societal demands. Career counseling can serve as a tool to help national workforces navigate uncertainty and changing skill demands (Baldi & Trigeorgis, 2020), including global-level challenges such as rapid technological advancement and climate change (Donald & Mouratidou, 2022; Mallis, 2023). To address these challenges, Hallpike et al. (2022) propose shifting from an individual-focused to a distributed-focused career decision-making approach. This acknowledges the malleable nature of employability (Rodrigues et al., 2020), influenced by employers and employees through agency and contextual factors over time (Fugate et al., 2021; Vermeeren & Van der Heijden, 2022).

Recent projections show that for every £1.00 the UK government invests in career guidance for young people, there is the opportunity for a significant return of £2.50 (Hooley et al., 2023). This underscores the importance of early intervention and continuous support to address inequality and prepare individuals to navigate dynamic labor markets (Donald & Manville, 2023). Parents, identified as influential in shaping education and career choices (Bowes et al., 2022), also require guidance to support their children effectively (CFE Research, 2023). In the education sector, schools play a pivotal role in identifying barriers to student progression (Atherton et al., 2019), including spotlighting localized challenges (CFE Research, 2023). Universities also need additional funding to offer comprehensive career support to all students. At the same time, existing metrics for league table rankings must be revisited to reduce barriers and actively incentivize collaborations between institutions (Buckholtz & Donald, 2022). Furthermore, providing consistent funding and career guidance can enhance academic achievement, increase employment rates, and raise tax revenue (Ho, 2023), while supporting entrepreneurship and fostering international partnerships can also enhance the sustainability of career ecosystems (Donald et al., 2022).

LIVED EXPERIENCE INSIGHTS

Our attention now turns to four lived experience insights, providing concrete examples illustrating the opportunities for enhanced collaboration among the various actors.

Lived Experience Insight

Shared By Aga Kelly, Nottingham Trent University, UK & Anna White, University of Nottingham, UK

The Challenge

In the years leading up to the 2017/18 academic year, Nottingham Trent University and the University of Nottingham collaborated with local digital marketing agencies to support the hiring of graduates and the growth of their businesses. However, when interviewing individuals for graduate roles, these agencies reported industry-specific knowledge gaps and a lack of understanding of career opportunities and routes for progression. Concurrently, Nottingham's digital marketing sector grew substantially, with many small agencies operating in the city and surrounding areas. Nevertheless, Nottingham City Council continued to report low graduate retention figures in the region, identifying technology as a priority sector for growth, and calling for universities to address the digital skills gap.

The Context

Nottingham Trent University and the University of Nottingham were keen to support their students and ensure they were equipped with relevant skills and knowledge required by industry to secure high-skilled graduate employment. The two universities sought to devise a solution to incorporate input from the growing number of local digital marketing experts and those interested in recruiting our graduates. We hoped that forging stronger links with digital marketing agencies could enable students to acquire digital marketing skills and provide viable alternative employment opportunities to corporate graduate schemes to help keep graduate talent in Nottinghamshire. The collaborative approach needed to be accessible and inclusive to foster social mobility and appeal to students from all university degrees.

Action Taken

In 2018/19, the two universities worked separately to design activities for our respective students with inputs from Nottingham-based digital marketing agencies. Then in 2019/20, we joined forces to launch a Nottingham 'Digital Marketing Academy' (DMA). We envisaged a joint initiative as more impactful whereby a single optimized program could offer students increased opportunities to gain real-life exposure, experience teamworking, and encourage peer-to-peer knowledge exchange between the university's students – regardless of the year of study or degree course. The DMA launched as an employer-led learning program, including industry-led workshops on digital marketing, elements of self-study, insight events, and a digital marketing challenge based on a real-world brief.

The Outcome

Nearly 1,000 students across the two universities have participated in the DMA since its launch in 2019/20. Many participants secured roles with partner agencies, other digital marketing businesses, or non-digital marketing businesses that recruit for digital marketing roles. The DMA has helped our employer partners enhance their wider on-campus activities and student communication strategies, including involvement with co-designing the curriculum and offering expert knowledge during guest lectures. The employer partners have also seen a dramatic increase in applications for their internship and graduate opportunities due to the DMA. Now in its 4th year, the two universities are continuing to collaborate on this scheme, which has been shortlisted for several sector awards.

Lessons Learned and Advice

The multi-stakeholder partnership is fundamental to the DMA's success. Collaboration helps to avoid clashes with coursework deadlines and exams, whilst the partnership approach saves employers time and money by eliminating repetition and enabling access to local graduate talent. Due to its accessible design, even during COVID-19-related restrictions, the DMA remained highly popular amongst students. The DMA is continually reviewed and updated based on feedback from students, employers and university partners. Our advice to others would be to develop a project or scheme that provides an authentic and valuable experience which truly meets the needs of all stakeholders involved.

Lived Experience Insight

Shared By Ruby Lawrence, Glasgow Caledonian University, UK

The Challenge

Students studying social sciences face a unique labor market challenge compared to other students in the 'School for Business and Society' since there is no standardized and defined career path based on their degree discipline. When discussing this challenge with academic teaching staff, it became apparent that many social science students aspire to work in the heritage sector (e.g., in museums and/or archives). However, the UK's heritage sector is highly competitive and getting a foot on the ladder can be difficult.

The Context

Glasgow Caledonian University (GCU) has a world-leading Archive Centre where students from other universities regularly seek work experience opportunities. Nevertheless, there was no formal collaboration process between the Archive Centre and the social sciences degree program at GCU. Additionally, the university archivist felt that students' knowledge of the archives was relatively low compared to the knowledge of work experience applicants from other institutions. However, discussions I led with academics and the university archivist showed a belief that collaboration between the Archive Centre and GCU's social sciences department could improve employability outcomes for students studying social sciences.

Action Taken

We designed an annual rolling work experience program ring-fenced for second-year social sciences students in collaboration with the university archivist. Participation in the program involved (i) valuable work experience in the Archive Center, (ii) contributing to displays and blogs, and (iii) participating in a workshop offering insights into study routes and careers related to museums/archives. Furthermore, as part of their MSc in Human Rights, experiential learning sessions took place in the Archive Centre embedded into the curriculum, including a general induction to the archive and a workshop in which students interacted with social movement history.

The Outcome

Student feedback on the work experience program was exceptional. Participants shared that they had significantly developed their career aspirations by forming specific and focused goals around the archiving work they wanted to do in the future. Students also reported that participation in the employability workshop (i) helped them understand how to navigate the university-to-work transition and (ii) showed them how to apply their knowledge and develop skills in diverse organizational settings. Consequently, students also reported feeling more confident and employable after completing the program.

Lessons Learned and Advice

As a university, we had overlooked the potential of our own Archive Centre as a collaborative partner in developing student employability. By creating an agreement of rolling annual activity that delivers benefits to all involved, we also helped to raise awareness of the Archive Centre amongst our students – addressing a broader university objective. Reputationally, it was fantastic to have our own students contributing their talent and developing their skills 'in-house', and we were also able to enhance the curriculum by embedding archive-related knowledge and experiences. Moreover, academic staff in the social sciences now use the Archive Centre as a research resource to inform their teaching and research. Consequently, I would advise considering opportunities for collaborative pursuits between actors operating within the university ecosystem to deliver various win-win outcomes.

Lived Experience Insight

Shared By Anne Meyer-Miner, University of Toronto, Canada &
David Sealey, Science Career Impact Project of Toronto, Canada

The Challenge

Graduate training programs in biomedical sciences are typically aimed at developing scientists who can make discoveries, publish in peer-reviewed journals, and secure grant funding. However, in the job market outside academia, graduates may struggle if they cannot demonstrate experience, capabilities and potential that employers can relate to. Furthermore, some students are unaware of viable career paths beyond academia.

The Context

Many universities have started addressing these gaps through experiential learning opportunities (e.g., internships, job shadowing and job simulation projects). Successful programs will raise awareness of career options and provide opportunities to gain practical experience and deliver value. The Science Career Impact Project (a volunteer organization in Toronto) and the Life Sciences Career Development Syndicate (a student-run professional development organization at the University of Toronto) established the Industry Team Case Study program to address this need.

Action Taken

In the program, which has been running since 2016, trainees design and develop biopharmaceutical sector projects with mentorship from industry professionals who serve as volunteers. Trainees identify a business or policy challenge, conduct research and analysis, propose a solution, and present their findings and lessons learned. Each cohort's engagements span four months, and focus areas have included regulatory affairs, market access, product development, and marketing. Trainees also attend industry seminars and one-to-one mentoring to deepen their knowledge and self-awareness.

The Outcome

Over 200 trainees (Masters, PhD, and Postdocs) have participated in this program. Trainees have reported that the program influenced their post-graduation career journey, and many have leveraged their projects to convince hiring managers of their potential and get hired. Moreover, based on metrics run in 2021, 55% of alums were first employed in industry – more than doubling the historical benchmark. Participation also broadens professional networks. From the employer perspective, mentors have been impressed by the caliber of case study projects and students' development of skills and capabilities.

Lessons Learned and Advice

Job simulation programs can be started at any institution. Their format, structure, and content can be developed in collaboration with trainees, employers, and administrators. Integrating experiential learning into degree programs can increase the employability of trainees and prepare them for diverse career paths. The employability outcomes can also translate into improved league table rankings and reputational standings, attracting future students and adding value through alum networks. Additionally, industry mentors can hone their coaching and leadership skills while scouting talent for their organizations. This collaborative, experiential learning initiative benefits universities, employers, and trainees. For more information about this lived experience insight, please see the work of Kozma et al. (2021).

Lived Experience Insight

Shared by Anjali A, SCMS Cochin School of Business, India & Nimmi P. Mohandas, Amrita School of Business, India

The Challenge

The popularity of the Masters in Business Administration (MBA) in India grew significantly from 1991 due to the revival of the business sector following liberalization, privatization, and increased globalization. Two prime decision-making parameters that encourage applicants to enroll in MBA programs are education quality and career outcomes (e.g., salary, promotion, satisfaction). Unfortunately, enrollment for MBA programs at business schools in India has declined recently, making it challenging to attract employers to run on-campus events.

The Context

Historically, an MBA was the key to accessing lucrative jobs in India. Strong employability outcomes gave an institution a competitive edge to attract prospective students. Recruiters in India generally prefer on-campus recruitment, yet, top talent is increasingly opting to pursue an MBA abroad. Consequently, university career services need help convincing organizations to visit their university in person due to reduced opportunities for securing top talent and the associated competitive advantage.

Action Taken

Business schools in India began to look for collaborative opportunities whereby MBA students from different universities would meet recruiters representing organizations in a central location. The aim was to build a sustainable rapport with specific organizations to increase students' chances of securing a role after their MBA. University career advisors helped develop these relationships with employers while supporting their MBA students to develop and signal employability.

The Outcome

Our MBA students experienced increased exposure to recruiters, which enabled them to increase their business acumen, develop networks, and identify areas for self-improvement. Accessing events with students from other universities also helped to increase their peer networks and social capital. Identifying areas for self-improvement also increased engagement with the university career service and enabled more tailored career-related support. Subsequently, the employability outcomes of our MBA students increased, with many receiving multiple job offers. The benefits to the students transcended to employers (via human capital) and our university (via rankings and attraction of future students and their associated tuition fees).

Lessons Learned and Advice

Encouraging collaboration between different universities can sometimes face barriers due to perceptions of direct competition and Tier rankings of business schools. However, such an approach often has more benefits than limitations. Enhancing self-perceived employability in MBA students and providing access to career support and recruiters optimizes the chances of positive employment outcomes. Access to networks of peers and organizations also helps to improve social mobility outcomes. Our advice would be that the sustainability of career ecosystems relies on identifying innovative ways to facilitate the collaboration of all actors, resulting in win-win-win outcomes.

Reflection on Lived Experience Insights

The four lived experience insights from Canada, India, and the UK highlight opportunities for greater collaboration between actors. A key finding emphasizes the potential for regional opportunities to promote such interactions. For example, universities in a specific city engaging with local employers, agencies, and city councils. Alternatively, university career services facilitating events and ensuring student participation by connecting students from various institutions with recruiters in a central location. These approaches create opportunities for students to network with their peers and employers, fostering professional relationships and providing access to mentoring and work experiences.

Another significant theme is the development of diverse talent pipelines, achieved by engaging and preparing all students for the transition from university into the workforce. It is worth noting that collaborative efforts between different actors can bring unique benefits to each party involved. Students can enhance their employability and work readiness through authentic and valuable real-world experiences, while universities can improve their rankings and generate revenue by showcasing positive graduate outcomes. Employers, in turn, gain strategic and competitive advantages, benefiting regional and national economies.

Recognizing the diverse goals and interests of all actors involved within a sustainable career ecosystem highlights their interconnected and interdependent nature. Successful and sustainable collaborative initiatives rely on open dialogue, continuous input, and feedback from all actors, as seen in the previous chapter and reiterated in this final set of lived experience insights.

CONCLUSION

This chapter considered the opportunities for greater collaboration among the various actors operating within a career ecosystem. The chapter began by advocating for greater collaboration between university career advisors and graduate recruiters before introducing the State Progress Checklist (SPC), consisting of the following nine themes grouped by three endeavor elements:

Endeavor Element I: Potential

- (i) Resources
- (ii) Motivations
- (iii) Interactions

Endeavor Element II: Agendas
- (iv) Assumptions
- (v) Scenarios
- (vi) Plans

Endeavor Element III: Effects
- (vii) Actions
- (viii) Outcomes
- (ix) Reuses

Subsequently, the chapter presented fifty questions for university career advisors and graduate recruiters to consider. Each actor can initially consider these questions separately before being discussed further in a meeting with both actors present. Additionally, the chapter explores the opportunities for five additional actors to operate collaboratively for the sustainability of the career ecosystem, including:

- (i) Students
- (ii) Lecturers
- (iii) Alums
- (iv) Professional bodies
- (v) National governments

Finally, the chapter concluded with four insights based on real-life experiences, providing concrete examples illustrating the opportunities for enhanced collaboration among the various actors.

If you are a university career advisor or graduate recruiter, you might like to consider the following questions:

- How can you use the fifty questions in this chapter to improve collaboration between actors?
- Are there any additional questions you can think of besides the fifty provided in this chapter?
- How can you promote the benefits of a sustainable career ecosystem to secure buy-in from other actors?

If you are one of the additional actors in the career ecosystem, then you might like to consider the following questions:

- What role can you play in enhancing the sustainability of the career ecosystem?
- What support do you need from other actors within the career ecosystem to achieve sustainable outcomes for everyone involved?
- How can you collaborate with other actors in the career ecosystem to enhance the likelihood of sustainable outcomes for all?

Section four of the book has thus far focused on the challenges (Chapter 8) and opportunities (Chapter 9) for greater collaboration between actors to strive for a sustainable career ecosystem. Chapter 10 now concludes Section four and the book by considering the future of work and providing some concluding thoughts.

REFERENCES

Aliu, J., & Aigbavboa, C. O. (2021). Structural determinants of graduate employability: Impact of university and industry collaborations. *Journal of Engineering. Design and Technology*, *19*(5), 1080–1100. doi:10.1108/JEDT-05-2020-0189

Apa, R., De Marchi, V., Grandinetti, R., & Sedita, S. R. (2021). University-SME collaboration and innovation performance. The role of informal relationships and absorptive capacity. *The Journal of Technology Transfer*, *46*(4), 961–988. doi:10.100710961-020-09802-9

Argent, G. (2016). *Real Collaboration Happens When Your Challenges Overlap*. Graduate Transitions. http://graduate-transitions.co.uk/real-collaboration-happens-when-your-challenges-overlap/

Arranz, N., Arroyabe, M. F., Sena, V., Arranz, C. F. A., & de Arroyabe, J. C. F. (2022). University-enterprise cooperation for the employability of higher education graduates: A social capital approach. *Studies in Higher Education*, *47*(5), 990–999. doi:10.1080/03075079.2022.2055323

Atherton, G., Boffey, R., & Kazim, T. (2019). *POLAR Opposite: How The Targeting of Learners for Widening Access to HE Work Could Be Improved*. Access HE. https://www.accesshe.ac.uk/ yYdIx0u7/SBT2142-London-Higher-Polar-Opposite-Report-Design-v3.pdf

Awwad, E., & Bose, S. (2023). *Moving from a Career Services Department to a Career Enablement Commitment*. Evolllution. https://evolllution.com/attracting-students/customer_service/moving-from-a-career-services-department-to-a-career-enablement-commitment

Baldi, F., & Trigeorgis, L. (2020). Valuing human capital career development: A real options approach. *Journal of Intellectual Capital, 21*(5), 781–807. doi:10.1108/JIC-06-2019-0134

Barnett, R. (2022). *The Philosophy of Higher Education: A Critical Introduction.* Routledge.

Baruch, Y. (2015). Organizational and labor market as career eco-system. In A. De Vos & B. I. J. M. Van der Heijden (Eds.), *Handbook of Research on Sustainable Careers* (pp. 164–180). Edward Elgar. doi:10.4337/9781782547037.00029

Baruch, Y., Ashleigh, M. J., & Donald, W. E. (2023). A sustainable career ecosystem perspective of talent flow and acquisition: The interface between higher education and industry. In W. E. Donald (Ed.), *Handbook of Research on Sustainable Career Ecosystems for University Students and Graduates* (pp. 177–194). IGI Global., doi:10.4018/978-1-6684-7442-6.ch010

Baruch, Y., & Rousseau, D. M. (2019). Integrating psychological contracts and ecosystems in career studies and management. *The Academy of Management Annals, 13*(1), 84–111. doi:10.5465/annals.2016.0103

Blackmore, P., Bulaitis, Z. H., Jackman, A. H., & Tan, E. (2015). *Employability in Higher Education: A Review of Practice and Strategies around the World.* YEA. https://yea.org.nz/wp-content/uploads/2020/07/Employability-in-Higher-Education-a-review-of-practice-and-strategies-around-the-world.pdf

Blokker, R., Akkermans, J., Tims, M., Jansen, P., & Khapova, S. (2019). Building a sustainable start: The role of career competencies, career success, and career shocks in young professionals' employability. *Journal of Vocational Behavior, 112*(1), 172–184. doi:10.1016/j.jvb.2019.02.013

Borah, D., Malik, K., & Massini, S. (2021). Teaching-focused university-industry collaborations: Determinants and impact on graduates' employability competencies. *Research Policy, 50*(3), 104172. doi:10.1016/j.respol.2020.104172

Bowes, L., Tazzyman, S., Birkin, G., & Roberts, J. (2022). *An Independent Evaluation of Uni Connect's Impact on Intermediate Outcomes for Learners: A Report for The Office for Students on the 2021/2022 (Wave 3) learner survey findings.* Office for Students. https://www.officeforstudents.org.uk/publications/ independent-evaluation-of-uni-connect-s-impact-on-outcomes/

Branicki, L., Steyer, V., & Sullivan-Taylor, B. (2019). HRM practices and impact on organizational performance and employee wellbeing. *International Journal of Human Resource Management, 30*(8), 1261–1286. doi:10.1080/09585192.2016.1244104

Buckholtz, T. J. (1995). *Information Proficiency: Your Key to the Information Age*. Van Nostrand Reinhold.

Buckholtz, T. J. (1996). *Evaluating the CEO: Computerworld Leadership Series*. IDG Enterprise.

Buckholtz, T. J. (2011). *Create Crucial Insight: Use Direct Outcomes Checklists. Think Well. Do Great*. Buckholtz & Associates.

Buckholtz, T. J., & Donald, W. E. (2022). Direct outcomes and win-win relationships between university careers advisors and graduate recruiters. *GiLE Journal of Skills Development*, *2*(1), 9–25. doi:10.52398/gjsd.2022.v2.i1.pp9-25

Cable, D. M., & Judge, T. A. (1996). Person-organization fit, job decisions, and organizational entry. *Organizational Behavior and Human Decision Processes*, *67*(3), 294–311. doi:10.1006/obhd.1996.0081

CFE Research (2023). *The benefits of and barriers to collaborative access activity by higher education providers*. The Office for Students. https://www.officeforstudents.org.uk/publications/benefits-of-and-barriers-to-collaborative-access-activity/

Clark-Ambrosini, J. L., Ashleigh, M. J., Higgs, M., & Baruch, Y. (2023). Quid pro quo? The future for graduate development programmes through the lens of talent management. *International Journal of Human Resource Management*, *34*(17), 3253–3276. doi:10.1080/09585192.2022.2117991

Clarke, M. (2018). Rethinking graduate employability: The role of capital, individual attributes and context. *Studies in Higher Education*, *43*(11), 1923–1937. doi:10.1080/03075079.2017.1294152

Cole, D., & Hallett, R. (2019). The language of employability. In J. Higgs, G. Crisp, & W. Letts (Eds.), *Education for Employability* (pp. 119-130). Brill. doi:10.1163/9789004400832_010

Cooke, F. J., Dickmann, M., & Parry, E. (2021). IJHRM after 30 years: Taking stock in times of COVID-19 and looking towards the future of HR research. *International Journal of Human Resource Management*, *32*(1), 1–23. doi:10.1080/09585192.2020.1833070

Craps, S., Pinxten, M., Knipprath, H., & Langie, G. (2021). Exploring professional roles for early career engineers: A systematic literature review. *European Journal of Engineering Education*, *46*(2), 266–286. doi:10.1080/03043797.2020.1781062

Creed, A., Dixon, M., & Schmitz, M. (2023). Enhancing Student Experience with Career Education. *2023 University of Melbourne Teaching and Learning Conference*. University of Melbourne.

Daubney, K. (2022). "Teaching employability is not my job!": Redefining embedded employability from within the higher education curriculum. *Higher Education. Skills and Work-Based Learning*, *12*(1), 92–106. doi:10.1108/HESWBL-07-2020-0165

De Wit-de Vries, E., Dolfsma, W. A., Van der Windt, H. J., & Gerkema, M. P. (2019). Knowledge transfer in university-industry research partnerships: A review. *The Journal of Technology Transfer*, *44*(4), 1236–1255. doi:10.100710961-018-9660-x

Dollinger, M., Arkoudis, S., & Marangell, S. (2019). University alumni mentoring programs: A win-win? *Journal of Higher Education Policy and Management*, *41*(4), 375–389. doi:10.1080/1360080X.2019.1617657

Donald, W. E. (2017). Students' perceptions of graduate employability: A sequential explanatory approach. Doctoral Thesis, University of Southampton. https://eprints.soton.ac.uk/id/eprint/415935

Donald, W. E. (2020). *Viewpoint: COVID-19 and the Future of Careers*. Graduate Recruitment Bureau. doi:10.13140/RG.2.2.19306.13760

Donald, W. E. (2021). *Conceptualisation of a new 'Early Careers Talent Pipeline' Framework: Enhancing Organisational Sustainability via Feedback-Seeking Behaviour*. Graduate Recruitment Bureau. doi:10.13140/RG.2.2.28278.47684

Donald, W. E. (2023a). Preface. In W. E. Donald (Ed.), *Handbook of Research on Sustainable Career Ecosystems for University Students and Graduates*, (Preface). IGI Global. doi:10.4018/978-1-6684-7442-6

Donald, W. E. (2023b). Application of career ecosystems theory and the new psychological contract to the field of project management: Toward a conceptual model. *Project Management Journal*, *54*(1), 7–18. doi:10.1177/87569728221118873

Donald, W. E., Ashleigh, M. J., & Baruch, Y. (2018). Students' perceptions of education and employability: Facilitating career transition from higher education into the labor market. *Career Development International*, *23*(5), 513–540. doi:10.1108/CDI-09-2017-0171

Donald, W. E., Ashleigh, M. J., & Baruch, Y. (2022). The university-to-work transition: Responses of universities and organizations to the COVID-19 pandemic. *Personnel Review*, *51*(9), 2201–2221. doi:10.1108/PR-03-2021-0170

Donald, W. E., Baruch, Y., & Ashleigh, M. J. (2019). The undergraduate self-perception of employability: Human capital, careers advice and career ownership. *Studies in Higher Education*, *44*(4), 599–614. doi:10.1080/03075079.2017.1387107

Donald, W. E., Baruch, Y., & Ashleigh, M. J. (2023). Construction and operationalisation of an Employability Capital Growth Model (ECGM) via A systematic literature review. *Studies in Higher Education*, 1–15. doi:10.1080/03075079.2023.2219270

Donald, W. E., & Ford, N. (2023). Fostering social mobility and employability: The case for peer learning. *Teaching in Higher Education*, *28*(3), 672–678. doi:10.1080/13562517.2022.2145467

Donald, W. E., & Hughes, H. P. N. (2023). How academics can play a more influential role during a year-in-industry placement: A contemporary critique and call for action. *Industry and Higher Education*. doi:10.1177/09504222231162059

Donald, W. E., & Jackson, D. (2023). Sustainable career ecosystems: Setting the scene. In W. E. Donald (Ed.), *Handbook of Research on Sustainable Career Ecosystems for University Students and Graduates* (pp. 1–13). IGI Global. doi:10.4018/978-1-6684-7442-6.ch001

Donald, W. E., & Manville, G. (2023). Fostering career agency via mindfulness and life coaching: A positive psychology sustainable career framework. In W. E. Donald (Ed.), *Handbook of Research on Sustainable Career Ecosystems for University Students and Graduates* (pp. 450–468). doi:10.4018/978-1-6684-7442-6.ch023

Donald, W. E., & Mouratidou, M. (2022). Preparing for a sustainable career: Challenges and opportunities. *GiLE Journal of Skills Development*, *2*(2), 3–5. doi:10.52398/gjsd.2022.v2.i2.pp3-5

Donald, W. E. & Scattergood, K. (2023). *Fostering student social mobility via social media: Opportunities for university career services*. Times Higher Education. doi:10.13140/RG.2.2.34483.71204

Ferns, A., Dawson, V., & Howitt, C. (2019). A collaborative framework for enhancing graduate employability. *International Journal of Work-Integrated Learning*, *20*(2), 99–111.

Fugate, M., Van der Heijden, B. I. J. M., De Vos, A., Forrier, A., & De Cuyper, N. (2021). Is what's past prologue? A review and agenda for contemporary employability research. *The Academy of Management Annals*, *15*(1), 266–298. doi:10.5465/annals.2018.0171

Gallow, M. L. (2018). How are graduates and alumni featured in university strategic plans? Lessons from Ireland. *Perspectives: Policy and Practice in Higher Education, 22*(3), 92–97. doi:10.1080/13603108.1397065

Gradleaders (2022). *16 Biggest Challenges Every Career Center Faces Today*. Gradeleaders. https://www.gradleaders.com/career-services-challenges

Hallpike, H., Vallee-Tourangeau, G., & Van der Heijden, B. I. J. M. (2022). A distributed interaction decision-making framework for sustainable career development. *Frontiers in Psychology, 12*, 790533. doi:10.3389/fpsyg.2021.790533 PMID:35250691

Ho, C. (2023). How Strong Career Development Can Lead to a Decent Work Future. *The Future Economy*. https://thefutureeconomy.ca/op-eds/career-development-decent-work-candy-ho-ceric/

Hooley, T., Percy, C., & Neary, S. (2023). *Investing In Careers. What is Career Guidance Worth?* Career Development Policy Group & University of Derby. https://adventuresincareerdevelopment.word press.com/2023/07/18/investing-in-careers-what-is-career-guidance-worth/

Hughes, M., Mouratidou, M., & Donald, W. E. (2023). Exploring the impacts of an industrial placement year on students' competency development: A three-cohort, longitudinal study. *Higher Education, Skills, and Work-Based Learning*. Advanced Online Publication. doi:10.1108/HESWBL-02-2023-0044

Izzo, F., Mele, S., & Mustilli, M. (2022). University to work transition: A literature review. *International Journal of Manpower, 43*(7), 1502–1515. doi:10.1108/IJM-07-2021-0398

Jackson, D., Riebe, L., & Macau, F. (2022). Determining factors in graduate recruitment and preparing students for success. *Education + Training, 64*(5), 681–699. doi:10.1108/ET-11-2020-0348

Jakubik, M. (2017). Solving business problems together case: A Master's degree programme in Finland. *Journal of Systemics, Cybernetics and Informatics, 15*(4), 53–57.

Jakubik, M. (2018). Masters bring business benefits-Proved by Finnish managers. *The Turkish Online Journal of Educational Technology*, 2, 65–77.

Jakubik, M. (2020). Enhancing human capital beyond university boundaries. Higher Education. *Skills and Work-Based Learning, 10*(2), 434–446. doi:10.1108/HESWBL-06-2019-0074

Jakubik, M. (2022). Education for life in Higher Education. *3rd Ferenc Farkas International Scientific Conference Proceedings, 3*, 21-31.

Kelly, C. M., Strauss, K., Arnold, J., & Stride, C. (2020). The relationship between leisure activities and psychological resources that support a sustainable career: The role of leisure seriousness and work-leisure similarity. *Journal of Vocational Behavior, 117*, 103340. doi:10.1016/j.jvb.2019.103340

Koen, J., Klehe, U.-C., & Van Vianen, A. E. M. (2012). Training career adaptability to facilitate a successful school-to-work transition. *Journal of Vocational Behavior, 81*(3), 395–408. doi:10.1016/j.jvb.2012.10.003

Kozhuk, D. (2023). *Why Higher Ed Should Invest in Career Services, Not Abolish It.* GOU Connect. https://www. gouconnect.com/career-everywhere/why-higher-ed-should-invest-in-career-services-not-abolish-it/

Kozma, K., Meyer-Miner, A., Chio, J., Mak, S., El-Boraie, A., & Sealey, D. (2021). Developing an industry job simulation program for graduate and postdoctoral trainees in the life sciences. *Canadian Journal of Career Development, 20*(2), 84–93. doi:10.53379/cjcd.2021.102

Mallis, A. (2023). *Close the Skills Gap by Learning New Ways of Working: RMIT Interim CEO.* https://www.digitalnationaus.com.au/news/close-the-skills-gap-by-learning-new-ways-of-working-rmit-interim-ceo-591689

Manville, G., Donald, W. E., & Eves, A. (2022). Can Embedding Authentic Assessment Into the Curriculum Enhance the Employability of Business School Students? *GiLE Journal of Skills Development, 2*(2), 73–87. doi:10.52398/gjsd.2022.v2.i2.pp73-87

Minocha, S., Hristov, D., & Reynolds, M. (2017). From graduate employability to employment: Policy and practice in UK higher education. *International Journal of Training and Development, 21*(3), 235–248. doi:10.1111/ijtd.12105

O'Regan, M., Carthy, A., McGuinness, C., & Owende, P. (2022). Employer collaboration in developing graduate employability: A pilot study in Ireland. *Education + Training, 65*(10), 1–13. doi:10.1108/ET-03-2022-0081

Okolie, U. C., Nwosu, H. E., & Mlanga, S. (2019). Graduate employability: How the higher education institutions can meet the demand of the labour market. *Higher Education. Skills and Work-Based Learning, 9*(4), 620–636. doi:10.1108/HESWBL-09-2018-0089

Padgett, R. C., & Donald, W. E. (2023). Preparing graduates for sustainable carers: A case of 'The Global Marketing Professional' module. *Higher Education, Skills, and Work-Based Learning*, *13*(1), 22–35. doi:10.1108/HESWBL-03-2022-0073

Pearson, J. (1999). Comprehensive research on alumni relationships: Four years of market research at Stanford university. *New Directions for Institutional Research*, *101*, 5–21. doi:10.1002/ir.10101

Petruzziello, G., Antonio, A. A., Chiesa, R., & Mariani, M. G. (2022). It takes more than agency: Linking support from teaching staff, career engagement, and movement capital among university students. *Frontiers in Psychology*, *13*, 1083698. doi:10.3389/fpsyg.2022.1083698 PMID:36600715

Pitan, O. S. (2023). Leveraging the triple helix system for effective employability delivery in Nigerian universities. In W. E. Donald (Ed.), *Handbook of Research on Sustainable Career Ecosystems for University Students and Graduates* (pp. 77–96). IGI Global. doi:10.4018/978-1-6684-7442-6.ch005

Reilly, P. (2021). *Collaborating with Employers to Create Work-Ready Graduates*. Higher Education. https://www.times highereducation.com/campus/collaborating-employers-create-workready-graduates

Rickmann, J., Perez-Encinas, A., & Fernadez-de-Pinedo, N. (2020). Addressing career services' internationalisation challenges through transnational consortia. In A. Curaj, L. Deca, & R. Pricopie, R. (Eds.), *European Higher Education Area: Challenges for a New Decade* (pp. 53-65). Springer. doi:10.1007/978-3-030-56316-5_4

Rodrigues, R., Butler, C. L., & Guest, D. (2020). Evaluating the employability paradox: When does organizational investment in human capital pay off? *International Journal of Human Resource Management*, *31*(9), 1134–1156. doi:10.1080/09585192.2019.1704825

Stevenson, J., McCaig, C., & Madriga, M. (2017). *Evaluation of the National Networks for Collaborative Outreach (NNCOs)*. Sheffield Hallam University. https://shura.shu.ac.uk/19106/

Tomlinson, M. (2017). Forms of graduate capital and their relationship to graduate employability. *Education + Training*, *59*(4), 338–352. doi:10.1108/ET-05-2016-0090

Tomlinson, M., & Anderson, V. (2021). Employers and graduates: The mediating role of signals and capitals. *Journal of Higher Education Policy and Management*, *43*(4), 384–399. doi:10.1080/1360080X.2020.1833126

Van der Heijden, B. I. J. M. (2005). No one has ever promised you a rose garden. *On shared responsibility and employability enhancing strategies throughout careers. Heerlen: Open University of the Netherlands*. Van Gorcum.

Van der Heijden, B. I. J. M., & De Vos, A. (2015). Sustainable careers: Introductory chapter. In A. De Vos & B. I. J. M. Van der Heijden (Eds.), *Handbook of Research on Sustainable Careers* (pp. 1–19). Edward Elgar Publishing. doi:10.4337/9781782547037.00006

Vermeeren, B., & Van der Heijden, B. I. J. M. (2022). Employability in the public sector: The impact of individual and organizational determinants. *Frontiers in Psychology*, *13*, 1041618. doi:10.3389/fpsyg.2022.1041618 PMID:36591038

Ybema, J. F., Van Vuuren, T., & Van Dam, K. (2020). HR practices for enhancing sustainable employability: Implementation, use, and outcomes. *International Journal of Human Resource Management*, *31*(7), 886–907. doi:10.1080/09585192.2017.1387865

ADDITIONAL READING

Ankrah, S. N., & Al-Tabbaa, O. (2015). Universities-industry collaboration: A systematic review. *Scandinavian Journal of Management*, *31*(3), 387–408. doi:10.1016/j.scaman.2015.02.003

Bruneel, J., D'Este, P., & Salter, A. (2010). Investigating the factors that diminish the barriers to university-industry collaboration. *Research Policy*, *39*(7), 858–868. doi:10.1016/j.respol.2010.03.006

Mgaiwa, S. J. (2021). Fostering graduate employability: Rethinking Tanzania's university practices. *SAGE Open*, *2021*(2), 1–14. doi:10.1177/21582440211006709

O'Leary, S. (2013). Collaborations in higher education with employers and their influence on graduate employability: An institutional project. *Enhancing Learning in the Social Sciences*, *5*(1), 37–50. doi:10.11120/elss.2013.05010037

Peel, S. (2022). Meeting student and employer expectations in the hybrid world. *Phoenix*, 166, 26-27.

Sheridan, R. (2022). Better together: Practising employer engagement as a community. *Phoenix*, 166, 16-17.

Siri, A., Leone, C., & Bencivenga, R. (2022). Equality, diversity, and inclusion strategies adopted in a European university alliance to facilitate the higher education-to-work transition. *Societies (Basel, Switzerland)*, *12*(5), 140. doi:10.3390oc12050140

Skute, I., Zalewska-Kurek, K., Hatak, I., & De Weerd-Nederhof, P. (2019). Mapping the field: A bibliometric analysis of the literature on university-industry collaborations. *The Journal of Technology Transfer*, *44*(3), 916–947. doi:10.100710961-017-9637-1

Thijssen, J. G. L., Van der Heijden, B. I. J. M., & Rocco, T. S. (2008). Toward the Employability-Link Model: Current employment transition to future employment perspectives. *Human Resource Development Review*, *7*(2), 165–183. doi:10.1177/1534484308314955

Chapter 10
Concluding Thoughts:
Future Workplace Trends and Implications

ABSTRACT

This chapter concludes the book with thoughts on future workplace trends and the implications that these might have for various actors operating within a sustainable career ecosystem. The chapter begins with a brief overview of recent developments and the current landscape. The focus then shifts to considering the future of work from the organization and graduate perspectives. Subsequently, implications for universities and employers are discussed before consideration of the implications for bridging the university-employer divide. The final part of the chapter summarizes the author's personal reflections, presents a future research agenda, and outlines the key takeaway message from each of the ten chapters.

RECENT DEVELOPMENTS AND THE CURRENT LANDSCAPE

Fifteen years ago, Brian Drive wrote the book The Accountable Leader: Developing Leadership Through Managerial Accountability (Drive, 2008). In the book, Drive identified 10 red flags of faulty organizational design, which Lewis (2022) developed into an image (Figure 1). When we look at these red flags, it becomes evident that they continue to be prevalent today.

DOI: 10.4018/978-1-6684-9827-9.ch010

Figure 1. Red flags for faulty organization design
Source: © 2023 HALO Psychology Ltd. Used with permission. Lewis (2022) based on Dive (2008).

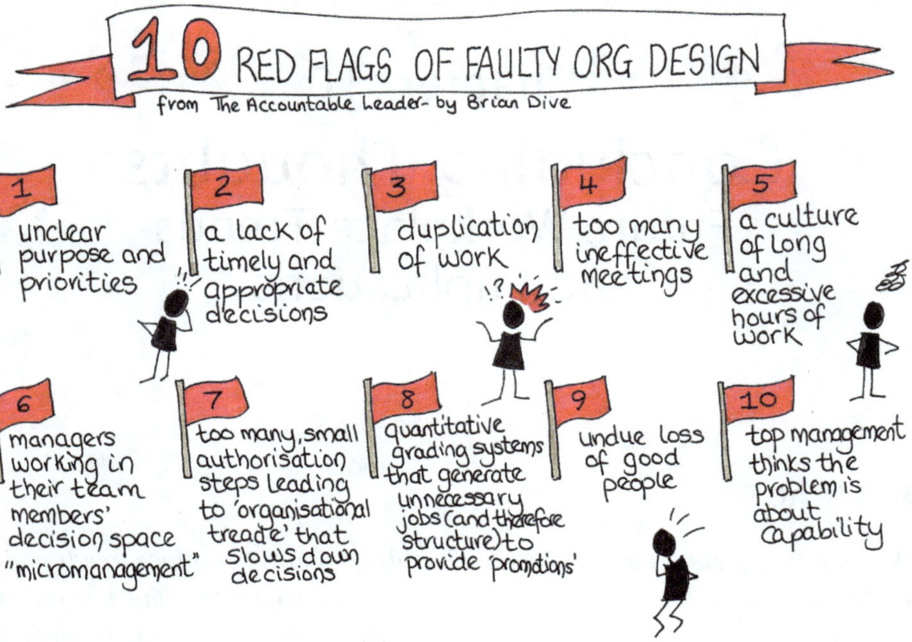

Why, then, when we have known about these issues for so long, has so little progress been made? Taking the UK as an example, the 2007-2008 Global Financial Crisis resulted in a decade of austerity politics, coupled with increased levels of immigration and wage growth suppression, whilst house prices, rent, and university tuition fees dramatically increased (Donald, 2020). On 23rd June 2016, the UK held a referendum with a slender majority voting for Brexit, whereby the UK departed the EU on 31st January 2020 after several years of uncertainty and volatile negotiations (Walker, 2021). A few weeks later, on 23rd March 2020, the UK went into lockdown due to the COVID-19 pandemic, causing unprecedented disruption to daily life to prevent the National Health Service from becoming overwhelmed (Donald, 2020). The following two years saw various policy approaches and restrictions, including furlough, lockdowns, and mask mandates, before most restrictions were lifted in March 2022. The economic impacts of the response to the pandemic were exacerbated by a significant escalation of the Russo-Ukrainian War, which began in 2014, whereby on 24th February 2022, Russia invaded Ukraine. In addition to the loss of life and the displacement of Ukrainians, economic sanctions on trade with Russia disrupted global energy supplies, driving the highest inflation levels in the UK for 40 years (Mendes, 2022). The failure of wages to keep up with the rising cost of living saw a reduction in living standards, with workers from the public and private sectors opting to strike. In 2022, nearly 2.5 million working days were lost to industrial action, the highest in a single year since 1989 (Office for National Statistics, 2023).

What we have witnessed is the occurrence of a series of chance events which are unforeseen or unexpected in nature (Bright et al., 2005). Chance events themselves are not a new phenomenon in that they have occurred throughout history (e.g., Financial Crises, Natural Disasters, Pandemics, Terrorism, Wars, etc.). However, the increased frequency of chance events and the increased timespan of one's career as retirement ages rise means that individuals will experience an increasing number of associated career shocks compared to previous generations (Akkermans et al., 2020). These career shocks can be either positive (e.g., an unexpected promotion) or negative (e.g., the sudden loss of a job) (Akkermans, Rodrigues et al., 2021). Different actors operating within a sustainable career ecosystem have different priorities (Baruch & Rousseau, 2019). Hence, the sustainability of a career ecosystem can come under threat from various chance events or career shocks (Donald et al., 2022). Moreover, a negative resource spiral occurs when an individual experiences the loss of one resource, subsequently leading to the loss of other personal resources (Hobfoll et al., 2018). For example, during the pandemic-related restrictions, individuals who unexpectedly lost their jobs experienced economic-related stress due to the loss of income, which increased the likelihood of financial hardship and negatively affected their wellbeing (Witteveen & Velthorst, 2020).

Additionally, the pandemic-related restrictions caused workers to re-evaluate their lives and priorities, which had ripple effects throughout the career ecosystem (Hughes & Thambar, 2023). The exodus of workers from the workforce due to early retirement or health reasons saw the loss of valuable knowledge and experience (Blustein, 2020). The depletion of human capital led to a 'War for Talent' (de Prada, 2022), whilst an increased desire for value and meaning in one's life led to the 'Great Resignation' (Serenko, 2022). Additionally, Serenko (2022) proposes that the COVID-19 pandemic can act as a catalyst for what he refers to as the 'Great Knowledge Revolution', whereby

Managers should learn how to use the available human capital more efficiently; realize the importance of universal succession planning programs; automate knowledge-centric business processes; facilitate knowledge-based IT initiatives by implementing self-functioning virtual communities, including enterprise social networks; restructure organizations to optimize intra-organizational knowledge flows; adjust strategies, products and target markets based on the available human capital; and create telecommuting conditions for people with disabilities who cannot be physically present. (p. 1)

Therefore, the future of work can likely be characterized as volatile, uncertain, complex, and ambiguous – particularly around technological advancement and climate change (Donald & Mouratidou, 2023; Gkeredakis et al., 2021). Rather than a 'one-size-fits-all approach', sustainability of the career ecosystem relies on evolution in different ways for different actors (e.g., at the industry, organization, job, and individual levels). Consequently, the power in the employee-employer relationship appears to be shifting away from the employer towards the employee, with employers struggling to attract and retain talent as actors operating within sustainable career ecosystems adapt to the new normal (Krammer, 2021).

Across the rest of this chapter, we consider the future of work from the organization and graduate perspectives before considering the implications it may have for universities and students. Potential implications for bridging the university-employer divide are then suggested before the book concludes with a summary of reflections, a future research agenda, and the key takeaway points from each chapter.

THE FUTURE OF WORK: THE ORGANIZATION PERSPECTIVE

Various commentators have examined current trends and speculated about what the future of work may look like. However, Dries et al. (2023) note that we must consider two questions when evaluating such claims: 1) Who is making the claim?, and 2) What is their agenda? Furthermore, Dries (2023) believes that the future of work does not exist, instead positioning it as "an arena for values, politics, ideology, and imagination… shaped by collective action and acts of resistance" (Video, Timestamp 00.00.55). The novel position of Dries aligns with the view that the future of work will encompass volatility, uncertainty, complexity, and ambiguity (Donald & Mouratidou, 2023).

Nevertheless, drawing together current trends and predictions from various resources can provide valuable insights into a general direction of travel to underpin pragmatic strategies for all actors operating within a sustainable career ecosystem. Figure 2 offers a cumulative summary of such insights drawn from 10 diverse sources (Career Thought Leaders, 2023; Cook, 2022; Deloitte, 2023; Emeritus, 2022; Gartner, 2021; Gibby, 2022; McRae & Aykens, 2022; Mercer, 2023; Offbeat, 2022; World Economic Forum, 2022).

Each of the three themes is now explored from the organization's perspective in the context of early-career talent.

Figure 2. The future of work (organization perspective)
Source: Author's own creation

Attraction and Selection

Organizations will continue to face what may appear to be two contradictory challenges. First, the increased participation in higher education combined with reduced or stagnant hiring during the period of pandemic-related restrictions means that in the short to medium term, organizations will continue to receive a high volume of applications for most of their vacancies (Donald et al., 2022). Second, the 'War for Talent' combined with an emerging skills gap will make it more difficult for organizations to secure talent ahead of competitors, whilst many applicants may lack the skills required to perform a specific role (Career Thought Leaders, 2023). Consequently, organizations may benefit by shifting from role-based recruitment to skills-based hiring, whereby they can deploy their employees more flexibly to offer organizational agility (Jesuthasan & Boudreau, 2021). There will also likely be a continuation of the recent trend of reducing academic barriers to entry for specific vacancies by removing mandates for specific degrees or particular degree classifications, leading to the pursuit of non-traditional candidates (Emeritus, 2023).

Automation and Artificial Intelligence (AI) will likely continue to play a significant role in managing high volumes of data by screening applicants and assessing for skills, motivations, and person-organization fit (Cook, 2022). However, organizations will need to learn from the early deployment of technology, whereby the diversity of hires was often hampered by unconscious bias encoded into the algorithms (Donald et al.,

2022). Additionally, early career talent responds poorly when their employer does not fulfil promises made around DEI during the attraction and selection process (Pohl et al., 2022). Therefore, DEI outcomes within organizations will take on increased significance despite ongoing resistance to such changes (McRae & Aykens, 2022).

Human-Centric Work Design

Idiosyncratic Deals (I-Deals) can benefit organizations and employees by optimizing human capital, leading to strategic advantage, and increased retention, performance, and job satisfaction (Rousseau et al., 2006). Therefore, Jakubik (2020) calls for a change in terminology from 'knowledge workers' and 'knowledge work' to 'intellectual workers' and 'intellectual work' to reflect the rise of human intellect. When combined with Automation and AI, the opportunity exists for strategic transformation and emphasis on employee wellbeing (Emeritus, 2022). We do not yet know how technology will advance and its future impact on workers and humankind (Dries et al., 2023). We may see increased opportunities for flexible working, a 4-day working week (where feasible/desirable for the organization and the employee), or the roll-out of a universal basic income. Alternatively, we may see a rise in unemployment, increased use of technology to monitor employee performance, or otherwise as yet unforeseen adverse impacts from technological advancement. Therefore, organizations must consider the consequences of their decisions on broader society rather than confining their focus to their shareholders, employees, or supply chains (Deloitte, 2023).

Organizations that embrace flexible working can also create inclusive cultures. For example, Kahn (2022) observes how working remotely can offer personal freedom, new employment opportunities, and improved quality of life, whilst Cook (2022) highlights increased accessibility to employment opportunities. Aksoy et al. (2023) found that, on average, a person saves 72 minutes each day they do not commute, offering opportunities for work, leisure, and caregiving whilst providing environmental benefits in the battle against climate change. Additionally, new graduates may prefer office-based working as a means of socialization and coworker support in managing their personal resources to adapt to workplace demands (Cai et al., 2023). Inclusive organizational cultures will also need to embed employee wellbeing as part of the culture, prioritize physical and mental health, and take action to address existing unhealthy work practices (Deloitte, 2023). Therefore, organizations with inclusive cultures will likely offer increased flexibility and personal autonomy, leading to competitive advantage (Gibby, 2022) by unlocking employee engagement, productivity, and growth opportunities (World Economic Forum, 2023).

Talent Retention

The 'War for Talent' and the 'Skills Gap' will likely exacerbate pre-existing retention challenges (Emeritus, 2022). Organizations will subsequently need to emphasize retaining their existing talent for sustainable competitive advantage (Career Thought Leaders, 2023). An emerging strategy to respond to such a challenge is focusing on upskilling and/or reskilling existing employees in preparation for the organization's future needs (Gibby, 2022). Developing an in-house talent pipeline can help address the skills gap among graduates and offer opportunities for 'Quiet Hiring' whereby an organization acquires new skill sets in response to evolving demands using existing talent (McRae & Aykens, 2022). However, Donald (2023) identifies how the evolution of person-organization fit over time means there can be instances where retaining talent is detrimental to the employee, the employer, or both parties. There may also be a risk of institutionalized thinking and a lack of fresh ideas via inter-organizational learning to maintain organizational competitiveness. Despite these potential risks, strategies of upskilling and/or reskilling can also address demands from graduates for opportunities to undertake lifelong learning (Offbeat, 2022), which has been linked to increased levels of career satisfaction and wellbeing (Heslin et al., 2020).

Furthermore, the pandemic has catalyzed early career talent to prioritize purpose, meaning, and autonomy via life crafting (Cook, 2023; De Jong et al., 2020). Organizations must focus on "creating an attractive work environment where employees are engaged at work, able to identify and solve complex problems with creative approaches and able to flourish as individuals" (Jakubik, 2022, p. 11). Developing personal resources can help with work-life balance, satisfaction, and talent retention (Fan & Potočnik, 2021). However, organizations must be aware of 'Faux Flex' whereby flexible working arrangements benefit the company rather than the employee (e.g., prescribed days working from home or being forced to work from home where the employee prefers to be in the office). The consideration particularly applies to early-career talent, who are more likely to want time in the office, compared to mid-career and late-career talent, who often prefer more flexibility (Donald, 2023; Hughes & Davis, 2021).

Additionally, aspects of upskilling/reskilling and a sense of purpose and autonomy must be combined with feedback strategies, promotion opportunities, and appropriate renumeration. We know that early career talent is looking for greater feedback on performance and development than previous generations (Chillakuri, 2020), whilst rising levels of student debt and the cost of living crisis are causing concern for financial wellbeing (Mercer, 2023). Therefore, successful organizations must emphasize continued employee growth, provide lateral and vertical career movement, and offer promotions and renumeration packages to retain talent (Emeritus, 2022; Jin & Waldman, 2020).

THE FUTURE OF WORK: THE GRADUATE PERSPECTIVE

Our attention now shifts to the graduate perspective of the future of work. The role of chance events and career shocks concerning the foundation of sustainable careers for young professionals is an emerging area of interest, sitting at the intersection of person, context, and time (Blokker et al., 2019; 2023). We also know that the pandemic-related restrictions are likely to have long-lasting impacts on the careers of individuals (Hamouche et al., 2023). Consequently, I led a research team that interviewed twenty-eight career professionals to explore how they believed the future of work would evolve (Donald, Jakubik, et al., 2023). One cohort graduated in 2008 during the 2007-2008 Global Financial Crisis, whilst the second cohort graduated in 2020 during the COVID-19 pandemic.

Interestingly, there was complete alignment between the themes offered by each cohort. The only evident difference came from the 2020 graduates tending to prefer working in the office to maximize opportunities for knowledge exchange and overcome loneliness or the lack of a suitable workspace at home. In contrast, the 2020 graduates tended to prefer to work from home, utilizing the time saved from the daily commute on care responsibilities, catching up on sleep, time with family and friends, and fitness-related activities.

Figure 3 presents our findings. Each of the four themes is subsequently detailed (using pseudonyms to maintain participant confidentiality), supplemented by additional research from scholars and practitioners. The lines in Figure 3 represent links between themes identified by participants in the study rather than an exhaustive mapping of links between themes (e.g., a growth mindset could be linked to career progression either directly or indirectly).

Figure 3. The future of work (graduate perspective)
Source: © 2023 Donald, Jakubik & Nimmi. Used with permission.

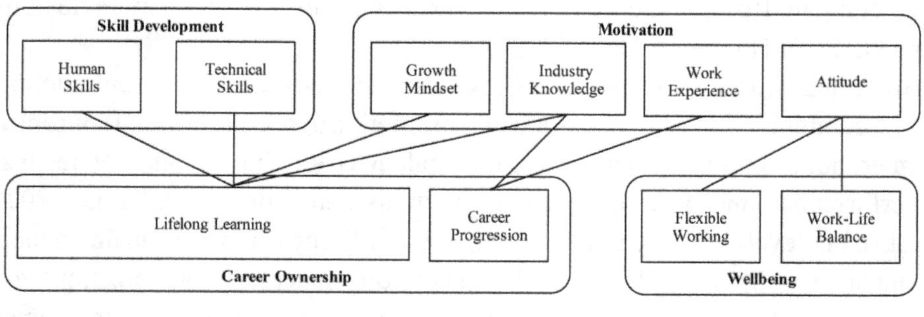

Skill Development

The graduates we interviewed believed the future of work would see an increased need for human skills (previously referred to in the literature as soft skills) and technical skills (previously referred to in the literature as hard skills). The dominant human skills mentioned included adaptability, communication, critical thinking, problem-solving, teamwork, and time management. The dominant technical skills were artificial intelligence, automation, cyber security, data analytics, process optimization, and robotics. The participants' views align with previous research showing how skills acquisition leads to increased self-perceived employability (Donald, 2017; Donald et al., 2019). Specifically, at the individual level, graduates discussed how "*skills are a personal asset, but every two to three years, they will diminish, which means they are also a liability requiring ongoing investment and development*" (Mohammed:2020). The graduates we interviewed also felt that organizations would need to make a "*huge investment in upskilling and reskilling employees*" (Natasha:2008) and enabling their employees to "*learn on the job as it broadens the range of people that can be considered for a role*" (Rose:2008). Flatt and Drewery (2023) support these views and posit an increased need for learning opportunities to be made available to graduates by their employers.

The dependence of the employee on the employer and the employer on the employee captures the continued evolvement of the New Psychological Contract (Rousseau, 1995) and its role in fostering a sustainable career ecosystem (Baruch & Rousseau, 2019; Donald & Jackson, 2023). The graduate perspective also reflects how, as a person, they contribute to and are dependent on the employer context, whereby their career evolves as a sequence of experiences over time (De Vos et al., 2020).

Motivation

Donald, Jakubik et al. (2023) defined the theme of 'Motivation' as "an individual possessing the capability to signal enthusiasm for a particular job based on past actions and future perspectives to enable individuals and organizations to assess the fit between their respective demands and resources" (p. 8). Graduates felt that the evolving nature of the future of work requires "*the motivation to learn, a willingness and drive*" (Clare:2020) and "*a growth mindset rather than a fixed mindset*" (David:2008). During the application and selection process, there would be an increasing need for the candidate to "*understand the industry*" (Isla:2008) and "*stay up to date with trends and the changing landscape*" (Noah: 2020). There was also the perception that attitude assessments will take on increased significance to ensure "*an individual fits into the work environment*" (Peter:2008) and is "*engaged and passionate*" (Helena:2008).

Furthermore, graduates felt that having work experience during one's degree will become increasingly necessary since "*someone with work experience who can show knowledge and passion for the industry will stand out*" (Peter:2008), whilst "*students who have not worked during their degree may be perceived as lazy*" (Suzanne:2020). However, there was a feeling that whilst beneficial, the value of "*voluntary work or extra-curricular activities to gain practical experience will depend on the sector*" (Eleanor:2008). Therefore, the view of Cole and Coulson (2022) of the need for lifewide learning appears to be supported, albeit with a caveat that the context can increase or decrease its influence during the application and selection process (i.e., having a moderation effect) when signaling employability to a prospective employer.

Career Ownership

Donald, Jakubik et al. (2023) defined the theme of 'Career Ownership' as "an ongoing process by which an individual commits to identifying areas for personal development and proactively takes action to acquire and retain resources to facilitate career progression based on the existing and future demands of their desired career path" (p. 8). Graduates suggested the uncertain and volatile nature of the labor market would mean an increased emphasis on being "*proactive in learning*" (Attila:2008) and "*considering what changes you think will happen*" (Jim:2008). The need for lifelong learning was also captured by participants who emphasized "*staying up to date with critical skills of the future*" (Payem:2020) and "*ensuring that if I want to move somewhere else, I have the best opportunity*" (Maria:2008). The findings are supported by other literature suggesting how the pace of change impacts career agency throughout one's career (Hughes & Thambar, 2023) and the need to embrace worker agency within a sustainable career ecosystem (Deloitte, 2023).

Additionally, graduates felt they needed to be proactive to ensure they are "*well-prepared for the next move, ensuring qualifications, experiences, and skills are an asset of today and the future*" (Mohammed:2020). For example, by considering "*what role I want to be doing in 10 years and developing a transition or career map to identify what steps need to be taken to get there*" (Julia:2008). The views were driven by the perceived future risk of losing one's job due to the increased prevalence of future chance events and by the consideration that "*it is easier to progress your career if you move between teams or companies fairly often*" (Payem:2020). The findings again map to other dominant views in the literature. We know that university students have increased levels of concern about future job loss (Hamouche et al., 2023) and that an increased need for career mobility via career transitions over time requires workers to be adaptable and adopt a growth mindset via lifelong learning (Sullivan & Al Arriss, 2021). We are also seeing an increased occurrence of boundaryless careers whereby individuals undertake a series of career decisions across the timespan of their career via career crafting rather than the traditional career approach of following a single career path (De Vos et al., 2019).

Wellbeing

Donald, Jakubik et al. (2023) define the theme of 'Wellbeing' as "a focus on enhancing an individual's physical, mental, and social states, thereby offering them health and prosperity, benefiting themselves and their employer" (p. 8). Graduates believe more employers, where feasible, will "*move to a four-day working week to offer flexibility*" (Beatrice:2020), whilst 2008 graduates are keen to increase their time spent working from home "*since the argument you cannot do your job unless you are sitting at a desk in an office is now null and void following the COVID-19 pandemic*" (Dianna:2008). However, 2020 graduates raised concerns about "*the social aspect where the pandemic has shed light on loneliness, depression, challenges of sitting at home and the impacts on mental health*" (Mehdi:2020). Their views are supported by Phillips et al. (2022), who found that the lockdown-related restrictions of the pandemic have had severe consequences for mental health and wellbeing, particularly for recent graduates. The variance in impacts of the restrictions to health and wellbeing suggested by our participants was also captured in a study of public sector employees in Germany, whereby some individuals reported lower levels of stress when they did not have to commute, whilst for others, working from home led to isolation and longer working hours (Seinsche et al., 2022). Subsequently, the overarching consensus of the graduates we interviewed seemed to be that the future of work "*will follow a hybrid working approach since some face-to-face interaction is still needed*" (Jim:2008), mainly "*to get the training right when onboarding new starters*" (Eleanor:2008).

Graduates from 2008 placed a much greater emphasis on work-life balance than graduates from 2020, perhaps reflecting the time element of a sustainable career (De Vos et al., 2020). As one participant noted, "*you see many people entering the industry, doing quite well in the first couple of years, jumping up the ladder quickly, and then experiencing burnout and dropping out of the industry altogether*" (Naomi:2008). There was also a desire to "*factor in things outside of work and careers – so how can you bring both together and have a bit of a plan about what you want to achieve?*" (David:2008). Finally, (Natasha:2008) explained how "*at the moment, I am just looking for something that fits around my family. When the kids are older, I can start to look at what I want. But sometimes, the needs of the family as a whole must influence what you can do as a career.*" The sentiments reflect other observations around how the future of work must move beyond a 'one-size-fits-all' approach and offer more flexible arrangements, providing worker autonomy and agency to benefit all actors operating in the career ecosystem (Deloitte, 2023; Krammer, 2021). For example, graduates we interviewed hoped the future of work would have "*more flexibility from employers regarding childcare, doing the school runs, and being more family-friendly*" (Naomi:2008) whilst "*increasing opportunities for equality, diversity, and inclusion*" (Rebecca:2008).

IMPLICATIONS FOR UNIVERSITIES

Our focus now shifts to considering how the perspectives from organizations and graduates of the future of work have implications for universities as actors operating within a sustainable career ecosystem. Four themes are addressed, including (i) a sense of belonging, (ii) creating global citizens, (iii) curriculum design, and (iv) the evolving role of career counselors.

A Sense of Belonging

A sense of belonging refers to "students' feelings of being accepted, included by and connected to their institutions" (Goodenow, 1993, p. 80). From the university perspective, fostering a sense of belonging can increase students' motivation, enjoyment, and achievement when pursuing undergraduate study (Pedler et al., 2022). Creative, supportive, and welcoming environments are crucial since mental health issues, disability, socio-economic status, and ethnicity can reduce the likelihood of student retention (O'Keeffe, 2013). Additionally, first-generation students often report lower scores for a sense of belonging than their peers, leading to lower motivation and enjoyment levels while studying (Pedler et al., 2022). Of concern, in Australia, 20% of students are considered to be at risk of not completing their degree (Meehan & Howells, 2019), whilst a study in Wales found that half of their participants expressed critical or less positive responses when asked to share their personal experience of a sense of belonging whilst at university (Ahn & Davis, 2020).

The attrition rate of such students is problematic because, at the university level, it reduces opportunities for integration and social mobility if students feel they cannot be their authentic selves or identify areas of commonality with their peers or academics (Fernández et al., 2023). Organizations are subsequently impacted because high attrition rates during undergraduate study make it more difficult to recruit diverse graduate talent (McRae & Aykens, 2022). Consequently, academic and social engagement has been targeted to offer students opportunities to interact with each other and develop a sense of belonging (Van Gijn-Grosvenor & Huisman, 2020). Nevertheless, two additional domains of surroundings and personal space are often neglected. "Surroundings equate to participants' living space, and geographical and cultural location, while personal spaces refer to life satisfaction, life attitudes, identity and personal interests" (Ahn & Davis, 2020, p. 622).

Creating Global Citizens

Alongside fostering a sense of belonging, universities will need to respond to the needs of employers by creating global citizens. The United Nations (2015) defines global citizenship as

the umbrella term for social, political, environmental, and economic actions of globally minded individuals and communities on a worldwide scale. The term can refer to the belief that individuals are members of multiple, diverse, local and non-local networks rather than single actors affecting isolated societies... The concept of global citizenship is embedded in the Sustainable Development Goals through SDG 4: Ensure Inclusive and Equitable Quality Education and Promote Lifelong Learning Opportunities for All, which includes global citizenship as one of its targets. (Online, Paragraphs 1-2)

Jakubik (2023) believes that to create global citizens, universities will need "to focus more on cultivating character, emancipatory competence, life-world becoming, values, justice, trust, truth, and intellectual virtues such as intellectual humility, curiosity, open-mindedness, and courage" (p. 45). Additionally, Smith et al. (2017) observe how the complex and evolving nature of labor markets will require universities to address five dimensions: (i) innovation, (ii) sustainability, (iii) integration, (iv) participation, and (v) inclusivity.

I believe that, taken together, the themes of a 'sense of belonging' and 'creating global citizenship' will be significant determinants for the sustainability of career ecosystems. Embracing these themes will enable universities to maintain relevance and to produce a diverse range of graduates who are (i) able to meet current and future organizational demands and (ii) capable of working together to tackle global-level threats (e.g. climate change) for the good of humankind.

Curriculum Design

Curriculum design will need to evolve, driven by the demands of employers and the evolution of technology. I believe such change will predominantly focus on hybrid delivery and assessment practices. From a delivery perspective, a hybrid setup can offer the additional flexibility of remote study where feasible whilst also ensuring that students who lack the technology or quiet study space for remote learning can continue to experience in-person content delivery (Bashir et al., 2021). The approach can also provide students with a sense of agency and alternative ways to flourish, preparing them for the hybrid world of work (Jakubik, 2022). Whilst in this book, our dominant focus has framed employment as within organizations, universities must also promote curriculum design and content that encourages students to prepare for entrepreneurial pursuits (Smith et al., 2017).

From an assessment perspective, I believe that universities must make their assessments more authentic and experience-orientated. Authentic assessment can help to develop personal skills such as teamwork and real-world problem-solving (Manville et al., 2022) and cultivate creativity (Jakubik, 2022) to address the evolving needs of the workplace. I also believe that authentic assessment can embrace technological advancements such as ChatGPT. Students can become familiar with utilizing innovative forms of technology to prepare themselves for such events across their career span, whilst the risks of plagiarism associated with more traditional assessment forms can be reduced. The curriculum design which will be most effective will supplement an authentic assessment approach with industry micro-placements whereby lecturers provide ongoing support and deploy reflective assessments to enhance the benefits of work placement learning on students' readiness for the university-to-work transition (Donald & Hughes, 2023; Okolie, 2022).

The Evolving Role of Career Counselors

Career decision-making continues to become more challenging and complex (Kulcsár et al., 2020; Nimmi et al., 2023). Additionally, the COVID-19 pandemic has led to unprecedented demand for career support from students and recent graduates (Donald et al., 2022). Subsequently, individuals have increased reliance on career counselors to support them in making better career decisions (Gati & Kulcsár, 2021) and to foster sustainable career paths linked to increased career satisfaction and wellbeing outcomes (Müller et al., 2023). Students will increasingly need tailored career support (Donald et al., 2022) to craft narratives and stories to signal employability and be capable of applying their experiences and abilities to the context of the hiring organization (Career Thought Leaders, 2023). Career counselors may also need to create an environment that mirrors the reality of the workplace, such as ensuring students are comfortable with remote and hybrid working practices and associated technologies (Thambar & Hughes, 2023).

I also believe that the selection processes adopted by organizations will undergo a continued transformation in the years ahead, requiring career counselors to stay up-to-date with industry practices. Universities will also need to provide additional funding and resources to career counselors since, in many cases, university career counselors cannot support their entire student body effectively. Without additional funding, career services will increasingly have to rely on the other actors operating in a career ecosystem if universities are to remain relevant and foster social mobility (Buckholtz & Donald, 2022).

IMPLICATIONS FOR STUDENTS

Next, we consider how the organization and graduate perspectives of the future of work have implications for students as actors operating within a sustainable career ecosystem. Four themes are addressed, including (i) university participation, (ii) lifewide learning, (iii) work experience, and (iv) a sense of purpose.

University Participation

Since World War II, the transition of higher education from 'elite' to 'mass' to 'universal' participation has seen increased student enrolments and the subsequent production of graduates (Trow, 2006). In countries such as Pakistan, where there are high levels of youth unemployment, the oversupply of graduates continues to place additional emphasis on the university's reputation as a proxy for graduate quality (Khan & Ali, 2022). In the UK, rising tuition fees are also problematic since they threaten students' perceived return on investment from participating in higher education (Donald et al., 2018). There is also a concern that due to Brexit, students will not have access to peers from as many different nationalities as before due to fewer European students enrolling in UK universities. Consequently, I believe that students will begin to question the value of higher education, particularly if employers provide alternative routes to employment without requiring such qualifications.

For those individuals who opt to pursue a university degree, there will be an increasing need to take ownership of preparing for entry into the labor market across all years of study (Raihan & Azad, 2023). Universities must also do more to address the socio-economic differences in the outcomes of their graduates undertaking the university-to-work transition (De Schepper et al., 2023), particularly given the negative impacts of the COVID-19 pandemic on social mobility outcomes (Donald et al., 2022).

Lifewide Learning

Complex and evolving labor markets mean an individual's learning is no longer confined to educational settings. Instead, learning must occur as a lifewide and lifelong pursuit (Cole & Coulson, 2022; Jackson, 2011). A challenge for students comes from uncertainty around the future trajectory of the world of work (Hughes &

Davis, 2021) whilst also needing to prepare to navigate transformative and disruptive technological innovations (Curşeu et al., 2021). Subsequently, students must acquire employability capital from various sources, including curricular, co-curricular, and extra-curricular opportunities (Jackson & Bridgstock, 2021).

Work Experience

Drawing together the notions of career agency and lifewide learning, students must also undertake work experience to enhance their employability capital and self-perceived employability (Jackson et al., 2022). Concerningly, the reduced opportunities to gain work experience during the lockdown phases of the COVID-19 pandemic caused a widening of pre-existing inequalities (Haelermans et al., 2022). Therefore, students must encourage universities to establish partnerships with organizations to remove barriers to accessing work experience during their degree studies (McCafferty, 2022). For example, the increased prevalence of micro-internships can help students gain skills and develop industry contacts to benefit all actors operating within a sustainable career ecosystem (Career Thought Leaders, 2023).

A Sense of Purpose

Additionally, the disruption to education, feelings of isolation, and increased time for reflection during the pandemic-related lockdowns saw students and recent graduates focus more on their wellbeing (Donald & Jackson, 2022). Consequently, I believe that students will increasingly seek employment opportunities that give them a sense of purpose and work-life balance, although naturally, some students will continue to focus more on salary in the initial stages of their careers (Christian, 2023). Therefore, students must use their time at university to understand their 'person-career fit' as an antecedent to a sustainable career (Chudzikowski et al., 2020). The position emphasizes the increased reliance on career counselors to support students in making informed career decisions (Gati & Kulcsár, 2021) and fostering sustainable career paths (Müller et al., 2023).

IMPLICATIONS FOR BRIDGING THE UNIVERSITY-EMPLOYER DIVIDE

Finally, we consider how the organization and graduate perspectives of the future of work have implications for bridging the university-employer divide. Four themes are addressed, including (i) dialogue between actors, (ii) sharing of resources, (iii) a broader range of employers, and (iv) recruitment agencies as intermediaries.

Dialogue Between Actors

Each actor depends on the other for the sustainability of the career ecosystem (Baruch, 2015). Active partnerships between universities and organizations will be needed to address the mismatch between students' perceptions and industry needs (Draissi et al., 2022). Such partnerships must focus on informing course pedagogy, improving assessment processes, and helping students secure work placements (Raihan & Azad, 2023). For example, as Khan and Ali (2022) suggest, "increasing industry-academia linkages, redesigning the curriculum to make it more industry-driven, and introducing pedagogical reforms towards innovative and technological skills development can maximize return on investment of students" (p. 1).

Organizations and graduate recruiters must also be clear about their current and future talent needs and how they plan to select early career talent. Additionally, Hughes and Thambar (2023) acknowledge that for the future evolution of the career ecosystem to benefit all actors, the needs of graduate talent must be balanced against the organization's needs. Consequently, psychological contracts must continue to evolve on both sides.

Sharing of Resources

The COVID-19 pandemic has seen record demand for career support by university students (Donald, Jakubik et al., 2023). Unfortunately, the lack of capacity for career services to manage the demand from their students is problematic given the need to confront human and technical skills gaps (McRae & Aykens, 2022). Subsequently, graduate recruiters as agents of the organization and career advisors as agents of the university need to look for win-win partnerships whereby the sharing of resources benefits all actors in the career ecosystem (Buckholtz & Donald, 2022). The State Progress Checklist provides a useful starting point (Appendix 1, Chapter 9). Universities must also re-consider perceived trade-offs concerning league table rankings and instead embrace opportunities to work together for the benefit of their collective students (Donald et al., 2022). I believe that universities and organizations working together to share expertise and resources can increase the employability of graduates to meet current and future organizational needs.

A Broader Range of Employers

When I interviewed university students and career advisors, a dominant theme was the need for a broader range of employers to be represented in events taking place at university campuses (Donald et al., 2018; 2022). These actors felt that SMEs and local organizations were underrepresented, with face time on university campuses dominated by multinational companies. I believe establishing local partnerships will be crucial to the sustainability of lower-ranked universities, whereby graduate talent can access local employment opportunities, subsequently providing regional benefits to society. Universities must also promote entrepreneurial and freelancing opportunities by informing students of expectations versus realities and providing personal and digital branding strategies. For example, the need for "a clear focus, consistent messaging, constant communication, and community-building to attract clients and referrals" (Career Thought Leader, 2023, p. 13).

Recruitment Agencies as Intermediaries

An additional opportunity to bridge the university-employer divide comes from using recruitment agencies as intermediaries between career services and organizations. Historically, university career services have been weary of agencies due to concerns that their role within a sustainable career ecosystem might be excluded (Donald et al., 2022). However, because agencies work with various universities and employers, they can be uniquely placed to understand the various trends and challenges, subsequently offering pragmatic solutions that benefit multiple actors. Moreover, recruitment agencies can provide students with access to employment opportunities, offer tailored preparation support for the application and selection process, and help foster social mobility by providing access to other networks of employers and peers (Higginbotham, 2021). Going forward, I believe that agencies will play an even greater role in bridging the university-employer divide, particularly as demand for career support increases and employability potential needs to be converted to employment outcomes for universities to remain relevant in the years ahead.

CONCLUSION

To conclude the chapter and the book, I now provide a series of ten reflections and four future research agenda suggestions concerning the book's central theme of strategic opportunities for bridging the university-employer divide. The book then draws to a close with a brief summary of the key takeaway messages from each of the ten chapters.

Reflections

Below are ten reflections I have about opportunities for bridging the university-employer divide. You may have other thoughts or opinions–which is great–since these reflections can act as a starting point for further discussion and debate.

1. Will universities still have an influential role to play in the future? Perhaps not unless they evolve with the changing needs of society, particularly as the cost versus benefits of participating in higher education continue to narrow. Perhaps the length of degree programs will be shortened/condensed.
2. How will universities overcome the staff retention problem in academia? Will increased workloads and the expectation of 'free labor' via service activities (e.g., peer review) continue to drive an exodus of staff from academia to industry?
3. Will we reach a point where the neoliberalization of higher education does more harm than good? Perhaps we already have due to an obsession with metrics and league table rankings rather than fostering collaborative environments and sharing knowledge and resources.
4. How will individual countries look to ensure national competitiveness and protect national interests? What impact will this have on the global labor market and the sustainability of career ecosystems?
5. Will countries re-visit and relax their visa policies, reversing a trend of tightening immigration rules in recent years? If so, how can national governments balance the risk of brain drain versus encouraging their populations to pursue studies abroad? Are career advisors sufficiently prepared to work with and support students from different cultures? Is there a mismatch between international students' expectations of employability, the process of gaining employment, and workplace culture? What assumptions might recruiters or employers hold about the selection process that is not clearly communicated and might be challenging for international students?
6. Will we see an increase in flexible learning and working opportunities? I suspect the answer will vary by institution, organizational culture, sector, and location.
7. How will national governments ensure that technological advances are beneficial, not detrimental to their populations? Has the time come for universal basic income? Would this damage productivity or increase wellbeing via a sense of purpose and meaning whereby an individual could pursue paid or voluntary work related to their values?
8. How will governments, organizations, universities, and individuals manage the increased prevalence of chance events and associated career shocks? How can students be best prepared to navigate increased volatility and uncertainty to enhance the likelihood of career sustainability?
9. Do academics and publishers need to re-think how they value research outputs? I would argue yes and suggest a need to promote the value of pragmatic publications underpinned by theoretical frameworks rather than dense theoretical publications for 'advancing theory', particularly in the so-called 'top-ranked'

journals (see Akkermans et al. 2023 for further discussion framed around bridging the graduate employability and worker employability literature).

10. Finally, have we missed the opportunity of the COVID-19 pandemic to remove barriers to inclusivity? As a disabled and housebound academic, it certainly feels like the return to in-person-only events and conferences leaves us a less inclusive community now than during the pandemic when virtual access was provided.

Future Research Agenda

I would also like to share four opportunities for future research to help outline an agenda to bridge the university-employer divide. Again, this is not meant to be an all-encompassing or prescriptive list, just a starting point to initiate further thought and discussion.

- There is a need for academic research to (a) embrace cross-discipline collaborations, (b) embrace the intersectionality of various theories, (c) increase the use of longitudinal and/or mixed methods studies, (d) consider the intersectionality of various demographics rather than looking at these in isolation (e.g., gender, ethnicity, sexual orientation, first-generation student status, etc.), and (e) demonstrate the real-world impact of specific interventions via empirical enquiry.
- We will need to increase our focus on wellbeing and mental health in response to the COVID-19 pandemic and the higher proportion of Generation Z struggling with these aspects compared to previous generations. For example, how can we promote wellbeing via technological advancement rather than exacerbate these pre-existing challenges? Additionally, can we use longitudinal studies to build a scientific understanding of the long-term impacts of office/school, hybrid, or virtual working/learning?
- With the rapid advancement of AI, we will need to consider how we evolve ethical guidelines around educational assessment, recruitment, and employee monitoring to safeguard all actors and provide benefits whilst maintaining integrity and promoting inclusivity.
- There is also a need for research to inform policy at institutional and government levels, particularly around higher education funding and the migration patterns of students and graduates. I believe that the sustainability of career ecosystems will rely on increased collaboration and knowledge sharing rather than protectionist instincts.

Key Takeaway Messages by Chapter

This book, consisting of four sections and ten chapters, aimed to draw together theoretical and practitioner insights to offer pragmatic strategies for university career advisers and graduate recruiters to act as agents for fostering sustainable graduate careers.

Section One provided an introduction and overview, whereby Chapter 1 set the scene by introducing contemporary universities, university career advisors, graduate recruiters, and sustainable graduate careers.

Section Two focused on the role of university career advisors in helping their students prepare for a sustainable career. Chapter 2 covered graduate employability and employability capital, including its operationalization and practical application. Chapter 3 explored student engagement strategies for university career services by highlighting current challenges and presenting pragmatic strategies to address them. Chapter 4 introduced the concept of signaling employability before discussing its application via personal branding and personal narratives.

Section Three shifted focus to the role of graduate recruiters operating as agents for organizations. Chapter 5 provided an overview of Generation Z and Industry 4.0, as well as the challenges and opportunities associated with attracting early career talent. Chapter 6 defined the concept of the university-to-work transition, considered the benefits to an organization of hiring graduates, and offered twenty-five activities grouped by six themes to enhance talent attraction efforts and prepare students for undertaking the university-to-work transition. Chapter 7 addressed person-organization fit by introducing the theoretical background, presenting challenges and strategies in assessing person-organization fit, and considering how person-organization fit can evolve over time.

Section Four drew together the various actors to consider challenges and opportunities for greater collaboration. Chapter 8 set out the challenges from the perspectives of university career advisors, graduate recruiters, and additional actors. Chapter 9 made a case for collaboration to bridge the university-employer divide by introducing the State Progress Checklist and considering the roles of additional actors in promoting the sustainability of career ecosystems. Chapter 10 concluded the book by considering future workplace trends, what they might look like from the perspectives of organizations and graduates, the implications for universities and students, and the implications for bridging the university-employer divide.

Moreover, the theoretical underpinnings across Chapters 2-9 were supplemented by 32 lived experience insights, which brought the book to life and helped provide complementary information to inform pragmatic strategies for bridging the university-employer divide.

To conclude, perhaps you might reflect on how your views have shifted after reading this book. Who else do you know who might benefit from the content? What additional thoughts do you have about the various themes and topics? Thank you for choosing to read this book. Now that you have the tools, go out there and play your role in bridging the university-employer divide to foster a sustainable career ecosystem.

REFERENCES

Ahn, M. Y., & Davis, H. H. (2020). Four domains of students' sense of belonging to university. *Studies in Higher Education*, *45*(3), 622–634. doi:10.1080/03075079.2018.1564902

Akkermans, J., Donald, W. E., Jackson, D., & Forrier, A. (2023). Are we talking about the same thing? The case for stronger connections between graduate and worker employability research. *Career Development International*. Advance Online Publication. doi:10.1108/CDI-08-2023-0278

Akkermans, J., Richardson, J., & Kraimer, M. (2020). The Covid-19 crisis as a career shock: Implications for careers and vocational behavior. *Journal of Vocational Behavior, 119*, a.103434. doi:10.1016/j.jvb.2020.103434

Akkermans, J., Rodrigues, R., Mol, S. T., Seibert, S., & Khapova, S. (2021). The role of career shocks in contemporary career development: Key challenges and ways forward. *Career Development International*, *26*(4), 453–466. doi:10.1108/CDI-07-2021-0172

Aksoy, C. G., Barrero, J. M., Bloom, N., Davis, S. J., Dolls, M., & Zarate, P. (2023). *Time Savings When Working From Home*. National Bureau of Economic Research. doi:10.3386/w30866

Baruch, Y. (2015). Organizational and labor market as career eco-system. In A. De Vos & B. I. J. M. Van der Heijden (Eds.), *Handbook of Research on Sustainable Careers* (pp. 164–180). Edward Elgar. doi:10.4337/9781782547037.00029

Baruch, Y., & Rousseau, D. M. (2019). Integrating psychological contracts and ecosystems in career studies and management. *The Academy of Management Annals*, *13*(1), 84–111. doi:10.5465/annals.2016.0103

Bashir, A., Bashir, S., Rana, K., Lambert, P., & Vernallis, A. (2021). Post-COVID-19 adaptions; the shifts towards online learning, hybrid course delivery and the implications for Biosciences courses in the higher education setting. *Frontiers in Education*, *6*, 711619. doi:10.3389/feduc.2021.711619

Blokker, R., Akkermans, J., Marciniak, J., Jansen, P. G. W., & Khapova, S. N. (2023). Organizing school-to-work transition research from a sustainable career perspective: A review and research agenda. *Work, Aging and Retirement*, *9*(3), 239–261. doi:10.1093/workar/waad012

Blokker, R., Akkermans, J., Tims, M., Jansen, P., & Khapova, S. (2019). Building a sustainable start: The role of career competencies, career success, and career shocks in young professionals' employability. *Journal of Vocational Behavior*, *112*, 172–184. doi:10.1016/j.jvb.2019.02.013

Blustein, D. L., Duffy, R., Ferreira, J. A., Cohen-Scali, V., Cinamon, R. G., & Allan, B. A. (2020). Unemployment in the time of COVID-19: A research agenda. *Journal of Vocational Behavior*, *119*, 103436. doi:10.1016/j.jvb.2020.103436 PMID:32390656

Bright, J. E. H., Pryor, R. G. L., & Harpham, L. (2005). The role of chance events on career decision making. *Journal of Vocational Behavior*, *66*(3), 561–576. doi:10.1016/j.jvb.2004.05.001

Buckholtz, T. J., & Donald, W. E. (2022). Direct outcomes and win-win relationships between university careers advisors and graduate recruiters. *GiLE Journal of Skills Development*, *2*(1), 9–25. doi:10.52398/gjsd.2022.v2.i1.pp9-25

Cai, D., Li, Z., Xu, L., Fan, L., Wen, S., Li, F., Guan, Z., & Guan, Y. (2023). Sustaining newcomers' career adaptability: The roles of socialization tactics, job embeddedness and career variety. *Journal of Occupational and Organizational Psychology*, *96*(2), 264–286. doi:10.1111/joop.12423

Career Thought Leaders. (2023). *2023 Careers Industry Trend Report: 5 Megatrends Impacting Careers in 2023*. Career Thought Leaders. https://www.careerthoughtleaders.com/whitepaper

Chillakuri, B. (2020). Understanding Generation Z expectations for effective onboarding. *Journal of Organizational Change Management*, *33*(7), 1277–1296. doi:10.1108/JOCM-02-2020-0058

Christian, A. (2023). *The Companies That Churn Through Young Workers*. https://www.bbc.com/worklife/article/20230111-the-companies-that-churn-through-young-workers

Chudzikowski, K., Gustafsson, S., & Tams, S. (2020). Constructing alignment for sustainable careers: Insights from the career narratives of management consultants. *Journal of Vocational Behavior*, *117*, 103312. doi:10.1016/j.jvb.2019.05.009

Cole, D., & Coulson, B. (2022). Through and beyond COVID-19, promoting whole person, lifelong and lifewide learning. *Journal of Innovation in Polytechnic Education*, *4*(1), 81–90.

Cook, J. (2022). *2023 Trends: What Do Experts Say About the Future of Work?* https://www.businessleader.co.uk/2023-trends-what-do-experts-say-about-the-future-of-work/

Curşeu, P. L., Semeijn, J. H., & Nikolova, I. (2021). Career challenges in smart cities: A sociotechnical systems view on sustainable careers. *Human Relations*, *74*(5), 656–677. doi:10.1177/0018726720949925

De Jong, E. M., Ziegler, N., & Schippers, M. C. (2020). From Shattered Goals to Meaning in Life: Life Crafting in Times of the COVID-19 Pandemic. *Frontiers in Psychology*, *11*, 577708. doi:10.3389/fpsyg.2020.577708 PMID:33178081

de Prada, A. C. (2022). *Winning the War for Talent by Becoming an Employer of Choice*. https://www.ukri.org/blog/winning-the-war-for-talent-by-becoming-an-employer-of-choice/

De Schepper, A., Clycq, N., & Kyndt, E. (2023). Socio-economic differences in the transition from higher education in the labour market: A systematic review. *Journal of Career Development*, *50*(1), 234–250. doi:10.1177/08948453221077674

De Vos, A., Akkermans, J., & Van der Heijden, B. I. J. M. (2019). From occupational choice to career crafting. In H. Hunz, M. Lazarova, & W. Mayrhofer (Eds.), *The Routledge Companion to Career Studies* (pp. 128-142). Routledge. doi:10.4324/9781315674704

Deloitte. (2023). *2023 Global Human Capital Trends*. Deloitte. https://www2.deloitte.com/us/en/insights/focus/human-capital-trends.html

Dive, B. (2008). *The Accountable Leader: Developing Leadership Through Managerial Accountability*. Kogan Page.

Donald, W. E. (2017). Students' perceptions of graduate employability: A sequential explanatory approach. Doctoral Thesis, University of Southampton. https://eprints.soton.ac.uk/id/eprint/415935

Donald, W. E. (2020). *Viewpoint: COVID-19 and the Future of Careers*. Graduate Recruitment Bureau. doi:10.13140/RG.2.2.19306.13760

Donald, W. E. (2023). Sustainable talent pipelines and person-organisation fit: Strategic insights from UK graduates. *Career Development International*, *28*(2), 234–249. doi:10.1108/CDI-10-2022-0285

Donald, W. E., Ashleigh, M. J., & Baruch, Y. (2018). Students' perceptions of education and employability: Facilitating career transition from higher education into the labor market. *Career Development International*, *23*(5), 513–540. doi:10.1108/CDI-09-2017-0171

Donald, W. E., Ashleigh, M. J., & Baruch, Y. (2022). The university-to-work transition: Responses of universities and organizations to the COVID-19 pandemic. *Personnel Review*, *51*(9), 2201–2221. doi:10.1108/PR-03-2021-0170

Donald, W. E., Baruch, Y., & Ashleigh, M. J. (2019). The undergraduate self-perception of employability: Human capital, careers advice and career ownership. *Studies in Higher Education*, *44*(4), 599–614. doi:10.1080/03075079.2017.1387107

Donald, W. E., & Jackson, D. (2022). Subjective wellbeing among university students and recent graduates: Evidence from the United Kingdom. *International Journal of Environmental Research and Public Health*, *19*(11), 6911. doi:10.3390/ijerph19116911 PMID:35682494

Donald, W. E., & Jackson, D. (2023). Sustainable career ecosystems: Setting the scene. In W. E. Donald (Ed.), *Handbook of Research on Sustainable Career Ecosystems for University Students and Graduates* (pp. 1–13). IGI Global., doi:10.4018/978-1-6684-7442-6.ch001

Donald, W. E., Jakubik, M., & Nimmi, P. M. (2023). Preparing university graduates for sustainable careers: Qualitative insights from the UK. In W. E. Donald (Ed.), *Handbook of Research on Sustainable Career Ecosystems for University Students and Graduates* (pp. 320–341). IGI Global., doi:10.4018/978-1-6684-7442-6.ch017

Donald, W. E., & Mouratidou, M. (2022). Preparing for a sustainable career: Challenges and opportunities. *GiLE Journal of Skills Development*, *2*(2), 3–5. doi:10.52398/gjsd.2022.v2.i2.pp3-5

Draissi, Zhanyong, Q., & Raguindin, P. Z. J. (2022). Knowledge mapping of skills mismatch phenomenon: A scientific analysis. *Higher Education. Skills and Work-Based Learning*, *12*(2), 271–293. doi:10.1108/HESWBL-02-2021-0019

Dries, N. (2023). *Imagining The (Distant) Future of Work*. [Video]. Youtube. https://www.youtube.com/watch?v=FP7jEAHIm6o

Dries, N., Luyckx, J., & Rogiers, P. (2023). Imagining the (distant) future of work. *Academy of Management Discoveries*, Advanced Online Publication. doi:10.5465/amd.2022.0130

Emeritus. (2022). *12 Workplace Trends to Expect In 2023*. Emeritus. https://emeritus.org/blog/the-future-of-work-workplace-trends/

Fan, Y., & Potočnik, K. (2021). The impact of the depletion, accumulation, and investment of personal resources on work-life balance satisfaction and job retention: A longitudinal study on working mothers. *Journal of Vocational Behavior*, *131*(1), 103656. doi:10.1016/j.jvb.2021.103656

Fernández, D. P., Ryan, M. K., & Begeny, C. (2023). Recognizing the diversity in how students define belonging: Evidence of differing conceptualizations, including as a function of students' gender and socio-economic background. *Social Psychology of Education*, *26*(3), 673–708. doi:10.100711218-023-09761-7

Flatt, A., & Drewery, D. (2023). How career development professionals can close the gap between human resources and Gen Z. In W. E. Donald (Ed.), *Handbook of Research on Sustainable Career Ecosystems for University Students and Graduates* (pp. 195–213). IGI Global., doi:10.4018/978-1-6684-7442-6.ch011

Gartner. (2021). *Digital Workers Say Flexibility Is Key to Their Productivity*. Gartner. https://www.gartner.com/ smarterwithgartner/digital-workers-say-flexibility-is-key-to-their-productivity

Gati, I., & Kulcsár, V. (2021). Making better career decisions: From challenges to opportunities. *Journal of Vocational Behavior*, *126*, 103545. doi:10.1016/j.jvb.2021.103545

Gibby, T. (2022). *Five Key Future of Work Trends In 2022*. Unleash. https://www.unleash.ai/hr-technology/5-key-future-of-work-trends-in-2022/

Gkeredakis, M., Lifshitz-Assaf, H., & Barrett, M. (2021). Crisis as opportunity, disruption and exposure: Exploring emergent responses to crisis through digital technology. *Information and Organization*, *31*(1), 100344. doi:10.1016/j.infoandorg.2021.100344

Goodenow, C. (1993). Classroom belonging among early adolescent students. *The Journal of Early Adolescence*, *13*(1), 21–43. doi:10.1177/0272431693013001002

Haelermans, C., Korthals, R., Jacobs, M., De Leeuw, S., Vermeulen, S., Van Vugt, L., Aarts, B., Prokic-Breuer, T., Van der Velden, R., Van Wetten, S., & De Wolf, I. (2022). Sharp increase in inequality in education in times of the COVID-19-Pandemic. *PLoS One*, *17*(2), e0261114. doi:10.1371/journal.pone.0261114 PMID:35108273

Hamouche, S., Kammogne, C. L., & Merkouche, W. (2023). Workforce's crisis-induced career shock, career preferences, job insecurity, layoff and perceived employability: Examining variations based on gender, education level and ethnic origin. *Higher Education. Skills and Work-Based Learning*, *13*(2), 264–282. doi:10.1108/HESWBL-05-2022-0101

Heslin, P. A., Keating, L. A., & Ashford, S. J. (2020). How being in learning mode may enable a sustainable career across the lifespan. *Journal of Vocational Behavior*, *117*, 103324. doi:10.1016/j.jvb.2019.103324

Higginbotham, D. (2021). *Recruitment Agencies*. Prospects. https://www.prospects.ac.uk/careers-advice/getting-a-job/recruitment-agencies

Hobfoll, S. E., Halbesleben, J., Neveu, J.-P., & Westman, M. (2018, January). Conservation of resources in the organizational context: The reality of resources and their consequences. *Annual Review of Organizational Psychology and Organizational Behavior*, *5*(1), 103–128. doi:10.1146/annurev-orgpsych-032117-104640

Hughes, H. P. N., & Davis, M. C. (2021). *Starting Your Career During a Pandemic: The Experience of Remote and Hybrid Working*. University of Leeds. https://business.leeds.ac.uk/dir-record/research-projects/1736/understanding-the-value-of-a-work-placement

Hughes, H. P. N., & Thambar, N. (2023). Graduate careers in a changing workplace: A fresh challenge? In W. E. Donald (Ed.), *Handbook of Research on Sustainable Career Ecosystems for University Students and Graduates* (pp. 469–487). IGI Global. doi:10.4018/978-1-6684-7442-6.ch024

Jackson, D., & Bridgstock, R. (2021). What actually works to enhance graduate employability? The relative value of curricular, co-curricular, and extra-curricular learning and paid work. *Higher Education*, *81*(4), 723–739. doi:10.100710734-020-00570-x

Jackson, D., Riebe, L., & Macau, F. (2022). Determining factors in graduate recruitment and preparing students for success. *Education + Training*, *64*(5), 681–699. doi:10.1108/ET-11-2020-0348

Jackson, N. J. (2011). *Learning for A Complex World: A Lifewide Concept of Learning, Education and Personal Development*. AuthorHouse.

Jakubik, M. (2020). Rise of intellectual workers and intellectual work. *International Journal of Management. Knowledge and Learning*, *9*(1), 59–73.

Jakubik, M. (2022). Work engagement – gateway to creativity. In D. Bylieva & A. Nordmann (Eds.), *Technology, Innovation and Creativity in Digital Society* (pp. 11–21). Springer. doi:10.1007/978-3-030-89708-6_2

Jakubik, M. (2023). Cultivating the future in higher education: Fostering students' life-world becoming with wisdom pedagogy. *Trends in Higher Education*, *2*(1), 45–61. doi:10.3390/higheredu2010004

Jesuthasan, R., & Boudreau, J. (2021). Work without jobs. *MIT Sloan Management Review*, *62*(2), 1–5.

Jin, X., & Waldman, M. (2020). Lateral moves, promotions, and task-specific human capital: Theory and evidence. *Journal of Law Economics and Organization*, *36*(1), 1–46.

Kahn, M. E. (2022). *Going Remote: How the Flexible Work Economy Can Improve Out Lives and Our Cities*. University of California Press.

Khan, F., & Ali, M. (2022). Exploring the gap between expected and actual return on investment of business graduates from employability: Evidence from a developing country. *International Journal of Management Education*, *20*(3), 100717. doi:10.1016/j.ijme.2022.100717

Krammer, S. M. (2021). Navigating the New Normal: Which firms have adapted better to the COVID-19 disruption? *Technovation*, *110*(1), 102368. doi:10.1016/j.technovation.2021.102368

Kulcsár, V., Dobrean, A., & Gati, I. (2020). Challenges and difficulties in career decision making: Their causes, and their direct effects on the process and the decision. *Journal of Vocational Behavior*, *116*(Part A), 103346. doi:10.1016/j.jvb.2019.103346

Lewis, H. (2022). *Sketchnote Summary of 10 Red Flags of Faulty Org Design*. HALO Psychology Limited.

Manville, G., Donald, W. E., & Eves, A. (2022). Can embedding authentic assessment into the curriculum enhance the employability of business school students? *GiLE Journal of Skills Development*, *2*(2), 73–87. doi:10.52398/gjsd.2022.v2.i2.pp73-87

McCafferty, H. (2022). An unjust balance: A systematic review of the employability perceptions of UK undergraduates from disadvantaged socio-economic backgrounds. *Research in Post-Compulsory Education*, *27*(4), 570–593. doi:10.1080/13596748.2022.2110774

McRae, E. R., & Aykens, P. (2022). *9 Future of Work Trends For 2023*. Gartner. https://www.gartner.com/en/articles/9-future-of-work-trends-for-2023

Meehan, C., & Howells, K. (2019). In search of the feeling of belonging in higher education: Undergraduate students transition into higher education. *Journal of Further and Higher Education*, *43*(1), 1376–1390. doi:10.1080/0309877X.2018.1490702

Mendes, L. (2022). *UK halts all fuel supplies from Russia, reports ONS*. Trade Finance Global. https://www.tradefinanceglobal.com/posts/uk-halts-all-fuel-supplies-from-russia-reports-ons/

Mercer. (2023). *Global Talent Trends 2022-2023*. Mercer. https://www.mercer.com/our-thinking/career/global-talent-hr-trends.html

Müller, C., Scheffer, A., Macke, J., & Vaclavik, M. C. (2023). Towards career sustainability: A systematic review to guide future research. *Brazilian Administrative Review, 19*(4), e220108. doi:10.1590/1807-7692bar2022220108

Nimmi, P. M., Mukundan, S. P., Jose, G., Tesi, A., & Alias, R. (2023). Future of work – apprehensions and excitement of management graduates. *Higher Education, Skills and Work-Based Learning*. Advanced Online Publication., doi:10.1108/HESWBL-08-2022-0181

O'Keeffe, P. (2013). A sense of belonging: Improving student retention. *College Student Journal*, *47*(4), 605–613.

Offbeat. (2022). *L&D Trends Map 2022*. Offbeat. https://www.offbeat.works/l-d-trends-map

Office for National Statistics. (2023). *Workplace Disputes and Working Conditions*. Office for National Statistics. https://www.ons. gov.uk/employmentandlabourmarket/peopleinwork/workplacedisputesandworkingconditions

Pedler, M. L., Willis, R., & Nieuwoudt, J. E. (2022). A sense of belonging at university: Student retention, motivation and enjoyment. *Journal of Further and Higher Education*, *46*(3), 397–408. doi:10.1080/0309877X.2021.1955844

Phillips, R., Seaborne, K., Goldsmith, A., Curtis, N., Davies, A., Haynes, W., McEnroe, R., Murphy, N., O'Neill, L., Pacey, C., Walker, E., & Wordley, E. (2022). Student loneliness through the pandemic: How, why and where? *The Geographical Journal*, *188*(2), 277–293. doi:10.1111/geoj.12438 PMID:35600138

Pohl, E., Ajadi, T., Soucy, T., Carroll, H., Earl, J., Verduyn, C., & Connolly, M. (2022). "Knowing nothing about EDI:" A collaborative autoethnography exploring how an anti-racist project was created, publicized, and silenced. *International Journal for Students as Partners*, *6*(1), 30–46. doi:10.15173/ijsap.v6i1.4882

Raihan, M. Z., & Azad, M. A. K. (2023). A bibliometric review on outcome-based learning for graduate employability: Mapping the research front. *Journal of Education*, *203*(1), 73–91. doi:10.1177/00220574211016444

Rousseau, D. M. (1995). *Psychological Contracts in Organizations: Understanding Written and Unwritten Agreements*. Sage (Atlanta, Ga.). doi:10.4135/9781452231594

Rousseau, D. M., Ho, V. T., & Greenberg, J. (2006). I-Deals: Idiosyncratic terms in employment relationships. *Academy of Management Review*, *31*(4), 977–994. doi:10.5465/amr.2006.22527470

Seinsche, L., Schubin, K., Neumann, J., & Pfaff, H. (2022). Employees' resources, demands and health while working from home during the COVID-19 pandemic – A qualitative study in the public sector. *International Journal of Environmental Research and Public Health*, *20*(1), 411. doi:10.3390/ijerph20010411 PMID:36612731

Serenko, A. (2022). The Great Resignation: The great knowledge exodus or the onset of the Great Knowledge Revolution? *Journal of Knowledge Management*, *27*(4), 1042–1055. doi:10.1108/JKM-12-2021-0920

Smith, A. M. J., Jones, D., Scott, B., & Stadler, A. (2017). Designing and delivering inclusive and accessible entrepreneurship education. *Entrepreneurship Education*, *7*, 335–357. doi:10.1108/S2040-724620170000007019

Sullivan, S. E., & Al Ariss, A. (2021). Making sense of different perspectives on career transitions: A review and agenda for future research. *Human Resource Management Review*, *31*(1), 100727. doi:10.1016/j.hrmr.2019.100727

Thambar, N., & Hughes, H. P. N. (2023). The robots are coming 2: Rise of the screens; The role of higher education careers professionals in disrupted times. *Journal of the National Institute for Career Education and Counselling*, *50*(1), 85–95. doi:10.20856/jnicec.5009

Trow, M. (2006). Reflections on the transition from elite to mass to universal access: forms and phases of higher education in modern societies since WWII. In J. J. F. Forest & P. G. Altbach (Eds.), *International Handbook of Higher Education* (pp. 243–280). Springer. doi:10.1007/978-1-4020-4012-2_13

United Nations. (2015). *Global Citizenship*. UN. https://www.un.org/en/academic-impact/global-citizenship

Van Gijn-Grosvenor, E., & Huisman, P. (2020). A sense of belonging among Australian university students. *Higher Education Research & Development*, *39*(2), 376–389. doi:10.1080/07294360.2019.1666256

Walker, N. (2021). *Brexit timeline: Events leading to the UK's exit from the European Union.* Commons Library. https://commonslibrary.parliament.uk/research-briefings/cbp-7960/

Witteveen, D., & Velthorst, E. (2020). Economic hardship and mental health complaints during COVID-19. *Proceedings of the National Academy of Sciences of the United States of America*, *117*(44), 27277–27284. doi:10.1073/pnas.2009609117 PMID:33046648

World Economic Forum. (2023). *How 'Everyday' Flexibility Can Unlock Engagement, Productivity and Growth.* WEF. https://www.weforum.org/agenda/2023/01/flexible-working-productivity-and-growth-davos23

Compilation of References

Ab Wahab, M., & Tatoglu, E. (2020). Chasing productivity demands, worker well-being, and firm performance: The moderating effects of HR support and flexible work arrangement. *Personnel Review, 49*(9), 1823–1843. doi:10.1108/PR-01-2019-0026

Adachi, C., Tai, J. H.-M., & Dawson, P. (2018). Academics' perceptions of the benefits and challenges of self and peer assessment in higher education. *Assessment & Evaluation in Higher Education, 43*(2), 294–306. doi:10.1080/02602938.2017.1339775

Afshari, L., & Nasab, A. H. (2021). Enhancing Organizational Learning Capability Through Managing Talent: Mediation Effect Of Intellectual Capital. *Human Resource Development International, 24*(1), 48–64. doi:10.1080/13678868.2020.1727239

Ahn, M. Y., & Davis, H. H. (2020). Four domains of students' sense of belonging to university. *Studies in Higher Education, 45*(3), 622–634. doi:10.1080/03075079.2018.1564902

Akkermans, J., Richardson, J., & Kraimer, M. (2020). The Covid-19 crisis as a career shock: Implications for careers and vocational behavior. *Journal of Vocational Behavior, 119*, a.103434. doi:10.1016/j.jvb.2020.103434

Akkermans, J., Blokker, R., Buers, C., Van der Heijden, B. I. J. M., & De Vos, A. (2021). Ready, set, go! In A. Marshall & J. Symonds (Eds.), *Adult Development at the School-to-Work Transition: International Pathways and Processes* (pp. 77–103). Oxford University Press. doi:10.1093/oso/9780190941512.003.0004

Akkermans, J., Brenninkmeijer, V., Huibers, M., & Blonk, R. W. B. (2013). Competencies for the contemporary career: Development and preliminary validation of the career competencies questionnaire. *Journal of Career Development, 40*(3), 245–267. doi:10.1177/0894845312467501

Akkermans, J., Collings, D. G., da Motta Veiga, S. P., Post, C., & Seibert, S. (2021). Towards a broader understanding of career shocks: Exploring interdisciplinary connections with research on job search, human resource management, entrepreneurship, and diversity. *Journal of Vocational Behavior, 126*(1), 103563. doi:10.1016/j.jvb.2021.103563

Akkermans, J., Donald, W. E., Jackson, D., & Forrier, A. (2023). Are we talking about the same thing? The case for stronger connections between graduate and worker employability research. *Career Development International*. Advance online publication. doi:10.1108/CDI-08-2023-0278

Akkermans, J., Rodrigues, R., Mol, S. T., Seibert, S., & Khapova, S. (2021). The role of career shocks in contemporary career development: Key challenges and ways forward. *Career Development International, 26*(4), 453–466. doi:10.1108/CDI-07-2021-0172

Akkermans, J., Tomlinson, M., & Anderson, V. (2023). Initial employability development: Introducing a conceptual model integrating signalling and social exchange mechanisms. *European Journal of Work and Organizational Psychology*, 1–13. doi:10.1080/1359432X.2023.2186783

Aksoy, C. G., Barrero, J. M., Bloom, N., Davis, S. J., Dolls, M., & Zarate, P. (2023). *Time Savings When Working From Home*. National Bureau of Economic Research. doi:10.3386/w30866

Alchin, C., McIlveen, P., & Perera, H. N. (2018). Negative career outlook and the working alliance in career counseling. *The Career Development Quarterly, 66*(3), 279–284. doi:10.1002/cdq.12149

Aliu, J., & Aigbavboa, C. O. (2021). Structural determinants of graduate employability: Impact of university and industry collaborations. *Journal of Engineering. Design and Technology, 19*(5), 1080–1100. doi:10.1108/JEDT-05-2020-0189

Allen, T. J., & Katz, R. (1986). The dual ladder: Motivational solution or managerial delusion? *R & D Management, 16*(2), 185–197. doi:10.1111/j.1467-9310.1986.tb01171.x

Anderson, V., & Tomlinson, M. (2021). Signaling standout graduate employability: The employer perspective. *Human Resource Management Journal, 31*(3), 675–693. doi:10.1111/1748-8583.12334

Apa, R., De Marchi, V., Grandinetti, R., & Sedita, S. R. (2021). University-SME collaboration and innovation performance. The role of informal relationships and absorptive capacity. *The Journal of Technology Transfer, 46*(4), 961–988. doi:10.100710961-020-09802-9

Argent, G. (2016). *Real Collaboration Happens When Your Challenges Overlap*. Graduate Transitions. http://graduate-transitions.co.uk/real-collaboration-happens-when-your-challenges-overlap/

Arnold, L., Mohamed-Ghouse, Z. S., & Wheeler, T. (2021). Role of the professional body in a pandemic. In A. Rajabifard, G. Foliente, & D. Paez (Eds.), *COVID-19 Pandemic, Geospatial Information, and Community Resilience* (pp. 161–169). Routledge. doi:10.1201/9781003181590-14

Arranz, N., Arroyabe, M. F., Sena, V., Arranz, C. F. A., & de Arroyabe, J. C. F. (2022). University-enterprise cooperation for the employability of higher education graduates: A social capital approach. *Studies in Higher Education, 47*(5), 990–999. doi:10.1080/03075079.2022.2055323

Arthur, M. B., Hall, D. T., & Lawrence, B. S. (1989). *Handbook of Career Theory*. Cambridge University Press. doi:10.1017/CBO9780511625459

Arthur, N., & Flynn, S. (2013). International students' views of transition to employment and immigration. *Canadian Journal of Career Development, 12*(1), 28–37.

Atherton, G., Boffey, R., & Kazim, T. (2019). *POLAR Opposite: How The Targeting of Learners for Widening Access to HE Work Could Be Improved.* Access HE. https://www.accesshe.ac.uk/yYdIx0u7/SBT2142-London-Higher-Polar-Opposite-Report-Design-v3.pdf

Awwad, E., & Bose, S. (2023). *Moving from a Career Services Department to a Career Enablement Commitment*. Evolllution. https://evolllution.com/attracting-students/customer_service/moving-from-a-career-services-department-to-a-career-enablement-commitment

Ayoubi, A. (2017). *The Tremendous Benefits of Connecting Academic and Career Advising*. The Career Leadership Collective.

Bakker, A. B., & Demerouti, E. (2007). The Job Demands-Resources model: State of the art. *Journal of Managerial Psychology*, *22*(3), 309–328. doi:10.1108/02683940710733115

Baldi, F., & Trigeorgis, L. (2020). Valuing human capital career development: A real options approach. *Journal of Intellectual Capital*, *21*(5), 781–807. doi:10.1108/JIC-06-2019-0134

Baluku, M. M., Mugabi, E. N., Nansamba, J., Matagi, L., Onderi, P., & Otto, K. (2021). Psychological capital and career outcomes among final year university students: The mediating role of career engagement and perceived employability. *International Journal of Applied Positive Psychology*, *6*(1), 55–80. doi:10.100741042-020-00040-w

Barnett, R. (2022). *The Philosophy of Higher Education: A Critical Introduction*. Routledge.

Baruch, Y. (2006). Career development in organizations and beyond: Balancing traditional and contemporary viewpoints. *Human Resource Management Review*, *16*(2), 125–138. doi:10.1016/j.hrmr.2006.03.002

Baruch, Y. (2015). Organizational and labor market as career eco-system. In A. De Vos & B. I. J. M. Van der Heijden (Eds.), *Handbook of Research on Sustainable Careers* (pp. 164–180). Edward Elgar. doi:10.4337/9781782547037.00029

Baruch, Y., Ashleigh, M. J., & Donald, W. E. (2023). A sustainable career ecosystem perspective of talent flow and acquisition: The interface between higher education and industry. In W. E. Donald (Ed.), *Handbook of Research on Sustainable Career Ecosystems for University Students and Graduates* (pp. 177–194). IGI Global. doi:10.4018/978-1-6684-7442-6.ch010

Baruch, Y., & Hind, P. (1999). Perpetual motion in organizations: Effective management and the impact of the new psychological contracts on 'Survivor Syndrome'. *European Journal of Work and Organizational Psychology*, *8*(2), 295–306. doi:10.1080/135943299398375

Baruch, Y., & Rousseau, D. M. (2019). Integrating psychological contracts and ecosystems in career studies and management. *The Academy of Management Annals*, *13*(1), 84–111. doi:10.5465/annals.2016.0103

Baruch, Y., & Sullivan, S. E. (2022). The why, what and how of career research: A review and recommendations for future study. *Career Development International*, *27*(1), 135–159. doi:10.1108/CDI-10-2021-0251

Bashir, A., Bashir, S., Rana, K., Lambert, P., & Vernallis, A. (2021). Post-COVID-19 adaptions; the shifts towards online learning, hybrid course delivery and the implications for Biosciences courses in the higher education setting. *Frontiers in Education*, *6*, 711619. doi:10.3389/feduc.2021.711619

Becker, K. L. (2021). We want connection and we do not mean wi-fi: Examining the impacts of Covid-19 on Gen Z's work and employment outcomes. *Management Research Review*, *45*(5), 684–699. doi:10.1108/MRR-01-2021-0052

Berezvai, Z., Lukáts, G. D., & Molontay, R. (2021). Can professors buy better evaluation with lenient grading? The effect of grade inflation on student evaluation of teaching. *Assessment & Evaluation in Higher Education*, *46*(5), 793–808. doi:10.1080/02602938.2020.1821866

Berger, J., & the Keller Fay Group. (2016). *Research Shows Micro-Influencers Have More Impact Than Average Consumers*. Experticity. https://go2.experticity.com/rs/288-AZS-731/images/Experticity-Keller FaySurveySummary_.pdf

Bertello, A., Ferraris, A., De Bernardi, P., & Bertoldi, B. (2022). Challenges to open innovation in traditional SMEs: An analysis of pre-competitive projects in university-industry-government collaboration. *The International Entrepreneurship and Management Journal*, *18*(1), 89–104. doi:10.100711365-020-00727-1

Bhaskar, A. U., Baruch, Y., & Seeta, G. (2023). Drivers of career success among the visually impaired: Improving career inclusivity and sustainability in a career ecosystem. *Human Relations*, *76*(10), 1507–1544. doi:10.1177/00187267221103529

Bikard, M., Vakili, K., & Teodoridis, F. (2019). When collaboration bridges institutions: The impact of university-industry collaboration on academic productivity. *Organization Science*, *30*(2), 426–445. doi:10.1287/orsc.2018.1235

Bilsland, C., Carter, L., & Wood, L. (2019). Work integrated learning internships in transnational education. *Education + Training*, *61*(3), 359–373. doi:10.1108/ET-07-2017-0094

Blackmore, P., Bulaitis, Z. H., Jackman, A. H., & Tan, E. (2015). *Employability in Higher Education: A Review of Practice and Strategies around the World.* YEA. https://yea.org.nz/wp-content/uploads/ 2020/07/Employability-in-Higher-Education-a-review-of-practice-and-strategies-around-the-world.pdf

Blackmore, P., & Kandiko, C. (2012). *Strategic Curriculum Change*. Routledge.

Blau, P. (1964). *Exchange and Power in Social Life*. Wiley.

Blokker, R., Akkermans, J., Marciniak, J., Jansen, P. G. W., & Khapova, S. N. (2023). Organizing school-to-work transition research from a sustainable career perspective: A review and research agenda. *Work, Aging and Retirement*, *9*(3), 239–261. doi:10.1093/workar/waad012

Blokker, R., Akkermans, J., Tims, M., Jansen, P. G. W., & Khapova, S. N. (2019). Building a sustainable start: The role of career competencies, career success, and career shocks in young professionals' employability. *Journal of Vocational Behavior*, *112*, 172–184. doi:10.1016/j.jvb.2019.02.013

Blustein, D. L., Duffy, R., Ferreira, J. A., Cohen-Scali, V., Cinamon, R. G., & Allan, B. A. (2020). Unemployment in the time of COVID-19: A research agenda. *Journal of Vocational Behavior*, *119*, 103436. doi:10.1016/j.jvb.2020.103436 PMID:32390656

Boffo, V. (2018). Employability and transitions: fostering the future of young adult graduates. In V. Boffo & M. Fedeli (Eds.), *Employability and Competences: Innovative Curricula for New Professions*, (pp. 117-128). Firenze University Press. doi:10.36253/978-88-6453-672-9.19

Borah, D., Malik, K., & Massini, S. (2021). Teaching-focused university-industry collaborations: Determinants and impact on graduates' employability competencies. *Research Policy*, *50*(3), 104172. doi:10.1016/j.respol.2020.104172

Bourdieu, P. (1983). The Forms of Capital. In J. G. Richardson (Ed.), *Handbook of Theory and Research for the Sociology of Education* (pp. 241–258). Greenwood Press.

Bowes, L., Tazzyman, S., Birkin, G., & Roberts, J. (2022). *An Independent Evaluation of Uni Connect's Impact on Intermediate Outcomes for Learners: A Report for The Office for Students on the 2021/2022 (Wave 3) learner survey findings.* Office for Students. https://www.officeforstudents.org.uk/publications/ independent-evaluation-of-uni-connect-s-impact-on-outcomes/

Branicki, L., Steyer, V., & Sullivan-Taylor, B. (2019). HRM practices and impact on organizational performance and employee wellbeing. *International Journal of Human Resource Management*, *30*(8), 1261–1286. doi:10.1080/09585192.2016.1244104

Brewer, R., & Movahedazarhouligh, S. (2018). Successful stories and conflicts: A literature review on the effectiveness of flipped learning in higher education. *Journal of Computer Assisted Learning*, *34*(4), 409–416. doi:10.1111/jcal.12250

Bridgstock, R., & Jackson, D. (2019). Strategic institutional approaches to graduate employability: Navigating meanings, measurements and what really matters. *Journal of Higher Education Policy and Management*, *41*(5), 468–484. doi:10.1080/1360080X.2019.1646378

Bright Network. (2022). *What do graduates want? 2022/23.* Bright Network. https://employers.brightnetwork.co.uk/what-do-graduates-want-report-and-video

Bright, J. E. H., Pryor, R. G. L., & Harpham, L. (2005). The role of chance events on career decision making. *Journal of Vocational Behavior*, *66*(3), 561–576. doi:10.1016/j.jvb.2004.05.001

Brooks, R., Gupta, A., Jayadeva, S., & Abrahams, J. (2021). Students' views about the purpose of higher education: A comparative analysis of six European countries. *Higher Education Research & Development*, *40*(7), 1375–1388. doi:10.1080/07294360.2020.1830039

Brown, J. L., Hammer, S. J., Perera, H. N., & McIlveen, P. (2021). Relations between graduates' learning experiences and employment outcomes: A cautionary note for institutional performance indicators. *International Journal for Educational and Vocational Guidance*, *22*(1), 137–156. doi:10.100710775-021-09477-0

Brown, P., & Hesketh, A. (2004). *The Mismanagement of Talent.* Oxford University Press. doi:10.1093/acprof:oso/9780199269532.001.0001

Bruner, J. (1986). *Actual Minds, Possible Worlds*. Harvard University Press. doi:10.4159/9780674029019

Buckholtz, T. J. (1995). *Information Proficiency: Your Key to the Information Age*. Van Nostrand Reinhold.

Buckholtz, T. J. (1996). *Evaluating the CEO: Computerworld Leadership Series*. IDG Enterprise.

Buckholtz, T. J. (2011). *Create Crucial Insight: Use Direct Outcomes Checklists. Think Well. Do Great*. Buckholtz & Associates.

Buckholtz, T. J., & Donald, W. E. (2022). Direct outcomes and win-win relationships between university careers advisors and graduate recruiters. *GiLE Journal of Skills Development*, *2*(1), 9–25. doi:10.52398/gjsd.2022.v2.i1.pp9-25

Bukodi, E. (2017). Cumulative inequalities over the life course: Life-long learning and social mobility in Britain. *Journal of Social Policy*, *46*(2), 367–404. doi:10.1017/S0047279416000635

Cable, D. M., & Judge, T. A. (1996). Person-organization fit, job decisions, and organizational entry. *Organizational Behavior and Human Decision Processes*, *67*(3), 294–311. doi:10.1006/obhd.1996.0081

Cai, D., Li, Z., Xu, L., Fan, L., Wen, S., Li, F., Guan, Z., & Guan, Y. (2023). Sustaining newcomers' career adaptability: The roles of socialization tactics, job embeddedness and career variety. *Journal of Occupational and Organizational Psychology*, *96*(2), 264–286. doi:10.1111/joop.12423

Career Thought Leaders. (2023). *2023 Careers Industry Trend Report: 5 Megatrends Impacting Careers in 2023*. Career Thought Leaders. https://www.careerthoughtleaders.com/whitepaper

Careers2032 Project. (2022). *An industry research project co-produced by AGCAS, ISE, Wonkhe and Handshake, looking at the careers sector of 2032 and the role technology could play in facilitating human connections*. Handshake. https://joinhandshake.co.uk/careers2032

Celani, A., & Singh, P. (2011). Signaling theory and applicant attraction outcomes. *Personnel Review*, *40*(2), 222–238. doi:10.1108/00483481111106093

CFE Research (2023). *The benefits of and barriers to collaborative access activity by higher education providers*. The Office for Students. https://www.officeforstudents.org.uk/publications/benefits-of-and-barriers-to-collaborative-access-activity/

CFE Research (2023). *The Benefits of And Barriers to Collaborative Access Activity by Higher Education Providers*. The Office for Students. https://www.officeforstudents.org.uk/publications/benefits-of-and-barriers-to-collaborative-access-activity/

Chan, G. (2023). 5 Reasons Why Building Your Personal Brand Will Land Your Next Job. *Forbes*. https://www.forbes.com/sites/goldiechan/2023/01/17/5-reasons-why-building-your-personal-brand-will-land-your-next-job/

Chartered Institute of Personnel and Development. (2022). *Growing proportion of UK graduates ending up in low-skills jobs, where they experience lower levels of job and life satisfaction.* CIPD. https://www.cipd.co.uk/about/media/press/041122-graduate-overqualification-cipd-report#gref

Chávez, K., & Mitchell, K. (2020). Exploring bias in student evaluations: Gender, race, and ethnicity. *PS, Political Science & Politics*, *53*(2), 270–274. doi:10.1017/S1049096519001744

Chillakuri, B. (2020). Understanding Generation Z expectations for effective onboarding. *Journal of Organizational Change Management*, *33*(7), 1277–1296. doi:10.1108/JOCM-02-2020-0058

Choi, E., Leroy, H., Johnson, A., & Nguyen, H. (2022). Flaws and all: How mindfulness reduces error hiding by enhancing authentic functioning. *Journal of Occupational Health Psychology*, *27*(5), 451–469. doi:10.1037/ocp0000327 PMID:35549505

Christian, A. (2023). *The Companies That Churn Through Young Workers.* https://www.bbc.com/worklife/article/20230111-the-companies-that-churn-through-young-workers

Chudzikowski, K., Gustafsson, S., & Tams, S. (2020). Constructing alignment for sustainable careers: Insights from the career narratives of management consultants. *Journal of Vocational Behavior*, *117*, 103312. doi:10.1016/j.jvb.2019.05.009

Clark-Ambrosini, J. L., Ashleigh, M. J., Higgs, M., & Baruch, Y. (2023). Quid pro quo? The future for graduate development programmes through the lens of talent management. *International Journal of Human Resource Management*, *34*(17), 3253–3276. doi:10.1080/09585192.2022.2117991

Clarke, M. (2018). Rethinking graduate employability: The role of capital, individual attributes and context. *Studies in Higher Education*, *43*(11), 1923–1937. doi:10.1080/03075079.2017.1294152

Clarke, M., & Scurry, T. (2020). The role of the psychological contract in shaping graduate experiences: A study of public sector talent management programmes in the UK and Australia. *International Journal of Human Resource Management*, *31*(8), 965–991. doi:10.1080/09585192.2017.1396545

Cody, E. E., Kryst, E. L., & Smith, K. K. (2018). Collaboration as a cornerstone for change. *Career Planning and Adult Development Journal*, *34*(2), 20–31.

Cole, D., & Hallett, R. (2019). The language of employability. In J. Higgs, G. Crisp, & W. Letts (Eds.), *Education for Employability* (pp. 119-130). Brill. doi:10.1163/9789004400832_010

Cole, D., & Coulson, B. (2022). Through and beyond COVID-19, promoting whole person, lifelong and lifewide learning. *Journal of Innovation in Polytechnic Education*, *4*(1), 81–90.

Cole, D., & Donald, W. E. (2022). Shifting the narrative: Towards a more holistic approach to learning. *GiLE Journal of Skills Development*, *2*(11), 3–4. doi:10.52398/gjsd.2022.v2.i1.pp3-4

Consiglio, C., Menatta, P., Borgogni, L., Alessandri, G., Valente, L., & Caprara, G. V. (2021). How youth may find jobs: The role of positivity, perceived employability, and support from employment agencies. *Sustainability (Basel)*, *13*(16), 9468. doi:10.3390u13169468

Cook, J. (2022). *2023 Trends: What Do Experts Say About the Future of Work?* https://www.businessleader.co.uk/2023-trends-what-do-experts-say-about-the-future-of-work/

Cooke, F. J., Dickmann, M., & Parry, E. (2021). IJHRM after 30 years: Taking stock in times of COVID-19 and looking towards the future of HR research. *International Journal of Human Resource Management*, *32*(1), 1–23. doi:10.1080/09585192.2020.1833070

Craps, S., Pinxten, M., Knipprath, H., & Langie, G. (2021). Exploring professional roles for early career engineers: A systematic literature review. *European Journal of Engineering Education*, *46*(2), 266–286. doi:10.1080/03043797.2020.1781062

Creed, A., Dixon, M., & Schmitz, M. (2023). Enhancing Student Experience with Career Education. *2023 University of Melbourne Teaching and Learning Conference*. University of Melbourne.

Creed, A. (2023). Development of the 'Transition Is A Becoming' metaphor: The perspectives of international students. In W. E. Donald (Ed.), *Handbook of Research on Sustainable Career Ecosystems for University Students and Graduates* (pp. 38–57). IGI Global. doi:10.4018/978-1-6684-7442-6.ch003

Creed, A., & Nacey, S. (2021). Qualitative and quantitative examination of metaphorical language use in career-life preparedness. In W. Murphy & J. Tosti-Kharas (Eds.), *Handbook of Research Methods in Careers* (pp. 283–298). Elgar. doi:10.4337/9781788976725.00023

Curşeu, P. L., Semeijn, J. H., & Nikolova, I. (2021). Career challenges in smart cities: A sociotechnical systems view on sustainable careers. *Human Relations*, *74*(5), 656–677. doi:10.1177/0018726720949925

D'Armagnac, S., Al Ariss, A., & N'Cho, J. (2022). Talent management in turbulent times: Selection, negotiation, and exploration of strategies for talent management in aeronautics and space industries. *International Journal of Human Resource Management*, *33*(13), 2767–2799. doi:10.1080/09585192.2021.1879205

Daniel, J. (2020). Education and the COVID-19 pandemic. *Prospects*, *49*(1), 91–96. doi:10.100711125-020-09464-3 PMID:32313309

Daubney, K. (2022). "Teaching employability is not my job!": Redefining embedded employability from within the higher education curriculum. *Higher Education: Skills and Work-Based Learning*, *12*(1), 92–106. doi:10.1108/HESWBL-07-2020-0165

Davies, H. (2014). *A Quick Guide to Society Sponsorship: Help Your Club and Your Career*. https:// careersblog.enterprise.co.uk/a-quick-guide-to-society-sponsorship-help-your-club-and-your-career/

de Blaquière, G., Nolan, J. E., & Wray, K. (2019). Joining up the dots: Telling the story of skills: How can students in Higher Education be supported to better understand and articulate their employability? *Journal of Teaching and Learning for Graduate Employability*, *10*(2), 15–35. doi:10.21153/jtlge2019vol10no2art699

De Jong, E. M., Ziegler, N., & Schippers, M. C. (2020). From Shattered Goals to Meaning in Life: Life Crafting in Times of the COVID-19 Pandemic. *Frontiers in Psychology*, *11*, 577708. doi:10.3389/fpsyg.2020.577708 PMID:33178081

de Prada, A. C. (2022). *Winning the War for Talent by Becoming an Employer of Choice*. https://www.ukri.org/blog/winning-the-war-for-talent-by-becoming-an-employer-of-choice/

De Schepper, A., Clycq, N., & Kyndt, E. (2023). Socio-economic differences in the transition from higher education in the labour market: A systematic review. *Journal of Career Development*, *50*(1), 234–250. doi:10.1177/08948453221077674

De Vos, A., Akkermans, J., & Van der Heijden, B. I. J. M. (2019). From occupational choice to career crafting. In H. Hunz, M. Lazarova, & W. Mayrhofer (Eds.), T*he Routledge Companion to Career Studies* (pp. 128-142). Routledge. doi:10.4324/9781315674704

De Vos, A., Van der Heijden, B. I. J. M. & Akkermans, J. (2020). Sustainable careers: Towards a conceptual model. *Journal of Vocational Behavior, 117*, a.103196. doi:10.1016/j.jvb.2018.06.011

de Wit-de Vries, E., Dolfsma, W. A., Van der Windt, H. J., & Gerkema, M. P. (2019). Knowledge transfer in university-industry research partnerships: A review. *The Journal of Technology Transfer*, *44*(4), 1236–1255. doi:10.100710961-018-9660-x

Dearing, R. (1997). *Higher Education in the Learning Society: Report of the National Committee of Inquiry into Higher Education*. Her Majesty's Stationary Office.

Del Corso, J., & Rehfuss, M. C. (2011). The role of narrative in career construction theory. *Journal of Vocational Behavior*, *79*(2), 334–339. doi:10.1016/j.jvb.2011.04.003

Deloitte. (2023). *2023 Global Human Capital Trends*. Deloitte. https://www2.deloitte.com/us/en/insights/focus/human-capital-trends.html

Dicker, R., Garcia, M., Kelly, A., & Mulrooney, H. (2019). What does 'quality' in higher education mean? Perceptions of staff, students and employers. *Studies in Higher Education*, *44*(8), 1425–1441. doi:10.1080/03075079.2018.1445987

Dive, B. (2008). *The Accountable Leader: Developing Leadership Through Managerial Accountability*. Kogan Page.

Dollinger, M., Arkoudis, S., & Marangell, S. (2019). University alumni mentoring programs: A win-win? *Journal of Higher Education Policy and Management*, *41*(4), 375–389. doi:10.1080/1360080X.2019.1617657

Donald, W. E. (2017). Students' perceptions of graduate employability: A sequential explanatory approach. Doctoral Thesis, University of Southampton. https://eprints.soton.ac.uk/id/eprint/415935

Donald, W. E. (2020). *Viewpoint: COVID-19 and the Future of Careers*. Graduate Recruitment Bureau. doi:10.13140/RG.2.2.19306.13760

Donald, W. E. (2022). *Overcoming Systemic Barriers to Inclusion in Academia: The Case for a Hybrid Conference Format*. Times Higher Education. doi:10.13140/RG.2.2.13284.65926

Donald, W. E. (2023a). Preface. In W. E. Donald (Ed.), *Handbook of Research on Sustainable Career Ecosystems for University Students and Graduates*, (Preface). IGI Global. doi:10.4018/978-1-6684-7442-6

Donald, W. E. (2021). *Conceptualisation of a new 'Early Careers Talent Pipeline' Framework: Enhancing Organisational Sustainability via Feedback-Seeking Behaviour.* Graduate Recruitment Bureau. doi:10.13140/RG.2.2.28278.47684

Donald, W. E. (2022). The Conceptualisation of Weather as a Career Metaphor. *Sustainability (Basel)*, *14*(14), 8856. doi:10.3390u14148856

Donald, W. E. (2023b). Application of career ecosystems theory and the new psychological contract to the field of project management: Toward a conceptual model. *Project Management Journal*, *54*(1), 7–18. doi:10.1177/87569728221118873

Donald, W. E. (2023b). Sustainable talent pipelines and person-organisation fit: Strategic insights from UK graduates. *Career Development International*, *28*(2), 234–249. doi:10.1108/CDI-10-2022-0285

Donald, W. E., Ashleigh, M. J., & Baruch, Y. (2018). Students' perceptions of education and employability: Facilitating career transition from higher education into the labour market. *Career Development International*, *23*(5), 513–540. doi:10.1108/CDI-09-2017-0171

Donald, W. E., Ashleigh, M. J., & Baruch, Y. (2022). The university-to-work transition: Responses of universities and organizations to the COVID-19 pandemic. *Personnel Review*, *51*(9), 2201–2221. doi:10.1108/PR-03-2021-0170

Donald, W. E., Baruch, Y., & Ashleigh, M. J. (2017). Boundaryless and protean career orientation: A multitude of pathways to graduate employability. In M. Tomlinson & L. Holmes (Eds.), *Graduate Employability in Context: Theory, Research and Debate* (pp. 129–150). Palgrave Macmillan. doi:10.1057/978-1-137-57168-7_6

Donald, W. E., Baruch, Y., & Ashleigh, M. J. (2019). The undergraduate self-perception of employability: Human capital, careers advance and career ownership. *Studies in Higher Education*, *44*(4), 599–614. doi:10.1080/03075079.2017.1387107

Donald, W. E., Baruch, Y., & Ashleigh, M. J. (2020). Striving for sustainable graduate careers: Conceptualization via career ecosystems and the new psychological contract. *Career Development International*, *25*(2), 90–110. doi:10.1108/CDI-03-2019-0079

Donald, W. E., Baruch, Y., & Ashleigh, M. J. (2023). Construction and operationalisation of an Employability Capital Growth Model (ECGM) via a systematic literature review (2016-2022). *Studies in Higher Education*, 1–15. doi:10.1080/03075079.2023.2219270

Donald, W. E., Baruch, Y., & Ashleigh, M. J. (2023). Technological transformation and human resource development of early career talent: Insights from accounting, banking, and finance. *Human Resource Development Quarterly*, *34*(3), 329–348. doi:10.1002/hrdq.21491

Donald, W. E., & Ford, N. (2023). Fostering social mobility and employability: The case for peer learning. *Teaching in Higher Education*, *28*(3), 672–678. doi:10.1080/13562517.2022.2145467

Donald, W. E., & Hughes, H. P. N. (2023). How academics can play a more influential role during a year-in-industry placement: A contemporary critique and call for action. *Industry and Higher Education*. doi:10.1177/09504222231162059

Donald, W. E., & Jackson, D. (2022). Subjective wellbeing among university students and recent graduates: Evidence from the United Kingdom. *International Journal of Environmental Research and Public Health*, *19*(11), 6911. doi:10.3390/ijerph19116911 PMID:35682494

Donald, W. E., & Jackson, D. (2023). Sustainable career ecosystems: Setting the scene. In W. E. Donald (Ed.), *Handbook of Research on Sustainable Career Ecosystems for University Students and Graduates* (pp. 1–13). IGI Global., doi:10.4018/978-1-6684-7442-6.ch001

Donald, W. E., Jakubik, M., & Nimmi, P. M. (2023). Preparing university graduates for sustainable careers: Qualitative insights from the UK. In W. E. Donald (Ed.), *Handbook of Research on Sustainable Career Ecosystems for University Students and Graduates* (pp. 320–341). IGI Global., doi:10.4018/978-1-6684-7442-6.ch017

Donald, W. E., & Manville, G. (2023). Fostering career agency via mindfulness and life coaching: A positive psychology sustainable career framework. In W. E. Donald (Ed.), *Handbook of Research on Sustainable Career Ecosystems for University Students and Graduates* (pp. 450–468). doi:10.4018/978-1-6684-7442-6.ch023

Donald, W. E., & Mouratidou, M. (2022). Preparing for a sustainable career: Challenges and opportunities. *GiLE Journal of Skills Development*, *2*(2), 3–5. doi:10.52398/gjsd.2022.v2.i2.pp3-5

Donald, W. E., & Scattergood, K. (2023). *Fostering student social mobility via social media: Opportunities for university career services*. Times Higher Education. doi:10.13140/RG.2.2.34483.71204

Dougherty, S. M., Ecton, W. G., Bonilla, S., & McGuinness, S. (2022). The effects of the COVID-19 pandemic and recession on career preparation during high school. *Peabody Journal of Education*, *97*(1), 326–343. doi:10.1080/0161956X.2022.2079911

Draissi, Zhanyong, Q., & Raguindin, P. Z. J. (2022). Knowledge mapping of skills mismatch phenomenon: A scientific analysis. *Higher Education. Skills and Work-Based Learning*, *12*(2), 271–293. doi:10.1108/HESWBL-02-2021-0019

Dries, N. (2023). *Imagining The (Distant) Future of Work*. [Video]. Youtube. https://www.youtube.com/watch?v=FP7jEAHIm6o

Dries, N., Luyckx, J., & Rogiers, P. (2023). Imagining the (distant) future of work. *Academy of Management Discoveries*, Advanced Online Publication. doi:10.5465/amd.2022.0130

Dries, N., & Pepermans, R. (2008). 'Real' high-potential careers: An empirical study into the perspectives of organisations and high potentials. *Personnel Review*, *37*(1), 85–108. doi:10.1108/00483480810839987

Emeritus. (2022). *12 Workplace Trends to Expect In 2023*. Emeritus. https://emeritus.org/blog/the-future-of-work-workplace-trends/

Employer Insights, Q. S. (2020). *QS Employer Insights Report 2020*. Employer Insights. https://www.qs.com/portfolio-items/qs-employer-insights-report-2020/

English, P., de Villiers Scheepers, M. J., Fleischman, D., Burgess, J., & Crimmins, G. (2021). Developing professional networks: The missing link to graduate employability. *Education + Training*, *63*(4), 647–661. doi:10.1108/ET-10-2020-0309

Etzkowitz, H., & Leydesdorff, L. (1995). The Triple Helix: University-Industry-Government relations: A laboratory for knowledge based economic development. *EASST Review*, *14*(1), 14–19.

Fakunle, O. (2021). International students' perspective on developing employability during study abroad. *Higher Education Quarterly*, *75*(4), 575–590. doi:10.1111/hequ.12308

Fan, Y., & Potočnik, K. (2021). The impact of the depletion, accumulation, and investment of personal resources on work-life balance satisfaction and job retention: A longitudinal study on working mothers. *Journal of Vocational Behavior*, *131*(1), 103656. doi:10.1016/j.jvb.2021.103656

Fernández, D. P., Ryan, M. K., & Begeny, C. (2023). Recognizing the diversity in how students define belonging: Evidence of differing conceptualizations, including as a function of students' gender and socio-economic background. *Social Psychology of Education*, *26*(3), 673–708. doi:10.100711218-023-09761-7

Ferns, S., Dawson, V., & Howitt, C. (2019). A collaborative framework for enhancing graduate employability. *International Journal of Work-Integrated Learning*, *20*(2), 99–111.

Fisher, J. F. (2023). *College Career Services Are Ailing-Networks Are the Cure*. Workshift. https://workshift.opencampusmedia.org/college-career-services-are-ailing-networks-are-the-cure/

Flat, A., & Drewery, D. (2023). How career development professionals can close the gap between human resources and Gen Z: The creation of sustainable relationships. In W. E. Donald (Ed.), *Handbook of Research on Sustainable Career Ecosystems for University Students and Graduates* (pp. 195–213). IGI Global., doi:10.4018/978-1-6684-7442-6.ch011

Forrier, A., De Cuyper, N., & Akkermans, J. (2018). The winner takes it all, the loser has to fall: Provoking the agency perspective in employability research. *Human Resource Management Journal*, *28*(4), 511–523. doi:10.1111/1748-8583.12206

Freire, C., & Bettencourt, C. (2021). The effect of work-family conflict and hindrance on nurses' satisfaction: The role of ethical leadership. *Personnel Review*, *51*(3), 966–979. doi:10.1108/PR-05-2020-0379

Fugate, M., Van der Heijden, B. I. J. M., De Vos, A., Forrier, A., & De Cuyper, N. (2021). Is what's past prologue? A review and agenda for contemporary employability research. *The Academy of Management Annals*, *15*(1), 266–298. doi:10.5465/annals.2018.0171

Galan-Muros, V., & Davey, T. (2019). The UBC ecosystem: Putting together a comprehensive framework for university-business cooperation. *The Journal of Technology Transfer*, *44*(4), 1311–1346. doi:10.100710961-017-9562-3

Gallow, M. L. (2018). How are graduates and alumni featured in university strategic plans? Lessons from Ireland. *Perspectives: Policy and Practice in Higher Education*, *22*(3), 92–97. doi:10.1080/13603108.1397065

Gartner. (2021). *Digital Workers Say Flexibility Is Key to Their Productivity*. Gartner. https://www.gartner.com/ smarterwithgartner/digital-workers-say-flexibility-is-key-to-their-productivity

Gati, I., & Kulcsár, V. (2021). Making better career decisions: From challenges to opportunities. *Journal of Vocational Behavior*, *126*, 103545. doi:10.1016/j.jvb.2021.103545

Ghani, E. K., & Muhammad, K. (2019). Industry 4.0: Employers' expectations of accounting graduates and its implications on teaching and learning practices. *International Journal of Education and Practice*, *7*(1), 19–29. doi:10.18488/journal.61.2019.71.19.29

Gibby, T. (2022). *Five Key Future of Work Trends In 2022*. Unleash. https://www.unleash.ai/hr-technology/5-key-future-of-work-trends-in-2022/

Gkeredakis, M., Lifshitz-Assaf, H., & Barrett, M. (2021). Crisis as opportunity, disruption and exposure: Exploring emergent responses to crisis through digital technology. *Information and Organization*, *31*(1), 100344. doi:10.1016/j.infoandorg.2021.100344

Goodenow, C. (1993). Classroom belonging among early adolescent students. *The Journal of Early Adolescence*, *13*(1), 21–43. doi:10.1177/0272431693013001002

Gorbatov, S., Khapova, S. N., Oostrom, J. K., & Lysova, E. I. (2021). Personal brand equity: Scale development and validation. *Personnel Psychology*, *74*(3), 505–542. doi:10.1111/peps.12412

Gradleaders (2022). *16 Biggest Challenges Every Career Center Faces Today*. Gradeleaders. https://www.gradleaders.com/career-services-challenges

Gradleaders. (2022). *16 biggest challenges every career center faces today*. GradeLeaders. https://www.gradleaders.com/career-services-challenges

Graduate Coach. (2020). *6 top graduate employability issues*. Graduate Coach. https://graduatecoach.co.uk/blog/graduate-employability-issues/

Graduate Recruitment Bureau. (2022). *What are the Biggest Challenges Recruiting Graduates?* Graduate Recruitment Bureau. https://www.grb.uk.com/employer-services/graduate-recruiter-faq/what-are-the-biggest-challenges-recruiting-graduates

Graduate Recruitment Bureau. (2023). *The 7 Benefits of Hiring Graduates*. GRB. https://www.grb.uk.com/recruiter-research/7-benefits-of-hiring-graduates

Greaves, L. (2021). *5 Student and Graduate Job-Hunting Pain Points*. Luminate. https://luminate.prospects.ac.uk/5-student-and-graduate-job-hunting-pain-points

Green, C. (2023). *How to Communicate About Your Career*. Browning York. https://www.browningyork.com/how-to-communicate-about-your-career/

Green, Z. A., Noor, U., & Hashemi, M. N. (2020). Furthering proactivity and career adaptability among university students: Test of intervention. *Journal of Career Assessment*, *28*(3), 402–424. doi:10.1177/1069072719870739

Grenny, J. (2017). *Great Storytelling Connects Employees to Their Work*. HBR. https://hbr.org/2017/09/great-storytelling-connects-employees-to-their-work

Gubler, M., Arnold, J., & Coombs, C. (2014). Reassessing the protean career concept: Empirical findings, conceptual components, and measurement. *Journal of Organizational Behavior*, *35*(S1), S23–S40. doi:10.1002/job.1908

Haelermans, C., Korthals, R., Jacobs, M., De Leeuw, S., Vermeulen, S., Van Vugt, L., Aarts, B., Prokic-Breuer, T., Van der Velden, R., Van Wetten, S., & De Wolf, I. (2022). Sharp increase in inequality in education in times of the COVID-19-Pandemic. *PLoS One*, *17*(2), e0261114. doi:10.1371/journal.pone.0261114 PMID:35108273

Hallpike, H., Vallee-Tourangeau, G., & Van der Heijden, B. I. J. M. (2022). A distributed interaction decision-making framework for sustainable career development. *Frontiers in Psychology*, *12*, 790533. doi:10.3389/fpsyg.2021.790533 PMID:35250691

Hamouche, S., Kammogne, C. L., & Merkouche, W. (2023). Workforce's crisis-induced career shock, career preferences, job insecurity, layoff and perceived employability: Examining variations based on gender, education level and ethnic origin. *Higher Education. Skills and Work-Based Learning*, *13*(2), 264–282. doi:10.1108/HESWBL-05-2022-0101

Handley, K., & den Outer, B. (2022). Learning to signal graduate employability: An exploratory study of UK students' experiences of online recruitment process. *Journal of Youth Studies*, 1–19. doi:10.1080/13676261.2022.2157252

Hawes, D. (2023). Navigating graduate recruitment in 2023: Diversity, skills shortages, AI and more. *Career Matters*, *11*(3), 42–43.

HazelkornE. (2019). University Rankings: There is room for error and "malpractice". *Elephant in the Lab*. doi:10.5281/zenodo.2592196

Healy, M. (2023). Careers and employability learning: Pedagogical principles for higher education. *Studies in Higher Education*, *48*(8), 1301–1314. doi:10.1080/03075079.2023.2196997

Healy, M., Hammer, S., & McIlveen, P. (2022). Mapping graduate employability and career development in higher education research: A citation network analysis. *Studies in Higher Education*, *47*(4), 799–811. doi:10.1080/03075079.2020.1804851

Heffernan, T. (2022). Sexism, racism, prejudice, and bias: A literature review and synthesis of research surrounding student evaluations of courses and teaching. *Assessment & Evaluation in Higher Education*, *47*(1), 144–154. doi:10.1080/02602938.2021.1888075

Hennings, M., Zhu, Y., & Van der Veen, R. (2022). Developing the capacity for a proactively self-managed career: An analysis of aspiring new-generation employees in Japan. *Asia Pacific Journal of Human Resources*, *60*(3), 682–699. doi:10.1111/1744-7941.12296

Heslin, P. A., Keating, L. A., & Ashford, S. J. (2020). How being in learning mode may enable a sustainable career across the lifespan. *Journal of Vocational Behavior*, *117*, 103324. doi:10.1016/j.jvb.2019.103324

Higdon, R. D. (2016). Employability: The missing voice: How student and graduate views could be used to develop future higher education policy and inform curricula. *Power and Education*, *8*(2), 176–195. doi:10.1177/1757743816653151

Higginbotham, D. (2021). *Recruitment Agencies.* Prospects. https://www.prospects.ac.uk/careers-advice/getting-a-job/recruitment-agencies

High Fliers. (2023). *The Graduate Market in 2023*. High Fliers. https://www.highfliers.co.uk/download/2023/graduate_market/GMReport23.pdf

Higher Ed Partners. (2021). *University career services: A critical tool in a competitive climate.* Higher Ed Partners. https://higheredpartners.co.uk/university-career-services-a-critical-tool-in-a-competitive-climate/

Ho, C. (2023). How Strong Career Development Can Lead to a Decent Work Future. *The Future Economy.* https://thefutureeconomy.ca/op-eds/career-development-decent-work-candy-ho-ceric/

Hobfoll, S. E. (1989). Conservation of resources: A new attempt at conceptualizing stress. *The American Psychologist*, *44*(3), 513–524. doi:10.1037/0003-066X.44.3.513 PMID:2648906

Hobfoll, S. E., Halbesleben, J., Neveu, J.-P., & Westman, M. (2018, January). Conservation of resources in the organizational context: The reality of resources and their consequences. *Annual Review of Organizational Psychology and Organizational Behavior*, *5*(1), 103–128. doi:10.1146/annurev-orgpsych-032117-104640

Hogarth, T., Winterbotham, M., Hasluck, C., Carter, K., Daniel, W. W., Green, A. E., & Morrison, J. (2007). *Employer and University Engagement in the Use and Development of Graduate Level Skills*. Department for Education and Skills.

Holmes, L. (2013). Competing perspectives on graduate employability: Possession, position or process? *Studies in Higher Education*, *38*(4), 538–554. doi:10.1080/03075079.2011.587140

Hooley, T., Percy, C., & Neary, S. (2023). *Investing In Careers. What is Career Guidance Worth?* Career Development Policy Group & University of Derby. https://adventuresincareerdevelopment.word press.com/2023/07/18/investing-in-careers-what-is-career-guidance-worth/

Hora, M. T. (2020). Hiring as cultural gatekeeping into occupational communities: Implications for higher education and student employability. *Higher Education*, *79*(1), 307–324. doi:10.100710734-019-00411-6

Hughes, H. P. N. (2020). *Understanding the Value of Internships*. University of Leeds. https://business. leeds.ac.uk/downloads/download/202/understanding_the_value_of_work_placements

Hughes, H. P. N., & Davis, M. C. (2021). *Starting Your Career During a Pandemic: The Experience of Remote and Hybrid Working*. University of Leeds. https://business.leeds.ac.uk/dir-record/research-projects/1736/understanding-the-value-of-a-work-placement

Hughes, H. P. N., Mouratidou, M., & Donald, W. E. (2023). Exploring the impact of an industrial placement year on students' competency development: A three-cohort, longitudinal study. *Higher Education, Skills and Work-Based Learning*. Advanced Online Publication. doi:10.1108/HESWBL-02-2023-0044

Hughes, H. P. N., & Thambar, N. (2023). Graduate careers in a changing workplace: A fresh challenge? In W. E. Donald (Ed.), *Handbook of Research on Sustainable Career Ecosystems for University Students and Graduates* (pp. 469–487). IGI Global. doi:10.4018/978-1-6684-7442-6.ch024

Illes, P., Chuai, X., & Preece, D. (2010). Talent management and HRM in multinational companies in Beijing: Definitions, differences and drivers. *Journal of World Business*, *45*(2), 179–189. doi:10.1016/j.jwb.2009.09.014

Ingram, N., & Allen, K. (2019). 'Talent-spotting' or 'social magic'? Inequality, cultural sorting and constructions of the ideal graduate in elite professions. *The Sociological Review*, *67*(3), 723–740. doi:10.1177/0038026118790949

Inkson, K. (2006). Protean and boundaryless career metaphors. *Journal of Vocational Behavior*, *69*(1), 48–63. doi:10.1016/j.jvb.2005.09.004

Inkson, K., & Amundson, N. E. (2002). Career metaphors and their application in theory and counseling practice. *Journal of Employment Counseling*, *39*(3), 98–108. doi:10.1002/j.2161-1920.2002.tb00841.x

Inkson, K., Dries, N., & Arnold, J. (2015). *Understanding Careers: Metaphors of Working Lives* (2nd ed.). Sage.

Institute of Student Employers, & International Network of Employers and University Career Services. (2020). *Covid-19: Global impacts on graduate recruitment*. Institute of Student Employers, & International Network of Employers and University Career Services https://cdn.ymaws.com/ise.org.uk/ resource/collection/78C3D824-D17B-4316-8E69-15A054E40F1E/Covid-19-international_final.pdf

Institute of Student Employers. (2023). *Where Should Universities Focus Employer Engagement to Support Their Unique Student Population?* Insights. https://insights.ise.org.uk/attraction-and-marketing/blog-where-should-universities-focus-employer-engagement-to-support-their-unique-student-population/

Izzo, F., Mele, S., & Mustilli, M. (2022). University to work transition: A literature review. *International Journal of Manpower*, *43*(7), 1502–1515. doi:10.1108/IJM-07-2021-0398

Jackson, D. (2020). Applying academic selection criterion to work-integrated learning programmes: Risk management or perpetuating inequality? *Teaching in Higher Education*, *25*(1), 98–115. doi:10.1080/13562517.2018.1541884

Jackson, D. (2020). The changing nature of graduate roles and the value of the degree. *Journal of Higher Education Policy and Management*, *43*(2), 182–197. doi:10.1080/1360080X.2020.1777634

Jackson, D., & Bridgstock, R. (2018). Evidencing student success and graduate employability in the contemporary world-of-work: Renewing our thinking. *Higher Education Research & Development*, *37*(5), 984–998. doi:10.1080/07294360.2018.1469603

Jackson, D., & Bridgstock, R. (2021). What actually works to enhance graduate employability? The relative value of curricular, co-curricular, and extra-curricular learning and paid work. *Higher Education*, *81*(4), 723–739. doi:10.100710734-020-00570-x

Jackson, D., & Cook, E. J. (2023). Benefits of work-integrated learning for students. In K. E. Zegwaard & T. J. Pretti (Eds.), *The International Handbook for Work-Integrated Learning*. Routledge / Taylor & Francis. doi:10.4324/9781003156420-8

Jackson, D., Riebe, L., & Macau, F. (2022). Determining factors in graduate recruitment and preparing students for success. *Education + Training*, *64*(5), 681–699. doi:10.1108/ET-11-2020-0348

Jackson, N. J. (2011). *Learning for A Complex World: A Lifewide Concept of Learning, Education and Personal Development*. AuthorHouse.

Jackson, N. J. (2018). Ecological perspectives on learning to practice in the arts in health and arts therapies fields. In C. Holmwood & J. Taylor (Eds.), *Learning as a Creative and Developmental Process in Higher Education: A Therapeutic Arts Approach and its Wider Application*. Routledge. doi:10.4324/9781315142142-18

Jakubik, M. (2017). Solving business problems together case: A Master's degree programme in Finland. *Journal of Systemics, Cybernetics and Informatics*, *15*(4), 53–57.

Jakubik, M. (2018). Masters bring business benefits-Proved by Finnish managers. *The Turkish Online Journal of Educational Technology*, *2*, 65–77.

Jakubik, M. (2020). Enhancing human capital beyond university boundaries. Higher Education. *Skills and Work-Based Learning*, *10*(2), 434–446. doi:10.1108/HESWBL-06-2019-0074

Jakubik, M. (2020). Rise of intellectual workers and intellectual work. *International Journal of Management. Knowledge and Learning*, *9*(1), 59–73.

Jakubik, M. (2021). Searching for practical wisdom in higher education with logos, pathos and ethos. Case: Finnish Universities of Sciences. *Philosophies*, *6*(3), 63. doi:10.3390/philosophies6030063

Jakubik, M. (2022). Education for life in Higher Education. *3rd Ferenc Farkas International Scientific Conference Proceedings, 3*, 21-31.

Jakubik, M. (2022). The role of higher education in solving global problems. *International Journal of Management. Knowledge and Learning*, *11*, 285–295. doi:10.53615/2232-5697.11.285-295

Jakubik, M. (2022). Work engagement – gateway to creativity. In D. Bylieva & A. Nordmann (Eds.), *Technology, Innovation and Creativity in Digital Society* (pp. 11–21). Springer. doi:10.1007/978-3-030-89708-6_2

Jakubik, M. (2023). Cultivating the future in higher education: Fostering students' life-world becoming with wisdom pedagogy. *Trends in Higher Education*, *2*(1), 45–61. doi:10.3390/higheredu2010004

Jakubik, M., & Müürsepp, P. (2022). From knowledge to wisdom. Will wisdom management replace knowledge management? *European Journal of Management and Business Economics*, *31*(3), 367–389. doi:10.1108/EJMBE-07-2021-0219

Jesuthasan, R., & Boudreau, J. (2021). Work without jobs. *MIT Sloan Management Review*, *62*(2), 1–5.

Jin, X., & Waldman, M. (2020). Lateral moves, promotions, and task-specific human capital: Theory and evidence. *Journal of Law Economics and Organization*, *36*(1), 1–46.

Kahn, M. E. (2022). *Going Remote: How the Flexible Work Economy Can Improve Out Lives and Our Cities*. University of California Press.

Kelly, C. M., Strauss, K., Arnold, J., & Stride, C. (2020). The relationship between leisure activities and psychological resources that support a sustainable career: The role of leisure seriousness and work-leisure similarity. *Journal of Vocational Behavior*, *117*, 103340. doi:10.1016/j.jvb.2019.103340

Khan, F., & Ali, M. (2022). Exploring the gap between expected and actual return on investment of business graduates from employability: Evidence from a developing country. *International Journal of Management Education*, *20*(3), 100717. doi:10.1016/j.ijme.2022.100717

Khedher, M. (2019). Conceptualizing and researching personal branding effects on employability. *Journal of Brand Management*, *26*(2), 99–109. doi:10.105741262-018-0117-1

Kinash, S., McGillivray, L., & Crane, L. (2018). Do university students, alumni, educators and employers link assessment and graduate employability? *Higher Education Research & Development*, *37*(2), 301–315. doi:10.1080/07294360.2017.1370439

Koen, J., Klehe, U.-C., & Van Vianen, A. E. M. (2012). Training career adaptability to facilitate a successful school-to-work transition. *Journal of Vocational Behavior, 81*(3), 395–408. doi:10.1016/j.jvb.2012.10.003

Kozhuk, D. (2023). *Why Higher Ed Should Invest in Career Services, Not Abolish It.* GOU Connect. https://www. gouconnect.com/career-everywhere/why-higher-ed-should-invest-in-career-services-not-abolish-it/

Kozma, K., Meyer-Miner, A., Chio, J., Mak, S., El-Boraie, A., & Sealey, D. (2021). Developing an industry job simulation program for graduate and postdoctoral trainees in the life sciences. *Canadian Journal of Career Development, 20*(2), 84–93. doi:10.53379/cjcd.2021.102

Krammer, S. M. (2021). Navigating the New Normal: Which firms have adapted better to the COVID-19 disruption? *Technovation, 110*(1), 102368. doi:10.1016/j.technovation.2021.102368

Kulcsár, V., Dobrean, A., & Gati, I. (2020). Challenges and difficulties in career decision making: Their causes, and their direct effects on the process and the decision. *Journal of Vocational Behavior, 116*(Part A), 103346. doi:10.1016/j.jvb.2019.103346

Labrecque, L. I., Markos, E., & Milne, G. R. (2011). Online personal branding: Processes, challenges, and implications. *Journal of Interactive Marketing, 25*(1), 37–50. doi:10.1016/j.intmar.2010.09.002

Lair, D. L., Sullivan, K., & Cheney, G. (2005). Marketization and recasting of the professional self: The rhetoric and ethics of personal branding. *Management Communication Quarterly, 18*(3), 307–343. doi:10.1177/0893318904270744

LaunchPad. (2022). *Key challenges in recruitment include expensive graduate schemes.* Launchpad. https://launchpadrecruits.com/insight-articles/grad-recruitment-strategies-and-challenges

Le Rossignol, K., & Kelly, M. (2023). A career ecosystem approach to developing student agency through digital storymaking. In W. E. Donald (Ed.), *Handbook of Research on Sustainable Career Ecosystems for University Students and Graduates* (pp. 158–175). IGI Global. doi:10.4018/978-1-6684-7442-6.ch009

Lee, S., Schmidt-Klau, D., & Verik, S. (2020). The labour market impacts of the COVID-19: A global perspective. *The Indian Journal of Labour Economics : the Quarterly Journal of the Indian Society of Labour Economics, 63*(S1), 11–15. doi:10.100741027-020-00249-y PMID:33041544

Lewis, H. (2022). *Sketchnote Summary of 10 Red Flags of Faulty Org Design.* HALO Psychology Limited.

Lisá, E., Hennelová, K., & Newman, D. (2019). Comparison between employers' and students' expectations in respect of employability skills of university graduates. *International Journal of Work-Integrated Learning, 20*(1), 71–82.

Lloyd, N. A., Paull, M., Clerke, T., & Male, S. A. (2019). *Access, Quality and Wellbeing In Engineering Work Integrated Learning Placements.* National Centre for Student Equity in Higher Education.

Lo Presti, A. L., Capone, V., Aversano, A., & Akkermans, J. (2022). Career competencies and career success: On the roles of employability activities and academic satisfaction during the school-to-work transition. *Journal of Career Development*, *49*(1), 107–125. doi:10.1177/0894845321992536

López-Miguens, M. J., Caballero, G., & Álvarez-González, P. (2021). Responsibility of the University in Employability: Development and validation of a measurement scale across five studies. *Business Ethics, the Environment & Responsibility*, *30*(1), 143–156. doi:10.1111/beer.12319

Lynch, J., & Lungrin, T. (2018). Integrating academic and career advising toward student success. *New Directions for Higher Education*, *184*(184), 69–79. doi:10.1002/he.20304

Maisuria, A., & Cole, M. (2017). The neoliberalization of higher education in England: An alternative is possible. *Policy Futures in Education*, *15*(5), 602–619. doi:10.1177/1478210317719792

Mallis, A. (2023). *Close the Skills Gap by Learning New Ways of Working: RMIT Interim CEO*. https://www.digitalnationaus.com.au/news/close-the-skills-gap-by-learning-new-ways-of-working-rmit-interim-ceo-591689

Manville, G., Donald, W. E., & Eves, A. (2022). Can Embedding Authentic Assessment Into the Curriculum Enhance the Employability of Business School Students? *GiLE Journal of Skills Development*, *2*(2), 73–87. doi:10.52398/gjsd.2022.v2.i2.pp73-87

Maree, J. G. (2020). How global change necessitates innovation in career counseling: Linking economic, industrial, psychology, and career counseling waves. In J. G. Maree (Ed.), *Innovating Counseling for Self- and Career Construction: Connecting Conscious Knowledge with Subconscious Thought* (pp. 67–84). Springer. doi:10.1007/978-3-030-48648-8_4

Martela, F., & Steger, M. F. (2016). The three meanings of meaning in life: Distinguishing, coherence, purpose, and significance. *The Journal of Positive Psychology*, *11*(5), 531–545. doi:10.1080/17439760.2015.1137623

Martin, L. L. (2016). Gender, teaching evaluations, and professional success in political science. *PS, Political Science & Politics*, *49*(2), 313–319. doi:10.1017/S1049096516000275

Maxwell, N. (2021). *The World Crisis – And What To Do About It: A Revolution for Thought and Action*. World Scientific.

McCafferty, H. (2022). An unjust balance: A systematic review of the employability perceptions of UK undergraduates from disadvantaged socio-economic backgrounds. *Research in Post-Compulsory Education*, *27*(4), 570–593. doi:10.1080/13596748.2022.2110774

McIlveen, P., & Creed, A. (2020). La conversation, métaphore de l'approche narrative du counseling d'orientation. In Masdonati, J., Massoudi, K. & Rossier, J. (Eds.) *Landmarks for Career Counseling (Repères pour l'orientation), Antipodes in Actualités Psychologiques Collection* (pp. 361-383). Lausanne, Suisse: Éditions Antipodes.

McMahon, M., & Watson, M. (2013). Story telling: Crafting identities. *British Journal of Guidance & Counselling*, *41*(3), 277–286. doi:10.1080/03069885.2013.789824 PMID:24009405

McRae, E. R., & Aykens, P. (2022). *9 Future of Work Trends For 2023*. Gartner. https://www.gartner.com/en/articles/9-future-of-work-trends-for-2023

Meehan, C., & Howells, K. (2019). In search of the feeling of belonging in higher education: Undergraduate students transition into higher education. *Journal of Further and Higher Education*, *43*(1), 1376–1390. doi:10.1080/0309877X.2018.1490702

Mendes, L. (2022). *UK halts all fuel supplies from Russia, reports ONS*. Trade Finance Global. https://www.tradefinanceglobal.com/posts/uk-halts-all-fuel-supplies-from-russia-reports-ons/

Mercer. (2023). *Global Talent Trends 2022-2023*. Mercer. https://www.mercer.com/our-thinking/career/global-talent-hr-trends.html

Miao, H. (2021). *College Students and Getting Valuable Career Experience Working as Brand Ambassadors for Companies like TikTok and Bumble*. CNBC. https://www.cnbc.com/2021/04/24/tiktok-bumble-others-are-hiring-college-students-as-brand-ambassadors.html

Michael Page. (2022). *Career Development Toolkit: Maximising your professional value*. Michael Page. https://www.michaelpage.co.uk/career-development-toolkit-maximise-professional-value

Michel-Schneider, U. (2021). *Challenges for University-Industry Collaboration – A Stakeholder View*. 12th Business & Management Virtual Conference, Prague. doi:10.20472/BMC.2021.012.007

Minocha, S., Hristov, D., & Reynolds, M. (2017). From graduate employability to employment: Policy and practice in UK higher education. *International Journal of Training and Development*, *21*(3), 235–248. doi:10.1111/ijtd.12105

Moore, T., & Morton, J. (2017). The myth of job readiness? Written communication, employability, and the 'skills gap' in higher education. *Studies in Higher Education*, *42*(3), 591–609. doi:10.1080/03075079.2015.1067602

Mulder, R. H. (2021). The impact of new technologies on work and its implication for human resource development research. *Human Resource Development Quarterly*, *32*(1), 105–109. doi:10.1002/hrdq.21447

MüllerC.SchefferA.MackeJ.VaclavikM. C. (2023). Towards career sustainability: A systematic review to guide future research. *Brazilian Administrative Review*, *19*(4), e220108. doi:10.1590/1807-7692bar2022220108

Munich Business School. (2022). *What is a "Working Student"?* Munich Business School. https://www.munich-business-school.de/insights/en/2022/what-is-a-working-student/

National Association of Colleges and Employers. (2022). *NACE 2021-22 Career Services Benchmarks Survey Report*. NACE. https://www.naceweb.org/store/2022/career-services-benchmark-and-compensation

Ng, E. S., Posch, A., Köllen, T., Kraiczy, N., & Thom, N. (2022). Do "one-size" employment policies fit all young workers? Heterogeneity in work attribute preferences among the Millennial generation. *Business Research Quarterly*. doi:10.1177/23409444221085587

Ng, T. W., & Feldman, D. C. (2007). The school-to-work transition: A role identity perspective. *Journal of Vocational Behavior, 71*(1), 114–134. doi:10.1016/j.jvb.2007.04.004

Nimmi, P. M., Mukundan, S. P., Jose, G., Tesi, A., & Alias, R. (2023). Future of work – apprehensions and excitement of management graduates. *Higher Education, Skills and Work-Based Learning*. Advanced Online Publication., doi:10.1108/HESWBL-08-2022-0181

Nimmi, P. M., Joseph, G., & Donald, W. E. (2022). Is it all about perception? A sustainability viewpoint on psychological capital and life wellbeing of management graduates. *Higher Education. Skills and Work-Based Learning, 12*(2), 384–398. doi:10.1108/HESWBL-01-2021-0004

Nimmi, P. M., Kuriakose, V., Donald, W. E., & Nowfal, M. (2021). HERO elements of psychological capital: Fostering career sustainability via resource caravans. *Australian Journal of Career Development, 30*(3), 199–210. doi:10.1177/10384162211066378

Nolan, J. E. (2020). *Narrating Employability from English Studies: An Ethnographic Study*. Doctoral Thesis, Newcastle University. https://theses.ncl.ac.uk/jspui/handle/10443/4940

O'Brien, G. (2022). Making campus attraction work for employers: Aligning employer-led experiences to the student journey. *Phoenix, 166*(2022), 6-7

O'Keeffe, P. (2013). A sense of belonging: Improving student retention. *College Student Journal, 47*(4), 605–613.

O'Regan, M., Carthy, A., McGuiness, C., & Owende, P. (2022). Employer collaboration in developing graduate employability: A pilot study in Ireland. *Education + Training, 65*(10), 1–13. doi:10.1108/ET-03-2022-0081

Offbeat. (2022). *L&D Trends Map 2022*. Offbeat. https://www.offbeat.works/l-d-trends-map

Office for National Statistics. (2023). *Workplace Disputes and Working Conditions*. Office for National Statistics. https://www.ons. gov.uk/employmentandlabourmarket/peopleinwork/workplacedisputesandworkingconditions

Ogbuanya, T. C., & Chukwuedo, S. O. (2017). Career-training mentorship intervention via the Dreyfus model: Implications for career behaviors and practical skills acquisition in vocational electronic technology. *Journal of Vocational Behavior, 103*, 88–105. doi:10.1016/j.jvb.2017.09.002

Okay-Somerville, B., & Scholarios, D. (2022). Focused for some, exploratory for others: Job search strategies and successful university-to-work transitions in the context of labor market ambiguity. *Journal of Career Development, 49*(1), 126–143. doi:10.1177/08948453211016058

Okolie, U. C., Nwosu, H. E., & Mlanga, S. (2019). Graduate employability: How the higher education institutions can meet the demand of the labour market. *Higher Education. Skills and Work-Based Learning, 9*(4), 620–636. doi:10.1108/HESWBL-09-2018-0089

Oliver, C. (2020). *The Complete University Guide: University and Subject League Tables Methodology*. https://www.thecompleteuniversityguide.co.uk/sector/insights/university-andsubject-league-tables-methodology

Orazbayeva, B., Plewa, C., Davey, T., & Muros, V. G. (2019). The future of university-business cooperation: Research and practice priorities. *Journal of Engineering and Technology Management*, *54*, 67–80. doi:10.1016/j.jengtecman.2019.10.001

Osmani, M., Weerakkody, V., Hindi, N., & Eldabi, T. (2019). Graduates employability skills: A review of literature against market demand. *Journal of Education for Business*, *94*(7), 423–432. doi:10.1080/08832323.2018.1545629

Padgett, R., & Donald, W. E. (2023). Preparing graduates for sustainable careers: A case of 'The Global Marketing Professional' module. *Higher Education, Skills, and Work-Based Learning*, *13*(1), 22–35. doi:10.1108/HESWBL-03-2022-0073

Parker, K., & Igielnik, R. (2020). *On the cusp of adulthood and facing an uncertain future: What we know about Gen Z so far*. Pew Research. https://www.pewresearch.org/social-trends/2020/05/14/on-the-cusp-of-adulthood-and-facing-an-uncertain-future-what-we-know-about-gen-z-so-far-2/

Parmentier, M. A., Fischer, E., & Reuber, A. R. (2013). Positioning person brands in establishing organizational fields. *Journal of the Academy of Marketing Science*, *41*(3), 373–387. doi:10.100711747-012-0309-2

Pearson. (2021). *Six Benefits of Professional Body Membership*. Pearson. https://www.pearson.com/uk/educators/fe-college-educators/btec-blog/2021/09/six-benefits-of-professional-body-membership.html

Pearson, J. (1999). Comprehensive research on alumni relationships: Four years of market research at Stanford university. *New Directions for Institutional Research*, *101*, 5–21. doi:10.1002/ir.10101

Pedler, M. L., Willis, R., & Nieuwoudt, J. E. (2022). A sense of belonging at university: Student retention, motivation and enjoyment. *Journal of Further and Higher Education*, *46*(3), 397–408. doi:10.1080/0309877X.2021.1955844

Petruzziello, G., Antonio, A. A., Chiesa, R., & Mariani, M. G. (2022). It takes more than agency: Linking support from teaching staff, career engagement, and movement capital among university students. *Frontiers in Psychology*, *13*, 1083698. Advance online publication. doi:10.3389/fpsyg.2022.1083698 PMID:36600715

Petruzziello, G., Chiesa, R., & Mariani, M. G. (2022). The storm Doesn't touch me!—The role of perceived employability of students and graduates in the pandemic era. *Sustainability (Basel)*, *14*(7), 4303. doi:10.3390u14074303

Pham, T., & Jackson, D. (2020). Employability and determinants of employment outcomes. In N. Tran, T. Pham, M. Tomlinson, K. Medica, & C. Thompson (Eds.), *Developing and Utilizing Employability Capitals: Graduates' Strategies Across Labour Markets* (pp. 237–255). Routledge. 10.4324/9781003004660-17

Pham, T. (2020). Reconceptualising employability of returnees: What really matters and strategic navigating approaches. *Higher Education*, *81*(6), 1329–1345. doi:10.100710734-020-00614-2

Pham, T. (2022). Preparing graduates for cross-country labor markets: What do we know about human and social capital work in Australia and Vietnam? In W. Lee, P. Brown, A. Goodwin, & A. Green (Eds.), *International Handbook on Educational Development in Asia-Pacific* (pp. 1–17). Springer.

Pham, T., & Sultani, B. (2021). *Enhancing Student Education Transitions and Employability: From Theory to Practice*. Routledge. doi:10.4324/9781003168737

Phillips, R., Seaborne, K., Goldsmith, A., Curtis, N., Davies, A., Haynes, W., McEnroe, R., Murphy, N., O'Neill, L., Pacey, C., Walker, E., & Wordley, E. (2022). Student loneliness through the pandemic: How, why and where? *The Geographical Journal*, *188*(2), 277–293. doi:10.1111/geoj.12438 PMID:35600138

Pitan, O. S. (2023). Leveraging the triple helix system for effective employability delivery in Nigerian universities. In W. E. Donald (Ed.), *Handbook of Research on Sustainable Career Ecosystems for University Students and Graduates* (pp. 77–96). IGI Global. doi:10.4018/978-1-6684-7442-6.ch005

Pohl, E., Ajadi, T., Soucy, T., Carroll, H., Earl, J., Verduyn, C., & Connolly, M. (2022). "Knowing nothing about EDI:" A collaborative autoethnography exploring how an anti-racist project was created, publicized, and silenced. *International Journal for Students as Partners*, *6*(1), 30–46. doi:10.15173/ijsap.v6i1.4882

Pryor, R. G. L., & Bright, J. E. H. (2009). Game as a career metaphor: A chaos theory career counselling application. *British Journal of Guidance & Counselling*, *37*(1), 39–50. doi:10.1080/03069880802534070

Raihan, M. Z., & Azad, M. A. K. (2023). A bibliometric review on outcome-based learning for graduate employability: Mapping the research front. *Journal of Education*, *203*(1), 73–91. doi:10.1177/00220574211016444

Reedy, F. (2022). Fostering connections between industry and universities. *Phoenix*, 166(2022), 13.

Reilly, P. (2021). *Collaborating with Employers to Create Work-Ready Graduates*. Higher Education. https://www.times highereducation.com/campus/collaborating-employers-create-workready-graduates

Rickmann, J., Perez-Encinas, A., & Fernadez-de-Pinedo, N. (2020). Addressing career services' internationalisation challenges through transnational consortia. In A. Curaj, L. Deca, & R. Pricopie, R. (Eds.), *European Higher Education Area: Challenges for a New Decade* (pp. 53-65). Springer. doi:10.1007/978-3-030-56316-5_4

Rodrigues, R., Butler, C. L., & Guest, D. (2020). Evaluating the employability paradox: When does organizational investment in human capital pay off? *International Journal of Human Resource Management*, *31*(9), 1134–1156. doi:10.1080/09585192.2019.1704825

Römgens, I., Scoupe, R., & Beausaert, S. (2020). Unraveling the concept of employability: Bringing together research on employability in higher education and the workplace. *Studies in Higher Education*, *45*(12), 2588–2603. doi:10.1080/03075079.2019.1623770

Rousseau, D. M. (1995). *Psychological Contracts in Organizations: Understanding Written and Unwritten Agreements*. Sage (Atlanta, Ga.). doi:10.4135/9781452231594

Rousseau, D. M., Ho, V. T., & Greenberg, J. (2006). I-Deals: Idiosyncratic terms in employment relationships. *Academy of Management Review*, *31*(4), 977–994. doi:10.5465/amr.2006.22527470

Rudolph, C. W., Zacher, H., & Hirschi, A. (2019). Empirical developments in career construction theory. *Journal of Vocational Behavior*, *111*(1), 1–6. doi:10.1016/j.jvb.2018.12.003

Sandvik, J., Saouma, R., Seegert, N., & Stanton, C. T. (2022). *Should Workplace Programs Be Voluntary or Mandatory? Evidence From a Field Experiment on Mentorship* (Working Paper 29148). National Bureau of Economic Research. doi:10.3386/w29148

Savickas, M. L. (2005). The theory and practice of career construction. In S. D. Brown & R. W. Lent (Eds.), *Career Development and Counseling: Putting Theory and Research to Work* (pp. 42-70). Wiley.

Savickas, M., & Porfeli, E. J. (2012). Career adapt-abilities scale: Construction, reliability, and measurement equivalence across 13 countries. *Journal of Vocational Behavior*, *80*(3), 661–673. doi:10.1016/j.jvb.2012.01.011

Schneider, B. (1987). The People Make The Place. *Personnel Psychology*, *40*(3), 437–453. doi:10.1111/j.1744-6570.1987.tb00609.x

Seinsche, L., Schubin, K., Neumann, J., & Pfaff, H. (2022). Employees' resources, demands and health while working from home during the COVID-19 pandemic – A qualitative study in the public sector. *International Journal of Environmental Research and Public Health*, *20*(1), 411. doi:10.3390/ijerph20010411 PMID:36612731

Serenko, A. (2022). The Great Resignation: The great knowledge exodus or the onset of the Great Knowledge Revolution? *Journal of Knowledge Management*, *27*(4), 1042–1055. doi:10.1108/JKM-12-2021-0920

Shtaltovna, Y., & Muzzu, C. (2021). Enhancing students' digital competencies within the Employability module of the University of Europe's skills-based curricula. In Proceedings of the first GiLE4Youth International Conference: The Development of Competencies for Employability (pp. 71-89). *GiLE Journal of Skills Development*. 10.56611/conf.proc.2021.1.71-89

Sjolander, C., & Dodd, J. S. (2022). *Career Centre Resources, Services and Metrics: A Pan-Canadian Benchmarking Survey*. Canadian Association of Career Educators and Employers.

Smith, A. M. J., Jones, D., Scott, B., & Stadler, A. (2017). Designing and delivering inclusive and accessible entrepreneurship education. *Entrepreneurship Education*, *7*, 335–357. doi:10.1108/S2040-724620170000007019

Smith, K. N., & Green, D. K. (2021). Employer internship recruiting on college campuses: 'the right pipeline for our funnel'. *Journal of Education and Work, 34*(4), 572–589. doi:10.1080/13639080.2021.1943333

Social Mobility Commission. (2017). *Unpaid Internships are Damaging to Social Mobility*. Social Mobility Commission. https://www.gov.uk/government/news/unpaid-internships-are-damaging-to-social-mobility

Soto-Acosta, P. (2020). COVID-19 pandemic: Shifting digital transformation to a high-speed gear. *Information Systems Management, 37*(4), 260–266. doi:10.1080/10580530.2020.1814461

Spence, M. (1973). Job market signalling. *The Quarterly Journal of Economics, 87*(3), 355–374. doi:10.2307/1882010

Spence, M. (1978). Job market signaling. In P. Diamond & M. Rothschild (Eds.), *Understanding in Economics* (pp. 281–306). Academic Press. doi:10.1016/B978-0-12-214850-7.50025-5

Stevenson, J., McCaig, C., & Madriga, M. (2017). *Evaluation of the National Networks for Collaborative Outreach (NNCOs)*. Sheffield Hallam University. https://shura.shu.ac.uk/19106/

Strauss, A. (1962). Transformation of identity. In A. M. Rose (Ed.), *Human Behaviour and Social Processes: An Interactionist Approach* (pp. 63–85). Routledge & Kegan Paul.

Sullivan, S. E., & Al Ariss, A. (2021). Making sense of different perspectives on career transitions: A review and agenda for future research. *Human Resource Management Review, 31*(1), 100727. doi:10.1016/j.hrmr.2019.100727

Super, D. E. (1957). *The Psychology of Careers*. Harper & Row.

Sylvester, R., & Donald, W. E. (2023). The Personal Brand V.A.L.U.E. Career Development Tool: A multi-perspective and interdisciplinary framework. In W. E. Donald (Ed.), *Handbook of Research on Sustainable Career Ecosystems for University Students and Graduates* (pp. 238–257). IGI Global. doi:10.4018/978-1-6684-7442-6.ch013

Tang, M. (2022). Challenges Associated with Employability Capitals Facing Chinese International Graduates in Australia. In B. Ng (Ed.), *Graduate Employability and Workplace-Based Learning Development: Insights from Sociocultural Perspectives* (pp. 83–99). Springer Nature Singapore. doi:10.1007/978-981-19-5622-5_6

Tang, M., & Jiang, W. (2023). Chinese international graduates in the Australian labor market: Employability capitals and wellbeing. In W. E. Donald (Ed.), *Handbook of Research on Sustainable Career Ecosystems for University Students and Graduates* (pp. 214–237). IGI Global. doi:10.4018/978-1-6684-7442-6.ch012

Teng, W., Ma, C., Pahlevansharif, S., & Turner, J. J. (2019). Graduate readiness for the employment market of the 4th industrial revolution: The development of soft employability skills. *Education + Training, 61*(5), 590–604. doi:10.1108/ET-07-2018-0154

Thambar, N., & Hughes, H. P. N. (2023). The robots are coming 2: Rise of the screens; The role of higher education careers professionals in disrupted times. *Journal of the National Institute for Career Education and Counselling*, *50*(1), 85–95. doi:10.20856/jnicec.5009

The Careers 2032 Project. (2022). *An Industry Research Project Co-Produced By AGCAS, ISE, Wonkhe and Handshake, Looking at The Careers Sector of 2032 and The Role Technology Could Play in Facilitating Human Connections*. Handshake. https://joinhandshake.co.uk/careers2032

The Complete University Guide. (2023). *University League Tables 2024*. https://www.thecompleteuniversityguide.co.uk/league-tables/rankings

The Graduate Project. (2023). *The Benefits of Hiring Graduates*. The Graduate Project. https://www.thegraduateproject.co.uk/news/2023/04/the-benefits-of-hiring-graduates/112

Thurab-Nkhosi, D., Williams, G., & Mason-Roberts, M. (2018). Achieving confidence in competencies through authentic assessment. *Journal of Management Development*, *37*(8), 652–662. doi:10.1108/JMD-12-2017-0413

Tims, M., & Akkermans, J. (2020). Job and career crafting to fulfill individual career pathways. In J. W. Hedge & G. W. Carter (Eds.), *Career Pathways: From School to Retirement* (pp. 165–190). Oxford University Press. doi:10.1093/oso/9780190907785.003.0010

Tomlinson, M. (2017). Forms of graduate capital and their relationship to graduate employability. *Education + Training*, *59*(4), 338–352. doi:10.1108/ET-05-2016-0090

Tomlinson, M., & Anderson, V. (2021). Employers and graduates: The mediating role of signals and capitals. *Journal of Higher Education Policy and Management*, *43*(4), 384–399. doi:10.1080/1360080X.2020.1833126

Tomlinson, M., & Jackson, D. (2021). Professional identity formation in contemporary higher education students. *Studies in Higher Education*, *46*(4), 885–900. doi:10.1080/03075079.2019.1659763

Tran, L. T., Ngo, N. T. H., Nguyen, H. T. M., Le, T. T. T., & Ho, T. T. H. (2022). "Employability in context": Graduate employability attributes expected by employers in regional Vietnam and implications for career guidance. *International Journal for Educational and Vocational Guidance*. doi:10.100710775-022-09560-0 PMID:35910080

Trendence. (2020). *Black Lives Matter Infographic: Racial Justice in the Workplace*. Trendence. https://trendence.co.uk/thoughtleadership/reports

Trow, M. (2006). Reflections on the transition from elite to mass to universal access: forms and phases of higher education in modern societies since WWII. In J. J. F. Forest & P. G. Altbach (Eds.), *International Handbook of Higher Education* (pp. 243–280). Springer. doi:10.1007/978-1-4020-4012-2_13

Ugiagbe-Green, I. (2023). Identity regulation through the whiteness of "Right Fit": Mitigating racism in graduate recruitment. In W. E. Donald (Ed.), *Handbook of Research on Sustainable Career Ecosystems for University Students and Graduates* (pp. 278–299). IGI Global. doi:10.4018/978-1-6684-7442-6.ch015

United Nations. (2015). *Global Citizenship.* UN. https://www.un.org/en/academic-impact/global-citizenship

Van der Heijden, B. I. J. M. (2005). No one has ever promised you a rose garden. *On shared responsibility and employability enhancing strategies throughout careers.* Heerlen: Open University of the Netherlands. Van Gorcum.

Van der Heijden, B. I. J. M., & De Vos, A. (2015). Sustainable careers: Introductory chapter. In A. De Vos & B. I. J. M. Van der Heijden (Eds.), *Handbook of Research on Sustainable Careers* (pp. 1–19). Edward Elgar. doi:10.4337/9781782547037.00006

Van Gijn-Grosvenor, E., & Huisman, P. (2020). A sense of belonging among Australian university students. *Higher Education Research & Development, 39*(2), 376–389. doi:10.1080/07294360.2019.1666256

Van Hooft, E. A. J., Kammeyer-Muller, J. D., Wanberg, C. R., Kanfer, R., & Basburg, G. (2020). Job search and unemployment success: A quantitative review and future research agenda. *The Journal of Applied Psychology, 106*(5), 674–713. doi:10.1037/apl0000675 PMID:32658493

Verhaest, D., Bogaert, E., Dereymaeker, J., Mestdagh, L., & Baert, S. (2018). Do employers prefer overqualified graduates? A field experiment. *Industrial Relations, 57*(3), 361–388. doi:10.1111/irel.12212

Vermeeren, B., & Van der Heijden, B. I. J. M. (2022). Employability in the public sector: The impact of individual and organizational determinants. *Frontiers in Psychology, 13*, 1041618. doi:10.3389/fpsyg.2022.1041618 PMID:36591038

Vincent, M., & Chahal, G. (2022). Supporting local SMEs to access talent. *Phoenix,* 166(2022), 8-9.

Violet. (2019). *What are the Advantages of Working as a Law Firm Campus Ambassador?* Violet. https://www.lawcareers.net/Explore/BlogPost/Violet/What-are-the-advantages-of-working-as-a-law-firm-campus-ambassador

Walker, N. (2021). *Brexit timeline: Events leading to the UK's exit from the European Union.* Commons Library. https://commonslibrary.parliament.uk/research-briefings/cbp-7960/

Wilensky, H. L. (1961). Orderly careers and social participation: The impact of work history on social integration in the middle mass. *American Sociological Review, 26*(4), 521–539. doi:10.2307/2090251

Winterton, J., & Turner, J. J. (2019). Preparing graduates for work readiness: An overview and agenda. *Education + Training, 61*(5), 536–551. doi:10.1108/ET-03-2019-0044

Witteveen, D., & Velthorst, E. (2020). Economic hardship and mental health complaints during COVID-19. *Proceedings of the National Academy of Sciences of the United States of America*, *117*(44), 27277–27284. doi:10.1073/pnas.2009609117 PMID:33046648

World Economic Forum. (2023). *How 'Everyday' Flexibility Can Unlock Engagement, Productivity and Growth*. WEF. https://www.weforum.org/agenda/2023/01/flexible-working-productivity-and-growth-davos23

Wright, P. M., Coff, R., & Moliterno, T. P. (2014). Strategic human capital crossing the great divide. *Journal of Management*, *40*(2), 353–370. doi:10.1177/0149206313518437

Ybema, J. F., van Vuuren, T., & van Dam, K. (2020). HR practices for enhancing sustainable employability: Implementation, use, and outcomes. *International Journal of Human Resource Management*, *31*(7), 886–907. doi:10.1080/09585192.2017.1387865

Yoon, H. J., & Hutchinson, B. (2018). Syntheses and future directions for career services, credentials, and training. In H. J. Yoon (Ed.), *International Practices of Career Services, Credentials, and Training* (pp. 217–238). National Career Development Association.

Zacher, H., & Froidevaux, A. (2021). Life stage, lifespan, and life course perspectives on vocational behavior and development: A theoretical framework, review, and research agenda. *Journal of Vocational Behavior*, *126*, 103476. doi:10.1016/j.jvb.2020.103476

Zhang, J., Yuen, M., & Chen, G. (2018). Teacher support for career development: An integrative review and research agenda. *Career Development International*, *23*(1), 122–144. doi:10.1108/CDI-09-2016-0155

Zhao, X., & Cox, A. (2022). Chinese students' study in the UK and employability: The views of Chinese employers, students and alumni, and UK teachers. *Journal of Education and Work*, *35*(4), 422–440. doi:10.1080/13639080.2022.2073339

Zhou, W., Li, M., Xin, L., & Zhu, J. (2018). The interactive effect of proactive personality and career exploration on graduating students' well-being in school-to-work transition. *International Journal of Mental Health Promotion*, *20*(2), 41–54. doi:10.32604/IJMHP.2018.010737

Zucker, R. (2019). *How to manage the emotional roller coaster of a job search*. HBR. https://hbr.org/2019/10/how-to-manage-the-emotional-roller-coaster-of-a-job-search

About the Author

William E. Donald is an Associate Professor in Sustainable Careers and Human Resource Management at the Ronin Institute (USA) and a Visiting Research Fellow at the University of Southampton (UK) as a guest of Professor Yehuda Baruch. Will's research interests include graduate employability, career development, and sustainable career ecosystems. He has published over 60 peer-reviewed works (journal articles, book chapters, and conference papers)–which have been read more than 30,000 times (ResearchGate) and cited over 1,000 times (GoogleScholar). According to the Scholar GPS Ranking Analytics 2023, based on a 5-year composite ranking for productivity, impact, and quality of research, Will featured in the top 9.45% of scholars across all fields, the top 7.06% for higher education, and the top 3.68% for career development. Will was the sole Editor of the 'Handbook of Research on Sustainable Career Ecosystems for University Students and Graduates', published by IGI Global in 2023. He is an international member of various Editorial Boards and Steering Groups and was previously the Managing Editor of the GiLE Journal of Skills Development. Will is a qualified Life and Performance Coach, a Fellow of the 'Learning and Performance Institute' (FLPI), an Associate Fellow of the 'Higher Education Academy' (AFHEA), and a Member of the 'National Council of Psychotherapists' (MNCP NP).

Index

P

R

S

U

W

www.ingramcontent.com/pod-product-compliance
Lightning Source LLC
LaVergne TN
LVHW080902300926
849162LV00003B/516